D0875680

TRAFFICKING JUSTICE

TRAFFICKING JUSTICE

How Russian Police Enforce New Laws,
from Crime to Courtroom

Lauren A. McCarthy

CORNELL UNIVERSITY PRESS   ITHACA AND LONDON

Cornell University Press gratefully acknowledges receipt of a publication subvention from the Office of Research Development, UMass Amherst, which aided in the publication of this book.

Copyright © 2015 by Cornell University

All rights reserved. Except for brief quotations in a review, this book, or parts thereof, must not be reproduced in any form without permission in writing from the publisher. For information, address Cornell University Press, Sage House, 512 East State Street, Ithaca, New York 14850.

First published 2015 by Cornell University Press
Printed in the United States of America

Library of Congress Cataloging-in-Publication Data

McCarthy, Lauren A., 1979– author.
   Trafficking justice : how Russian police enforce new laws, from crime to courtroom / Lauren A. McCarthy.
      pages cm
   Includes bibliographical references and index.
   ISBN 978-0-8014-5389-2 (cloth : alk. paper)
   1. Human trafficking—Russia (Federation)   2. Law enforcement—Russia (Federation)   3. Human trafficking—Law and legislation—Russia (Federation)—Criminal provisions.   I. Title.
      HD4875.R9M33 2015
      364.15—dc23   2015012304

Cornell University Press strives to use environmentally responsible suppliers and materials to the fullest extent possible in the publishing of its books. Such materials include vegetable-based, low-VOC inks and acid-free papers that are recycled, totally chlorine-free, or partly composed of nonwood fibers. For further information, visit our website at www.cornellpress.cornell.edu.

Cloth printing   10 9 8 7 6 5 4 3 2 1

This book is dedicated to my mother, Mary Ann McCarthy, whose grace, kindness, and beauty will forever live in the memory of those who knew her.

You have supported this project in more ways than you could have possibly imagined.

Contents

Figures

Tables

Preface

In March 2008, about halfway through my fieldwork in Russia, I may have unwittingly aided in a trafficking situation. I was flying to Munich for a much needed break, and on the airplane I sat next to a woman in her late twenties who was traveling from Blagoveshchensk in the Russian Far East. We struck up a conversation. She was easygoing and pleasant to talk to. She told me about her job, which was shuttle trading in clothing from China to her hometown where she sold her wares at the market, her kids—she had a son and a daughter—and her life. She in turn asked me what I was doing in Russia and more about my life. When we finally got around to asking why the other was traveling to Munich, I got a surprising answer. To get married, she said. My trafficking radar immediately went up, so I asked more. She had met her future husband in China at a bar. He was a German who worked for a major international company, and they had started seeing each other when they were both there on business. They spoke in broken English, neither knowing the other's native language. Over time, they fell in love, and she had decided to come to Germany to get married. Eventually, they planned either to bring her children over or to move back to China to be closer to them. Her anxiety was clear, but so was her enthusiasm about her new life. She asked me if I thought she was making the right decision. I deferred to her judgment and told her that if she was sure about it, then I thought she was making a good decision. I gave her my contact information and told her to stay in touch once she was settled in Germany after the wedding.

When we landed at the airport in Munich, things became a little more worrisome. I passed through passport control easily, the German guard brusquely asking the required questions before stamping my passport. I waited on the other side for her. She did not go through so easily. The German guard, having been trained to ask a set of questions that would uncover trafficking victims before they made it into Germany, asked her whom she was visiting, where she was staying, how much money she had with her, and what date was on her return ticket. Seeing that she looked confused, I stepped back to translate for her. She said she was visiting a friend—a white lie, but not completely egregious considering that saying she would be getting married would require a fiancé visa rather than a tourist one, a much bigger hassle to procure—but the address of the place she would be staying, she said, was in her checked luggage, so she didn't know. She didn't have a lot of money on her but said that she had some in her luggage as well. She made up a date for the return ticket, knowing full well that she did not plan to come back. Though the guard made his own decision to let her through, the fact that I implicitly vouched for her I am sure helped. She thanked me profusely, visibly flustered.

We came out of the terminal where her fiancé was meeting her. She wanted to introduce me and told me that he could give me a ride to my hotel. It was late, but I didn't want to accept, thinking that I would be intruding on their first moments together after their separation. She insisted, and I told her that she should talk to him privately about it; if it was all right with him, I would go. He agreed, and so did I. We drove to my hotel in the center of Munich, me in the front seat chatting with him in English and her in the back seat trying to follow along. I did my best to translate the conversation so she could participate. I assessed him as a good guy. He didn't seem like a trafficker. After all, what kind of trafficker would give me a ride to my hotel just because she asked him to? He could have easily said no. When we got to the hotel, I said my goodbyes and thank yous and wished them all the best. They drove off, and I never heard from her again. It is entirely possible that she married, moved to Germany with her children, and lived a happy life. But to this day, the situation nags at me. I think of the things I should have done just in case: asked for her phone number or her e-mail address, taken down his license plate number, figured out a way to contact his company and see if he really did work there.

Several months later, another experience showed me just how wrong my assessment could have been about her fiancé being a nice guy and therefore not a trafficker. I had a unique opportunity to interview a convicted trafficker in his temporary holding facility as he awaited transfer to prison to serve his nine-year sentence. The story of his case is at the beginning of the introduction to this book, so I will not reprise it here. Though I thought he would be a monster, he was kind, polite, talkative, and easy to get along with. We spoke for almost an hour. It was hard to see him as anything other than a genuine person even though

I had seen the video evidence and heard the telephone recordings that confirmed his participation in the trafficking ring. Seeing me as a human rights activist who could potentially expose his case to the European Court of Human Rights in Strasbourg, he told me about the conditions of the prison and the abuse he felt he had suffered at the hands of the police. He neglected to tell me, as I later found out, that he had on several occasions tried to bribe them to release him—a fact that law enforcement had video evidence to prove. In our conversation, he insisted that he had not trafficked anyone. He explained his actions in a straight-forward manner. He ran a brothel in Spain, where prostitution was legal. When he paid his Russian partners for the women to come over to work in his brothels, he was just ordering supplies for his business. Trafficking, he said, was what happened to Africans in the eighteenth and nineteenth centuries, and he insisted that he had done nothing of the sort. Furthermore, he insisted, the women knew what awaited them in Spain. They had all approached his Russian partners looking for work abroad and willingly agreed to be prostitutes.

Throughout my years of traveling to Russia prior to, during, and after my fieldwork, I have been amazed at the number of women I know who have put themselves at risk by entering into online relationships with foreign men they have never met and then eventually going to visit them. Even more astounding was the number of women I knew in the context of anti-trafficking work who were engaging in the same sort of behavior. I never questioned their decisions. Their enthusiasm was so contagious and their conviction that there were no good Russian men so convincing. Some of these relationships have worked out and as far as I know, none of these women have been trafficked. My Russian women friends now live in places as diverse as England, Italy, Turkey, and Switzerland, all as a result of online dating.

I begin with these stories to show the complexities of trafficking. In the media's portrayal of trafficking, we see innocent women victims who were duped. Movies like *Taken* and *Eastern Promises*, television shows like *The Wire* and books like the *Girl with the Dragon Tattoo* all portray trafficking victims in this way. The reality is somewhat different. The women and men who are trafficking victims have agency. They desire to make a better life for themselves and their families. Sometimes that includes working in prostitution. Sometimes it includes working in low-wage jobs in unsafe and unsanitary conditions. I do not take a moral position on their choices. While it is certainly possible that they could or should have known better, most people realize that only with the clarity of hindsight.

This book lies at the sometimes uncomfortable intersection of law, bureau-cratic process, and real-life stories. Behind the data, statistics, and interviews that I use in the research are stories of individuals making choices and what happens when those choices are constrained because of the illegal actions of others. After collecting and combing through all these data, I can say with conviction that although there are certainly other pressing problems in Russia, I believe that the legal system needs to prioritize prosecuting traffickers and educating its agents to identify and assist victims. The amount of cruelty and degradation experienced by many of the victims in the stories I examined for this book is unimaginable. As one of my interviewees suggested, there is something more insidious and cynical about this crime than many others. At its heart, it is not just an offense against a person but a business—the business of buying and selling people and exploiting their potential as laborers, whether in farming, prostitution, factory work, or construction, without giving them the choice about when and whether to leave. This deprivation of freedom lies at the heart of what makes trafficking so awful. But it is also worth noting that the solution is found not only in the criminal justice system, the focus of this book, but in an approach that involves making progress in a host of other policy areas, including immigration, welfare provision, gender discrimination, violence against women, crime victim rights, and care for the disabled, orphaned, mentally ill, and addicted. It also includes an increase in societal empathy for marginalized populations rather than a tendency to blame the victims for their situations.

I collected the data that appear throughout the book, either from interviews or through the assembly of a data set from news media reports on trafficking (see appendix A for more detail). Though I reproduce official Russian law enforcement statistics in appendix B, I do not use these figures for several reasons. First, law enforcement statistics do not separate trafficking crimes into type or have any detail about what actually happened in the trafficking situation. Although these categorizations do not particularly matter for law enforcement's statistical accounting purposes, they are immensely important for helping us understand how trafficking happens in Russia, the typical forms of exploitation that occur, and who the traffickers are. Second, because trafficking may be investigated by multiple agencies, there is often a disconnect among the statistics registered, as each agency counts cases slightly differently. It is therefore difficult to track what happens to cases as they make their way through the criminal justice system. Finally, official law enforcement statistics are extraordinarily difficult to obtain (see appendix A for my somewhat humorous attempt to get them from the police). Only the judiciary has a reliable search mechanism; even then, statistics before 2008 have to be obtained through an official request. The information reproduced in appendix B has been obtained either through informal channels or pieced together from books and articles written in Russian and is therefore incomplete.

To protect my sources, I do not use any names throughout the book, instead referring only to the city where they work and their role in the system and giving each interviewee a letter and number designation. Translations of interviews, legislative and conference transcripts, laws, and news articles are my own. Due to space limitations, basic information on each of the trafficking cases used in the construction of my data set is available online at http://people.umass.edu/laurenmc/traffickingjustice. The case numbers in parentheses throughout the book correspond to their identification number in my database.

This book would not have been what it is without the help and support of many people along the way. Acknowledging their contributions here can only scratch the surface of my gratitude for the patience, encouragement, and necessary pushing that they provided at various times. I would first like to thank Kathryn Hendley, whose scholarship and approach to research have been an inspiration to me. She has always pushed me to think outside the box and find my own path. Her no-nonsense advice and encouragement have been instrumental in helping me navigate graduate school, my career, and this book.

This research would not have been possible without the generous support of the Fulbright Institute for International Education and the Foreign Language and Area Studies (FLAS) program. The former funded my fieldwork in Russia, and the latter gave me the language skills to do it. My eight months as a Title VIII Research Fellow at the Kennan Institute in the Woodrow Wilson Center in Washington, DC, in 2013 gave me the physical and intellectual space to puzzle out how to write the book. My affiliation with Timothy Frye and Andrei Yakovlev's International Center for the Study of Institutions and Development at the Higher School of Economics in Moscow has given me the ability to continue to travel to Russia to conduct follow-up interviews and begin new research projects.

Thank you to the many people who have read the book manuscript in part or in whole, some multiple times. Jeb Barnes, Mary Buckley, Jessica Clayton, Howard Erlanger, Scott Gehlbach, Ralph Grunewald, Valerie Hennings, Yoshiko Herrera, Alisha Kirchoff, Sida Liu, MJ Peterson, William Pomeranz, Kerry Ratigan, Mitra Sharafi, Katie Sticca, Brian Taylor, Alexei Trochev, Anna van Santen, and two anonymous reviewers have all provided invaluable feedback during the transformation of my work into a publishable manuscript. Emily Sellars has always been there at the right moments to come up with a catchy phrase or help me streamline my thoughts and visualize my data. So many parts of this book are better for her help. Stewart Macaulay, Peter Solomon, and Aili Tripp participated at the early stages of my research and set it on a path to success with their thoughtful comments about where to go next. Brian Schaffner generously provided the funding to invite people to a manuscript review workshop in Madison and to feed them. The University of Massachusetts Amherst's Office of Research Development also provided funds to underwrite the costs of publication. I could not have asked for a better editor than Roger Haydon, who has graciously answered all my questions, given pointed and thoughtful comments on the manuscript, and shepherded it through production. Thanks also to my copyeditor, Carolyn Pouncy, and production editor, Susan Specter, whose meticulous editing significantly improved the final manuscript. Dina Dineva prepared the index.

Thanks also to my incredible research assistant Dakota Irvin, who waded through hundreds of Russian news media articles to help construct the data set for this book and then was willing to sign on again for the final push to complete the data entry. Without his diligent and careful detective work, I would have only about half as many cases to discuss. Thanks also to my research assistants at the University of Massachusetts Amherst: Arkadiy Chapko, who sorted through years of topic e-mail messages from Yandex; and Sarish Siddiqui, who helped in the preparation of references for the manuscript. Peter Roudik at the Law Library of Congress helped me find all of the Russian legal commentaries that were used in this book.

My fieldwork would not have been possible without the help of a number of people. I am extremely grateful to Thomas Firestone, Terry Kinney, and Alexei Trepikhalin at the US Embassy in Moscow, who answered all my questions and invited me to their trafficking conferences. Alberto Andreani, Dmitrii Babin, and Kirill Boychenko at the International Organization for Migration not only helped me gain access to law enforcement, but also patiently answered my millions of questions about the way the institutions worked. Louise Shelley helped facilitate many of my meetings with experts throughout Russia. The most important thank you, however, goes to my interviewees. They generously shared their experiences and knowledge about human trafficking, the legal system, and law enforcement with me and helped me understand the nuances and intricacies of their working environment. In particular, I would like to mention Elena Tiurukanova, who was the first to research human trafficking in Russia and served as an inspiration for my own work, and Tatiana Kholshchevnikova, who did most of the drafting of the trafficking law and helped walk me through the intricacies of the lawmaking process. Both passed away during the writing of this book.

I am grateful to the participants at the many conferences and workshops where I have had the opportunity to present these ideas, receive feedback, and meet people who have become colleagues and collaborators: two Social Science Research Council dissertation development workshops; the Havighurst Center at Miami University's Young Researchers' Conference; IREX's Regional Policy

Symposium; the University of Wisconsin-Madison's Law, Politics and Society brownbag; and multiple Association for Slavic, East European, and Eurasian Studies and Law and Society Association conferences.

Thanks also to the people who have provided the moral support, encouragement, and sense of humor that is inevitably needed to complete a project of this magnitude: Diana Varat, Laura Singleton, Melanie Getreuer, Kate McCarthy, Ann Gripper, Noah Buckley, Daniel LaChance, Marta Murray Close, Debra Sondak, Monica Dorman, Kristyn Peck, Annie Sovcik, Jennifer Walker, Marissa Padilla, Alexander Borisovich (Shurik), and my many other friends and colleagues from the University of Wisconsin-Madison, University of Massachusetts Amherst, and Columbia University.

Last but certainly not least, thank you to my family for their love and support. My parents, Tom and Amanda, brother Peter, and sister Brighid have been my most consistent fans. And to Dan Kost, I'm so very grateful that our paths crossed when they did.

Note on Transliteration

For Russian names and titles in the references and notes and for Russian words in the text, I use the Library of Congress transliteration system (e.g., iu and ia rather than yu and ya). I have also used the familiar English form for place and personal names in the text (e.g., Chelyabinsk rather than Cheliabinsk) and omitted soft signs (e.g., Perm rather than Perm') to enhance readability. If a Russian author has also published in English, I retain the English transliteration for all of his or her works (e.g., Paneyakh rather than Paneiakh).

Abbreviations

AC   Administrative Code [Kodeks Rossiiskoi Federatsii ob administra-
     tivnykh pravonarusheniiakh]
CC   Criminal Code of the Russian Federation [Ugolovnyi kodeks Ros-
     siiskoi Federatsii]
CPC Criminal Procedure Code of the Russian Federation
     [Ugolovno-protsessual'nyi kodeks Rossiiskoi Federatsii]
FMS Federal Migration Service [Federal'naia migratsionnaia sluzhba]
FSB Federal Security Service [Federal'naia sluzhba bezopasnosti]
IOM International Organization for Migration
MVD Ministry of Internal Affairs [Ministerstvo vnutrennykh del]
SK   Investigative Committee [Sledstvennyi komitet]
SZ RF Collected Legislation of the Russian Federation [Sobranie
     zakonodatel'stva Rossiiskoi Federatsii]

Criminal Code Articles Referenced

Article 126	Kidnapping
Article 127	False Imprisonment
Article 127.1	Human Trafficking
Article 127.2	Use of Slave Labor
Article 152	Trafficking in Minors (removed from Criminal Code 12/2003)
Article 210	Organizing or Participating in a Criminal Conspiracy or Criminal Organization
Article 240	Recruitment into Prostitution
Article 241	Organizing Prostitution
Article 285/286	Abuse of Authority/Official Position
Article 322	Illegal Border Crossing
Article 322.1	Organizing Illegal Migration

TRAFFICKING JUSTICE

INTRODUCTION

In May 2008 in Yoshkar Ola, I watched as three men sat in the defendant's cage in a Russian courtroom for the judge's reading of their sentences.[1] The men, two Russians and an Albanian, were sentenced to between seven and nine years in prison for trafficking women to Europe and distributing them to brothels in Spain, France, Belgium, and Germany. On June 22, 2006, two years after they had sent their first victim abroad, the Russian ringleader and his Albanian partner were arrested at a traffic checkpoint on their way to take two new victims to the airport. The other Russian, who ran the tourist agency that facilitated the trafficking, was arrested in his office later that day. Their conviction was one of the first in Russia under new laws criminalizing human trafficking.

Many of the women victims in this case had gone willingly, signing loan agreements with the traffickers to help get them to Europe to work as prostitutes. Some of them had not, thinking they were going to work as waitresses or dancers. Once there, each woman was required to pay back the brothel owner for the money he or she had spent on her in addition to the debts she owed to the traffickers in Yoshkar Ola for her documents and transportation. When the women would stop sending money to pay off their debts in Russia, the traffickers would threaten to plaster their parents' neighborhoods with posters showing

---

1. Yoshkar Ola is the capital city of Mari El, a small republic in the Volga region of Russia. Most Russian courtrooms keep defendants in actual cages where their handcuffs are removed during their time in the courtroom.

photographs of the women and reading, "Seeking the swindler, Tatiana Vladi-mirovna Marchenko, born on XX, who lives at XX and who borrowed a large amount of money to go abroad and work as a prostitute and did not pay her creditors back!" Although the victims kept approximately 20 percent of what they earned as prostitutes, most of it was used to pay off their debts to the traf-fickers in Yoshkar Ola and to feed and clothe themselves.

The investigation, undertaken by Mari El's regional security services, had taken over two and a half years and began after they received a flood of reports from foreign law enforcement agents about arrests of women from Mari El who were carrying fake documents and engaging in prostitution. After the sentencing, I was party to a conversation among several male FSB agents as they discussed the outcome of the case. Referring to the sentence, one of the agents said, "[the judge] gave them very little." Another disagreed, "[the women] knew what they were getting into. They signed the papers saying that they owed the money." The first agent responded, "it doesn't matter whether they signed the papers or what they agreed to, they were still bought and sold."

In December 2003, the Russian government passed a law criminalizing human trafficking and the use of slave labor.[2] The law was intended to make it easier for Russian law enforcement to pursue human trafficking cases, but implementation has been difficult. As illustrated by the story above, even two agents within the same agency working on the same case disagreed on how to interpret the law. Does the consent of the victim at the beginning stages of the trafficking process matter? Does the exchange of money mean that trafficking has definitely taken place? In this book, I examine how Russian law enforcement has made sense of the new laws in order to investigate and prosecute sex trafficking, labor traffick-ing, and child trafficking for illegal adoption. The passage of a new law is only the first step in its implementation. New laws are layered onto existing formal and informal practices in the institutions that must implement them. The in-stitutional machinery—its structure, culture, and incentive systems—causes law enforcement agents to act in predictable ways, not only in response to human trafficking but throughout the criminal justice system. Without taking these fac-tors into account, it is impossible to understand why Russia's law enforcement agencies have had such difficulty implementing human trafficking laws. For the purposes of this study, law enforcement is defined as encompassing four indepen-dent agencies, each of which plays a role in pursuing trafficking cases: the police (Ministry of Internal Affairs/MVD—Ministerstvo vnutrennykh del), the Inves-tigative Committee (SK—Sledstvennyi komitet), the state prosecuting agency

---

2. Federal Law no. 162-FZ, "O vnesenii izmenenii i dopolnenii v Ugolovnyi kodeks Rossiiskoi Federatsii" of December 8, 2003. SZ RF 2003, no. 50, item 4848.

(General Procuracy—General'naia prokuratura) and the Federal Security Service (FSB—Federal'naia sluzhba bezopasnosti).

Human Trafficking and the Russian Federation

Human trafficking, especially of women and children, is an issue that has engaged the international community at several points since the nineteenth century. Defined by the United Nations (UN) as the "recruitment, transportation, transfer, harboring or receipt of persons, by means of the threat or use of force or other forms of coercion, of abduction, of fraud, of deception, of the abuse of power or of a position of vulnerability or of the giving or receiving of payments or benefits to achieve the consent of a person having control over another person, for the purpose of exploitation," trafficking has been called "a grave threat to the security, stability, values and other interests of the entire world community" by the National Security Council (1997) and is often referred to as the "modern day slave trade" and "white slavery."[3]

Estimates of the number of trafficking victims are difficult to calculate. The crime is intentionally hidden, and the criminal networks are dispersed, often across borders (Laczko 2005; Andreas and Greenhill 2010). As of 2012, the International Labor Organization (ILO) estimated that worldwide 18.7 million people are being exploited at any one time in the private economy, with 4.5 million of them victims of sexual exploitation (98 percent women) and 14.2 million of them being exploited in forced labor in the agriculture, construction, domestic work, or manufacturing sectors (60 percent men). Many of these people cross borders before they are exploited, but even more are trafficked within their own countries (ILO 2012). As of 2007, the annual profits from all forms of trafficking were estimated at $91.2 billion per year, with sexual slavery being by far the most profitable (Kara 2008, 19). A woman trafficked into sexual exploitation brings in an average annual revenue of $42,000 for her exploiter (Kara 2008, 21).

Russia has three major types of trafficking: sex trafficking, labor trafficking, and child trafficking for illegal adoption. The sex trafficking problem came to Russia in the aftermath of the Soviet Union's dissolution (Hughes 2000; Erokhina and Buriak 2002; Granville 2004; Orlova 2004). During the 1990s, Slavic women, the so-called "Natashas," were trafficked out of the countries of the former Soviet Union into Western Europe, Asia, North America, and the Middle

---

3. "Exploitation shall include, at a minimum, the exploitation of the prostitution of others or other forms of sexual exploitation, forced labor or services, slavery or practices similar to slavery, servitude, or the removal of organs" (UN 2000).

East.[4] Today, Russian women are still found in all the same places abroad, but there has also been an increase in internal sex trafficking of Russian women from smaller provincial towns to large provincial centers and to the megalopolises, St. Petersburg and Moscow. Children throughout Russia are bought and sold for illegal adoption. The economic boom of the 2000s increased the amount of labor trafficking in Russia (ILO 2009a). Men and sometimes women come to Russia from Central Asia (mainly Kyrgyzstan, Uzbekistan, and Tajikistan), Moldova, Belarus, and sometimes as far as China and Vietnam, looking to make money to support themselves and their families in low-wage manual labor in the construction, agriculture, and manufacturing sectors. There are also cases of internal labor trafficking in which Russians, usually homeless people and/or alcoholics, are exploited in slave-like conditions by locals.

Estimates of the severity of the problem in Russia vary wildly, but even the most conservative appraisals are staggering. In 2013, the Global Slavery Index estimated that between 490,000 and 540,000 people were enslaved in Russia.[5] Gerber and Mendelson's 2008 survey suggests that over 175,000 women currently living in Russia are former trafficking victims. Additionally, anywhere between 10,000 and 60,000 Russian women are said to be trafficked abroad each year (Lehti and Aromaa 2006, Danilkin 2006). In a 2006 study, the sociologist Elena Tiurukanova estimated that up to 1 million migrants in Russia were experiencing some form of trafficking or slavery-like exploitation (35).

In the early 2000s, pressure on Russia to deal with this issue was building from both international and domestic sources. In 2000, 117 countries, including Russia, signed the UN Protocol to Prevent, Suppress, and Punish Trafficking in Persons, Especially Women and Children, as a supplement to the UN Convention against Transnational Organized Crime. The protocol required signatories, at a minimum, to criminalize trafficking and related activities and recommended that they develop a comprehensive strategy for fighting it. Also in 2000, the US Department of State began ranking countries on their efforts to combat human trafficking. For the first two years of this annual report, Russia fell in the lowest-ranked tier (Dept. of State 2001, 2002). Other international organizations to which Russia belongs, the Organization for Security and Cooperation in Europe (OSCE) and the

---

4. The term "the Natashas" comes from the eponymously named book by Victor Malarek (2004), one of the earliest journalistic investigations of Slavic women in the sex trade. Not all women who left Russia in the 1990s to work in prostitution were trafficked. Some were agents working on their own behalf and were able to manage the conditions of their work in the sex industry. In a situation of limited opportunities at home, many women saw migrating for sex work as a way to make money and gain independence and empowerment.

5. By the index's estimates, Russia is one of the top ten countries in absolute number of people enslaved (Walk Free 2013, 11).

Council of Europe (CoE), also issued directives for their members to follow on human trafficking (OSCE 2003; CoE 2005). International pressure was coupled with pressure from domestic nongovernmental organizations (NGOs) involved in women's issues and from law enforcement agencies. For law enforcement, officially making trafficking a crime would allow its agents to pursue crimes they had been seeing on the ground but lacked sufficient legal authority to handle.

In 2003 the Russian legislature passed changes to the Criminal Code making human trafficking and the use of slave labor criminal offenses (Articles 127.1 and 127.2). In addition, the law made significant changes to the criminal offenses of recruitment into prostitution (Article 240) and organizing prostitution (Article 241).[6] The new laws on human trafficking were meant to ease the burden of pursuing trafficking cases by giving law enforcement a statute that combined all the component parts of trafficking into one. Despite asking for a law to help combat this new crime, law enforcement's usage of these new tools has been low compared to the number of trafficking cases thought to involve Russia each year. From January 2004 through December 2013, a total of 889 instances of human trafficking and the use of slave labor were officially registered by law enforcement (see appendix B).[7] Unfortunately, many of these cases never made it any farther into the criminal justice system than the registration stage.

At the same time, the number of prosecutions under recruitment into and organizing prostitution charges exploded after the new laws were passed—in 2004 there was a 187 percent increase in crimes registered under the former and a 174 percent increase under the latter. The result has been a policy of prosecuting *human traffickers* but not *human trafficking*. When agents encounter a situation in which they could use the new laws, they have chosen to register only about half as trafficking. In the other half, they have defaulted back to prosecuting component parts of the crime—including organizing or recruitment into prostitution, migration violations, kidnapping, and/or false imprisonment—precisely the charges they complained about as being insufficient when they asked for trafficking to be made an official crime.

So why have law enforcement officials used the human trafficking laws so infrequently even though they recognize the problem and have asked for these new tools? To answer this question, we must also explore the institutional context in which law enforcement operates. Only by understanding these forces and their

---

6. *Ugolovnyi kodeks Rossiiskoi Federatsii* of June 13, 1996, no. 63-FZ. SZ RF, 1996, no. 25, item 2954, hereafter Criminal Code (CC).

7. My data was collected from December 2003 through December 2013, covering the first ten years that the law was on the books. However, because the trafficking law was passed in December 2003, the opening of cases under these statutes and collection of official law enforcement data does not begin until January 2004.

effect on decision making can we make sense of the way Russian law enforcement has handled human trafficking and how the trafficking law's meaning has been constructed in everyday practice.

Explaining Law Enforcement Practice

Russia's law enforcement agencies are its largest but most closed and secretive bureaucracies, yet some of the most important because of their tremendous power in the everyday lives of the population. Despite their ubiquity, their everyday functioning is poorly understood and often mischaracterized. Although there are several excellent studies of Soviet-era law enforcement agencies (Smith 1978; Shelley 1996; Solomon 1996), few works delve deeply into the day-to-day practices of law enforcement agencies in the post-Soviet context (Favarel-Garrigues 2011; Taylor 2011; Paneyakh et al. 2012; Paneyakh 2014). Consequently, we have little knowledge of how Russian law enforcement operates within formal rules while using informal rules and practices to do its work.

Casual observers may assume that Russian law enforcement agencies have been unsuccessful at combating human trafficking because they are lazy, corrupt, indifferent, or hostile to the victims, who tend to come from marginalized populations. Many of these concerns are true. Russia's law enforcement institutions have consistently been rated as untrustworthy and ineffective in the post-Soviet period by the public they are supposed to be serving.[8] They have also been described as predatory, interested primarily in self-enrichment rather than serving and protecting the people (Gerber and Mendelson 2008). That corruption is endemic to Russian law enforcement has been well established in both the academic literature and popular media. Since the 1990s, law enforcement agencies have been closely connected with organized crime and political elites (Varese 2001; Volkov 2002; Taylor 2011). In the Putin era in particular, the legal system has often been mobilized in the service of the state—to eliminate opposition by charging them with crimes—and in the service of the wealthy—to steal assets from rivals and/or protect themselves from legal action (Burger and Holland 2008; Firestone 2010; Levy 2010a–c; Taylor 2011). Given all this, perhaps it is unsurprising that Russian law enforcement's efforts on trafficking have been inadequate. However, law enforcement actors are not homogenous. I argue that even agents who are honest, dedicated to their jobs, and committed to fighting human trafficking are constrained by the institutional machinery with which they must contend in their day-to-day practice and have obvious incentives not to use trafficking laws.

---

8. See, in English, Davis et al. 2004; Griaznova 2007; Reynolds et al. 2008; Zernova 2012b; Semukhina and Reynolds 2013.

Trafficking is a difficult crime to interdict, requiring significant training and resources for law enforcement. But the capacity of Russia's law enforcement agencies has grown significantly over the past decade, with a dramatic increase in funding for the police force and other law enforcement services (Taylor 2011). When combined with declining crime rates, in theory, this growth in state capacity should free up law enforcement strength to combat more complex crimes such as money laundering, tax evasion, organized crime, and human trafficking (Massal'skii and Levin 2009).

There are also concerns that the government lacks the political will to push law enforcement to implement human trafficking laws. Absent clear signals from above that a new policy is a priority, agents on the ground may not take new laws or policies seriously given the multitude of other tasks they are responsible for (Khozhdaeva 2011; McCarthy 2014a). For most of the 1990s, the government refused to even recognize that human trafficking was a problem for Russia. The changes incorporating human trafficking into the Criminal Code were only a small part of a comprehensive bill on trafficking that was scuttled due to cost and political considerations, demonstrating that perhaps the political will for a true anti-trafficking campaign was lacking. Furthermore, guaranteeing the rights of the most likely victims of human trafficking—women, migrants, and other marginalized groups—has not historically been a high priority in Russia. As of 2014, Russia remains the only country in the region without any state-funded victim protection services and without a national action plan for combating human trafficking, both considered crucial for an effective response to the problem (Dean 2014). Instead, domestic NGOs largely financed by foreign funding have intermittently provided these services since the early 2000s.

At the same time, human trafficking has become a fixture in official discourse about "modern threats and challenges" (*sovremennye vyzovy i ugrozy*) to the Russian state at the highest levels.[9] It is frequently mentioned in the same breath as money laundering, tax evasion, and organized crime and has been identified as a funding source for terrorist activity (Massal'skii and Levin 2009).[10] Russia has been quite active on human trafficking in the international organizations in which it occupies a leading role, in particular the Commonwealth of Independent States. Russian law enforcement agencies have also worked with agencies in other countries to develop and implement agreements on human trafficking, including data sharing and joint investigative activities. The state has pushed local law enforcement to bring in more trafficking cases by including the crime

---

9. See, for example, interviews with President Vladimir Putin (Mikhailova, Vladimirov, and Kuz'min 2007) and Minister of Internal Affairs Rashid Nurgaliev (Vesti.ru 2008).

10. In an interview with *Rossisskaia gazeta* in 2005, Minister of Internal Affairs Rashid Nurgaliev noted that human trafficking was one of several activities that provided a funding base for terrorism, although there has as yet been no evidence released to support this claim (Falaleev 2005).

as a separate entry in its yearly evaluation criteria and has invested in human trafficking education programs for agents.

Overall, there continue to be valid concerns about the level of political will to fight human trafficking and the general efficacy of law enforcement agencies in Russia. However, these explanations can provide only a partial answer to the question of why Russian law enforcement has underperformed in implementing human trafficking laws. A more important aspect of the story is the institutional machinery of law enforcement, which has a greater impact on day-to-day choices and behavior than political will, resources, or corruption.

The Role of Institutional Machinery

When new criminal justice policies are passed anywhere in the world, the agents tasked with the laws' implementation must work out what they mean, how and when they should be used, and whether they are actually a priority for their superiors. This process takes place in an already established institutional context in which the behavior of actors is shaped and constrained by the institution's structure, culture, and system of incentives—what I term the institutional machinery. Getting street-level bureaucrats to implement new laws and policies into their daily practice is a perennial concern for policy makers, practitioners, and legal scholars alike (Feeley 1973; Lipsky 1980; Macaulay 1984).[11] Although bureaucrats are technically bound to follow rule changes that come from above, the institutional machinery in which officials find themselves often makes them reluctant to modify practices that have become comfortable over time. This pattern is precisely what we see in Russian law enforcement's implementation of human trafficking laws.

My argument about the effects of the institutional machinery on law enforcement draws on insights about the behavior of organizations and actors within those organizations from organizational theory, new institutionalism, and law and society.[12] These fields all emphasize the importance of examining the institutional context, both formal and informal, in which actors make their decisions. On one hand, understanding the formal context in which actors operate—the

---

11. "Street-level bureaucrats" are unelected government agents who interact with the public on a day-to-day basis and implement policy (Lipsky 1980).

12. This research takes a similar theoretical and methodological approach to Amy Farrell and her colleagues (2008, 2012, 2014), who study the implementation of human trafficking laws by law enforcement in the United States, focusing on the ways in which new laws are experienced by street-level implementers and how their institutional context plays an important part in the way human trafficking cases are pursued.

official rules and policies of the agency—shows how the institution works to limit the discretion of agents operating on the ground and directs their behavior toward fulfilling the institution's goals (Wilson 1989; Boyd et al. 1996). On the other hand, examining the informal norms and practices—the routines that develop over time to help make day-to-day work more efficient—gives us a greater appreciation of how actors become bound to particular ways of thinking and acting that tend to reproduce themselves, even if they do not conform to official agency policy (Lipsky 1980). Even in a strongly hierarchical system like Russia's, where it might be expected that the system has a homogenizing effect on the behavior of those who implement policy, discretion and informal decision-making criteria still play important roles.

Together, the formal and informal aspects of an institution's working environment lead to a set of routines and standard operating procedures within the agency (Allison 1971) and create the boundaries within which agents can imagine solutions to new situations they encounter, including new policies and laws (Simon 1957; March and Simon 1958). Because organizations such as law enforcement agencies mediate between the laws passed by the legislature and the people who actually apply them, the way that these organizations behave and the decisions they make have an important impact on the way that citizens experience the law and by extension the state (Feeley 1973; Lipsky 1980; Macaulay 1984; Jenness and Grattet 2005). This is no less true in the area of criminal justice, where police and other law enforcement agents have the discretionary power to decide to whom the state's protection and enforcement resources are allocated.

The structure of formal rules and procedures imposed on actors within bureaucracies drives them toward the minimization of uncertainty (March and Simon 1958; Allison 1971). Implementing new laws and policies carries an inherent degree of risk. Research, primarily done in the United States, has suggested that police and prosecutors have been particularly hesitant to implement laws that are ambiguously worded, not accorded high priority by agency heads, do not give them any strategic advantage in court, contradict their personal beliefs about the severity of the crime, or do not line up with what they think a "typical" instance of a particular crime looks like.[13] Additionally, with a new law actors in the system may disagree on its meaning and what it encompasses or, equally important, does not encompass.

Because of their risk aversion, most actors in bureaucracies tend to hew as closely as possible to existing organizational norms and procedures simply

---

13. On ambiguous wording, see Boyd et al. 1996; and Cronin et al. 2007. On prioritization, see Mastrofski and Ritti 1992; and Hill 2003. On strategic advantage, see Albonetti 1986, 1987; Ma 2002; Jenness and McPhail 2005; and Boyne 2014. On severity of the crime and typical instances, see Sudnow 1965; Mastrofski and Ritti 1992; and Farrell and Pfeffer 2014.

because they are familiar. This tendency may lead to the ossification of institutional norms and practices rather than dynamic change and adaptation to new situations as they arise. Although organizations remain capable of responding to new problems, policies, or rules, their response often takes the form of incremental steps away from the agency's existing standard operating procedures. In other words, bureaucratic actors think inside the box before thinking outside it. Departure from existing routines and practices requires some aspect of the situation to be outside the norm, shaking up law enforcement's standard operating procedures in a way that induces some sort of behavioral change (Allison 1971; Vaughan 1998) or specifically incentivizing them to do so (Bayley 2001, 2002).

Actors within organizations, including law enforcement agencies, are generally limited with regard to the time and resources they can spend on any individual problem. When they are faced with time, resource, and cognitive capacity constraints, they will look for the first "good enough" solution that will get them to the end goal rather than weighing the entire universe of possible alternatives to find the optimal one (Simon 1957).

When uncertainty and vagueness about a new policy combines with significant levels of discretion, street-level bureaucrats are likely to develop informal criteria to use as shortcuts to categorize cases or help process them more efficiently through the system (Lipsky 1980; Frohmann 1991). By the nature of their jobs interacting with citizens on a day-to-day basis, street-level bureaucrats have a significant amount of discretion in applying policy.[14] As a new criminal law is used in practice, the crime goes through "normalization" (Sudnow 1965). Agents combine the text of the laws and their own interpretations of those laws with existing beliefs and stereotypes about what a typical instance of a particular type of crime looks like to create a set of informal criteria for judging if the crime has actually taken place. Additionally, street-level workers enforce moral judgments, not just rules and laws (Maynard-Moody and Musheno 2003). They make normatively based decisions about whether victims are deserving based on their identity and behavior, thereby constructing to whom and when the state's resources are given (Gordon 2001). Finally, law enforcement's discretionary decisions not only create the meaning of the law as it is applied in practice but also lead to "produced" crime rates that are based on officer perceptions rather than crime rates that represent the reality on the ground (Black 1970).

---

14. Research on the impact of discretion and informal decision-making criteria has been more limited in civil law systems. The emphasis on certainty and clarity of the law makes scholars and practitioners alike unwilling to admit that discretion and informal decision-making criteria exist, let alone can play an important role in the outcomes of the criminal justice system. For exceptions, see Boyne (2014) on German prosecutorial discretion; and Ma (2002) on prosecutorial discretion in France, Germany and Italy.

The experiences of street-level bureaucrats in their early encounters with new laws create path dependencies at the local level. When encountering their first case, it is standard procedure for law enforcement officials to ask colleagues for advice and investigate what has been done before with similar cases. Initial decisions made at the local level during the early years of implementation can thus have persistent effects on the understanding and application of the new law over time. The on-the-ground construction of policy by street-level bureaucrats may not actually conform to the law's goals or even the agency's interpretation of the law but will nonetheless become part of the standard operating procedure and be reproduced if it is effective enough to get the job done (Skolnick 1966; Feeley 1973; Lipsky 1980).

Though the particulars of the institutional context vary from agency to agency and country to country, without an understanding of the formal and informal environment in which street-level bureaucrats operate, it can be difficult to make sense of their behavior. It is to the specifics of Russian law enforcement's institutional machinery that I now turn.

Russian Law Enforcement's Institutional Machinery

Despite twenty years of post-Soviet police practice and numerous institutional reforms, the institutional machinery for processing criminal cases still retains much of its Soviet character.[15] The first aspect of the institutional machinery is the system of incentives for its workforce. Russian law enforcement operates under a system of strict statistical performance assessment indicators called the *palochnaia sistema* (stick system). The system focuses on the number of activities completed by law enforcement (cases cleared, citations written, searches conducted, suspects arrested, etc.) to assess whether agents are performing their duties adequately, at both the individual and department level. Three statistical indicators form the core of this assessment system: (1) number of cases cleared; (2) number of cases investigated within time limits set by the Criminal Procedure Code;[16] and (3) number of cases/activities in comparison to the previous reporting period. The system is characterized by extremely detailed and time-consuming documentation requirements. Success in this system is a conviction. Anything else is viewed as failure. Consequently, at all stages of an

---

15. The term "institutional machinery" is particularly appropriate for Russia's law enforcement agencies as they tend to describe the processing of cases in a very mechanistic way as a "production chain or an assembly line" (Paneyakh 2014, 7).

16. *Ugolovno-protsessual'nyi kodeks Rossiiskoi Federatsii* of December 18, 2001, no. 174-FZ. SZ RF 2001, no 52 (Part 1), item 4921, hereafter Criminal Procedure Code (CPC).

investigation, agents are incentivized to look for cases that are familiar, in which the charges and evidence collection are straightforward and quick and that have a fairly certain chance of conviction (Paneyakh 2014).

Statistics are aggregated up the hierarchy, so lower-level officials face significant pressure from above to clear cases. This tension can lead to failure to perform police duties and to manipulation and falsification of statistics and evidence. Unlike statistical assessment systems that are used by law enforcement agencies in other countries, the Russian system sets rigid targets from the center and punishes those who do not meet them (Taylor 2014a). Failure to meet statistical targets can affect an agent's own prospects for career advancement as well as that of his superiors by limiting their opportunities for salary bonuses and movement up the ranks.

The second element of the institutional machinery is the basic structure of the law enforcement bureaucracy. In Russia, investigative and prosecutorial functions are strictly separated among multiple and often overlapping agencies, creating a situation in which no one can take ownership of a case, become invested in its outcome, and see it through to completion. This structure creates a series of barriers that deters prosecution of many crimes, not just human trafficking. Making the situation even more difficult, some crimes, including human trafficking, fall under the jurisdiction of multiple investigative agencies. As a result, a case can bounce back and forth among them with no one wanting to take responsibility for it. There are also significant institutional rivalries among the different law enforcement agencies over investigative jurisdiction and prestige, especially as power and resources have shifted among them over time. These rivalries have erupted in several public battles as usually secretive agencies pursue tit-for-tat misconduct charges against one another's agents (Taylor 2011). More generally, agents work against rather than with one another to pursue criminal cases. Overall, this structure drives law enforcement agents to do the minimum necessary to pass the case to the next person in the criminal justice chain, thereby moving it into the cleared column on their reporting sheets. Yet they are all dependent on one another, leading to institution-wide collusion to do the minimum amount possible but still move the case toward a "successful" resolution—a conviction (Paneyakh 2014).

The third element of the institutional machinery is the culture of the bureaucracy. In Russian law enforcement this culture prioritizes strict hierarchical subordination of its agents to those above them in the chain of command. Superiors are held accountable for the statistical performance of their departments and therefore put pressure on their subordinates to meet the targets, which are supposed to improve from year to year in accordance with the goals set from above (Maksimova 2011; Khozhdaeva 2011; Paneyakh et al. 2012). In this system individual agents are more likely to be punished for taking initiative than rewarded, even if that initiative is within the bounds of the law and may help an investigation. The orgranizational culture of law enforcement also dictates the norms of acceptable behavior for its agents. New agents are socialized into a culture in which corrupt behaviors and practices are tacitly accepted or outright encouraged by superiors. Given the pressure from superiors, even honest agents may find it difficult to resist joining in or at least turning a blind eye. The logic of appropriateness (March and Olsen 1984) that has developed in Russian law enforcement tends to lead to informal norms and practices that have a corrosive effect on the effective operation of the criminal justice system and the administration of justice. For example, because the performance assessment system emphasizes clearing cases, agents quickly learn that falsifying evidence or pinning crimes on marginalized people is a quick and easy way to accomplish that goal (Paneyakh 2014). Once they begin to have better statistics as a result of this practice, it tends to persist and reproduce itself over time and, more important, becomes widely accepted within the institution as a legitimate shortcut and normal behavior (Vaughan 1998).

Taken together, the three parts of the institutional machinery—performance incentives, structure, and culture—lead to predictable behaviors and strategies when Russian law enforcement encounters new laws or policies. Although often portrayed as lawless, Russian law enforcement agents are in fact acutely attuned to the intricacies of both the formal and informal requirements of their jobs. Their incentives are to process cases quickly while minimizing the risk of nonconviction or nonclearance, and they must figure out how to balance these competing demands when implementing a new law. In the absence of heavy political pressure to use a new law, agents try to minimize risk by avoiding it and sticking with familiar standard operating procedures. When they do use new laws, they apply informal criteria to determine what counts. These shortcuts are reproduced over time because they increase efficiency, a particularly high priority for Russian law enforcement given the emphasis on completing investigations in a specified time period. The result is a "race to the bottom," where law enforcement agents settle on doing the bare minimum to move the case forward and check the necessary boxes, rather than a "race to the top," where they strive to find ways to innovate and implement new policies well.

Human Trafficking Laws and the Institutional Machinery

The nature of human trafficking as a crime exacerbates the tendencies that the institutional machinery creates. Human trafficking cases have none of the characteristics that Russian law enforcement agents look for in an ideal case. Trafficking is a complex, multistage crime with multiple component parts, many of which are criminal offenses in and of themselves. And while traffickers are not limited by national borders, law enforcement is. Once the trafficking moves elsewhere, local agents must rely on other countries' law enforcement or Interpol to gather evidence, adding another layer of bureaucratic procedure to the investigative process. Witnesses are difficult to work with, as they often come from marginalized groups about which law enforcement already has negative opinions. They may speak another language, be mistrustful, or be addicted to drugs or alcohol. This complexity means that pursuing human trafficking cases is a drain on the time and resources of a department, time and resources that could instead be used to clear many other cases.

The Russian law on human trafficking also creates a great deal of uncertainty for law enforcement agents. The definition of key terms in the law, in particular buying/selling and exploitation, are vague and subject to multiple interpretations. As noted above, different people who deal with a case may disagree about whether it falls into the category of human trafficking at all. This uncertainty may lead to a case categorized as human trafficking not being successfully processed through the system, leaving a black mark on the agency's record. Using the human trafficking law, then, slows down the processing of cases and creates inefficiencies that, in the Russian context, may actually be punished.

When encountering a case for the first time, law enforcement agents are primed to look for what they already know. For example, encountering a sex trafficking victim in prostitution still triggers the organizational repertoire associated with prostitution. Rather than thinking about a trafficking violation, agents will rely on existing routines and practices to deal with situations of prostitution—fining the victim and possibly investigating the brothel owner. They may also overlook the offense entirely, since it has been common practice since the 1990s for local law enforcement to be paid in cash or in kind for benign neglect of prostitution operations. If agents encounter a labor trafficking situation involving migrants, their organizational repertoire surrounding migrants kicks in. They will check registration documents, issue fines, take the migrants into custody, and probably pursue deportation proceedings. They will be unlikely to stop to check if people from either of these groups might be victims rather than offenders. Police officers accustomed to viewing members of marginalized groups as having low moral reputations may consider victims of trafficking not deserving of aid and largely responsible for their own situations.

Ultimately, law enforcement usually invokes human trafficking statutes only when a situation clearly fits its notions of what constitutes trafficking—innocent victims who were forced into prostitution completely against their will; victims for whom money was exchanged in a direct transaction; victims who were chained up and beaten; and any transactions involving children—and would be objectively recognized as such by any actor in the criminal justice system. These determinations of what counts as trafficking have relied heavily on informal, extralegal criteria like officers' conceptions of what the ideal-typical victim looks like and how he or she should behave. These criteria are often gendered and racialized, focusing on previous sexual behavior, degree of resistance, and level of agency in entering the trafficking situation.

Thus, despite the new laws that theoretically make the job of prosecuting trafficking cases easier, agents still default to the previous standard operating procedures and prosecute human trafficking cases with alternative Criminal Code articles. In the case of sex trafficking, this approach was enabled by stronger laws against organizing and recruitment into prostitution in amendments passed at the same time as the trafficking laws. These other crimes are easier to prove, are more familiar to law enforcement agents, and often carry similar or harsher punishments, allowing them to successfully punish traffickers without having to negotiate the uncertainty and confusion surrounding the new laws on trafficking. And because many of the stages of human trafficking constitute crimes in and of themselves, a law enforcement agent would not be wrong to charge a case of sex trafficking as recruitment into prostitution or a case of labor trafficking as organizing illegal entry or false imprisonment. With infinite time and resources, perhaps agents would be able to spend the time to distinguish how the charges differ, legally speaking (Simon 1957). However, with limited time and the need to hit statistical markers, they prefer to choose from a familiar menu of options which allows them to clear the case quickly, easily, and more efficiently. Given the incentives to clear cases and the fear of punishment for not meeting performance targets, it is perhaps unsurprising that prosecuting traffickers under other, good enough, Criminal Code articles has been one of law enforcement's solutions to dealing with the human trafficking problem.

Recognizing the difficulty of using human trafficking laws, many scholars and international organizations explicitly encourage law enforcement to use other statutes to pursue human trafficking crimes in the interest of protecting human rights and combating organized crime (Gallagher and Holmes 2008). So, why does it matter if Russian law enforcement is using the human trafficking laws if traffickers are being imprisoned in other ways? The importance of using these laws is both practical and symbolic. Practically, the trafficking laws were passed to overcome many of the difficulties reported by law enforcement in pursuing human trafficking crimes (Rosbalt.ru 2002). The trafficking charge includes all stages in the process under one Criminal Code article. Without it, agencies must charge each individual member at each stage of the trafficking under a different statute. In addition, by prosecuting trafficking under other laws, law enforcement deals with only one part of the trafficking organization, usually the exploiter. This approach does not allow prosecution of each link in the trafficking chain or the

entire ring. Much like the unsuccessful strategy of trying to control drug trafficking by prosecuting street-corner drug dealers, this method is unlikely to be effective over the long run. The links in the chain are easily replaced with new people
and the trafficking rings continue to operate. Finally, the Russian government
looks at law enforcement statistics to estimate the severity of crimes and if these
activities are not charged as human trafficking, the scale of the trafficking problem in Russia will be underestimated. Symbolically, using the trafficking law is
important because it sends a signal that law enforcement takes the crime seriously,
especially if the convictions result in meaningful sentences for traffickers. Non-
enforcement and nonuse of the laws on human trafficking will allow this growing
problem to continue unchecked by legal regulation that was intended to curtail it.

Although the institutional machinery acts to drive law enforcement officers
away from charging cases as human trafficking, each year since the new laws
were passed, they have managed to register between fifty and a hundred cases
(see appendix B, table B.1). How do we explain this? Most of the cases where
agents do use human trafficking laws fit stereotypical notions of what trafficking
looks like, as described above. In this sense, the informal criteria do their job,
helping to filter in certain types of cases that clearly fit both the legal definition and the popular cultural conception of what trafficking is. In addition, the
same performance incentive structures and organizational hierarchies that lead
law enforcement agents to avoid using trafficking laws also give them a small
push to produce trafficking cases. Because trafficking has been separated out as
a distinct category on yearly performance assessment forms, it reflects poorly on
agency superiors when they fill those boxes with zeroes year after year. Choosing
a trafficking charge, at least in cases of sex trafficking, also gives law enforcement
more investigative tools because it qualifies as a grave crime (punishable by over
five years in prison). Finally, there are some dedicated law enforcement agents
who are in high-ranking positions and are sufficiently moved by the human costs
of trafficking that they are willing to pursue these cases regardless of the incentive
structures they face. Overall, though, while a few factors incentivize agents to look
for trafficking cases, the more salient pressures push them to find other means
of prosecuting traffickers. This process is explored in greater detail in the rest of
the book where I examine the impacts of the institutional machinery at the stages
of finding and identifying a case, investigating a case, and trial and sentencing.

Broader Implications

This book uses the case of human trafficking to anatomize the day-to-day workings of the Russian state's most secretive and closed set of institutions, its law

enforcement agencies. In doing so, it highlights the importance of understanding the institutional context, both formal and informal, within which these bureaucratic actors carry out their functions and the limitations that this context places on their abilities to implement new policies. But it also gives insight into two other important areas of inquiry, which I briefly mention here. In particular, it adds to a nascent but growing literature on the challenges that law enforcement faces in combating human trafficking through the criminal justice system. Additionally, it demonstrates the important role that law enforcement plays in constructing the meaning of new laws as they are implemented in practice. This is relevant not only in the issue area of human trafficking but also for laws and policies aimed at addressing other complex, international policy issues, including drug trafficking, money laundering, terrorism, and intellectual piracy.

Implementing Laws on Human Trafficking

The primary response to human trafficking around the world has been a policy of criminalization, making law enforcement agencies the primary organizations responsible for dealing with it. Yet although almost all countries now have laws on human trafficking, it remains a difficult crime to find, investigate, and prosecute.[17] An effective criminal justice response to the problem requires extensive government investment of resources both to enable law enforcement to interdict it successfully and to ensure that victims are cared for and protected (Gallagher and Holmes 2008). There is significant variation in how much success states have had in implementing their domestic human trafficking laws. But even in countries with strong, effective criminal justice institutions and a general respect for the rule of law, law enforcement agents face similar problems in combating human trafficking. In numerous country contexts, researchers have noted how uncertainty about what the laws mean, what law enforcement should be looking for, and concerns about time and resources have led law enforcement to be extremely reluctant to pursue trafficking cases.[18] A deeper understanding of the problems that law enforcement faces during the investigation and prosecution of human trafficking cases can help shine light on gaps in practice that need to be filled for a more effective criminal justice response.

---

17. According to the 2013 *Trafficking in Persons Report*, 178 countries now have criminal laws fully or partially prohibiting all forms of trafficking, some out of real concern for the problem, others out of fear of US sanctions (DeStefano 2008; Gallagher 2011). However, the total number of human trafficking prosecutions worldwide in 2012 was only 7,705 (Dept. of State 2013b).

18. On the United States, see Clawson et al. 2006, 2008; Farrell et al. 2008, 2012; and Farrell and Pfeffer 2014. On Germany, see Herz 2006, 2011; and on the Netherlands, see Verhoeven and van Gestel 2011.

Law Enforcement as Policy Implementers

As David Bayley suggests, "Judgments about the nature of rule, the ethos of government, and the quality of political life can be enriched for any country by observing how the police act . . . to ignore authoritative rule enforcement would be a profound mistake in evaluating how government is accomplished in any country" (1971, 102). Together with the military, law enforcement agencies are the "legitimate use of force" that Weber refers to in his definition of the state.[19] Without confidence in law enforcement agencies, it is difficult to build a state based on the rule of law. In the most general sense, the rule of law requires that laws are transparent and evenly applied to everyone: rich and poor; government officials and ordinary citizens. On the ground, law enforcement is most often tasked with the job of applying the laws. Thus they are the primary link between criminal justice policies as passed by the government and their implementation. Lower-level state bodies such as beat cops and trial courts are where the majority of individuals interact with the state (Feeley 1973). In effect, they are the face of the law. Interactions with these street-level bureaucrats can either help enhance the state's legitimacy when the bureaucrats act fairly or can undermine it when they do not (Tyler 1990, 2004, 2007; Sunshine and Tyler 2003). Without this basic level of trust and legitimacy, people will not approach law enforcement to ask for help and agents will not be able to conduct criminal investigations.

This book adds a comparative dimension to a rich body of scholarly work developed primarily in the US context, which connects state legitimacy with the behavior of actors in the criminal justice system.[20] Comparative work on these topics can give rich insight into how behaviors of street-level bureaucrats—in this case, law enforcement personnel—can perpetuate or undermine a belief in basic concepts that help maintain state legitimacy. Understanding the incentives inherent in the career structure of Russian law enforcement is all the more important in the context of a state that is consistently rededicating itself, at least on the official level, to eradicating corruption in the ranks of street-level bureaucracies and moving toward the rule of law.[21] Without a sufficiently nuanced understanding of the incentives underlying bureaucratic behavior, it is difficult to prescribe adequate and workable reform measures that might accomplish this goal.

Whereas law enforcement's duties are carried out at the domestic level, their role in policy implementation is far broader. As criminal problems have become

---

19. According to Weber, the state is a "human community that (successfully) claims the monopoly of legitimate use of physical violence within a particular territory" (2004, 35).

20. Exceptions include Boyne in Germany (2014), Hodgson in France (2005), Johnson in Japan (2002), and Taylor in Russia (2011).

21. Most notably put forth in then President Dmitrii Medvedev's 2009 article "Forward, Russia!" See also Hendley 2006 and 2009 for discussion on the rule of law in the Russian context.

increasingly global in character, domestic law enforcement agencies have had to also take responsibility for implementing international criminal justice agreements at the state level. Human trafficking is representative of a new class of crimes that also includes terrorism, organized crime, and money laundering. These are complex, multi-actor crimes, unfolding over time and place and sometimes requiring law enforcement to cooperate with colleagues around the world to undertake successful investigations. Russia, along with most other countries, has committed to fighting these crimes by signing international conventions, protocols, and bilateral agreements that obligate the state to do its part.

This book suggests that there may be important limitations on the efficacy of these agreements in practice. Actual compliance with international obligations on human trafficking depends not on the leaders' commitments or the legislature's incorporation of treaty provisions into domestic law but instead on the institutional machinery of the domestic agencies that need to implement the policies. No matter the level of commitment in the upper echelons of government, it is still up to local police, prosecutors, and judges to investigate, indict, convict, and sentence human traffickers. In a world in which criminal activity is becoming more transnational and countries are committing themselves to international agreements that require domestic criminal justice responses, understanding the limitations placed on domestic law enforcement agents by their own institutional environment can help us understand why many of these agreements are so poorly implemented in practice and why cooperation on these issues is inherently difficult.

HISTORY, TRENDS, AND CONTOURS
OF HUMAN TRAFFICKING IN RUSSIA

In the mid-1990s, Russian nongovernmental organizations and the West started to raise the issue of human trafficking in Russia. The domestic anti-trafficking movement grew largely out of an active shelter movement focused on violence against women—particularly domestic violence and rape—that developed in the aftermath of the collapse of the Soviet Union.[1] These organizations learned about trafficking victims from their colleagues abroad who reported helping Slavic women, "the Natashas," who had been forced to work as prostitutes. They also began receiving calls on their own domestic violence and rape hotlines from women who had returned from being trafficked abroad.

In Russia, women had been disproportionately affected by the transition away from communism and toward the free market. Policies that once existed to support women's employment like child care and maternity leave disappeared, and the lack of legal protections for women led to discrimination in hiring and expectations of sexual availability at the workplace (Bridger and Kay 1996; Orlova 2004; Ashwin 2006). At the same time, the 1990s saw sex work become increasingly destigmatized, public, and glamorized by the media (Averignos 2006). With good job opportunities few and far between, many women decided to pursue sex work either full time or as a way to supplement their income in the difficult

---

1. See Sperling 1999; Kay 2000; Hemment 2004, 2007; Kuehnast and Nechemias 2004; and Johnson 2005a for more discussion of this point.

economic transition, especially in economically depressed areas where wages were often delayed or not paid at all (Aral et al. 2003).

Others decided to take advantage of the new opportunities for work and travel abroad and found work as strippers, dancers, or prostitutes, jobs that were rumored to be more lucrative in the West than in Russia.[2] Some were successful, but others became victims of human trafficking. These women were recruited for jobs as nannies, maids, or waitresses, only to find out once they reached their destination countries that they would have to work as prostitutes. Others went to their destinations knowing they would be working as prostitutes but were deceived about the pay, working conditions, length of service, and ability to leave the situation. Many of the women became stuck, unable to pay back their debts or escape. Often they were resold over and over until they were no longer healthy. At this point, they either returned to Russia physically and psychologically damaged or stayed illegally in the destination countries, often trying to find work as prostitutes on their own. For most, when they returned, nothing had changed. They were still in desperate situations and had little social support. Many were retrafficked, returned to their traffickers willingly, or continued working in prostitution in Russia (Tverdova 2011).

Initially, the Russian government was unwilling to admit that as a source country for victims of trafficking, it too needed to play a role in combating it. Instead, government officials saw it as an issue for Western destination countries to deal with (Repetskaya 1999; Buckley 2008). Early Russian newspaper coverage blamed the West's "sex mania" and wealth for taking advantage of Slavic women and highlighted incidents of non-Russians exploiting Russians (Buckley 2007). Internal trafficking in Russia was understood by the government as something that happened only in the North Caucasus, where, officials argued, the people were culturally disposed to hold and trade slaves. There was also significant skepticism from officials about the fact that many foreign-funded NGOs were so closely involved in the issue (Hughes 2002). From the NGO side, however, many suggested that law enforcement's disinterest in dealing with human trafficking was because agents were making money in the business or at least were protecting those who were (Buckley 2008; Khodyreva 1997; Shelley 2002).

The first official discussion about human trafficking occurred in 1997 with a hearing in the Duma's Security Committee. In it, trafficking was framed as

---

2. One of the aspects of trafficking from countries of the former Soviet Union that sets it apart from trafficking elsewhere is the generally high level of education of the victims, many of whom have college degrees (Stoecker 2005; Tverdova 2011).

a national security issue rather than a violation of human rights, though there were also paternalistic appeals to Russian pride to protect "their" women and children from being taken advantage of in this way (Johnson 2009a; Shelley and Orttung 2005; Shelley 2005). In November of the same year, a conference sponsored by the Western NGO the Global Survival Network, the International League for Human Rights, and the Moscow women's organization Sestry took place in Moscow. The conference, a gathering of over 100 NGO activists and Russian and US government officials, showcased a report and documentary film based on a two-year investigation—using both traditional and undercover research methods—of the trafficking of Russian women into prostitution abroad. The report focused on the cases of Japan, Switzerland, Germany, the United States, and Macau, interviewing trafficked women, their traffickers, government officials, and local aid organizations. Members of the investigative team also worked undercover setting up a fake company for trafficking. This research exposed the existence of connections between trafficking and marriage agencies, trafficking and organized crime, and trafficking and corrupt government officials (Caldwell, Galster, and Steinzor 1997; Caldwell 1997).

At this conference, the only government participation was from the Ministry of Labor's Department on the Family, Women, and Children and the Ministry of Justice.[3] There was no participation from either the Foreign Ministry or law enforcement agencies, which activists considered to be the primary government organs that needed to deal with trafficking. At the conference, the Ministry of Justice representative made it clear that consular officials should be aware of trafficking, but that it was the Foreign Ministry's job to deal with it, highlighting the predominant belief that combating human trafficking was a task to be undertaken in the destination countries, not the countries of origin (Zavadskaya 1997). This buck passing between agencies continued to be a feature of negotiations over a trafficking law for the next several years.

In 2000 the OSCE reported that in the previous five years, more than five hundred thousand women had been trafficked from the former Soviet Union into sex slavery in fifty different countries. Many of these victims came from Russia. At about the same time, the issue became a higher priority for the United States and Europe. Foreign governments and other donor organizations poured money into Russia in attempts to stop the outflow of trafficking victims at the source,

---

3. Unlike in many other countries, Russia's Ministry of Justice is not in charge of prosecuting crimes. This task is done by the Procuracy. Among other things, the Russian Ministry of Justice oversees the court system and ensures that criminal punishments are carried out and payments from decisions in civil and arbitrazh courts are made. It also is in charge of registering organizations (commercial and nongovernmental) and political parties.

before they needed assistance in their destination countries.[4] Programs were mainly aimed at sex trafficking and were undertaken in cooperation with domestic NGOs throughout Russia. They included educational programming for at-risk groups (high-school- and college-aged women), law enforcement agencies, journalists, and doctors and other first responders; information hotlines for those seeking employment abroad; brochures and public service announcements warning women about potential trafficking situations and providing information and phone numbers of consulates and other contacts in destination countries; and a series of conferences and roundtables to discuss the issue. There was also funding for shelters for trafficking victims in several regions.

As the government became more aware of the problem, so too did society. In 2003 Yaroslava Tankova, a reporter at *Komsomol'skaia pravda* made a splash when she wrote a first-person narrative of being trafficked. In her series "I Was a Sex Slave," she described her harrowing experience going undercover and being trafficked to Israel through the Egyptian desert (Tan'kova 2003). This series sparked significant discussion and debate among the readership of this daily intended for younger readers, and a number of television programs devoted to the issue soon followed (Buckley 2007, 2009). By 2008 a survey conducted by Mendelson and Gerber among women aged eighteen to thirty-four showed that while most women (64 percent) had seen advertisements for highly paid work abroad, very few would answer such an ad (less than 2 percent). When asked why they would not, over 70 percent responded that it was probably a way to trick women into forced prostitution. An even larger number of respondents (84 percent) said that they had heard of women going abroad and being forced to work in prostitution against their will, usually from the media. In a 2008 interview with an NGO that provided medical services to prostitutes, I was told that most street prostitutes had become wary of offers of easy money in prostitution abroad and consequently preferred to stay in their own towns or travel within the boundaries of Russia (N6). However, increased awareness has also resulted in a greater tendency to blame the victims, seeing them as "libido driven, lazy people" who know what they are getting into when accepting a job abroad and therefore agree to the risk of being forced into prostitution (Tverdova 2011, 335).

---

4. Between the fiscal years 2003 and 2012, the US government obligated over $12 million for anti-trafficking activities in Russia (Dept. of State 2004a–2013a). Selected other grants from European governments include the International Organization for Migration's (IOM) $2.5 million anti-trafficking project sponsored by the European Commission (EC) and the Swedish International Development Agency (SIDA); a 99,900 euro project sponsored by the EC through the Angel Coalition for a network of anti-trafficking NGOs throughout Russia; a project in northwestern Russia ($400,000) sponsored by SIDA; and a Swiss government funded project implemented by the IOM and the Angel Coalition ($500,000) (IOM 2007a).

Issues of labor trafficking have been much slower to grab the public's attention and are usually spotlighted only in large, high-profile cases. For example, in 2013, a rescue operation performed by the civic activist group Alternativa freed twelve women from Central Asia who were being forced to work in a shop in Moscow. The widespread press coverage showed the connection between migrant labor and trafficking, especially since charges were never brought against the owners of the shop. However, as the discourse on migrants becomes more heated and tolerance falls, it seems less likely that exploited migrant laborers will be seen as a group needing special protection.

Contours of Human Trafficking in Russia

But what has human trafficking looked like in Russia since the early 2000s? The discussion that follows draws on a unique data set that relies primarily on publicly available Russian news media articles (television transcripts, newspapers, online reporting) and information from court Web sites in which Russians were involved as either victims or perpetrators and/or if the destination country was Russia (see appendix A for methodological details). The discussion here focuses on cases that law enforcement charged under trafficking statutes.[5] The data set includes other instances described as trafficking and containing clear trafficking-like elements that were not pursued by law enforcement as trafficking. Where relevant, I discuss these as well. As this book shows, looking at both types of situations together reveals clear patterns of what law enforcement sees as "counting" as human trafficking. These patterns exhibit how the institutional machinery and the incentives it creates play out in the on-the-ground practice of law enforcement agents.

Although these data show the breadth and variety of human trafficking crimes that have taken place in Russia, there is unfortunately no way to know how well the number of media reports and cases pursued by law enforcement reflect the true incidence of trafficking. Depending on the identity of the victims and the method of trafficking employed, certain types of cases may be less likely to catch the attention of law enforcement or be reported at all. Trafficking in Russia can be divided into three main types: sex and labor trafficking—both with domestic

---

5. Cases were considered to have been charged as trafficking if a specific trafficking charge (including both article number and/or aggravating factors as worded in the Criminal Code article) was mentioned in any of the newspaper articles referring to that case or the case was reported as opened (*vozbuzhdeno*) as either human trafficking (*torgovlia liud'mi*) or use of slave labor (*ispolzovanie rabskogo truda*), using the specific language of the Criminal Code.

and international manifestations—and child trafficking for illegal adoption.[6] In domestic cases the victims are Russian, and the exploitation takes place in Russia. In international cases the victim crosses the border either into or out of Russia before being exploited. There are two cases of organ trafficking in the data set, but both were interdicted before the organ transplant took place. However, a 2013 report from the OSCE indicates that Russians may have been victims in several organ trafficking cases in the OSCE region (OSCE 2013).

Of the 279 cases that law enforcement charged under human trafficking statutes (Article 127.1 and Article 127.2), the majority of them (64 percent) had to do with domestic sexual and labor exploitation (see table 1.1).[7] If child trafficking is included as a type of domestic trafficking, because all known cases have happened within Russia, the percentage of domestic trafficking cases rises to 81 percent. The charges in these cases tend to break down consistently with Article 127.1 (human trafficking) used primarily for cases of sex trafficking and child trafficking, and Article 127.2 (use of slave labor) used for cases of forced labor. Five cases were charged with both articles; in four the primary form of exploitation was labor, and in one it was prostitution. While law enforcement has sometimes understood labor exploitation as falling under Article 127.1 (ten cases were charged this way), agents have hardly ever seen forced prostitution as a use of slave labor.

TABLE 1.1 Cases charged under trafficking laws, 2004–2013 (n=279)

TYPE OF TRAFFICKING	NUMBER OF CASES	PERCENT OF TOTAL
Sex trafficking	130	46
Domestic	102	36
International	28	10
Labor trafficking	101	36
Domestic	78	28
International	23	8.5
Child trafficking	46	17
Organ trafficking	2	0.7
Domestic	1	0.4
International	1	0.4

---

6. It is important to differentiate between trafficking and legal adoption, for which there is a regulated process, although it often involves bribery in the form of gifts to the orphanage. The selling of children to which I refer here takes place completely outside normal channels. Although there are a number of cases in which minors were sold into prostitution, I include discussion of those cases in the section on sex trafficking since the primary form of exploitation was sexual.

7. This reflects findings in the International Labor Organization's 2012 report on victims of forced labor (including sexual labor) worldwide, in which most victims were trafficked domestically (ILO 2012).

Sex Trafficking

The data set includes 130 cases of sex trafficking, most of which led to convictions.[8] However, in a number of cases the human trafficking charge was either dropped or changed during the investigation or trial. The status and resolutions of these cases can be found in table 1.2.

In the majority of sex trafficking cases pursued by law enforcement under human trafficking charges, the women victims were Russian and exploited in Russia. Even then, law enforcement tended to use trafficking charges in domestic cases only when there was clear evidence of a monetary transaction having taken place. The primary form of exploitation in both international and domestic cases was prostitution, with two cases of exploitation for pornography. Let us examine the domestic situation first.

DOMESTIC SEX TRAFFICKING CASES

A close analysis of court documents and news media reports from the data set reveals a basic narrative about what happens in these cases. All the prostitution operations had some sort of recruitment scheme, qualifying them as trafficking according to the law. The victims in most of these cases came from impoverished or broken homes or had graduated from state orphanage facilities; many had experienced abuse at home. They were usually recruited while hanging out

TABLE 1.2 Outcomes of sex trafficking cases charged under trafficking laws (n=130)

	DOMESTIC CASES CHARGED AS HUMAN TRAFFICKING	INTERNATIONAL CASES CHARGED AS HUMAN TRAFFICKING
Closed	2	0
At least one defendant convicted of human trafficking	48	25
At least one defendant convicted, not of human trafficking	14	1
At least one defendant convicted, not clear under what charge	2	1
Acquitted	1	0
Ongoing	7	0
Unclear[a]	28	1

[a] I define a case as having an unclear resolution if there was no news media coverage of the ultimate outcome of the case.

___

8. There were an additional 111 cases that contained elements of sex trafficking but were not charged as such by law enforcement.

on the street with friends, at railroad stations, or after they had run away from home. Traffickers specifically target these types of vulnerable populations, who are unlikely to go to the police or to have people report them missing. In 58 of the 102 domestic sex trafficking cases, there was at least one minor victim, defined in Russian law as under eighteen.

Traffickers often went from cities to neighboring villages to recruit the women. This tactic made it more difficult for the women to return home if they were to run away, because they would have no money and no way to get there. The recruitment schemes usually involved plying the women with alcohol, then inviting them to go somewhere with the traffickers. Women were sometimes involved in the recruitment phase to make the victims feel safer. Traffickers often took advantage of the women's difficult financial situations, knowing that they were having difficulty finding a job or paying rent. The initial meetings involved a proposal to the women to work as prostitutes, sometimes having another woman convince them how profitable the job could be. However, it was rare for victims to accept the proposition right away. Usually the traffickers applied some pressure, either psychological or physical. If victims did accept without force, it was often because the recruiters had painted an unrealistic picture of the fairy-tale (*skazochnyi*) nature of the profession and the ability to live well and earn a lot of money. The trafficking occasionally began with kidnapping, but that was not the primary way in which women became involved in trafficking situations.

The exploitation of the victims followed similar patterns and usually took place in a town or city. Domestic trafficking operations were fairly small but organized, with functions divided up among the various participants. The number of traffickers in each operation ranged between 1 and 26, with an average of 4.5 traffickers per ring. The prostitution rings had clearly defined roles: an organizer who ran the operation, divided profits among the members, set the schedule, decided on a system of fines, and chose the exact places where the women would stand and ply their trade; a madam (often a former prostitute) who took the phone calls, accompanied the women to their calls, and took the money from clients; one or more security personnel who resolved any conflicts with clients, looked over the clients' apartments to make sure that the women would be safe while on their calls, and watched over and sometimes physically intimidated the women; and one or more drivers, who usually knew that the women were engaged in prostitution but did not form part of the criminal group, since they were replaced frequently (often they ended up being witnesses in the case). Prostitutes were not considered members of the group unless they were acting as the madam. If they received anything, it would be a small amount of money for food, clothes, and living expenses. Half of the cases (61) involved women traffickers, many of them former prostitutes who either joined with their pimps to exploit new women or acted as recruiters. Sometimes the women traffickers continued to work in prostitution alongside the victims but had more responsibility in the operation. In several cases, women were the primary organizers of the prostitution operations.

These operations were focused either on street prostitution or on private callers, sometimes both. The operations targeting private callers usually advertised their services by leaving business cards with taxi drivers or at local hotels and saunas. These were usually run out of one or several apartments (often belonging to a member of the group), which also housed prostitutes who did not live locally. Prostitutes who did live locally reported to the main apartment for work each afternoon to await calls from clients with the other women. Other prostitution operations were street-based, with the women standing at a designated location during working hours. In both types of operations, when a call came in or a client stopped for a prostitute on the street, one of the women or the madam watching over them discussed the price. After an agreement was made and a prostitute chosen, she was then driven to the client's house, a hotel, or an apartment rented by the organizers. The prostitution operations had different prices, based on type of service and location where the service would be rendered. The money was never given directly to the prostitute herself, always to the madam or the security guard who accompanied her to her call.[9] The number of prostitutes in each operation varied. Sometimes women worked willingly alongside those who were forced, complicating identification of victims and determining their number. Table 1.3 shows the number of victims in these cases, which ranged from one to forty (average seven).

TABLE 1.3   Number of victims in domestic sex trafficking cases (n=102)

NUMBER OF VICTIMS[a]	NUMBER OF CASES
1	28
2–5	41
6–10	10
11–15	9
>15	14

[a] For cases where the number of victims is uncertain, I count the lowest number, so this may underestimate the true number of victims in each case. This is in addition to the underestimation that occurs because many of the victims are not found or identified. This is the case for all victim counts from here on.

9. These recruitment practices and patterns of organizing prostitution have been fairly consistent since the late 1990s, when a small study of commercial sex work was carried out in Moscow (Aral et al. 2003).

In many cases, the court documents and news media reports describe in graphic detail the extensive cruelty inflicted on the victims. They were subjected to multiple rapes, beatings, and other abuse in the process of getting them to accept or continue work in prostitution. Almost all the trafficking operations had systems of fines if the women were late for work or refused to service clients, if the clients expressed dissatisfaction, or for other violations, usually between 500–1,000 rubles ($18–$36) per offense. The debts they incurred through this system kept them tied to prostitution. There was usually a "buyout" price by which a woman could leave the prostitution business. It was equal to a specified number of rubles (usually 7,500–10,000 rubles, $268–$357) or one month's work without pay, assuming no other fines were levied in the meantime. Another way for a woman to leave was to bring in two women to replace her. If the prostitute were to join another brothel, however, the buyout price was much steeper (usually 30,000 rubles, $1,071).[10] In reality, women almost never left prostitution in this way, but the traffickers used the possibility to give victims hope and as a stimulus to get them to work more to earn the buyout money faster.

When the women made their intentions to leave prostitution known, the organizers exerted significant physical and psychological pressure on the women to stay and continue working. Many of the court documents mentioned that women feared for their lives or well-being. To get them to continue in prostitution, the women were often threatened with sale to brothels run by ethnic groups—Turks, Koreans, or Chinese—who were rumored to be more perverse in the sexual acts they would force prostitutes to perform and more cruel. If a woman came into the prostitution operation with a friend, as often happened, the group might threaten to kill the friend if the woman ran away. Their families were also threatened. In one case, the victim had been brought under false pretenses to Moscow from Ulyanovsk along with her three-year-old daughter. When she expressed a desire to leave, they took her daughter to a separate apartment and held her there until the victim agreed to continue working in prostitution (no. 519).

Despite the threats and the fear, many did try to run away. Often they were chased down by their pimps, even all the way back to their hometowns. Some of them went to the police right after escaping; some (usually the minors) told their mothers, who then went to the police.[11] Others did nothing. Trafficking rings were also brought down by undercover law enforcement operations aimed at dismantling local prostitution businesses or at combating minors in prostitution.

---

10. All calculations are made with the ruble/dollar exchange rate at 28:1, the average for the time period of my study.

11. While going to the police is not always effective, especially with women and sexual violence claims, in the cases to which I refer in this section, the initial report to the police was what got the investigation underway.

INTERNATIONAL SEX TRAFFICKING CASES

International sex trafficking cases, all for prostitution, are usually the biggest, most extensive, and most resource-intensive of the trafficking cases investigated by law enforcement. The data set includes twenty-eight of these cases. Women were trafficked into Russia from Uzbekistan, Belarus, Ukraine, Kyrgyzstan, and Tajikistan. Women were sent abroad or caught in the process of being sent abroad to European Union (EU) countries (Spain, Germany, Italy, Greece, the Netherlands, Norway, Cyprus, Malta), the Middle East (United Arab Emirates, Turkey, Bahrain, Israel, Egypt, and Lebanon), and to Asia (China, South Korea, and Kazakhstan). Many of these trafficking operations sent their victims to more than one country, diversifying their trade. International trafficking operations differed in size and scope from domestic ones. Whereas in domestic trafficking cases, the number of victims usually tended to be small (average 7), in the international cases, there were usually significantly more (average 23.6), as seen in table 1.4.[12] In four of the cases, over forty victims had been sent abroad. International cases are reported to have taken place over a much longer period of time.

Newspaper articles about these cases specifically noted that each of them likely had even more victims than they had discovered, but that they had either not returned from abroad or had not come forward once they did return. This is also a testament to the more sophisticated and organized nature of groups that engage in international trafficking (Shelley 2010). International trafficking requires a significantly greater investment of resources, including money for travel and obtaining travel documents, often fraudulently. Ten of the international sex trafficking cases had at least one minor as a victim. Though minors are legally not allowed to go abroad without parental consent, those that did had documents that falsified their age.

TABLE 1.4 Number of victims in international sex trafficking cases (n=28)

NUMBER OF VICTIMS	NUMBER OF CASES
1	4
2–5	11
6–10	2
11–15	5
>15	6

---

12. This number drops to 13.5 if we exclude one case in which over 300 victims were trafficked abroad (no. 324).

Despite the fact that these international trafficking rings are very large and complex, the number of traffickers per case, between 1 and 13 (average 3.3) does not seem to be that different from domestic cases and if anything, is slightly lower. This reflects the difficulties inherent in bringing down an international trafficking ring, rather than the few people who were caught being extremely sophisticated and organized.[13] At the same time, it is somewhat easier to run a smaller operation if the main partners are abroad and all the traffickers in Russia need to do is recruit women to be sent abroad and arrange for their travel or run the brothel once the women are brought into Russia.

One notable exception is the case of Dmitrii Strykanov, a military intelligence officer, and his accomplices who, operating out of Moscow, trafficked over a hundred women from various regions of Russia to Italy, Germany, Greece, Holland, Israel, and the United Arab Emirates from 1999 to 2007 for prostitution (no. 33). They received from $1,500 to $8,000 per woman from their partners abroad. Strykanov and ten other defendants were convicted to prison sentences ranging from five to nineteen years. News articles mentioned that there could still be as many as seven more defendants at large, mostly partners in foreign countries. Later, this case was tied to an Israeli organized crime boss, Rami Saban, who had his hand in trafficking operations throughout the EU, the Middle East, and the former Soviet Union. In fact, while investigating another large trafficking operation involving women sent from Khabarovsk to South Korea, China, Greece, Cyprus, and Israel, police found three additional trafficking rings connected to Saban working in the Russian Far East in Khabarovsk, Komsomolsk-on-Amur, and Amursk (no. 342). Saban himself was later arrested in Israel with ten of his accomplices. The sheer size and scope of these investigations and the deep connections with organized crime give an indication of how complicated the investigation of international cases can be. In the Far East cases, the investigation went for two years and the case file was 140 volumes (at 500 pages per volume). Over five hundred witnesses were interviewed, and dozens of searches and forensic analyses were done. In the Strykanov case, the case file was 266 volumes. The indictment alone was twenty-five thousand pages.[14] In both of these cases,

---

13. This reflects a broader pattern in Russian law enforcement practice regarding organized criminal groups, in which usually only one or a few people are caught (Ovchinskii 2007). This strategy, of course, is a common means of structuring organized criminal groups, in which the removal of one person does not bring down the whole group. This situation may change somewhat because of the new law on cooperating witnesses passed in October 2009, which offers incentives to the one person who is caught to inform on the other members of the group (Tumanov and Shmaraeva 2009).

14. In Russia, the indictment must outline in detail all of the proof that exists for each separate charge for each separate person being charged. This makes the indictment documents long and very repetitive.

Russian law enforcement worked with Interpol and foreign law enforcement agencies in the destination countries to free the women and to conduct investigative activities.

International trafficking cases follow a fairly stereotypical narrative, one that law enforcement and the population at large would likely recognize as trafficking as it is portrayed in the media. Women are recruited—sometimes under false pretexts, sometimes with the clear intention to be prostitutes—and are then sent abroad to existing contacts to be distributed to brothels or sold to brothel owners in the destination country. They are often recruited by women who have returned from abroad with fancy clothes, jewelry, expensive cars, and so on and tell the potential victims how easy it is to make money. In cases where the women have agreed to be prostitutes, they are sometimes asked to write an IOU to the trafficker for facilitating the trip. Once in their destination country, they usually have their passports taken away and are forced to work for little or no pay. Most of their income goes to pay off the debts that were allegedly incurred to send them abroad. Debt amounts are often inflated, and as in domestic cases, prostitutes are subject to a system of fines for misbehavior, leaving them with ever-increasing debt. They are further trapped because many of them do not speak the language of the country where they have ended up or have overstayed their visas and therefore are there illegally. Traffickers often get victims tourist visas, telling them they will be changed into working visas when they arrive; this discrepancy can also make the women afraid to seek help.

There are two types of international sex trafficking that occur in Russia: women trafficked out of Russia for exploitation and women trafficked into Russia for exploitation. An example of each follows.

Trafficking out of Russia: The Mari El case (no. 29) mentioned in the introduction involved trafficking out of Russia. Starting in 2004, Nikolai Shirchenko and his associate Vadim Petrov found women to work as prostitutes in EU countries. Taking advantage of their victims' dire financial situations, Shirchenko and Petrov recruited women specifically for the purpose of prostitution, telling them they would make significant amounts of money abroad. Petrov owned a tourist agency, Puma, and with the help of Shirchenko's son, put together false travel documents for the women they recruited. Over time, the group grew to include a network of pimps in various European countries as well as a middleman/courier in Moscow who made sure the documents got to the relevant embassies and the women were met and taken care of before they left Russia. The women took out loans from Petrov and Shirchenko to finance their trips with the belief that they would earn enough money to pay them back quickly and then save money. Once abroad, they kept only about 30 percent of their earnings, so they could not save any money. Instead, they were stuck paying back the loans, which the traffickers extorted through threats of plastering their parents' neighborhoods with revealing information about their engagement in prostitution. In June 2006 Shirchenko and Petrov were arrested with one of their foreign partners, Alberto Spakhiu, a Spaniard with Albanian citizenship, who was in Yoshkar Ola to accompany two of the women to Spain to work in one of his brothels. They were eventually sentenced to between eight and nine years in prison each.

Trafficking into Russia: In another case, eight women were trafficked into the city of Ussuriisk in the Primorskii region from Uzbekistan for exploitation in prostitution (no. 87). Acting on intelligence about a trafficking operation from law enforcement colleagues in Tashkent, Russian agents started investigating the trafficking operation. In April 2004 Igor Khvan, who was living in Ussuriisk, wired his friend in Tashkent, Uzbekistan, money to buy plane tickets and a recruitment fee of $300 to send him several women to work in prostitution. When the women arrived in Russia, they were met at the airport by Khvan. He took their passports under the guise of needing to register them, took them to an apartment, and forced them into prostitution. After several months, one of the women, Liudmila Kim, struck a deal with Khvan, saying that she would recruit more women (including her cousin!) if he would send her back to Uzbekistan. They began a business whereby Khvan would send Kim a recruitment fee and money to pay for the women's plane tickets to Ussuriisk, where they were then forced into prostitution. Eventually, in December 2004, the police conducted a raid, freed the women, and arrested Khvan. A separate case was opened by Uzbek law enforcement to prosecute Kim for her role in the operation. Khvan was convicted to seven years in prison in January 2006.

Labor Trafficking

Human trafficking into forced labor situations generally occurs in industries that are less regulated and therefore more likely to have informal employment practices (Tiurukanova 2005a, 10). In Russia, the informal economy is enormous, accounting for anywhere between 49 and 70 percent of the country's gross domestic product, depending on the estimate (Schneider 2004; Sharapenko 2009). There are a number of sectors in which noncontract work has become the norm, particularly construction, agriculture, and the service sector (for domestic services, repairs, etc.). The informal nature of this work makes people vulnerable to being used as slave labor.

In the data set, there are a total of 101 labor trafficking cases.[15] In all of them, the labor exploitation occurred in Russia. There were no cases of Russians being

---

15. An additional 121 cases had elements of labor trafficking but were not charged as such.

trafficked out of Russia for labor purposes. Here I define international cases as those where the victims were recruited into trafficking situations from their countries and usually brought illegally into Russia for exploitation. There are also a number of cases in which foreign victims are already present, legally or illegally, in Russia. Victims in labor cases were usually men, although there were several cases where women were trafficked for domestic servitude or factory work or alongside men to help cook and clean for them. The status and resolutions of the cases in the data set can be found in table 1.5.

Labor trafficking cases tend to involve two types of victims. The first group comprises Russians and/or other local residents who are homeless, alcoholics, drug addicts, or of similarly marginalized status. These are usually men who have fallen on hard times and do not have families or friends who might search for them when they disappear. They are usually exploited by locals living in their region or a nearby one. Many of them do not have identity documents or places to live.

The second and more frequent group is foreign migrant workers. Sometimes these victims are exploited by members of their own ethnic groups, sometimes by Russian citizens or a combination of the two. Most workers who were brought into Russia specifically for labor exploitation were from Uzbekistan (ten cases) and Ukraine (six cases). Others came from Vietnam (two), Kazakhstan (two), Tajikistan (two), Moldova (one), and China (one). In one enormous case from Moscow, over seven hundred workers were brought in from Morocco, Egypt, Syria, Kyrgyzstan, Uzbekistan, Azerbaijan, and Vietnam to work in a sewing factory producing fake brand-name goods (no. 561).

A number of characteristics make migrants particularly vulnerable to becoming victims of forced labor. Most of them have chosen to migrate for economic reasons. The forced labor situations usually begin as recruitment, masquerading

TABLE 1.5 Outcomes of labor trafficking cases charged under trafficking laws (n=101)

	DOMESTIC CASES	INTERNATIONAL CASES
Closed	1	1
At least one defendant convicted of human trafficking	46	9
At least one defendant convicted, not of human trafficking	12	2
Acquitted	2	0
Ongoing	3	3
Unclear	14	7
Suspended	0	1

as employment for an ordinary job (Tiurukanova 2005a, 11). Recruitment often takes place through existing relationships and networks, giving the recruited person an automatic basis for trust in the information that the recruiter is providing. Although some accept the jobs because they promise good pay and good working conditions, many migrants are quite willing to work in flexible working conditions. A surprisingly large number accept jobs abroad without knowing what type of work, what hours, and what conditions it will entail. As Tiurukanova explains based on her interviews with migrant workers, this is because they see their situations as temporary and are therefore willing to accept discomfort and misery if their family stands to gain from the money they can earn (2005a, 66). One victim's lawyer from a case in Orel described this well: "Their [the traffickers'] greed did them in. If they had just paid them money, the Uzbeks would have been ready to tolerate inhuman working and living conditions" (Svetova 2008).

Frequently the migrants' only pay is that they return safely to their countries and even that sometimes happens only because they have been deported by unscrupulous bosses who call the migration police so they do not have to pay the migrant laborers their wages. Given their willingness to accept jobs in less than ideal conditions, victims' understandings of exploitation are often subjective, which means they may not see themselves as being exploited at all (Brunovskis and Surtees 2007; Surtees 2008, 24). Foreign victims are also easy to exploit because they are often in Russia illegally and therefore less likely to go to law enforcement because they do not have proper documentation.

Most slave labor cases have multiple victims, ranging from one to forty-nine (table 1.6). In the international cases, the number of victims per case was significantly higher, an average of thirteen, compared to an average of five victims in domestic trafficking cases.[16] This reflects the practice of traffickers recruiting an entire work brigade at a time (Surtees 2007a). In many of the cases, law enforce-

TABLE 1.6 Number of victims in labor trafficking cases charged under trafficking laws (n=101)

NUMBER OF VICTIMS	NUMBER OF DOMESTIC CASES	NUMBER OF INTERNATIONAL CASES
1	26	3
2–5	32	5
6–10	11	3
11–15	3	5
>15	6	7

---

16. I have left out the case with 700 victims mentioned above (no. 561) so as not to skew the average.

ment noted that the victims could not all be found or did not all agree to testify, so usually the number of officially recognized victims was much lower than the true number of victims.

The number of traffickers in each operation ranged from 1 to 21 (average 2.6), with all but 9 cases involving between 1 and 4 traffickers. There is no difference in the average number of traffickers in domestic and international cases. Labor trafficking operations are usually run by men and exploit men, unlike sex trafficking operations where there is significant involvement by women. There were thirteen labor trafficking cases that had women victims and eighteen cases in which women were involved as suspects.

Most victims of slave labor work excessively long hours, live in poor conditions, do not eat regularly, and are not paid for their labor. Kidnappings that lead to trafficking situations are rare. The predominant forms of subordination in labor trafficking cases do not differ significantly from those used in sex trafficking cases: physical violence, debt bondage, confiscation of identity documents, and isolation. As soon as victims enter the trafficking situation, traffickers ask for their passports and other identity documents under the guise of registering them for work. Such requests are common practice in Russia and countries of the former Soviet Union and are unlikely to raise any sort of suspicion in the victims. The traffickers then keep the documents, making it difficult for the workers to leave the situation or go for help.

Victims' inability to leave the situation is further guaranteed by the fact that many of them are locked up, chained, or guarded by human or canine minders. In one case in the Perm region, the victims were reportedly placed on a 1-kilometer long chain that allowed them to cover the entire grounds of the factory where they were forced to work (no. 248). In addition, most labor trafficking takes place in locations that are far from cities or in small villages where the traffickers are well connected with local authorities and sometimes local organized crime groups. This makes the victims afraid to seek help and the neighbors too scared to help. One railroad station employee in the Novosibirsk region stated in a media interview that he regularly witnessed the initial stages of labor trafficking at the train station: "Of course we see them selling foreigners into slavery, but we can't help them. Many of us have families and children and if the criminals find out that we turned them in or tried to help [the foreigners], we'll have to answer for it with the health and lives of our families" (Ol'shanskii and Kochemin 2007). When the labor takes place in cities, the victims are kept isolated from contact with the outside world, usually living on the premises where they are exploited.

Victims are kept in check by threats of or actual physical violence to themselves or to their families. They are beaten for mistakes, poor work, or attempts at running away, and these beatings often take place in front of others to serve as an example. Beatings can be exceptionally vicious. In one case in the Kurgan region (no. 354), where over fifty people from Russia and abroad had been used as slaves in factory and agricultural work, victims reported that the accused beat them with bats if they tried to escape or worked poorly and sometimes put plastic bags over their heads to mimic suffocation. One woman who tried to escape was placed in a small room, chained to the bed, and not fed or given water for several days. Others were punished by having to spend up to twenty-four hours in a cistern barrel without food and water. Another victim in this case described his punishment for working poorly: "I was supposed to maintain the temperature of the stove where the steam came from to make the boots, but the pressure wouldn't go up. They came in and started to yell, and then they grabbed me and shoved me in. I was chest-deep in the hot stove. I was lucky that at the moment they threw me in, it was burning low. I resisted as much as I could. All of this went on for about fifteen minutes, and then they let me go and I pulled myself out of the stove" (Zadvornykh and Panov 2013).

News articles report in harrowing detail the level of trauma experienced by the victims and the long-term consequences to their health from both the working conditions and the physical abuse they suffered at the hands of their traffickers. In several cases there was speculation that other victims had died in these conditions but their bodies had not yet been found. Murder charges were also pursued in three cases in which the traffickers beat the workers to death because they refused to perform the work demanded of them or had become too injured to continue working (nos. 39, 92, 367).

Debt bondage is frequently used as a way to make victims continue to work. In cases where men are brought to Russia from abroad, they are told they must repay the costs of their transport. Usually these costs are inflated. In several cases, workers were originally told that they would owe a certain amount for transport and could work it off when they arrived. As soon as they arrived in Russia, however, the traffickers announced that the transportation costs were actually much higher and they would have to work that amount off instead. In a case from the Volgograd region (no. 126), the victim was tending horses on an oral contract. When several of them died, he was told that the value of the animals was 100,000 rubles ($3,571) and that he now owed the trafficker for his carelessness in letting them die. His passport was confiscated, and he was beaten when he tried to leave, turning what was an ordinary working situation into exploitation. In several other cases, the victims were told that they ostensibly owed money to the trafficker as a result of some business dealing they had had in the past, after which the trafficker kidnapped them and forced them to work off the debts.

In a creative way to get as much as possible from their victims, traffickers have also tried to extort money or property. In one case in the Chelyabinsk region (no. 328), an enormous labor trafficking case was originally uncovered during an investigation of an attempt by the traffickers to fraudulently obtain an apartment in the city of Karabash. They had promised to help one of their employees sell his inherited apartment and instead tried to appropriate it for themselves. He went to the police, and in the search of the traffickers' apartment, the police found documents of people who were being held as slaves and forced to work at their trash dump, sorting recyclable materials. In another case in the Kostroma region, the accused used the victims' passports to take out loans to buy luxury items (no. 269).

The types of labor that trafficking victims performed were varied (see table 1.7). The primary labor activities were agriculture, factory work, and construction.[17]

The following example cases give a good sense of how labor exploitation works in different industries in Russia. In a typical case of slave labor in agriculture—the first case prosecuted in the Chelyabinsk region—a father and son, Vladimir and Yuri Simonyan, were convicted in absentia for using slave labor (no. 13). They found unemployed men in the city of Magnitogorsk and promised them well-paid work with housing and food. From October 2006 to January 2007 they held four victims and forced them to work on their property under threat of death. The victims did difficult physical labor looking after livestock, cleaning stalls, and carrying water. They lived in an unheated shed during the winter,

TABLE 1.7   Labor trafficking cases by primary type of labor (n=101)

TYPE OF EXPLOITATION	NUMBER OF CASES
Agriculture/animal husbandry	30
Factory	17
Construction	14
Domestic labor (gardening, miscellaneous household services)	12
Forestry/gathering	4
Automotive (car wash, repair)	4
Begging	4
Salvage/trash	2
Fishing/maritime	2
Other/unspecified[a]	12

[a] This includes four cases of soldier/prisoner labor and eight in which the type of labor performed could not be ascertained.

17. A report from Human Rights Watch in 2013 detailed a number of foreign migrant workers in situations of labor exploitation during the construction of venues and other infrastructure for the 2014 Winter Olympics in Sochi, including holding identity documents, nonpayment or withholding of wages, excessive work hours, and inadequate housing and food (HRW 2013).

guarded by dogs, and were fed food unsuitable for human consumption. They were humiliated, insulted, and beaten if they did not work. Several ended up with broken bones. In trial, one of the victims said: "We were beaten worse than their cattle. They didn't beat their cattle like that. They felt bad for them" (Pinkus 2007). The case was opened after one of the victims managed to run away and contact the police, who then found the rest of the workers. The father and son attempted to pay the victims their lost wages (6,000–25,000 rubles, $214–$892) to get them to drop the case, after which the victims disappeared. Only through dedicated investigative work were they found and their statements taken. Though the Simonyans' lawyer made the argument that the men agreed to the work and therefore were not victims, the defendants were still convicted to 3.5 years in prison each. Unfortunately, the sentence never took effect. The convicted men fled and have been on the wanted list ever since.

One of the most publicized cases of international labor trafficking happened in 2008 in the region of Orel (no. 90).[18] In this case Alexei Prygunov and Pyotr Shmakov, two Orel locals, used their contact, a police officer in Uzbekistan, to recruit men to work at their carwash with promises of good salaries and good working conditions. From September through December 2006, they brought twenty-four Uzbeks to Orel via Moscow. When the victims arrived, their documents were taken away under pretense of registration. The men were forced to work for sixteen to twenty hours a day for no pay until April 2007. The victims' lawyer suggests that there may have been more than sixty victims, but many disappeared after the MVD raided the carwash. Those who tried to call home for help were beaten and forced to call their relatives and tell them everything was fine. They slept on metal cots, were fed only pasta and bread (once they were so hungry they had to eat dog), and were under constant guard. They were beaten for anything they did wrong and fined if they did not wash the cars fast enough. The system of debt bondage worked, as they racked up debt for transportation, bedding, uniforms, and registration to work legally in Russia. To ensure discipline, the traffickers kept guns and frequently displayed them to the victims.

The slaves were finally released after one of them managed to call the authorities. However, the MVD only showed up after the FSB pressured them. This is likely because one of the traffickers involved was a member of the regional elite—the head of the region's freestyle wrestling federation and a member of the region's anticorruption committee. In one newspaper article, the reporter speculated on how the traffickers got away with it: "The officers said that the owner of the car wash, Aleksei Prygunov, was a known criminal authority in the

---

18. The following account is a combination of news sources and a presentation by the victims' lawyer, Dionys Lomakin, at a conference I attended in Vladivostok.

past. In the last few years, he managed to move his way up into the local elite. He headed the freestyle and Greco-Roman wrestling federation and was on the public council for fighting corruption. Probably, he felt confident that no one would see anything unnatural about his 'business'" (Svetova 2008).

Because of the elite status of the defendants and their connections, both the victims and their lawyers experienced significant pressure from procurators and the defense lawyers to drop their complaint. In the end, of the twenty-four victims who were found, six stayed in Orel to testify. Even this required the help of a local NGO that was able to provide the men with a place to stay. The NGO was also threatened. Finally, after a long and grueling trial, Prygunov and Shmakov were acquitted of using slave labor. Instead, they were convicted of organizing illegal migration, given three-year conditional sentences, and released in the courtroom.

In cases of exploitation in factories, the industries range from garments to canning to preparation of processed foods. In Dagestan numerous slave labor situations have been discovered in brick factories. This problem came to the attention of the public and law enforcement in 2009, when several men were featured on the missing persons television program *Zhdi Menia* (Wait for Me), which tries to unite missing people with people searching for them. Some of the men were eventually found working as slaves in brick factories in Dagestan. Over the next several months, Dagestani law enforcement looked into violations on the premises of brick factories in the region and eventually uncovered over two hundred violations of labor law, mostly administrative and sanitary violations (Aledzieva 2009). There were a number of civil claims for compensation and one criminal case opened for use of slave labor. In this case (no. 320), through friends, the accused had recruited mostly homeless men to work at the factory. Once they arrived, he took their documents, would not let them leave the premises, and did not pay them.[19] In 2013, a civic activist organization—Alternativa, headed by the twenty-six-year-old Oleg Melnikov—brought the issue of slave labor in brick factories to the public's attention once again when he and his rescue squad began freeing men and women from brick factories in Dagestan who had gone missing. The early operations were undertaken with the support of the mayor of Makhachkala and in cooperation with local law enforcement, but none seem to have resulted in any criminal cases being opened against the factory owners (Aronov 2013; Kolesnikova 2013; Pustovoitov 2013).

Two large trafficking cases involved victims forced to dig through piles of trash and look for recyclable materials (nos. 241, 328). According to an article

19. As of the writing of this book, the outcome of this case is still unclear. The investigation was reported as ongoing as of August 14, 2009, but there is no further information available.

in the *Moscow Times* (Smirnova 2013), recycling has the potential to become a very profitable business in Russia, as reports from a case in Chelyabinsk show (no. 328). The owners of the trash dumps were estimated to be making about 200,000 rubles ($7,142) a month from the labor of local homeless men (Interfax 2013). One of the slaves in this case described his ordeal: "The trash dump was my workplace. We collected trash from 5 a.m. to 11 p.m. every day without weekends or holidays. You weren't allowed to be sick—they'd force you to work. We had to tear open every bag of trash and take out the plastic bottles and tin cans. Nonferrous metals were considered the most valuable. If I missed one of these, they punished me, took me to the guard post or right in front of everyone else and hit me in the head and the chest" (Vystavkina 2013). The slaves in both of these cases were forced to forage for food and water in the dump.

A 2013 speech by the head of the Investigative Committee, Alexander Bastrykin, identified labor trafficking for exploitation on fishing boats as an increasing problem in Russia (ITAR-TASS 2013). In that year alone, there were three different boats whose captains were charged with using slave labor, all connected with the same ownership group based in Vladivostok (no. 578). Prior to that, however, there was only one case of this type, which occurred in 2005 when twenty-eight Ukrainian fishermen were forced to illegally fish crabs in the Pacific Ocean off the Sakhalin coast (no. 86). Begging is a form of labor trafficking that occurs primarily in large cities. In the three begging cases that are included in the data set, men and women, usually handicapped, are recruited from the provinces or from other countries with promises of jobs, brought to the city, and stationed in the metro or on the street to beg (nos. 59, 211, 413). They are expected to bring in a certain amount of money each day and are punished if they do not. Although there are too few cases of this type to make any generalizations, all three are identified as having Roma exploiters.

Most cases of labor trafficking come to law enforcement's attention because the victims escape and report them. Usually a successful escape follows several previous attempts and involves some daring. In one trafficking situation women from Vietnam were forced to work in a garment factory on the outskirts of Moscow, and they tied together the shirts they had sewn to lower themselves from the fourth floor (no. 500). Unfortunately, the shirts did not hold together and several of them ended up with broken bones, which is what finally alerted the police to the situation. Similarly, in a case in Murmansk (no. 78) several victims broke their legs in an escape attempt from the second floor of an alcohol factory. In other cases, the victims are reported to have walked for days, usually under cover of night, because they feared they would be tracked down by the traffickers and forcibly returned to the slave labor situation. In one particularly desperate and creative move, a victim saw a truck driver going by with license plates from his home region and managed to slip him a note containing the address where he was being held to deliver to his wife, who then called police (no. 297). In some cases, the families or friends of victims filed missing person reports which the police then checked into and found the victims. In others, neighbors who lived near where the exploitation was taking place called the police or the FSB.

SOLDIER AND PRISONER LABOR

One subset of cases is conspicuously absent from the charging practices of law enforcement under Article 127.2: the use of conscripted soldiers as slave labor by either their commanders or someone to whom their commander has rented their services. The military has a reputation for treating its conscripts poorly, and stories of abuse are widespread. Although the media refers to these cases as slave labor, they are rarely prosecuted as such. If criminal charges are brought against a commander, they are usually under abuse of official position/authority statutes (CC Article 285 or 286). Occasionally there have been slave labor charges attached, but only once has law enforcement successfully convicted anyone involved. The soldier cases are part of a larger group of cases in the data set, forty-two in total, in which people in positions of power including police, prison officials, heads of state orphanages, and so on unlawfully used the labor of people under their care.

The one case where slave labor was prosecuted successfully took place in the Krasnodar region. A commander rented a nineteen-year-old soldier under his command to a local for agricultural work for five months (November 2005–March 2006). The soldier was not paid for his work; all the money he earned went to the commander. He finally managed to run away but did not return to his unit because he was afraid the commander would send him back. Instead, after spending the day at the train station without any money, he asked the cashier to call the police. In 2007 the local who had rented him was convicted of use of slave labor and received a two-year conditional sentence (no. 26). No news articles mentioned what happened to the commander who rented him out. In a similar case in 2005 in Vladikavkaz (no. 201), the soldier Oleg Tereshkin from Bashkortostan was rented to a local for 700 rubles or a piglet every week. While working, he was fed cow heads and innards and was beaten. He was forced to write to his parents every month saying that things were going fine in his service. He tried to run away several times, but when he got back to his camp, the commander returned him. He managed to call home with the cell phone of a passerby and his father came to rescue him. Initially, he was considered a deserter, a common response by the military to accusations of exploitation, but the charges were eventually dropped. The local, who had been renting soldiers for over seven years, was charged with using slave labor, but the case does not seem to have gone anywhere.

In other cases, the soldiers' lawyers have tried to make the argument that slave labor charges are appropriate but have not had much success convincing procurators. In the case of Andrei Rudenko, a soldier who was rented out together with a bulldozer to help a Chita man construct roads, the victim was paralyzed in an accident as a result of the slave labor. After several trials, his superior was convicted of four counts of abuse of authority, sentenced to three years in prison, and banned from the military for several years. Rudenko's lawyer vehemently disagreed with the classification: "We think that . . . [the commander] ought to be held responsible for trafficking and using forced labor. The majority of the witnesses stated that the soldier was, at a minimum, in the [subordinate] position of guard and mechanic when he was working on the bulldozer. What is that if it's not forced labor?" (Regnum.ru 2007b). In 2007 an all-Russian assembly of NGOs focused on alternatives to compulsory military service suggested in an open letter to the procurator general and the head military procurator that they use these Criminal Code articles more frequently to deal with commanders who had committed these crimes (Za demokraticheskuiu AGS 2007).

Child Trafficking

In Russia, the idea that "children represent the country's future and the continuation of the Russian nationality resonates . . . powerfully" (McKinney 2009, 300–301). At the same time, seven hundred thousand children were in state care as of 2008, two-thirds of whom still had at least one living parent (Rudnicki 2012). There continues to be significant concern about exploitation of Russian children by foreign adoptive parents, which is marked by strongly protectionist rhetoric and, as of 2013, bans on adoption of Russian children to particular countries including the United States.[20] Despite the insistence that it is easy for foreign adoptive parents to simply pay money to buy Russian children and take them for whatever purposes they want (usually the implication is some sort of sexual abuse), in the period from 2004 to 2013, there were no cases of this type opened under human trafficking laws.[21] The only exception is a case from December 2013 (no. 555), when, based on an investigative report by Reuters, the Investigative Committee opened a case against twenty-six families in the United States who had adopted Russian children and later given them away or traded them on an Internet exchange.

---

20. This fire is stoked every time there is a reported death or abuse of a child that was adopted from Russia. In fact, the US government representatives with whom I attended conferences were so used to this accusation that they were always ready with statistics about how many children had been adopted by Americans in contrast to how many had been harmed by their adoptive American parents.

21. Russia does have a provision in the Criminal Code prohibiting illegal adoption (CC Article 154), but it must take place multiple times or with the intent to profit. Punishment for the offense can be a fine up to 40,000 rubles or equivalent to three month's pay, community service up to 350 hours, corrective labor up to a year, or arrest for up to six months.

There are two main types of child trafficking in Russia. The first is the stereotypical child trafficking ring. These well-organized groups sell newborn babies to childless couples for illegal adoption. A total of twelve trafficking rings of this type have been uncovered by law enforcement, five in Chechnya (one was a cross-regional case between Dagestan and Chechnya, though it was prosecuted in Chechnya), two each in Stavropol and North Ossetia, and one each in Dagestan, Moscow, and Ulyanovsk. All but three of these were charged under the human trafficking statutes. The other type of child trafficking that occurs in Russia is one-off situations in which mothers and/or fathers who are in difficult financial or life situations decide to sell their child to get money to pay debts, make purchases, or otherwise get rid of the financial burden that a child brings. Forty-three of these types of cases have taken place, with all but five charged as human trafficking. Unlike cases of both sex and labor trafficking, child trafficking cases usually only have one or two defendants. The biggest child trafficking ring in the data set consisted of four people.

Organized child trafficking rings are fairly small, but they have a clear working scheme. They all have at least one member of the group (usually a woman) who is connected to a maternity hospital as a doctor, nurse, or midwife or has close connections with one of these people. These medical professionals are in a position to convince women or girls who are giving birth at the hospital to give up their babies at the hospital by signing away parental rights. Other members of the group then help as middlemen or falsify paperwork to enable the illegal adoption to take place. In all but one of these cases, the children were newborns when they were sold, most less than a week old. In almost all cases of organized trafficking, the price for children was mentioned in the news coverage. The prices for children appear to be more or less fixed by the group, sometimes with differential pricing for boys and girls. For example, in a 2006 case from Chechnya, the price for newborn boys was 110,000 rubles ($3,928) and for girls, 80,000 rubles ($2,857) (no. 11). By 2012, when another case was discovered in the same region (no. 420), the price had increased fourfold. Newborn boys were being sold for 500,000 rubles ($17,857) and newborn girls for between 350,000 and 400,000 ($12,500–$14,285).

Most of the women who give their babies to these trafficking rings are not paid by the traffickers but instead did not want their children or were already planning to give up their babies at the hospital. In one case (no. 421), a mother, who had given birth to a baby in the region of Kabardino-Balkaria, had already given up her baby at the hospital when she was approached by a woman trafficker, Liubov Dashaeva. Dashaeva offered to pay her 50,000 rubles ($1,785) for the child and hire a lawyer to do the legal work of reinstating her parental rights. The baby was then sold to a family in Chechnya by Dashaeva who was later sentenced to a three-year prison term for her activities. In other cases the babies are obtained through deception. In a case that was ongoing in Chechnya as of the writing of this book (no. 420), a young girl gave birth in a Dagestan hospital, after which the nurse told her that the child had a congenital disorder when in fact he was perfectly healthy. Consequently, she signed away her parental rights in the hospital, and the child was taken by the trafficker, Umalat Amaeva, and sold in Chechnya. In this particular trafficking ring, Amaeva, acting as the middleman, had connections with other medical professionals in hospitals throughout Dagestan who targeted young mothers to convince them to give up their babies. They were rumored to have sold at least twelve babies in this fashion.

In defending their actions, members of these groups always note that they are simply trying to find good homes for unwanted children or helping infertile couples. They insist that they screen the adoptive families carefully to make sure that they have financial stability and can take care of the children. In one case in Stavropol (no. 266), Tamara Konova, a former maternity clinic employee, offered her services as a middleman, matching up buyers and mothers. She charged between 40,000 and 100,000 rubles ($1,428–$3,571), with an initial payment of 50,000 rubles ($1,785) to arrange the fake documents at the time of the birth. Her fees included an honorarium to be paid to the mother, payoffs for the doctors for filling out false documents about the birth, and payments for the delivery of the child and the mother's hospital stay. During the trial she admitted her guilt but said: "I did not want anything bad for the newborns. The birth mother wanted to kill the child, I convinced her to have the baby and leave it in the hospital. I wanted the baby to grow up in a proper family" (Stavropolye.tv 2009). Although this case was not prosecuted as human trafficking, the woman was sentenced to two years in a prison colony for fraud and giving bribes (CC Articles 159, 291). In another case in Moscow (no. 38), the defendant, Liudmila Verzhbitskaya, defended herself by saying:

> I didn't sell any children. It's all a lie. I just really wanted to help childless parents find happiness. Those who approached me about abortion, I helped them rethink it. I hoped that once their babies were born, it would awaken a maternal instinct and they would keep the baby. If they refused the child, I tried to place it in a good family. Surely this didn't hurt anyone. About the money, yes, I took it, but it was only for expenses connected with the birth and necessary documents. I placed all the children with parents who were participating in the surrogate mother program but for various reasons it didn't work out. All the children are in good families. And you see how many abandoned children we have [in Russia] and what their fate is like. (Korablev 2005)

In the one-off situations of child trafficking, parents usually put the word out on the street that they are looking for a buyer for their child, sometimes trying to arrange the transaction before the baby is even born. Usually they begin looking for buyers among their friends, neighbors, or communities; only rarely do they advertise publicly. There is usually negotiation over the price for the child, and because the parents are so desperate, there seems to be a lot of room for negotiation. Articles on several of these cases mentioned how the parent started with a much higher asking price but quickly came down to meet the potential buyer at whatever price they were offering, often by over half. In one example, the buyer, who was cooperating with the police at the time of the purchase, had originally agreed to pay 26,000 rubles ($928) for the child but showed up to make the purchase with only 6,000 rubles ($214) in cash. The mother took the money and gave her the baby (no. 509). In contrast to the organized groups, in the one-off sales asking prices vary widely. Children were sold for as little as 60 rubles ($2) and as much as 4 million rubles ($142,000).

The transactions in these cases usually take place at some semipublic place: outside a bar, at a train station, or in a parking lot. The money is exchanged for the child in a very straightforward transaction. News media coverage of these cases places particular emphasis on the lack of emotion and indifference shown by the parents at the moment when they hand their child over to the buyer. Sometimes the children themselves are in bad shape. In several cases the children who were sold were described as half-naked, dirty, underfed, or sick.

As for the people selling their children, the common thread is desperation. In almost every one of these cases, once caught, the parent (usually the mother) identifies financial difficulties as the reason for selling the child. In one case in the town of Bikin in the Khabarovsk region, the police learned from local residents that a woman was looking to sell her five-year-old son so that she could invest the money in her shuttle trade business bringing goods from China to Bikin (no. 340). In another case in Perm, the parents were reported to be selling their eighteen-month-old daughter for money to buy an apartment so they would not have to live with their parents any longer (no. 390).

Some of the sellers are described as alcoholics or drug addicts. Many of them have had previous run-ins with the law, and almost all of them are unemployed. Fathers are usually absent, and there may be other children at home already. In several cases, the people selling their children are later found not mentally fit to stand trial and are remanded to a psychiatric institution. Some of the children are even sold while the parents are intoxicated.

In some cases, children are born to women who are temporarily in Russia for work (legally or illegally) and are barely subsisting on their own or with the other children that they already have. In Kaluga, law enforcement got wind of a couple's plan to sell their baby and staged a fake purchase. The woman, Gulnora Karaboeva, had come to Russia from Uzbekistan for work but became unemployed and was trying to support her children who still lived in Uzbekistan. She had met the father of the baby while working in St. Petersburg, after which they moved to Kaluga together. But because they were not registered, they could not get medical care or find a place to live. At the time Gulnora gave birth, they had been living in basements and sleeping on the streets. In its decision, the court recognized the difficult life circumstances of both parents as mitigating factors in sentencing (no. 333). Nevertheless, they were each sentenced to four years in prison, and the baby was put into state care.

Cases of child trafficking are usually discovered either through undercover work in which law enforcement agents pose as potential buyers or are reported to the police by people who have been offered the child for sale. In these latter types of cases, the police then help arrange the purchase, which occurs under law enforcement observation. In rare cases the trafficking is reported to police by people who have already bought the child, fearing for its safety if it stayed with its parents or fearing who else might buy the child and for what purposes. In one particularly remarkable case in Ulyanovsk (no. 510), a drunk couple approached a twenty-two-year-old male passerby and offered him their eighteen-month-old son for 60 rubles ($2). Fearing for the child's safety, the young man bought the child and immediately went to the police.

In several of the larger cases in the North Caucasus, interagency investigative groups were formed that included representatives of the FSB, the Investigative Committee, the MVD, and the Procuracy (nos. 420, 473, 511). This indicates how seriously Russian authorities take the issue of child trafficking. Even officials get involved in these cases, if only to defend the reputation of their republics by denying that selling children is a Caucasus phenomenon. In one case in North Ossetia (no. 473), the head of the republic, Taimuraz Mamsurov, commented on a large case of child trafficking in which the head of Vladikavkaz's maternity hospital was arrested for selling a three-week-old baby girl for 500,000 rubles ($17,857). "As they have reported to me, this went on for years, behind all our backs. This used to happen in the past, but then, children were taken into families and it was kept secret so that the child's future wasn't ruined, so that when he grew up, no one would say that he was unwanted. And now, unfortunately, it's a business" (Chumarnaia 2013). His concerns were not misplaced, as this arrest appeared to be only the tip of the iceberg of a much larger child trafficking operation. In June 2013, another head doctor at a different maternity hospital, also in Vladikavkaz, was arrested on suspicion of selling at least two children, one in 2008 and one in 2010 (no. 523). In another case in Ingushetia (no. 448), the spokesperson for the Investigative Committee, Zurab Geroev, said: "It is difficult for me to talk about this topic—this is the first instance of child trafficking in the republic in many years. In Ingushetia there are no abandoned children. According to our culture's rules, if children are left without parental care their relatives take them and raise them, even very distant relatives. That's why the population is completely shocked by this barbarous fact" (Larina 2012).

Initially, law enforcement agents had a difficult time prosecuting child trafficking because of a widespread mistaken interpretation of the law that made them think that they could not hold parents responsible for selling their children because the children were not intended for exploitation. Consequently, of the seventeen cases of child trafficking that occurred before a 2008 amendment to correct this, only ten were charged with human trafficking, and five resulted in guilty verdicts. After the amendment, the number of child trafficking cases that were charged and prosecuted successfully under trafficking laws increased significantly.

Corruption and Human Trafficking

An outline of the contours of trafficking in Russia would be incomplete without a discussion of the role that corruption plays in facilitating the trafficking process. Corruption has been identified as both an "underlying root cause and a facilitating tool" for human trafficking, ensuring that it "remains a low-risk, high profit crime" (UNODC 2008). There are many ways that corruption can feature in human trafficking (Shelley and Orttung 2005; Tiurukanova 2006; Zhang and Pineda 2008). Corrupt officials can be involved in falsifying travel documents and can be paid off at border crossings to facilitate illegal entry of human trafficking victims. Local law enforcement can be bribed to turn a blind eye to what is happening, and investigators, prosecutors, and judges can be bought off during the criminal investigation (Shelley and Orttung 2005; UNODC 2008). In the data set, eleven trafficking cases included some sort of official involved in facilitating the trafficking, usually the police.[22] In these cases official involvement came to the media's attention only because the offenders were caught and prosecuted.

Most prostitution operations in Russia operate with protection from law enforcement agents, an arrangement that is called a *krysha* (roof). The brothel owners pay a monthly fee to ensure that their operations are not disturbed. The monthly price of a krysha can range from $300 to $2,800 (Golianova 2008; nos. 551, 302). Other reports have suggested that local police can earn about $60 per location per night guarding spots where street prostitution takes place (*tochki*). In addition, law enforcement officers often extort money from the

---

22. An additional thirteen cases that did not end up being charged as trafficking had officials involved. This does not include situations that involve soldiers, prisoners, or others in state care who are forced to perform labor by state officials.

prostitutes' clients, about $20 per client (Kanev 2007). Another common exchange for protection is in-kind, often involving a brothel owner sending women from his or her brothel to participate in a *subbotnik*, a day with the police in a sauna.[23] Police frequently enter these arrangements with brothel owners after threatening them with a criminal case. Traffickers also use their connections with local law enforcement as a threat to the victims, saying that if the victims go to the police they will be returned. In several cases in the data set, police were reportedly bribed to return escaped slaves (nos. 560, 587) or prostitutes who had run away (nos. 302, 550, 584).

In three instances, defendants tried to bribe law enforcement officials to close the case. In one case of slave labor in Altai, a relative of the accused offered a bribe of 300,000 rubles ($10,715) to the investigator to close the case and release his relatives from prison (no. 122). He was arrested for attempted bribery but did not confess, insisting that it was bail money to get his relatives out of jail. He was convicted of giving bribes to an official in June 2008 (CC Article 291[2]), though it was unclear what his punishment was (Regnum.ru 2008b). In a case in Mari El, a secret camera worn by the FSB agent interrogating one of the traffickers caught the trafficker offering a bribe to let him return home to Spain (no. 29; O30, P3). In a case in Ulyanovsk (no. 197), the defendants tried to pay off the victims so that they would not testify and pay the police to close the case. When the officer refused, the criminals threatened him with violence (Snezhina 2007). In a case like this last one, if the bribe is successful and happens soon enough in the process, the case would not even register in my data set or be registered by the MVD—as, for example, would have happened in the Uzbek slave labor case in Orel described above if the FSB had not pressured the MVD to raid the car wash and open the case.

Law enforcement personnel may also take on a more active role in prostitution rings. In one case in Cheboksary in the Chuvash Republic (no. 319), the head of a local police unit Andrei Kakorlatov helped resolve conflicts between group members and other area brothel owners and with unhappy clients in addition to receiving regular payments from the brothel owner of between 3,000 and 8,000 rubles eleven times over three years and in kind. He and his subordinates were caught only because the brothel owner, Elena Bronnikova, agreed to cooperate with law enforcement in exchange for a lesser sentence. In another case from the Samara region (no. 428), a woman investigator was on the payroll of the prostitution ring. When the first complaints came in from victims, the investigator

---

23. In Soviet times, a subbotnik was a day for the people to clean public places throughout the country. This is obviously a serious perversion of the good deeds that were done under the name *subbotnik* during the Soviet period.

refused to open a case and falsified statements to help the accused.[24] In both of these cases, the officers were convicted to prison time for abuse of authority (CC Article 286), lost rank, and were barred from service in law enforcement. In a case in Saratov (no. 584) several officers were involved in a local prostitution ring. The first officer was the main recruiter, convincing young women from at-risk groups to work in prostitution. When the women decided that they no longer wanted to do it, his colleague would plant drugs on them and threaten them with prosecution for drug offenses if they did not continue working. A third officer provided advanced warnings to the brothel owner about upcoming police raids. And in one of the biggest international sex trafficking cases in Russia, an active military intelligence officer, Dmitrii Strykanov, was convicted along with ten others of sending women to Europe and the Middle East (no. 33; Regions.ru 2011; Sokovnin 2011).

Law enforcement agents have also been actively involved in labor trafficking. In one case in Astrakhan (no. 173) two transportation police employees colluded with traffickers to illegally detain incoming migrants from Tajikistan and Uzbekistan to extort money for the return of their passports taken at the document checkpoint. When the migrants refused to pay for the return of their passports, they were sold to traffickers for 3,300 rubles ($117) each. The traffickers then held the migrants, forcing them to work, and released them only when they paid them 800 rubles ($29). The defendants were all sentenced to approximately four years in prison, including the transportation police employees (Mizulina 2006; Procuracy RF 2008; Regnum.ru 2008a). In another case, a beat officer stopped a local man at the market in Astrakhan, and asked him to sit in the police car for a document check. Then after threatening him with a gun, the officer drove him to the neighboring region of Kalmykia where he was sold into slavery (no. 297).

In the Bashkortostan, the wife of the head procurator in the Buraevskii region was accused of organizing illegal entry for thirteen Uzbek citizens, who were then forced into agricultural work and had their passports taken away (no. 4). There was suspicion that the procurator himself was also involved, since the wife was easily able to get registration papers for the migrants, even though they had entered the country illegally. The procurator was forced to resign over the allegations, though it is unclear what eventually happened in the case (Panfilova 2007; Regnum.ru 2007a).

There are also examples of law enforcement agents making noncorrupt choices. In one remarkable case, given the belief that law enforcement is easily bought off

---

24. In an interesting twist to this case, the investigator said that the case against her had been fabricated because the procurator, who had just been transferred from another region, was looking to raise his new department's ratings by increase his prosecution statistics.

in the shadow economy, the Krasnodar agent who was asked to be the group's krysha instead went to his superiors, who authorized him to act undercover. The agent then collected evidence and documented the group's illegal activities. When the group ran short of money, they decided to sell one of their prostitutes and asked him to help them find a buyer. He agreed and set up a sting operation in which the undercover buyer said he would pay 50,000 rubles ($1,785) to use the woman for organs. Not only did the sellers not flinch, but they even offered the buyer two women. After the money was exchanged, they were promptly arrested, charged with attempted trafficking, and sentenced to nine to ten years in prison (no. 27).

Since the early 2000s, awareness of the human trafficking problem has increased in both official circles and in society more generally. As this chapter shows, the trafficking situation in contemporary Russia is quite complex. Though law enforcement is pursuing some cases that fit the trafficking stereotype—Russian women being sent abroad for exploitation in prostitution—the majority of cases being pursued involve domestic trafficking. International cases are significantly more complex to investigate and therefore present a disincentive to law enforcement to pursue. Child trafficking for illegal adoption has been pursued quite aggressively by Russian law enforcement in cases of both organized child selling and one-off cases of desperate parents selling their children for cash. Finally, despite initial denials that labor slavery could take place outside the Caucasus, law enforcement has pursued cases of labor trafficking of migrants and people at the margins of society in regions throughout Russia.

Analysis of court documents and news reports shows quite clearly that all types of trafficking operations use similar tactics to ensure that their victims remain in the trafficking situation: debt bondage, confiscation of identity documents, threats, and violence. There are also some clearly discernible patterns in the profiles of victims and trafficking schemes. Traffickers themselves show more variation. Some are highly organized, and others are less so. Men primarily exploit men in labor trafficking situations, and both women and men exploit women in sex trafficking situations. Finally, there is no question that corruption has an impact on the pursuit of human trafficking cases. It may inhibit initial registration and investigation at the stage when there is some flexibility in law enforcement decision making. But perhaps more important, corruption is often what allows the exploitation to continue for as long as it does undetected.

THE HUMAN TRAFFICKING LAWS

Before 2003, the absence of a trafficking law impeded Russian law enforcement in two important ways. First, law enforcement had no way to assess or show the government the size and scope of the problem because there was nothing in the Criminal Code under which they could categorize the offenses. Without hard numbers it was difficult to convince the government that a problem existed and that resources were necessary to solve it, especially when there were many other pressing problems that also needed resources (Yaroslavl 2002, 62). As Elena Mizulina highlighted in a 2002 presentation to conference participants gathered at the Duma, "[We] ran into a completely paradoxical thing. Those people who should be fighting [human trafficking]—warning us, finding it, ringing the warning bells that look, we're being seized by prostitution, the trade in sex for exploitation—instead said 'but we don't have any criminal cases and it's not a problem.' There won't be any criminal cases as long as there is no criminal responsibility [prescribed by law]" (Moscow 2003a).

When pressed for information on the size and scope of the problem, law enforcement agencies offered a number of imprecise estimates and proxies, such as the number of companies recruiting women for prostitution abroad,[1] the

---

1. During a meeting of the Duma Security Committee in 1997, Deputy Chair Sergei Boskholov noted that in 1994, over 100 organizations were involved in recruiting women for prostitution abroad and more than twenty criminal cases had been opened under Article 226 of the RSFSR Criminal Code (operation of prostitution) (Highlights 1999). After the fall of the Soviet Union, Russia continued to operate under the Soviet Union's Criminal Code until 1996 when a new code was passed.

number of women stopped at the border with false documents,[2] the number of people who had been given jobs abroad by legally registered agencies,[3] and the number of kidnapping cases per year. But none of these estimations provided a clear picture of the trafficking situation. One academic in Saratov to whom I spoke recalled painstakingly contacting individual procurators in regions across Russia to see if they had seen trafficking cases so she could assess the scope of the phenomenon (A3). Finally, at one conference, Elena Tiurukanova, a sociologist and migration expert, explained that it was simply not feasible to expect that law enforcement could provide numbers on human trafficking crimes from statistics on existing Criminal Code articles that officers had been using to prosecute traffickers (Yaroslavl 2002, 112).

Second, although Russian law enforcement agencies had cooperated with international colleagues in bringing down human trafficking operations in other countries (Demin 2004), they were hampered at home by the lack of a legal definition of trafficking that could be applied to adult victims. One of the fundamental tenets of a system based on Roman law—a civil law system—is the principle of *Nullum crimen, nulla poena sine praevia lege poenali*, which translates as "no crime, no punishment without a previous penal law." If a case does not fit precisely under the elements outlined in a specific article of the Criminal Code, it cannot and should not be charged. In practice, this meant that without a legal definition of human trafficking, law enforcement agents could not prosecute or punish it.[4] One NGO representative from Chelyabinsk confirmed this through her own experience. She had brought the police multiple victims who had been trafficked to Cyprus for prostitution by the same firm and were willing to help law enforcement to bring down the trafficking ring, but the police said they had no statute with which they could prosecute (Yaroslavl 2002, 102).

Though law enforcement could prosecute component parts of the crime, those charges did not always fit comfortably with the evidence its agents had collected. As one academic told me in an interview in Saratov, "They were charging

---

2. Vladimir Dantin, First Deputy Chief of Border Control, said that in 1996 and the first half of 1997, there were 4,326 of these situations (Highlights 1999).

3. At a conference in 2002, Sergei Pushkarev, an MVD officer from the Primorskii region, said that in the first half of 2002, 3,837 people from the region were placed in jobs abroad by legally registered employment agencies, 263 women into show business in Japan and Korea, and 3,574 sailors onto foreign-flagged ships (Golitsyno 2002, 102-3).

4. The first attempt to legislate on human trafficking took place in 1999. In September of that year, in a meeting of the Legislative Committee, two Duma deputies, Vladimir Zhirinovsky and V. A. Lisichkin, proposed amendments to several articles of the Civil Code to create civil penalties for human trafficking, but not criminal. These legislative proposals were heard in the Duma in a first reading in June 2001 but in November of that same year, they were rejected (Legislative Committee, State Duma of the Russian Federation 2001).

[people] with kidnapping and other things, but often the proof that they had didn't fall under the classification of kidnapping" (A3). In speeches, law enforcement representatives confirmed this (Ukolov 2002). These charges also did not get to the part of the crime that they felt was at its heart, the buying and selling of people. To highlight the inadequacy of the existing statutes, Tatiana Moskalkova, a deputy head of the legal division in the MVD, listed the articles that existed in Russian law that could encompass human trafficking: "What do we have in Russian law today? Kidnapping, false imprisonment, rape, forced sexual activities. . . . Now we know that in reality this problem is increasing in scope and goes deep into the heart of the country. What does this mean? That we haven't found a legal or practical way to deal with it" (Yaroslavl 2002, 80).

This chapter outlines the situation in which law enforcement found itself before the trafficking laws were passed, including the ways that officers tried—sometimes successfully, sometimes not—to combat trafficking through existing law by charging offenders with kidnapping or false imprisonment, administrative violations, or prostitution-related offenses. I then turn to the various pressure points that developed in the early 2000s that pushed Russia toward developing and eventually passing a law criminalizing trafficking. Even though an interagency working group drafted a comprehensive law that would have included provisions to protect victims and prevent trafficking, in the end the only changes that occurred were to the Criminal Code, fulfilling the minimum requirements that Russia had taken on as a signatory to the UN Protocol on trafficking. Finally, I examine the content of the new law passed in 2003 and amendments to it that were passed in 2008.

Law Enforcement Practice before the Trafficking Law

Despite having no legal definition of human trafficking that covered adults, law enforcement still tried to pursue trafficking cases when they found them. According to one MVD official I interviewed, "Until 2003, Russia did not have any laws against human trafficking, and we worked well enough on this issue [without them]" (M22). Officers did this in four ways: (1) prosecuting trafficking in minors; (2) using statues on kidnapping and false imprisonment; (3) using statutes on prostitution; or (4) using statutes on administrative violations committed by businesses.

Prosecuting Trafficking in Minors

Before the December 2003 laws were passed, only trafficking in minors (under eighteen) was criminalized under Russian law. This was covered in Article 152

TABLE 2.1   Article 152—trafficking in minors

BASIC DEFINITION	1ST-LEVEL AGGRAVATING FACTORS	2ND-LEVEL AGGRAVATING FACTORS
Buying/selling of a minor or the commission of any transactions involving giving or receiving a minor Punishment: imprisonment up to 5 yrs.	• multiple times; • 2 or more people; • premeditated agreement; • use of official status; • illegal transport to or from abroad • goal of recruitment into criminal, antisocial or sexual activities[a] • intent to use for organ or skin transplant Punishment: imprisonment 3–10 yrs.	• leading to accidental death or severe consequences to health or other severe consequences Punishment: imprisonment 5–15 yrs.

[a] Federal Law no. 92-FZ "O vnesenii izmenenii i dopolnenii v Ugolovnyi kodeks Rossiiskoi Federatsii" of June 25, 1998, added "activities of a sexual nature" (SZ RF 1998, no. 26, item 3012).

TABLE 2.2   Cases under Criminal Code Article 152—trafficking in minors

	2000	2001	2002	2003
Cases registered	37	16	10	21
Number of accused	31	31	22	22

Source: MVD statistics 2000–2003, on file with author.
Note: Volchetskaia and Usenko (2000) additionally report that four cases of child trafficking in 1995 and seventy-four in 1997 were prosecuted under Article 152.

(see table 2.1), which was removed from the Criminal Code with the passage of the new human trafficking articles because it was considered redundant.[5]

This statute was used throughout Russia to prosecute offenders who trafficked children under the age of eighteen (table 2.2). According to some scholars, the wide interpretation of the phrase "transactions involving . . . a minor" to include minors being used as collateral in loans, given as gifts, lent to perform services or to commit antisocial activities, or used as a medium of exchange allowed law enforcement to be quite successful in pursuing these cases (Dolgolenko, 2004, 24; Girko 2005). Others argued that law enforcement had a difficult time investigating them (Volchetskaia and Usenko 2000; Nesterova 2003).

In one example of the successful use of this law, from 1997 through 1999 an organized criminal group from Kabardino-Balkaria took nine pregnant Russian women to Israel to give birth. Their babies (the minors) were then sold to childless Israeli couples. In 2003 the members of the group were convicted of

---

5. Russian/Soviet law has a long history of criminalizing the buying and selling of children. The first mention was in the 1960 Soviet Criminal Code under kidnapping of a minor, specified in 1995 as "trafficking of a minor" (Volkov 2007).

trafficking in minors, as well as other crimes, and sentenced to between 2.5 and 8 years in prison.[6] In another example from Rostov, Zaur Mamedov, along with his mother and sister, organized a business to send Russian women, including minors, to Dubai with promises of good jobs and then sold them into prostitution. The three offenders were convicted in 2004 of recruitment into prostitution and trafficking in minors for the counts in which the victims were under eighteen (Regions.ru 2004; Mizulina 2006; Zhuravlev and Krepysheva 2007).

Charging Kidnapping or False Imprisonment

When the victims were not minors, law enforcement tried to use statutes on kidnapping and false imprisonment (Articles 126 and 127) if victims were kidnapped into the trafficking situation or held against their will. For example, in one 2002 labor trafficking case in the Penza region (no. 182), six people were forced to tend livestock by a local man, working from 6 a.m. to 9 p.m. every day with little food. They were held behind a tall fence guarded by dogs and threatened with death if they attempted escape. One day, one of the victims, an elderly man, was sent by the trafficker to collect his pension, which the trafficker planned to keep for himself. Instead he went to the police. The trafficker was charged with false imprisonment (Ladnyi 2002; Regions.ru 2002).

Despite some successes, there were also problems in using these articles for prosecuting trafficking cases. In a 2003 newspaper article, the journalist Olga Nesterova, based on a conversation with the police, outlined several instances in which it would be impossible to prosecute trafficking or the use of slave labor under existing law. In one situation, a man had been enslaved in Chechnya for seven years during which he was traded among several people. He was eventually found by a journalist who took him to the police, but they said they could not open a case under false imprisonment because he had no idea where he had been held. In addition, the people who actually used his labor could not be held criminally responsible because there was no law criminalizing the use of slave labor.

Nesterova's police informant also noted the shortcomings in using the kidnapping statute in cases of labor trafficking, telling the story of a criminal group from Central Asia that operated at a train station in Moscow, recruiting their newly arrived countrymen who were seeking work. Two new arrivals got in the car with the group, who promised them a ride. Once in the car, the migrants were forced to hand over their money and passports, then one of the migrants was

---

6. Five of the nine were then released under an amnesty for the fifty-fifth anniversary of the Soviet Union's victory in World War II (Dvorkin 2007).

released on the promise that he would bring 3,000 rubles ($100) to free his companion. When he failed to come up with the money, his companion was sold into a construction brigade and forced to work. According to the reporter, "Formally, he wasn't kidnapped. Didn't he get into the car himself? Didn't they agree on the money? That means there's no element of the crime although in fact, he was sold for 1,500 rubles [$53]" (Nesterova 2003).

Charging with Administrative Violations

Another way that law enforcement dealt with trafficking was to pursue firms that were sending trafficking victims abroad under the guise of providing legitimate services, including marriage agencies, tourist agencies, and employment firms. Sergei Pushkarev, an MVD officer from the Primorskii region, described how these businesses operated: "Hiding behind their licenses and using the holes in Russian legislation, many firms provide marketing and consulting services in close cooperation with Moscow tourist firms, but in reality they're middlemen. In Moscow, the person signs a contract for provision of tourist services and goes to Europe on a tourist visa, where they find out that special permission is needed in that country to work, a work visa. Then they're there illegally with all the consequences: sale, resale, horrible sexual exploitation, and so on. In a word, slavery" (Golitsyno 2002, 105).

These firms could be blacklisted on official government registries, criminally charged with knowingly using false information in an advertisement (CC Art. 182), or fined under the Administrative Code for illegal business activities.[7] In one example from Kazan, a woman was trafficked to South Korea and exploited in prostitution. She had used a registered firm that promised to find her a legitimate job abroad. When she returned, the police opened a case under laws prohibiting fraud (N44). But there were many other cases where fraud charges were pursued with no success. Violations of the licensing regime were cited by a number of law enforcement agents as some of the major holes through which traffickers could take their victims abroad. Pushkarev continued:

---

7. Article 182 of the Criminal Code was removed in December 2003. This article stated that using false information about goods, work, or services in an advertisement as well as the preparation of such advertisements done with mercenary interests and causing significant harm would be punished by a fine or imprisonment up to two years. Article 14.1 of the Administrative Code covers licensing violations. The Administrative Code contains violations that are criminal but not defined as socially dangerous and are mostly petty in nature. They may include things like traffic violations, disorderly conduct, and public drunkenness. Violators go through a less formal procedure and can be punished by warnings, fines, community service, and occasionally administrative detention for up to fifteen days (Burnham, Maggs, and Danilenko 2012). *Kodeks Rossiiskoi Federatsii ob administrativnykh pravonarusheniiakh* of December 30, 2001, no. 195-FZ (SZ RF 2002, no. 1, item 1, hereafter AC).

The firm will get several licenses. Having gotten a license from us [the MVD] to find jobs for people abroad, they then get a license from the Employment Service Department to find people jobs and then a license as a tourist agency. Putting together these three types of activities allows them to fly under the radar of Russian law [because they are being monitored by three separate agencies]. One example is of the tourist agency Nika-Tour—2000, which had an agreement with a Moscow firm, Zolotoi Kliuch, that had a license to send people abroad for work. The end result was the deportation of Russian citizens from South Korea. When the tax police looked into the activities of this firm, it annulled their license. I should say, though, that this was the only time that we have succeeded in uncovering and monitoring the activities of a firm conducting these activities. (Golitsyno 2002, 106)

In some regions, NGOs and sometimes the local migration authorities were actively engaged in publicizing lists of firms that were officially authorized to issue tourist visas and find employment placement abroad so that people could verify whether the firm they were using was on the list. Administrative violations could also be used to punish those who benefited from using forced labor. They could be fined under the Administrative Code for not paying wages or benefits for their workers (Tiurukanova 2005a, 22). In reality these laws were rarely used to deal with slave labor cases.

Charging with Prostitution-Related Activities

Before the human trafficking law was passed, police also tried to prosecute sex trafficking cases under charges related to prostitution. This was done under Criminal Code Articles 240 (recruitment into prostitution) and 241 (organizing prostitution). This approach came with its own set of problems, most of which were later alleviated by changes in the wording of these statutes alongside the passage of the human trafficking laws.

In 2003 the Amur regional police presented a report in which they outlined the problems that they had encountered when using Article 240 to prosecute in cases where women had been trafficked abroad to China for prostitution (UVD Amurskoi Oblasti 2003). In this region, recruiters looked for street prostitutes in the city center and told them that they could make more money being prostitutes in China. When they agreed, the recruiters organized groups of women and sent them to Chinese pimps, receiving large sums of money in exchange. The women ended up with no legal rights, no documents, and no money and were subjected to violence, forced drug use, and other forms of abuse. At the time of the report, the police had identified at least seven Russian women who had died under these circumstances in China. The problem with using the recruitment into prostitution statute in this situation, they said, was that the women went voluntarily, and the statute required that the women be recruited through "violence or the threat of violence, blackmail, destruction or harm to property, or through deceit."[8] Law enforcement could not prove any of these elements and therefore the accused could not be pursued under existing law (UVD Amurskoi Oblasti 2003).

More generally, law enforcement had difficulty prosecuting under these statutes when Russian women were exploited abroad because the violations and the exploitation technically took place out of Russian jurisdiction and agents could not use Russian law to prosecute foreigners who lived abroad (N24, UVD Amurskoi Oblasti 2003). In cases in which people were sold multiple times, only the person who committed the original recruitment act could be prosecuted and only if that act was committed in Russia (P2). Furthermore, using prostitution-related statutes punished only the end exploiter or the recruiter, not necessarily all the people in the trafficking chain.

Even so, there were some examples of Russian law enforcement working successfully under these laws to prosecute human trafficking crimes. In 2003 the FSB in the Vladimir and Kaluga regions cooperated to bring down a trafficking ring that had been sending Russian women to the United Arab Emirates (UAE) and Thailand for sexual exploitation (Mizulina 2006; Tiurukanova 2005b; Newsru.com 2005a). The ring advertised for nannies and dancers in local newspapers; when women responded, they were transported to St. Petersburg or Astrakhan (their two bases of operation) and only then told that they would either need to pay back the money that was spent on them for transportation ($2,000–3,000) or work as prostitutes in Thailand or the UAE. When the masterminds of the trafficking ring, the Dzhelyalov brothers, were arrested, police found falsified passports to take the women abroad and photos of the victims which were sent to potential purchasers in the destination countries. A total of thirty-four women, including six minors, were sent between 2001 and 2003. Through cooperation with Interpol in the UAE and Thailand, most of them were returned to Russia.

The Dzhelyalovs were making approximately $20,000 a month from the operation. They were charged with recruitment into prostitution, false imprisonment, organizing a criminal group, and involving a minor in criminal activities. They were sentenced to between six and eight years in prison and required to pay

---

8. Although one could imagine a legal argument that the women were deceived here, the statute was interpreted to mean that the deceit had to occur during recruitment. Since the women knew they were going to work as prostitutes, law enforcement believed that this provision did not apply.

between 15,000 and 20,000 rubles ($535–$715) in damages to several of the victims. One of the brothers appealed his sentence to the Russian Supreme Court, requesting that his sentence be lowered, but the Supreme Court concurred with the ruling of the lower court and by extension the procurator's argument that these articles sufficiently covered the activities undertaken by Dzhelyalov—that is, human trafficking.[9] Although the conviction was a success, this example shows how law enforcement had to deal with human trafficking before it was criminalized—stringing together a series of charges that corresponded to each stage of trafficking—rather than having one statute that encompassed the entire process.

Passing the Law

Pressure for a law on trafficking came from many sources. As noted above, law enforcement believed that its existing tools were inadequate to combat the problem. Domestic and international NGOs also pushed Russia to pass a comprehensive law on human trafficking to enable them to stop the crime and assist victims. Additional pressure came from other governments—particularly the United States, which began ranking foreign governments on their efforts to combat human trafficking yearly, starting in 2000. Finally, Russia itself had taken on the obligation to pass a law by signing the 2000 UN Transnational Organized Crime (TOC) convention and its optional protocol on human trafficking: the Protocol to Prevent, Suppress, and Punish Trafficking in Persons, Especially Women and Children (known commonly as the Palermo Protocol).

The TOC standardized definitions of organized crime and included provisions to enhance domestic law enforcement capabilities and facilitate international cooperation in dismantling organized crime groups (Vlassis 2002). In large part due to problems during the 1990s with the Russian Mafia, Russia was one of the first signatories to the convention. The Palermo Protocol defined trafficking as including acts (recruitment, transportation, transfer, harboring, or receipt of persons), means (threat or use of force or other forms of coercion, abduction, fraud, deception, the abuse of power or of a position of vulnerability, or the giving or receiving of payments or benefits to achieve the consent of a person having

---

9. Dzhelyalov was protesting that the court of first instance's decision to prosecute him for actions committed outside the borders of the Russian Federation was a violation of Criminal Code regulations on punishment. See Decision of the Criminal Division of the Supreme Court of Russia from April 28, 2005, Case 86-005-5 (Opredelenie Sudebnoi kollegii po ugolovnym delam Verkhovnogo suda RF ot 28 aprelia 2005 g. no. 85-005-5).

control over another person), and purpose (exploitation), taking a broad view on the categories of exploitation that should be included.[10] This protocol obligated Russia, at a minimum, to incorporate penalties for human trafficking and related activities into its domestic criminal law but also strongly advised signatory states to adopt more comprehensive anti-trafficking policies that focused on prevention and victim rehabilitation services (Gallagher 2010). Louise Shelley (2005), an American academic heavily involved in discussions about the Russian law, credits Russia's accession to the convention as a major driving force for speeding up the passage of domestic anti-trafficking laws.

International pressure on Russia also came from the United States. In 2000 the United States passed its first domestic anti-trafficking law, the Victims of Trafficking and Violence Prevention Act (TVPA).[11] In addition to creating a framework for fighting trafficking on US soil, the TVPA required the US Department of State's new Office to Monitor and Combat Trafficking in Persons to issue an annual report rating other countries on their efforts to deal with human trafficking. The TVPA defined a set of minimum standards for foreign governments to meet, requiring that they "prohibit severe forms of trafficking in persons and punish acts of such trafficking," "prescribe punishment (for traffickers) commensurate with that for grave crimes, such as forcible sexual assault," and "prescribe punishment that is sufficiently stringent to deter" traffickers.[12]

Countries are grouped into one of three tiers. Tier 1, the best ranking, indicates that the country's government fully complies with the TVPA's minimum standards. Tier 2 indicates that the country's government does not fully comply but is making significant efforts to do so. In the 2004 *Trafficking in Persons Report*, a Tier 2 watch list was added to account for countries whose governments do not fully comply and are making efforts to do so but have significant trafficking

---

10. There was strong disagreement during the protocol's development about the precise language to use to cover exploitation in the form of prostitution, which was resolved by a broad definition that took account of the range of prostitution regulation regimes in signatory countries (Gallagher 2001, 2010; Raymond 2002).

11. The legislation was reauthorized and amended in 2003, 2005, and 2008 (TVPRA 2003, 2005, 2008).

12. "Severe forms of trafficking" are defined as (1) sex trafficking in which a commercial sex act is induced by force, fraud, or coercion, or in which the person induced to perform such an act has not attained eighteen years of age; or (2) the recruitment, harboring, transportation, provision, or obtaining of a person for labor or services, through the use of force, fraud, or coercion for the purpose of subjection to involuntary servitude, peonage, debt bondage, or slavery. The report judges countries based on "(1) the extent to which the country is a country of origin, transit, or destination for severe forms of trafficking; (2) the extent to which the government of the country does not comply with the TVPA's minimum standards including, in particular, the extent of the government's trafficking-related corruption; and (3) the resources and capabilities of the government to address and eliminate severe forms of trafficking in persons." (Dept. of State 2008b).

problems (based on number of victims) and have failed to provide evidence that they are increasing their efforts to combat trafficking, or those that have committed to take steps to combat trafficking over the next year but have not yet done so. Tier 3 countries do not fully comply with the TVPA's minimum standards and are not making significant efforts to do so (Dept. of State 2004b). A Tier 3 rating can lead to withholding of nonhumanitarian, nontrade related foreign assistance for the following fiscal year and US encouragement to the International Monetary Fund and other international financial institutions to vote against further aid to the country.[13]

For the first two years the report was issued, 2001 and 2002, Russia was rated a Tier 3 country (Dept. of State 2001, 2002). Lack of legislation specifically dealing with human trafficking was one of the major reasons. Russian officials were livid at this designation, calling it "libel" and suggesting that the information presented in the report was not verifiable (Johnson 2009a, 132). Nevertheless, it did appear to spur some action on Russia's part.

In April 2002, in response to an order from President Vladimir Putin to fix the law to deal with human trafficking, the Ministry of Internal Affairs created a Working Group to draft legislation (Ukolov 2002). On August 27, 2002, at a press conference, the MVD Directorate on Fighting Organized Crime (UBOP) announced that it had submitted a legislative proposal to the Duma to create both criminal and administrative penalties for people who participated in and enabled trafficking (Rosbalt.ru 2002; Ukolov 2002). The directorate also called for tighter regulation of businesses that could enable trafficking such as marriage, tourist, and employment agencies. Similar proposals were also being developed by the Ministry of Justice and circulated among the relevant ministries.

In the fall of 2002, soon after the Russian government received its second Tier 3 rating, it asked the US government for assistance and financial support for a working group to develop trafficking legislation (Johnson 2009a). This project was part of a larger investment in anti-trafficking activities that the US government had been making in Russia with the hope of stopping trafficking at the source rather than after exploitation had taken place in the destination countries. The working group was headed by Duma deputy Elena Mizulina, who had been

13. While it has turned out that sanctions are rarely issued, especially for countries with which the United States has a friendly relationship or to which it already provides aid, the fear of sanctions was significant when they were first introduced and resulted in many countries passing anti-trafficking laws (Chuang 2006; DeStefano 2008; Gallagher 2011). According to the TVPA, the president can provide a waiver to a country that would otherwise be subject to sanctions by issuing a memorandum justifying the decision.

instrumental in helping to pass a new Criminal Procedure Code in 2001 that had also been developed in a series of US government-funded working groups (Spence 2005).[14] Special Representative of the Presidential Administration to the Central Federal District Georgii Poltavchenko, an old friend of President Putin's from his days in the KGB, sponsored the working group (Taylor 2011; Shelley and Orttung 2005).[15] This high-level support gave legitimacy to the project and access to the president, considered by advocates to be crucial for passing any future law. The working group had fifteen members and included representatives of the Duma; high-ranking representatives from the ministries of Internal Affairs, Labor, and Justice; and domestic and international NGOs. It did not include representatives from the Procuracy, although they did participate in all the conferences.

The working group held a series of conferences and roundtables throughout Russia in late 2002 and early 2003 to discuss the proposed legislation. In just four months, they drafted comprehensive legislation based on the successful experiences of other countries and the input of key domestic actors, including law enforcement. The full package of proposed legislation called for, among other things, creation of a country-wide network of rehabilitation shelters for victims; a protection program for victims regardless of their willingness to participate as witnesses; educational programs for students, teachers, and various government agencies; the addition of seven new articles to the Criminal Code to criminalize trafficking and related activities; and the shuttering of employment firms participating in fraudulent recruitment of job candidates (Draft Law 2003). It was hailed as a model law for all countries. Financing was to come from a combination of ministries at the federal and regional level—Internal Affairs, Health and Social Development, Education and Science, Defense, Foreign Affairs, the Federal Border Service, and the General Procuracy—with each department implementing measures in its sphere of competence. According to several members of the working group, without the financial support from the US government for the roundtable discussions and conferences, the draft law would not have gone anywhere, because there would have been no one to pay for the discussions (Johnson 2009a; A9). On February 13, 2003, a hearing was scheduled in the Duma's Legislative Committee, after which the committee recommended that the working

---

14. Later in her legislative career, Mizulina, as the head of the Duma's Committee on Women, Family, and Children, was instrumental in championing the law that restricted Americans' ability to adopt Russian children and the law banning propaganda of "nontraditional sexual relations" to minors (Volchek 2013).

15. Russia is divided into eight federal districts. Each district has a presidentially appointed head who oversees the regions within the district.

group make some additional revisions to the law and officially present it to the Duma for a first reading in April.[16]

Throughout the discussions on the law, the touchiest subject by far was financing. While each ministry's representatives expressed support for the law in the abstract, they were very reluctant to commit the resources necessary to implement its provisions, in part because no one knew the true size of the problem and what resources it would require. In the end, Elena Mizulina and the Legislative Committee decided that the resistance from the ministries to financing the bill was too great of a hurdle. As Mizulina noted at a conference in May: "The law is at [the highest levels] because they take it very seriously, but the question is about money. This law requires money. And for that reason, since the [Presidential] Administration supports us, and they sent us a proposal to create the financial justification for the project . . . we need to write [the law] to minimize the cost of it at least in the first stages. Because if it turns out that the law is very expensive, it won't pass, and we need it to pass" (Moscow 2003a, 37).

The April reading in the Duma never happened. By May 2003, when another roundtable discussion on trafficking was held in the Duma, Mizulina and the members of the working group, in consultation with the Presidential Administration, had decided to attach several of the draft law's provisions criminalizing human trafficking to a bill that was already in the process of moving through the Duma rather than pursuing adoption of the draft law as a whole. Mizulina stated: "We agreed provisionally, that is, provisionally for all interested parties, to include in the second reading [of the bill already in process] amendments connected with combating human trafficking and connected with criminal responsibility for abetting prostitution" (Moscow 2003a, 12).[17] The omnibus bill, "On Amendments to the Criminal Code," which had been passed in a first reading on April 23, 2003, was focused on overhauling sentencing practices and dealing with recidivism. Mizulina later blamed the Presidential Administration for holding

---

16. Russian legislation goes through three readings in the lower house, the State Duma, during which changes and amendments can be made to the legislation. Usually most changes are added after the first reading, and the second and third readings are often done on the same day. After passing in the third reading, the bill moves on to the upper house, the Federation Council, where it is voted on. After both houses pass the legislation, it is forwarded to the president who signs it. It is then published in the federal register (*Sobranie zakonodatel'stvo*) and goes into effect.

17. The importance of having the bill presented by the Presidential Administration came up repeatedly throughout the conferences about the draft law. This emphasis reflects the understanding common in Russia that only bills that originate from the Presidential Administration are taken seriously by the Duma. Even bills that originate at the initiative of Duma deputies are not seriously considered unless they have consulted with the Presidential Administration first (Johnson 2009a, N24, A9).

up the draft law because it was unwilling to commit to creating a coordinating committee to oversee the work of the police and NGOs to help victims, one of the bill's provisions (Kolesnichenko 2004a).

Despite the careful work by those involved in crafting the draft law's language for changes to the Criminal Code so that the wording would fit seamlessly within existing law, the final formulation of the amendments on human trafficking was primarily the result of negotiations between representatives of the Presidential Administration and US government officials. Thomas Firestone, the Department of Justice's resident legal adviser, insisted that the articles envisioned by the draft law be rephrased to give them "more teeth" (Johnson 2009a, 134).[18] In the same negotiations, Firestone told the Russian officials that if they did not pass a trafficking law, Russia would be in danger of being penalized under the TVPA's provisions that applied to Tier 3 countries which would include cancellation of study tours to the United States for senior government officials, which had been paid for by the United States government for the previous fifteen years (Johnson 2009a, 134).

In October 2003, following these backroom negotiations, Vladimir Putin announced that it was time for Russia to pass a law on human trafficking:

> Today I introduced amendments to Russia's Criminal Code to the Duma. They create a system of norms prescribing harsh punishments for human trafficking, especially of children, using slave labor and other associated crimes. . . . Human trafficking is a modern form of slavery that is accompanied by the most base and cruel violations of human rights. . . . In Russian law, this problem is not systematically regulated, which allows the unchecked growth of this dangerous situation. . . . The introduction of amendments fixes this hole in our legislation. I ask the leadership of law enforcement to give the most serious attention to these problems and use all means and opportunities provided by law to fight this evil. I want to note that the sanctions under these articles are quite harsh—up to fifteen years imprisonment, and I especially want to note that the law will punish those who thrive on the exploitation of people and not those who, in difficult life situations, have fallen into the dirty hands of traffickers. (Putin 2003)

The amendments criminalizing human trafficking ended up being two of over one hundred proposed amendments that were added to the omnibus bill between

---

18. In the final version of the Criminal Code articles, punishments were significantly harsher than those included in the draft law. In the draft law, there were a range of options for punishment from fines to imprisonment. In the final version, imprisonment was the primary method of punishment for trafficking violations.

its first and second readings. A hastily drafted explanatory note (*poiasnitel'naia zapiska*) which circulated along with the bill before its second reading outlined the dangers that trafficking presented and the urgency of combating it by making it a criminal offense, pointing out that other "civilized" countries in the West already had laws against it. The note contained several examples of sex and labor exploitation, with the latter restricted to stories from the Caucasus, including slave markets of Russian soldiers in Chechnya (*Poiasnitel'naia zapiska* 2003; Buckley 2008). In both the second and third readings in the Duma and its reading in the Federation Council, human trafficking was mentioned only once, in passing, during the Federation Council senator's introduction of the bill. The bill was approved by the Duma on November 21, 2003, and passed by the Federation Council on November 23, 2003.[19] It was signed by President Putin on December 8 and officially went into effect on December 11, 2003 (Federal Law no. 162-FZ of 2003). The Federation Council officially ratified the Transnational Organized Crime convention and its protocol on trafficking on April 26, 2004.[20]

Momentum for passing the rest of the provisions of the draft law continued into 2004 with an assembly of Russian NGOs working against trafficking, to which Putin sent his blessing and at which US Secretary of State Colin Powell spoke (Buckley 2008). At this conference Boris Gavrilov, the head of the MVD's Investigative Division, called trafficking "so serious a problem for Russia that it threatens the genetic foundations of the nation" (Kolesnichenko 2004b). Another hearing was held at the Duma in November of that year (Kolesnichenko 2004a). There was also a push for a separate piece of legislation on protection for trafficking victims, but this initiative did not go anywhere. This drive was stymied primarily by a reluctance to fund protection measures for victims of a particular crime, in this case human trafficking, rather than creating a set of measures for protection of all crime victims (N24, A8).[21] However, legislation establishing a

19. Arguments came up in the Duma about the desirability of other parts of the bill, but no one mentioned the addition of human trafficking or slave labor at all. The bill was passed in a second reading with 64 percent voting yes, 0.2 percent voting no, and 35.8 percent not participating. In its third reading on November 21, 2003, the bill was passed with 60.9 percent of the deputies voting for it, 6.7 percent against it, and 32.4 percent not participating (Federation Council 2003; State Duma 2003).

20. The president and/or his administration negotiates and signs international treaties (Constitution, Article 86). The Federation Council, the upper house of the Russian legislature, then must ratify all international treaties (Constitution, Article 106). Federal Law no. 26-FZ, "O ratifikatsii Konventsii Organizatsii Ob"edinennykh Natsii protiv transnatsional'noi organizovannoi prestupnosti i dopolniaiushchikh ee Protokola protiv nezakonnogo vvoza migrantov po sushe, moriu i vozdukhu i Protokola o preduprezhdenii i presechenii torgovli liud'mi, osobenno zhenshchinami i det'mi, i nakazanii za nee," of April 26, 2004 (SZ RF 2004, no. 18, item 1684).

21. A law to protect crime victims was finally passed in December 2013. Federal Law no. 432-FZ, "O vnesenii izmenenii v otdel'nye zakonodatel'nye akty Rossiiskoi Federatsii v tseliakh sovershenstvovaniia prav poterpevshikh v ugolovnom sudoproizvodstve," of December 28, 2013 (SZ RF 2013, no. 52 [part 1], item 6997).

witness protection program, which could apply to human trafficking victims and their families, was passed in 2004.

In 2006 there was another roundtable of NGOs working on trafficking in Moscow as well as another Duma hearing on potential changes to the law. During this time, the trafficking legislation's key proponent, Elena Mizulina, was not in the Duma, leaving the bill without an advocate in the legislature.[22] In 2007 she joined a new party, A Just Russia, and was reelected to the Duma. However, by 2008, most people I interviewed who had participated in the working group believed that comprehensive legislation on human trafficking was no longer a realistic option. The focus had shifted to the implementation of and amendments to the existing Criminal Code articles to make them more usable. Throughout this time, high-level MVD personnel remained involved in pushing for more legislative changes to make the law more functional, including expressing continued support for passage of the draft law.[23]

The New Trafficking Law

The law passed in December 2003 established the offenses of human trafficking (Article 127.1) and use of slave labor (Article 127.2) for the first time in Russian criminal law. The provision that had previously covered trafficking in minors, Article 152, was removed to avoid overlap.[24] In addition, there were significant changes to the Criminal Code articles on organizing and recruitment into prostitution. While the draft law had envisioned adding seven articles to the Criminal Code to cover all aspects of human trafficking, in the end, according to my interviewees, these changes were all that were politically feasible.[25] According to one member of the working group, the representative of the Presidential Admin-

22. Mizulina's party, Yabloko, did not get enough votes to make it over the threshold for parliamentary representation in the party list system.

23. On May 16, 2006, Deputy Head of the MVD's Criminal Investigation Department Andrei Shilovskii asked the Duma to pass the draft law in a briefing on human trafficking, noting that it was already fully developed and ready to go (Regnum.ru 2006).

24. This was not part of the suggested changes in the draft law. Instead, the draft law proposed to add a list of aggravating factors to Article 152. Dolgolenko (2004, 24) suggests that Article 127.1 was an improvement. By outlining concrete actions that, when taken, constituted commission of the crime (buying/selling, recruitment, transfer, receipt, harboring, etc.), Article 127.1 allowed suspects to be caught before the transaction had taken place, whereas Article 152 required that the transaction actually be completed before law enforcement could take action.

25. The original seven criminal code articles envisioned in the draft law were human trafficking; revealing confidential information about human trafficking victims; use of slave labor; debt bondage; illegal activities concerning documents with the goal of human trafficking; recruitment of people for the goal of exploitation; and falsification, preparation, or sale of documents for use in human trafficking (Draft Law 2003).

istration with whom this deal was being struck was willing to add only two of the proposed Criminal Code amendments because he was "malicious"—that is, insulted that he had not been included in the working group from the start (A9).

In the Russian legal system, as in most civil law systems, interpretation of the code's provisions is aided by commentaries (*kommentarii*) written by legal academics. Although these commentaries are not binding and not uniform in their interpretations, they are often consulted by investigators and procurators in the preparation of an indictment or by judges in their decisions, especially if the law is new and/or they have no experience with it. The following analysis of the laws on human trafficking is based both on the text of the Criminal Code articles and commentaries about them.

Article 127.1—Human Trafficking

In addition to the basic definition and aggravating factors laid out in table 2.3, Article 127.1 has two explanatory notes (*primechanie*). The first outlines the circumstances under which someone suspected of human trafficking can be exempted from criminal prosecution for his actions. The second defines the term exploitation. As in the UN Palermo Protocol, the term exploitation is defined widely to include using the prostitution of others and any other form of

TABLE 2.3 Article 127.1—human trafficking

BASIC DEFINITION (AS OF 2003)	1ST-LEVEL AGGRAVATING FACTORS	2ND-LEVEL AGGRAVATING FACTORS
Buying/selling of a person, or the recruitment, transportation, transfer, harboring, or receiving of a person for the purpose of their exploitation	• 2 or more people; • known minor; • use of official status;[a] • transport across Russian borders or illegal holding of someone abroad;[c] • use of false documents or taking, hiding, or destruction of identity documents;	• leading to accidental death or severe consequences to health or other severe consequences;[b] • actions that endanger the life and health of multiple people;
Punishment: imprisonment up to 5 yrs.	• violence or threat of violence;[d] • goal of removing organs or skin Punishment: imprisonment 3–9 yrs.	• organized group Punishment: imprisonment 8–15 yrs.

[a] This could include the use of any professional status, including state employees (civilian and law enforcement), heads of organizations, doctors, and so on (Chekalin 2006).

[b] A wide range of consequences falls into this classification, including suicide of the victim or someone close to the victim, infection with HIV or other sexually transmitted diseases, murder, rape, and forced abortions. It is, however, necessary to prove that the consequences were a direct result of the trafficking and not incidental to it (Tomin 2010).

[c] Whether the border crossing is done legally or illegally.

[d] Investigators need to prove that the threat was considered real by the victim. Whether the accused would have realistically been able to carry out the threat is not important (Lebedev and Galakhov 2009; Borisov 2012).

sexual exploitation, slave labor or services, servitude, or the removal of organs or skin.[26]

The first explanatory note states that a trafficker will be exempt from criminal prosecution if he or she is a first-time trafficker, voluntarily releases the victim(s), helps in the investigation, and has not committed any other crimes in the trafficking process.[27] This seemingly strange exemption is a direct response to fears that people in Chechnya would not otherwise release Russians (especially soldiers) whom they had taken prisoner. The second war in Chechnya was winding down at the time the law was being introduced, so the safety of Russian soldiers was a very salient concern, especially given media reports that described slave markets throughout Chechnya. Unsurprisingly, international and Russian experts expressed great concern about this, considering it to essentially be an "immunity clause" (Moscow 2003b) with little clarity on to whom it would apply or when and for how long releasing the victims would be an option.[28] But Mizulina, law enforcement agents, and government officials insisted on keeping this clause, saying that it could spur a mass release of existing slaves in Chechnya. These concerns were largely unfounded. In the first ten years after the passage of the human trafficking law, there is no record of this provision having ever been used (Serdiukova 2013).

The phrasing of the law and the absence of wording specifying what types of activities counted as human trafficking and what would be required to prove them created significant roadblocks for implementation in the first several years. The phrase "buying/selling," created confusion among law enforcement because it could be interpreted in two different ways. In the broader interpretation, any of the activities listed in the law (recruitment, transportation, transfer, harboring, or receipt) would have to be done with the goal of exploiting the victim, but the buying or selling of a person would be considered a crime on its own, regardless of whether the buyer/seller had the goal of exploiting the victim. This would allow the prosecution of people who sold others for nonexploitative purposes (e.g., mothers who illegally sold their babies for adoption). This interpretation

---

26. In 2004, removal of organs or skin was removed from this list of types of exploitation to avoid overlap with Article 120 of the Criminal Code (Forced Removal of Organs or Skin for Transplant) and to eliminate confusion, because it was also included as an aggravating factor for trafficking (Girko 2005).

27. This exemption applies only to trafficking which falls under the first part of the Criminal Code article or part 2, section a (trafficking two or more people).

28. Several academics have suggested amendments to deal with these problems. Alikhadzhieva (2006, 6) proposed specifying that the exemption applied only if the exploitation had not yet taken place. Buriak (2006) suggested adding a grace period during which the trafficker could free the victim(s) after which he or she would still be held criminally responsible. At present, there does not appear to be any discussion about amending this part of the law (Antonov 2011; Serdiukova 2013).

would require law enforcement to show that a transaction had taken place, that the object being bought/sold was a person, and that the intent of the trafficker was to sell the person and thereby make profit from the sale. Alternatively, agents could show that any of the other activities had resulted in the actual exploitation of the victim or had been done with the goal of exploiting the victim.

In the narrower interpretation of the law, any of the activities listed in the law (recruitment, transportation, transfer, harboring, or receipt *and* buying/selling) would have to be done with the goal of exploitation. This would require law enforcement to prove not only that the accused intended to sell the victim, but also that he or she intended for the victim to be exploited (although not necessarily directly by him or her). Most commentaries supported this interpretation of the law, though not all.[29] The practical consequence of this interpretation was that the buying and selling of children for nonexploitative purposes was decriminalized, since the crime of trafficking a minor had been removed from the Criminal Code. If law enforcement agents wanted to prosecute someone for selling a child, they first had to establish that the person knew that the child would be exploited, which was often impossible as most children were sold to childless couples for adoption or, as I heard over and over, by irresponsible and impoverished parents "for a bottle of vodka."[30] While this difference may seem minor, it had a huge impact on practice. Proving intent to exploit turned out to be very difficult for law enforcement.

More mundane but also affecting implementation practice was that several of the words included in the legal definition of human trafficking existed elsewhere in Russian legal codes with different meanings already attached to them. The most frequently cited example of this is the term buying/selling (*kuplia-prodazha*). As a concept, buying/selling exists in the Civil Code in a provision that governs business transactions, but only those having to do with objects.[31] Because a human is not an object, critics argued, he or she is not buyable and/or sellable in the traditional sense of buying and selling. This has caused problems with interpretation, even though the type of transaction that takes place is very often a direct buying and selling of a human as if he or she were an object

---

29. Academics adopting a narrow interpretation of the law noted that to prove the crime, both intent to traffic and the goal of exploitation had to be present (Chekalin 2006; Dolgolenko 2004; Alikhadzhieva 2006). Those who supported a broader interpretation noted that proving intent to traffic, not the intent to exploit, was key (Lebedev 2004; Gromov 2005; Zhuravlev and Krepysheva 2007).

30. There is actually one case in the data set from the Sverdlovsk region where a baby was sold for money to buy a bottle of vodka (no. 171; Newsru.com 2005b; Mizulina 2006).

31. Chapter 30, *Grazhdanskii kodeks Rossiiskoi Federatsii*, part 2, of January 26, 1996, no. 14-FZ (SZ RF 1996, no. 5, item 410).

(Dolgolenko 2004, 23; Chekalin 2006). The term buying/selling does not exist anywhere in the UN Protocol but instead mirrors the formulation of Article 152, the Russian Criminal Code statute prohibiting trafficking in minors, which was removed with the passage of the new trafficking laws. Alikhadzhieva (2006) suggests that this was done to ease law enforcement's transition by making the wording of the new article as close as possible to the old one so agents would better understand how to implement it. This term did not seem to raise nearly the same level of scrutiny or criticism when it was part of Article 152.

This overlap in definitions is even more of a problem when the same term appears twice in one code with multiple meanings. For example, the term recruitment (*verbovka*) appears twice in the Criminal Code. In the human trafficking statute, "recruitment" implies something nefarious or deceitful, but in the other place where it appears, Article 359 (mercenary activities), there is no intimation of deceit. Recruitment in this case is simply the hiring of mercenaries (also illegal). Although these debates may seem academic, they created confusion and inconsistency in the legal system, which is meant to be a unified whole and not to have conflicting terminology across or within codes. These discrepancies especially affected law enforcement personnel looking for guidance on how to use the new law.

Why did Russian lawmakers fail to work out these inconsistencies when drafting the law, and why did law enforcement fail to identify these problems? In part, the fact that the final formulation of the law came out of a backroom deal meant that the wording was largely out of the hands of legal experts and law enforcement agents who might use it. It was also added in a rush to a bill that was already more than halfway through the legislative process, thereby skipping the stage when it might have received closer scrutiny. Additionally, one of the drafters of the law, Tatiana Kholshchevnikova, explained to me that legislators felt hemmed in by the wording of the UN Protocol as translated by the Ministry of Foreign Affairs. Another academic echoed this, explaining that it is less important for an international convention to pay attention to these technicalities of wording, since conventions stand on their own, but in a code that fits into a national legal system, terminology needs to be consistent (A4). Direct translation ended up being a significant issue when not contextualized for Russia. As one of my interviewees in the MVD told me, "the new Russian law is mostly from the Palermo Protocol . . . but it took the norms straight from that protocol without making them Russia-specific. In Russian law, one letter or comma can completely change the law enforcement practice here, and that was not really taken into account [by the drafters of the law]" (M9).

The definition of human trafficking codified in Russian law was, in some ways, broader than the international definition contained in the UN Palermo

Protocol. The UN protocol specifies that trafficking is a transnational crime and must be committed by an organized group (UN 2000, Article 4). The Russian law, however, does not create these restrictions, which means that both internal and small-scale trafficking can be prosecuted. However, complicating implementation practice were two ways that the Russian definition of trafficking diverged from the UN protocol. The UN protocol defines trafficking as "the recruitment, transportation, transfer, harboring, or receipt of persons, *by means of the threat or use of force or other forms of coercion, of abduction, of fraud, of deception, of the abuse of power or of a position of vulnerability, or of the giving or receiving of payments or benefits to achieve the consent of a person having control over another person*, for the purpose of exploitation" (UN 2000).[32] Although the Russian legislation used the elements of the crime and types of exploitation outlined in the protocol, it did not specify the means by which the crime could be committed, despite the fact that they were included in the draft law. Instead, two of the means outlined in the protocol were added as aggravating factors (threat or use of force and abuse of power).

On one hand, as a procurator pointed out to me, by leaving out the means by which human trafficking could be committed, the Russian law could be used more broadly, especially since the means by which traffickers commit their crimes change over time. But in reality, he admitted, without a basic outline of what the crime looks like, law enforcement is hamstrung because its agents do not know what they are looking for (P2). Having a list of the means by which trafficking can be committed is not only important for helping law enforcement identify a case as human trafficking. It can also help judges who are uncertain about what trafficking is by giving them a clear set of criteria to look for as definitive proof. In fact, I heard several stories of particularly committed law enforcement agents who looked to Russia's international obligations under this convention to help show other actors in the legal system the proper way to understand human trafficking, including the means by which it could be committed.

The second issue that the Russian law did not deal with was the victim's consent to his or her exploitation. If the victim initially agrees to be a prostitute or to work in a job that turns into exploitation, is he or she still a victim of trafficking? According to the UN protocol, "The consent of a victim of trafficking in persons to the intended exploitation . . . shall be irrelevant where any of the means . . . [outlined above] have been used" (UN 2000). Consent, then, depends on defining the means that would render consent irrelevant. This is another consequence of Russian law not defining the means by which trafficking could be committed.

---

32. Italics mine.

The issue of consent came up frequently during conferences about the draft law but was never incorporated into the law. Even law enforcement representatives noted that the agency's policies toward sex trafficking had long been driven by its belief that women knew what they were getting into (Golitsyno 2002, 107). Regardless of its inclusion, consent mattered when law enforcement made its decisions about whether to pursue cases or not. Without any guidance from the law, consent has continued to be an important informal criterion that both law enforcement and judges use to determine whether a victim is "real" or not.

Article 127.2—Use of Slave Labor

Although the human trafficking statute includes forced labor as one possible type of exploitation, in practice, cases of forced labor are rarely prosecuted under it. Instead, the new Article 127.2, use of slave labor, has been the go-to article for trafficking cases involving forced labor. Some scholars make the argument that forced sexual labor in prostitution could also be prosecuted under this statute (D'iakov and Kadnikov 2008; Tomin 2010). This has never happened. Table 2.4 outlines the definition of slave labor and its aggravating factors.

Unlike the Criminal Code article on human trafficking, there are no explanatory notes whereby traffickers may be exempted from criminal prosecution.[33] There does not seem to be a significant amount of controversy over how this law should be interpreted, given the minimal focus on this particular legal provision in the Russian legal academic literature. The most significant complication in interpreting and implementing this Criminal Code article is that Russian law has a separate legal definition of forced labor in the Labor Code (which can be punished

TABLE 2.4 Article 127.2—use of slave labor

BASIC DEFINITION	1ST-LEVEL AGGRAVATING FACTORS	2ND-LEVEL AGGRAVATING FACTORS
Use of the labor of a person over whom one has authority akin to ownership, in which that person cannot refuse to perform labor (services) for reasons unrelated to himself Punishment: imprisonment up to 5 yrs.	• 2 or more people; • known minor; • use of official status; • use of blackmail, violence, or the threat of violence; • taking, hiding, or destruction of identity documents; Punishment: imprisonment 3–9 yrs.	• leading to accidental death or severe consequences to health or other severe consequences; • organized group Punishment: imprisonment 8–15 yrs.

33. Although Serdiukova (2013) suggests that the same should be true with this article.

as an administrative violation but is not criminal).[34] In practice, differentiating the two is not easy. Although all slave labor is considered forced labor, not all forced labor is considered to take place in slave-like conditions (Brilliantov 2010). In addition, violations of the Labor Code do not come under the competence of the police; instead they are the responsibility of labor inspectors to enforce.

Proving the use of slave labor under Article 127.2 requires showing that the accused knowingly made use of such labor.[35] In addition, the accused must have had the intent to enslave, have created conditions of slavery, ensured that the victim was stuck in a slave-like situation, and have personally appropriated the results of the slave labor, either directly (prostitution, building a house, etc.) or indirectly (selling the results of the slave labor to make a profit) (D'iakov and Kadnikov 2008; Brilliantov 2010; Tomin 2010).[36] Also key to prosecuting a case under this article is proving that the victim could not refuse to perform the labor/services demanded of him or her by the trafficker. This can happen for economic reasons (paying off debt, in exchange for land use) or noneconomic reasons (physical or psychological force) (Brilliantov 2010; Zhalinskii 2010). Most of the aggravating factors found in Article 127.2 mirror those in the human trafficking article and are interpreted the same way. The only exception is that blackmail is specified as one of the ways by which a person could be put in a slave labor situation or kept there (Lebedev 2004; Girko 2005; Novikov 2006).[37]

Changes to Laws on Enabling Prostitution

Whereas criminal laws on organizing and recruitment into prostitution were considered inadequate by law enforcement before the human trafficking laws were passed, changes in the wording of these laws significantly increased their utility in prosecuting traffickers by broadening them to include more aggravating

---

34. Article 4 of the Labor Code defines forced labor as: "all work done under threat of punishment (or physical pressure) with the goal of maintaining labor discipline; punishing participation in a strike; mobilizing labor for economic development purposes; as a punishment for expressing political views or ideological convictions that are in opposition to the political, social, or economic system; as a way of discriminating based on racial, social, national, or religious origins." See *Trudovoi kodeks Rossiiskoi Federatsii* of December 30, 2001, no. 197-FZ (SZ RF 2002, no. 1 [part 1], item 3).

35. Labor is defined widely in commentaries to the law and can include physical, intellectual, or sexual labor.

36. The length of the exploitation does not make a difference, legally speaking. The fact that slave labor was used is enough to prosecute under this statute (Lebedev 2004; Girko 2005; Novikov 2006; D'iakov and Kadnikov 2008; Brilliantov 2010; Zhalinskii 2010).

37. Blackmail is primarily defined in this article as threatening to reveal compromising information about the person or the person's family that could lead to serious harm if revealed. It does not matter whether the information is true or false or whether the blackmailer actually has the information, only that the victim believes that the blackmailer does (Brilliantov 2010).

factors. Whether inadvertently or purposely, these changes made it even less likely that law enforcement would choose to use the new human trafficking laws, at least in cases of sexual exploitation for prostitution, since the new formulations of Articles 240 and 241 (summarized in tables 2.5 and 2.6) gave them the ability to cover a wider number of situations under a law they already knew how to use.

The new formulation contained several key changes that made this article more attractive for law enforcement to use in human trafficking situations. The first was the addition of "or forcing someone to continue in prostitution" as part of the basic definition of the crime. This clause could encompass a much broader range of situations. Also, the changes meant that recruiting or forcing someone

TABLE 2.5 Changes to Article 240—recruitment into prostitution

	BASIC DEFINITION	1ST-LEVEL AGGRAVATING FACTORS	2ND-LEVEL AGGRAVATING FACTORS
240 old	Recruitment into prostitution committed by means of: • violence or threat of violence; • blackmail; • destruction or harm to property; • deceit Punishment: fine up to 200–500 times the minimum monthly wage[a] or amounting to salary or income for a period of 2–5 months; imprisonment up to 4 yrs.	• organized group Punishment: fine up to 700–1,000 times the minimum monthly wage or amounting to salary or income for a period of 7 months to 1 year; imprisonment 3–6 yrs.	None
240 new	Recruitment into or forcing to continue in prostitution Punishment: fine up to 200,000 rubles or amounting to salary or income for a period of 18 months; compulsory labor up to 3 yrs.; or imprisonment up to 3 yrs.[b]	• violence or threat of violence; • transport across Russian borders or illegal holding of someone abroad; • premeditated agreement Punishment: imprisonment up to 6 yrs. with or without 2 yrs. of probation	• organized group • minor Punishment: imprisonment from 3–8 yrs. with possible loss of rights to hold a particular job up to 15 yrs. and with or without probation up to 2 yrs.

[a] The minimum monthly wage (MROT) was an amount standardized by the government. 1 MROT = 450 rubles in 2002 and 600 rubles in 2003 http://www.rg.ru/2003/09/11/Minimumzarplatyvyrastetvoktyabre.html/, accessed 2/21/11.
[b] In 2011, compulsory labor was added as a possible punishment. Everything else has remained the same since the 2003 laws. Federal Law no. 420-FZ "O vnesenii izmenenii v Ugolovnyi kodeks Rossiiskoi Federatsii i otdel'nye zakonodatel'nye akty Rossiiskoi Federatsii" of December 7, 2011 (SZ RF 2011, no. 50, item 7362).

TABLE 2.6   Changes to Article 241—organizing prostitution

	BASIC DEFINITION	1ST-LEVEL AGGRAVATING FACTORS	2ND-LEVEL AGGRAVATING FACTORS
241 old	Organization or maintenance of a place of prostitution Punishment: fine up to 700–1,000 times the minimum monthly wage or amounting to salary or income for a period of 7 mos.–1 yr.; imprisonment up to 5 yrs.	None	None
241 new	Activities aimed at organizing the prostitution of others, at keeping a place of prostitution, or systematically providing a place for prostitution to take place Punishment: fine between 100,000 to 500,000 rubles or amounting to salary or income for a period of 1–3 yrs.; compulsory labor up to 5 yrs.; imprisonment up to 5 yrs.	• use of official position; • violence or threat of violence; • known minor Punishment: imprisonment up to 6 yrs. with possible loss of rights to hold a particular job up to 10 yrs. and with or without probation up to 2 yrs.	• use of person known to be under 14 Punishment: imprisonment 3–9 yrs. with possible loss of rights to hold a particular job up to 15 yrs. and with or without probation up to 2 yrs.

to stay in prostitution was a crime in and of itself. Previously even the basic crime required recruitment with "violence or threat of violence, blackmail, destruction of property, or through deceit." This was difficult to prove, especially because women often went into prostitution voluntarily.

The new formulation of Article 240 divided the crime into three levels of aggravating factors and added several new ones which were important for trafficking, including (1) transport of the victim across Russian borders; (2) recruitment into prostitution by means of a premeditated agreement (which is easier to prove than commitment by an organized group, which was the previous requirement and is the requirement for the highest aggravating factor in the human trafficking statute); and (3) recruitment of a known minor into prostitution. However, the changes to Article 240 removed deceit, blackmail, and destruction of property as means by which the crime could be committed, which might have given law enforcement guidance in identifying these situations. The new formulation left only violence or the threat of violence as aggravating factors. Perhaps including the means was not as important, considering that the crime itself now stood alone and many law enforcement agents had experience using the old version of the law, so they understood the requirements.

Article 241 was also broadened significantly. In its earlier formulation, it had been a crime with no aggravating factors, defined as organizing or maintaining a place of prostitution. In the new formulation, the words "or systematically providing a place for prostitution to take place" were added to the basic definition. In addition, two levels of aggravating factors were added to the crime. Some of these specified the means by which the crime could be committed (use of an official position; violence or the threat of violence), whereas others stated that the crime was more serious if committed with respect to a minor, especially one under the age of fourteen. This statute is rarely used on its own in human trafficking cases, because if there is any element of force, the defendant is usually charged under recruitment into prostitution. Nevertheless, it does provide an additional charge to be used against the people facilitating the exploitation of victims of sex trafficking and is often used in that way.

Amending the Human Trafficking Law

In addition to the legal commentaries mentioned above, there are two official ways to clear up uncertainty surrounding a law's interpretation: a resolution from the Plenum of the Supreme Court (*postanovlenie*) or an amendment to the law. Of course, law enforcement also relies on internal agency directives to explain how agents are supposed to interpret and apply a law, but those are not always distributed evenly throughout the country.

In civil law systems, precedent does not formally play a role in binding lower courts to particular interpretations and applications of the law.[38] Judicial decision making and reasoning can, and often do, vary from court to court and from region to region. Decisions of the highest courts, the Supreme Court and the Supreme Arbitrazh Court, however, can have informal precedential value in that lower court judges generally abide by them for fear of having their decisions overturned on appeal.[39]

---

38. In contrast, common law legal systems such as those in the United States and the United Kingdom are guided by precedent. In these systems, law enforcement agents are aided by the development of case law over time, which sets precedents for how statutes will be interpreted by the court in the future. When there are conflicts between courts, they are usually settled by appeals courts whose rulings are binding on all future cases in courts below them (Merryman and Perez-Perdomo 2007).

39. The Supreme Court is the highest court in the Russian courts of general jurisdiction, which deal with criminal and civil cases. Until August 2014 when it was merged with the Supreme Court, the Supreme Arbitrazh Court was the highest court in the system of arbitrazh courts, which deal with business disputes. The possibility of precedent playing a more formal role in the Russian legal system has been debated by the Russian legal community at various times (Maggs 2002; Smirnov 2008; Kornia 2010; Pomeranz and Gutbrod 2012).

When there is a significant amount of conflicting practice among interpretations of a particular law, the Plenum of the Supreme Court can choose to issue a resolution on the proper interpretation of the law, which is then binding on future practice throughout the court system. Both law enforcement professionals and academics have stressed the need for a resolution on the human trafficking law to provide needed clarification for confused practitioners and ensure some level of consistency in the application of the new law. Unfortunately these resolutions are usually only issued after there has been enough judicial practice on a law to show that there is confusion, which requires a large number of cases reaching the appellate level. Because there are so few trafficking cases overall, the Plenum is unlikely to consider the human trafficking laws particularly problematic. But many law enforcement agents say that they are hesitant to use the law without the explanation this resolution would provide. Ambiguity thus creates a vicious circle in which no new judicial practice is created, so no resolution can be issued.

The most decisive way to clear up uncertainty about a law is for the legislature to amend it.[40] After the laws on trafficking were passed in December 2003, various legislators initiated attempts to improve the law. Their activities were driven by a deep concern over the perceived inability of law enforcement to prosecute child trafficking under the existing law. The most publicized case that showed the hole in the human trafficking law occurred in 2005 (no. 38). A Moscow woman, Liudmila Verzhbitskaya, approached friends who worked in abortion clinics to find women who were in late stages of pregnancy and did not want their babies. She convinced them to give up their babies, rather than having abortions, and falsified their participation in a surrogate mother program. Verzhbitskaya paid each of the women $1,000–$1,500 for their participation, then sold their babies to childless couples for $20,000–$25,000 each. Although Verzhbitskaya was originally charged with human trafficking, the charge could not be sustained according to the investigator, Sergei Nesterkin, and instead was reclassified as kidnapping:

> According to the law, as soon as a mother gives up her baby, the state becomes responsible for the baby, and the baby should be located with them. In this situation Verzhbitskaya hid the children at the houses of her friends, and if the babies had died, no one would have known. Her activities had to be charged under this article [kidnapping] because in

---

40. The underlying philosophy of civil law legal systems like Russia's is a strong division of functions between the legislative and judicial branches of government. In an ideal civil law system, codes are complete, coherent, and clear. Legislatures make and amend the law, and judges apply it. If there are gaps in the law, it is the legislature's responsibility to amend it rather than to allow judicial decisions to fill in the gaps as in a common law system (Merryman and Perez-Perdomo 2007).

THE HUMAN TRAFFICKING LAWS

the Russian Criminal Code, there is simply no article that deals with criminal responsibility for the trafficking of minors. A person can be punished under Article 127.1 only if the fact of exploitation is proven. But how can you "exploit nursing babies" which is what Verzhbitskaya did? (Korablev 2007)

Though decriminalizing the sale of minors was clearly not the intent of the law's drafters, this interpretation of the law created a heated argument between legislators and law enforcement agents. In response to accusations by law enforcement agencies that the Duma had de facto legalized child trafficking, Pavel Krasheninnikov, the head of the Duma's Legislative Committee, accused law enforcement of incompetence:

> There has been no legalization of child trafficking in our country. . . . If earlier there was a "partial" law, Article 152 (child trafficking), now there is a broader and more "general" law, Article 127.1 (human trafficking), which provides for harsh punishment. The number of the statute has changed but not its content; the statute reads "human trafficking," so if trafficking takes place, a criminal case should be opened. And buying/selling, that's separate. What is written after that should be read as "or recruitment with the goal of exploitation, or transfer with the goal of exploitation, or harboring with the goal of exploitation." It is a legal technicality. And those who don't know that ought to relearn the basics. It's not a problem with the Criminal Code but with the Procuracy. (Korablev 2008)

This problem was also noted in media reports on almost every case of child trafficking between 2004 and 2008, when the law was amended to clarify that buying/selling could stand alone as a crime without the goal of exploitation. By this time, Krasheninnikov had softened his tone. When discussing the amendments he stated, "from the academic point of view, 'with the purpose of exploitation' is not a required element [of the crime], but in practice, we have gone down a path where implementers of the law always look for transactions with the goal of exploitation" (State Duma 2008a).

Three separate legislative proposals, two from Duma representatives and one from the Presidential Administration, were eventually combined into one new law, passed in November 2008 to amend the trafficking laws.[41] Now the buying or

---

41. Pavel Krasheninnikov's proposal, project no. 270443-4, "O vnesenii izmeneniia v stat'iu 127.1 Ugolovnogo kodeksa Rossiiskoi Federatsii" was removed from consideration on March 19, 2008. The proposal from Vladimir Zhirinovsky and his colleagues, project no. 430557-4, "O vnesenii izmenenii v Ugolovnyi kodeks Rossiiskoi Federatsii (po voprosu ob ugolovnoi otvetstvennosti za torgovliu nesovershennoletnimi" was voted down the same day (both on file with author).

selling of a person is a crime in and of itself, as is any transaction with regard to a person. This was meant to cover situations in which, as one Federation Council senator pointed out, "a person was given as a gift or exchanged for a person who was kidnapped; if someone was sold for later resale, but not exploitation; if someone was sold as a consequence of losing a card game; if parents sold their children" (Federation Council 2008).[42] The law's wording now reads "buying/selling a person, any transaction involving a person, and likewise the recruitment, transportation, transfer, harboring, or receiving of a person for the purpose of their exploitation." Another change raised the minimum level of punishment for human trafficking from five to six years, thereby making it qualify as a grave crime.[43] When a crime is classified as grave, it changes the types of investigative activities that are authorized by law and changes the type of prison sentence that the accused may have to serve if convicted.[44] Finally, the new law added two aggravating factors, trafficking a known pregnant woman and trafficking a person in a dependent state, both intended to deal with issues surrounding child trafficking.

Throughout discussions of the amendments, there were frequent references made to the problems of implementation. Deputy Andrei Nazarov noted that of the eighty-three cases registered from 2004 to 2006, only thirteen were opened (State Duma 2008b).[45] The explanatory note to the draft of the law from the Presidential Administration provided statistics that showed only ten cases had been fully investigated by the MVD, of which only six had resulted in sentences under the human trafficking statute.[46]

There were fairly heated debates in both the Duma and the Federation Council about whether this wording change was the best, though all were adamant in expressing their support for making the law more usable. During the debates, a number of other proposals were brought up but ultimately rejected. Some legislators

---

42. Other than the final item in this list, it is unclear how often any of these other types of transactions have occurred.

43. There are four levels of crime in Russian law: (1) minor crime (*prestuplenie nebol'shoi tiazhesti*), which has a maximum punishment of two years in prison; (2) moderately grave crime (*prestuplenie srednei tiazhesti*), which has a maximum punishment of five years in prison; (3) grave crime (*tiazhkoe prestuplenie*), which has a maximum punishment of ten years in prison; and (4) especially grave crime (*osobo tiazhkoe prestuplenie*), crimes punishable by ten years to life in prison (CC Articles 15 and 58).

44. CC Articles 15 and 58 and Federal Law no. 144-FZ, "Ob operativno—rozysknoi deitel'nosti," of August 12, 1995 (SZ RF 1995, no. 33, item 3349), which allows intrusive investigative actions to take place without the prior approval of a judge to prevent grave and especially grave crimes, provided that the operativnik inform a judge within twenty-four hours and get a warrant within forty-eight hours.

45. Registering a crime is what happens when a violation first comes to law enforcement's attention. There is a separate official procedure that must take place to actually open the case for further investigation.

46. Three had had convictions under other statutes (Articles 240 or 241) but were acquitted of human trafficking, and one had not been forwarded to trial (*Poiasnitel'naia zapiska* 2008).

argued for a definition of trafficking that added the term "against his or her will" after the buying and selling so that things like sports trades would not fall within the purview of the law (see Kotenkov in Federation Council 2008). Many argued for reinstating a separate statute that specifically criminalized trafficking in minors, which they considered to be a far more serious crime deserving of greater punishment than the trafficking of adults. There was also discussion of adding in the means by which trafficking could be committed as outlined in the UN protocol so that the traffickers no longer could make the argument in court that their victims went voluntarily (see Ivanov in State Duma 2008a). Other members argued for a change in the wording that added "or for profit motives" in addition to the goal of exploitation (see Krasheninnikov in State Duma 2008a).

In the end, debates notwithstanding, the Presidential Administration's version of the wording was passed with minor changes.[47] However, Pavel Krasheninnikov gave himself and other initiators of the legislation credit, saying "without the other legislative proposals, it is hardly likely that the administration would have put forth its own proposal, probably. In any case, the administration was given impulse by the Duma" (State Duma 2008a).

Although several other amendments have been made to the human trafficking law since 2008, they have not changed the substance and were primarily connected with reforms of the system of punishments for convicts. The only additional substantive change made to Article 127.1 was in 2012, when the term "known" was removed from the aggravating factor "a known minor," during a push by the Duma to more harshly criminalize crimes against minors.[48] This change underwent vigorous debate in the Duma and Federation Council during the discussions on the 2008 amendments. As one Duma member noted, judges had a difficult time assessing whether or not the trafficker knew that the victim was a minor and that traffickers usually got out of this by denying they knew the victim's age (see Ivanov in State Duma 2008a). There have been no substantive changes to Article 127.2, use of slave labor, since it was first passed in 2003.

In sum, as of 2003, the laws on the books did not seem sufficient to deal with human trafficking for sexual or labor exploitation. If the victim was not a minor, law enforcement had to find ways to prosecute cases using the statutes at its disposal or let the traffickers go because there were no elements of a crime in their

---

47. Federal Law no. 218-FZ, "O vnesenii izmenenii v stat'iu 127.1 Ugolovnogo kodeksa Rossiiskoi Federatsii," of November 25, 2008 (SZ RF 2008, no. 48, item 5513).

48. This was also removed in Articles 240 and 241. See Federal Law no. 14-FZ, "O vnesenii izmenenii v Ugolovnyi kodeks Rossiiskoi Federatsii i otdel'nye zakonodatel'nye akty Rossiiskoi Federatsii v tseliakh usileniia otvetstvennosti za prestupleniia seksual'nogo kharaktera, sovershennye v otnoshenii nesovershennoletnikh," of February 29, 2012 (SZ RF 2012, no. 10, item 1162).

activities. Because Russian law specifically prohibits reasoning by analogy in criminal law, it was impossible to expand the understanding of one of these other crimes to include trafficking (Constitution Article 54; CC Article 3[2]). Despite agents' attempts to prosecute trafficking by cobbling together several Criminal Code articles that each dealt with different stages of the crime, only the 2003 law gave law enforcement a definition of human trafficking that covered all the stages in one statute.

However, just because agents had been given these new laws did not mean that they chose to use them. Law enforcement agents operate within an institutional machinery that has made pursuing human trafficking cases under trafficking laws undesirable. Changes in Criminal Code articles on recruitment into and organization of prostitution increased the utility of using these articles to prosecute sex trafficking cases. This choice gave law enforcement the advantage of being able to use previous experience and recognized investigative techniques to pursue these crimes. In cases of uncertainty about the proper laws to use, agents could use these laws to pursue human trafficking violations rather than engage with the ambiguity of the human trafficking laws.

Once the law was passed in 2003, law enforcement quickly identified additional problems with the law: confusing wording, and the absence of a resolution from the Supreme Court standardizing judicial practice. In particular, these concerns focused on what law enforcement considered the de facto legalization of child trafficking, a problem that was solved in November 2008 with an amendment to the human trafficking statute. After these changes, law enforcement made good on its promises, pursuing cases of people selling children for illegal adoption quite successfully. This is a bright spot in what has otherwise been a challenging law to implement in practice.

LAW ENFORCEMENT'S INSTITUTIONAL MACHINERY AND THE CRIMINAL PROCESS

As one NGO activist who had worked with law enforcement made clear in an interview,

> There is very little praise or recognition if you do something right, but a significant amount of punishment for failure, especially since promotions are based primarily on the number of cases opened and closed. This makes investigators unwilling to open a case unless they believe they can close it. Sometimes they will investigate a case for a year or so before opening it, but if they never open it, all that time was wasted, and it does not show up on the statistics that they [their supervisors] look at when they review promotions. There are some risk takers, but they are few and far between. The incentive is to drop the charges down to what you know you can get the person on. They almost always go with what is safe. (N31)

The fear of failure described in this quotation refers not to failure as we might define it—failure to stop crime, keep society safe, or find criminals. Instead it refers to the failure to fulfill prescribed targets and plans for law enforcement activity set from above for a given time period. This is one of the most enduring legacies of the Soviet-era law enforcement structure and has caused today's Russian law enforcement agencies to retain an emphasis on self-preservation and service to the state over public service. Understanding why this is the case requires knowing how the system in which these agencies are embedded influences and normalizes particular ways of thinking and acting (Vaughan 1998). Statistical indicators assessing performance, along with an extremely hierarchical organizational structure and culture—what I term the institutional machinery—create a series of barriers that deters the prosecution of many crimes in Russia, not only human trafficking. This chapter outlines the institutions of law enforcement, the incentives created by their institutional machinery, and how those incentives play out in the criminal justice process.[1]

Law Enforcement Agencies

For the purposes of this study, I define Russian law enforcement as including four agencies: the police (Ministerstvo vnutrennykh del, MVD), the Procuracy (Prokuratura), the Federal Security Service (Federal'naia sluzhba bezopasnosti, FSB), and the Investigative Committee (Sledstvennyi komitet pri Prokurature, later the Sledstvennyi komitet, SK). I also include a brief description of the Federal Migration Service (Federal'naia migratsionnaia sluzhba, FMS) because of its involvement in some human trafficking cases, although it is technically not a law enforcement agency.[2] All these agencies are organized hierarchically into three territorial levels. The local (*raion*) agents answer to their regional (*sub"ekt*) superiors who answer to the federal-level agency heads.[3] Law enforcement agents do not answer to anyone outside their agencies, except for the courts and the Procuracy under its powers of general oversight. Local governments are prohibited by law from interfering with the activities of law enforcement organs on their territories (Paneyakh et al. 2012, 14). Trafficking is usually dealt with at the local level by local agents and courts, unless it is a large or complex case, in which case it is dealt with at the regional level.

---

1. Throughout the chapter, I use the gender pronoun that reflects the predominant gender makeup of each institution: he for the MVD, Investigative Committee, Procuracy, and FSB; and she for judges. As of 2013, women make up 20 percent of the MVD force (MVD 2013); as of 2010, they accounted for 40–45 percent of the Procuracy (Kolosov 2010). As of 2011, two-thirds of judges were women (Zakatnova 2011). There are no available statistics on the number of women in the Investigative Committee.

2. There are a number of other law enforcement agencies in Russia, including the Federal Drug Control Service (FSKN), Federal Penitentiary Service (FSIN), Federal Customs Service (FTS), Federal Bailiff Service (FSSP), Federal Fire Service (FPS), Federal Guard Service (FSO), and Foreign Intelligence Service (SVR). I have chosen to exclude them from the description here because they are unlikely to be involved in human trafficking cases.

3. As of 2013, there were eighty-three regions (*sub"ekty*) in the Russian Federation of six different types: twenty-one republics, nine krais, forty-six oblasts, two federal cities (Moscow and St. Petersburg), one autonomous oblast, and four autonomous okrugs. For convenience, I refer to them as regions or republics throughout the book. Each region is divided into a number of local municipalities (*raiony*).

Each agency is responsible for different aspects of investigating and prosecuting criminal activities as outlined by the Criminal Procedure Code (CPC). During any investigation, there are two types of law enforcement agents involved, operative investigators (*operativniki*) and criminal investigators (*sledovateli*).[4] Both the MVD and the FSB have operativniki and the MVD, FSB, and Investigative Committee all have investigators. Several other specialized agencies are empowered to do investigative activities according to the Criminal Procedure Code and the Law on Operational-Investigative Activities, but in this chapter, I concentrate only on the agencies that can be involved in human trafficking cases.

Ministry of Internal Affairs

The Ministry of Internal Affairs oversees the police (*politsiia*), called the *militsiia* through 2011, which is the most structurally complex of the law enforcement agencies. The institution employs 1.1 million people throughout the country, 780,000 of them on-the-ground agents (Paneyakh et al. 2012, 16). In the Soviet system, the primary purpose of law was to protect the state from the people—specifically, deviant individuals who, by not conforming to the state's ideological and behavioral dictates, threatened to destroy the system. The main function of the police under communism, then, was to ensure the social and political status quo and prevent economic and political crimes that might undermine the state's power. Although the investigations of dissidents, organized criminals, and those committing other serious crimes against the state was entrusted to the "high police," the KGB (Committee for State Security—Komitet gosudarstvennoi bezopasnosti), the MVD played an important role in combating lower-level economic and political crime (Shelley 1996). They were helped in these tasks by citizen's brigades (*druzhina*), who took on some responsibility for routine patrolling, especially in rural areas, and policing major events or state-initiated campaigns (Galeotti 1993; Williams and Serrins 1993; Shelley 1996).[5] Most police work was done through informants and forced confessions. In fact, after the breakup of the Soviet Union, one of the flaws that quickly became obvious was the MVD's inability to carry out basic policing tasks (Tanner 2000). They had relied on coercive tactics for so long that they did not know how to do anything else.

---

4. I use the Russian word for the operatives (*operativniki*) throughout to distinguish them from the criminal investigators (*sledovateli*), whom I call simply investigators (Burnham, Maggs, and Danilenko 2012).

5. According to Galeotti (1993), in 1989 there were fourteen million people registered as *druzhinniki*, a number that dropped precipitously in the early 1990s.

After 1991, pressure increased for the MVD to work more effectively. Consequently, a number of structural reorganizations took place, and regulations were issued to regulate police conduct (Robertson 2004; Beck and Robertson 2005). Nevertheless, very few resources were dedicated to training, equipping, and reeducating the police (Williams and Serrins 1993). Because the MVD was so short-staffed, superiors tolerated low-level corruption because it was one of the few perks to the job for lower-level police agents. Even so, the poor salaries, low respect from the public, and increased risk of harm led to significant turnover within the MVD's forces, especially experienced officers who could easily find jobs in private security or organized crime (Shelley 1996, 1999; Varese 2001; Volkov 2002; Robertson 2004). The exodus of qualified law enforcement professionals in the 1990s meant that the MVD had to recruit new officers quickly. To do so, the training period for new police was halved, and a new two-year course was introduced which included the possibility of training through correspondence courses. This led to a number of problems including using falsified diplomas, officers who could not pass health requirements, and overall decreased professionalism (Newsru.com 2009).

During the 2000s, several efforts were made to reform the MVD to increase its professionalism and competence. The penitentiary system and fire department were moved out of the MVD's purview to reduce agents' responsibilities and keep their focus on policing activities like uncovering and investigating crime, regulating traffic, and maintaining general order (Robertson 2004; Solomon 2005). The MVD has become more centralized in the 2000s. During the 1990s, law enforcement agencies were responsible to locally elected officials, but now they answer only to their agency superiors, a return to the Soviet-era setup. In addition, whereas in the 1990s, much of the funding for law enforcement activities came from regional governments, funding has become more centralized, making local law enforcement less dependent on the local and regional governments (Taylor 2011).

In 2011, the MVD experienced its first serious reorganization in over a decade, based on the law "On the Police," signed into law in February 2011.[6] The most visible change was the renaming of the police force from *militsiia* to *politsiia*. Other important reforms included recertifying police officers, reducing the police force by 20 percent, and raising salaries for those who remained (Taylor 2014b). Despite these reorganizations, overall quality and level of professionalism remains low, and nepotistic hiring practices continue. Work in the MVD is not considered to be a particularly high-status profession in terms of salary or respect unless done as part of one of the elite investigative units (Taylor 2011).

---

6. Federal Law no. 3-FZ, "O Politsii," of February 7, 2011 (SZ RF 2011, no. 7, item 900).

The MVD is conscious of this perception and is constantly making efforts to change it by introducing reforms such as a new behavior code and increased training requirements.[7] Nevertheless, the MVD has been unable to develop legitimacy in the eyes of the populace or an effective system of public accountability, both considered important aspects of moving away from its authoritarian past.[8] Trust in the police remains low, and beliefs that the institution is corrupt persist (see Semukhina and Reynolds 2013 for an overview).

The MVD's current organizational structure consists of four levels: federal, federal district (*okrug*), regional, and local.[9] The federal-level MVD is made up of a number of subdivisions whose functions are replicated almost exactly at the regional level (e.g., traffic control, investigations, and operative activities).[10] There are also several federal-level operative units, the operative-investigative bureaus (*operativno-rozysknoe biuro*) that do not have equivalents at the regional or local levels. These are focused on specific problems, cross-regional crimes, and the improvement of interagency cooperation. In 2007 the MVD established a subdivision in one of these units specifically trained to investigate human trafficking and kidnapping crimes: the Third Division of Operative-Investigative Bureau no. 2 (Tretii otdel Operativno-rozysknoi biuro no. 2). This federal unit offers logistical support and expertise to agents working on trafficking cases in regions throughout Russia. In some particularly difficult cases, they have sent their agents out to work directly with agents in other regions.

Putin's post-2004 recentralization drive installed an intermediary level of federal government oversight, the federal district, of which there are eight throughout the country.[11] An MVD division was also created at this level. These federal district units are technically a part of the federal-level MVD and do not fall between the federal and regional levels in the hierarchy of subordination. These

---

7. The behavior code forbids cursing, drinking at work or the night before, casual sexual affairs, or smoking in public, among other things (Arutunyan 2009). The training requirements now include first aid, being able to operate construction equipment, reciting the national anthem and anti-corruption rules as well as having to re-pass a driving test (Krainova 2009; MT 2009b).

8. See Shelley 1996; Caparini and Marenin 2004; Robertson 2004, 2005; Solomon 2005; Taylor 2011.

9. Based on the 2011 law "On the Police." In the next several paragraphs, I draw heavily on Paneyakh et al. 2012 for a description of the current structure of law enforcement.

10. It also has some subdivisions that exist only at the federal level (e.g., analytical units, international cooperation units). The transportation police, which oversees safety on mass transit, has nine subdivisions throughout Russia overseen by a federal-level head.

11. They are the Central, Southern, Northwestern, Far Eastern, Siberian, Ural, Volga, and North Caucasus. The creation of the districts was part of Putin's consolidation of power in 2004 after a terrorist attack on an elementary school in Beslan, North Ossetia. It was justified as an important step toward eliminating regional corruption and thereby being better able to prevent future terrorist attacks (Taylor 2011).

units perform a coordinating function within and among federal district law enforcement agencies and have one investigative and two operative units to deal with extremely serious or cross-regional cases. If for some reason a case cannot be handled in the place where it took place (i.e., corruption or official involvement), it can be investigated by the federal-district-level MVD. The federal district level also has a division that deals with kidnapping and human trafficking.

Most law enforcement activity takes place at the regional and local levels in cities and towns. There are about 2,000 local departments (*upravlenie*) in Russia, each with 100–150 employees covering 50,000–100,000 residents (Paneyakh et al. 2012, 19).[12] Although most of these employees are involved in various types of day-to-day patrol work, two departments within the MVD are more directly involved in criminal investigations: operativniki and investigators.

OPERATIVNIKI

The MVD is one of several Russian law enforcement agencies where operative investigators are located. The MVD's operativniki are usually the ones who would be involved in any trafficking investigation. Their main responsibilities are to develop relationships with informants, uncover crimes, conduct preliminary investigative activities, and find and detain suspected criminals. Operativniki are governed not by the Criminal Procedure Code but by a separate piece of legislation that delineates their duties and responsibilities (CPC Article 89; Federal Law no. 144-FZ of 1995). Their activities are overseen by the Procuracy. Operativniki have broad powers and are free of most regulation over their activities, with the tradeoff that much of the evidence they collect cannot be admitted in court unless it either follows the dictates of the Criminal Procedure Code or is reobtained in a manner that follows the code. Investigators can order operativniki to gather more information in the course of the investigation once a case is formally opened.[13] In turn, operativniki can use lower-level police to help them fulfill various tasks (e.g., going door to door to look for witnesses to a crime) or if they are hot on a suspect's trail.[14]

In a typical police department, there are several subunits of specialized operativniki covering property crimes, serious and violent crimes, economic crimes/corruption, missing persons, and so on (Paneyakh et al. 2012, 23). When the

---

12. Before 2007 individual cities and towns each had their own MVD divisions, but organizational reform has centralized some of these units into interregional (*mezhregional'nyi*) units, which cover several municipalities.

13. Because helping investigators takes operativniki away from their other official duties, they usually try to get all relevant information before bringing the case to the investigator (Paneyakh et al. 2012, 22).

14. Lower-level police includes the beat police (Uchastkovyi upolnomochennyi politsii), patrol police (Patrul'no-postovaia sluzhba) and truant officers (inspektory po delam nesovershennoletnikh).

human trafficking law was passed, the MVD issued an edict to the specialized unit for fighting organized crime—UBOP (Upravlenie po bor'be s organizovan-noi prestupnost'iu)—assigning them responsibility for investigating traffick-ing cases.[15] This edict required that at least one UBOP agent in each region has human trafficking as one of his specified duties. This does not mean that he would work only on human trafficking, but that if a case was uncovered, it would fall within his competence. The UBOP was disbanded under a presidential order from Dmitrii Medvedev in September 2008, but the requirement that each region have at least one person specializing in human trafficking remains.[16] Regional MVD heads decide how to organize their specialized units, including those on human trafficking and how many people are assigned to them. This means that there is significant variation at the regional level in the composition of units that have trafficking as one of their specializations. For example, in 2006, the Moscow region created a vice squad, the Department for Fighting Crimes against Public Morality and Human Trafficking, which still operates today.

INVESTIGATORS

Operativniki pass the evidence they have gathered to an investigator who man-ages the preliminary investigation (*predvaritel'noe rassledovanie*) and builds the case file (*delo*). Investigators have extensive powers when putting the case file together, including subpoenaing witnesses and compelling them to give testi-mony and conducting some types of searches without judicial authorization.[17] Although technically part of the MVD, investigators have desk jobs, unlike the rest of the MVD divisions, which are mostly involved in on-the-ground police work (Paneyakh et al. 2012, 38).

---

15. The corresponding federal level unit was called DBOPiT (Department for Fighting Orga-nized Crime and Terrorism, Departament po bor'be s organizovannoi prestupnost'iu i terrorizm)

16. The order reassigned the specialized operativniki back into the general pool of operativniki investigating all crimes, into antieconomic crime units, or into new units meant to fight extremism. According to one informant to whom I spoke in the summer of 2012, many of the agents from UBOP who were transferred into the general pool left the police force entirely and went into private security or organized crime, since they no longer had elite status (M17). For those who remained, the change seems to have left the same people in charge of working on trafficking, simply changing to whom their units are subordinated. There is some belief that these units were shut down, ironically, because of excessive corruption in the ranks, but the official reason given was that because of their success, they had eradicated the most serious organized crime groups and were now needed for other duties like preventing extremism and to staff the witness protection program (Abdullaev 2008a; Bernstein 2008; Ovchinskii 2008; Hahn 2010; Taylor 2011).

17. It is a criminal offense not to give testimony when requested in a criminal investigation unless it is against oneself, a spouse, or a close relative. Refusal is punishable by a fine or in some cases arrest (CPC Articles 188[3], 111[2]; CC Article 308). Before 2007, investigators had to go through procura-tors to get arrest warrants, but now they can request them directly from the court (Paneyakh et al. 2012, 84).

Nationwide, the MVD has approximately forty-five thousand investigators. But, like operativniki, investigators are also found in three other law enforcement agencies: the FSB, the Federal Narcotics Service, and the Investigative Committee. The Criminal Procedure Code outlines which agency's investigators have jurisdiction over which articles of the Criminal Code (CPC Article 151). Investigative jurisdiction for human trafficking cases is split between the MVD (trafficking without aggravating factors) and the Investigative Committee (trafficking with aggravating factors), as described in more detail below. Cases of organizing prostitution or recruitment into prostitution with aggravating factors are assigned to the MVD's investigators.[18]

The Procuracy

Established under Peter the Great, the Procuracy has been one of the most powerful law enforcement institutions in the Soviet and post-Soviet period. Its agents, procurators, were intended to serve as the "eye of the tsar," ensuring that all government agencies, departments, officials, and courts conformed to the laws of the land. They maintained this function until the 1864 judicial reforms, when they were explicitly given the in-court prosecutorial role and their supervisory role was reduced. During the Soviet period, their supervisory functions were renewed and expanded while they kept the in-court prosecutorial role. In a system in which law was often used instrumentally by the state to pursue its own goals, the Procuracy's power of general oversight (*nadzor*) was an important way for the government to control the outcomes in the courts. Its agents' close relationship with judges, who generally followed whatever the procurator recommended in criminal cases, cemented their powerful position in Soviet law (Kaminskaya 1982; Simis 1982; Solomon 1996). This power also ended up making the Procuracy a complaints bureau for citizens about the conduct of administrative agencies and other citizens.[19]

According to the 1993 Russian Constitution, the Procuracy stands independent of both the judicial and executive branches. During all the reforms of the legal

---

18. Cases of organizing and recruitment into prostitution without aggravating factors as well as cases of illegal border crossing and organizing illegal migration without aggravating factors are not required to have a full preliminary investigation. Instead they go through the process of inquiry (*doznanie*), a less involved investigatory process usually conducted by a specialized inquiry officer (*doznavatel'*) (CPC Article 150[3]). Inquiries have a shorter time period—thirty days—which in exceptional cases can be extended to twelve months (CPC Article 223). If the inquiry is not completed when the time is up, it is usually transferred to an investigator for full investigation. It can also be transferred by a procurator to an investigator if the case is complex or important (CPC Article 27[211–12]).

19. For more on the history of the Procuracy, see Smith 1978; Solomon 1996; Thaman 1996; and Kazantsev 1997.

system in the post-Soviet era, the Procuracy fought hard to keep its Soviet-era powers intact (Smith 2005). However, the 2001 Criminal Procedure Code shifted a significant amount of power away from the Procuracy to the courts. Under the Soviet Criminal Procedure Code, procurators could issue arrest warrants, decide on the period of detention for suspects, and order and conduct searches, seizures of evidence, and wiretaps without permission of the courts. The new code requires judicial approval of all these activities. The Procuracy still retains its powers of general oversight and its reputation as a general complaints bureau (Holmes 1999; Mikhailovskaya 1999; Pomeranz 2009).[20] During the Soviet period, the goal of finding the truth (istina) in each criminal case meant that procurators were supposed to be neutral, examining both incriminatory and exculpatory evidence. The introduction of a hybrid system in the 2001 Criminal Procedure Code brought adversarial procedure into the courtroom. Procurators are now solely on the side of the state, and their courtroom role has changed from being passive participants as the judge reviewed the case file to active participants who have to prove their case before the judge or jury.

Through 2007, the Procuracy had to approve all "intrusive" investigative actions (those that encroach on confidentiality of communications or the sanctity of the home) during the pretrial investigation stage and had the power to demand that the investigator undertake additional investigation. However, major changes in the Procuracy's structure in 2007 transferred these responsibilities to the head of the investigative agency doing the investigation.[21] Before these changes, the Procuracy had its own investigative division with jurisdiction over serious crimes, including human trafficking with aggravating factors. Now, the Procuracy's role in human trafficking cases is limited to supervising the criminal process and signing off on the indictment as well as prosecuting trafficking cases as the state's representative in court. They also have the power to close and reopen cases.

The Procuracy has always been very centralized, with an identical structure at the local, regional, and federal levels. All procurators ultimately answer to the procurator general, who is appointed by the Federation Council, the upper house of the Russian Parliament, based on the president's recommendation.[22] As of January 25, 2011, the Procuracy employed 45,021 people throughout Russia.[23]

---

20. In the post-Soviet period, complaints to the Procuracy, especially about administrative decisions, have proven significantly less successful than challenging them in court (Solomon 2004).
21. Federal Law no. 87-FZ, "O vnesenii izmenenii v Ugolovno-protsessual'nyi kodeks Rossiiskoi Federatsii i o prokurature Rossiiskoi Federatsii," of June 5, 2007 (SZ RF 2007, no. 24, item 2830).
22. Article 12, Federal Law no. 2202–1, "O prokurature Rossiiskoi Federatsii," of January 17, 1992 (SZ RF 1995, no. 47, item 4472).
23. Presidential Order no. 90, "Ob obshchei shtatnoi chislennosti organov prokuratury Rossiiskoi Federatsii," of January 25, 2011 (SZ RF 2011, no. 5, item 710).

At the local level, there are usually between five and eight procurators in each office, although larger municipalities may have as many as thirty (Paneyakh et al. 2012, 46).

The Investigative Committee

The 2007 overhaul of the Procuracy separated its investigative functions from its general oversight function and placed them in a newly created agency—the Investigative Committee of the Procuracy—with a head appointed by the Federation Council via a recommendation from the president and subordinate to the procurator general (Burger and Holland 2008; Taylor 2011; Burnham and Firestone unpublished). In January 2011, the Investigative Committee (SK) was separated from the Procuracy entirely. It now answers directly to the president, and its head serves at the pleasure of the president.[24] Like the Procuracy, it is strictly hierarchical, with the federal agency replicated at the local and regional levels. The SK employs 21,156 people as of January 2012, with 3–10 people in each local office.[25] There are fewer local divisions than there are of the local-level MVD, which means that many departments are interregional.

The SK's investigators are sledovateli and therefore perform the same functions as their counterparts in the MVD, but for more serious crimes. The SK handles the investigation of grave and especially grave crimes—those punishable by over five years imprisonment—and crimes committed by procurators (Abdullaev and Bratersky 2010; Feifer 2010; MT 2010a, 2010b). It is also responsible for independently verifying reports of crimes in other categories, including verification of dead bodies, crimes committed by officials, and violence directed at or committed by police (Paneyakh et al. 2012, 29). Since 2009 its investigative jurisdiction has continued to widen. In 2011 it was given jurisdiction over all tax crimes, and in 2012 all crimes committed by or against minors. Any case, regardless of its investigative jurisdiction as assigned by the Criminal Procedure Code, can be transferred to the SK at any stage for further investigation.

---

24. Federal Law no. 404-FZ, "O vnesenii izmenenii v otdel'nye zakonodatel'nye akty Rossiiskoi Federatsii v sviazi s sovershenstvovaniem deiatel'nosti organov predvaritel'nogo sledstviia," of December 28, 2010 (SZ RF 2011, no. 1, item 16). For speculation that this change is part of a longer struggle among various Kremlin factions vying for increased power, see Galeotti 2010a. The Investigative Committee and the Procuracy have had a significant institutional rivalry since the Investigative Committee was created; they have repeatedly tried to investigate each other's higher-ups (Abdullaev 2009, Taylor 2011).

25. This figure does not include another 2,034 investigators who are in charge of investigating crimes committed within the military. See Presidential Order no. 38, "Voprosy deiatel'nosti Sledstvennogo komiteta Rossiiskoi Federatsii," of January 14, 2011 (SZ RF 2011, no. 4, item 572).

Today, the SK is the primary agency doing human trafficking investigations, since trafficking is rarely found without aggravating factors. In addition, the agency has jurisdiction over other serious crimes such as kidnapping, false imprisonment, and abuse of authority/official position. So if a trafficking case includes elements of one of these other crimes, it will be investigated by the SK. Most trafficking cases are investigated by the local SK, but if the case is big, cross-regional, or complicated by the involvement of organized crime, it may be investigated at the regional level.

The SK is also responsible for international cooperation on law enforcement activities. It is in charge of executing requests for assistance under existing mutual legal assistance treaties (MLAT). This includes information exchange and carrying out investigative activities requested by foreign law enforcement agencies (though some still require a warrant issued by a domestic Russian court). It is also empowered to conclude its own agreements with foreign law enforcement bodies and inherited all such agreements that were made by the Investigative Committee of the Procuracy.

The Federal Security Service

During the Soviet period, the KGB was the most feared element of law enforcement with a broad mandate that included domestic and foreign intelligence gathering, border security, protection of the Communist Party leadership, repression of dissidents and other enemies of the state, monitoring of communications, and ensuring the security of government communications (Taylor 2011). After the fall of the USSR in 1991, the KGB's functions were broken up into several smaller units. The FSB inherited the domestic intelligence functions of the KGB along with several special forces units. As an agency it has grown increasingly powerful under the presidency of Vladimir Putin, himself a former KGB agent.[26]

In 2003, the FSB took over border protection duties from the Federal Border Service.[27] As such, it has played an important role in dealing with cases of extremism, terrorism, economic and organized crime and corruption. Though the responsibility for investigating most trafficking crimes falls to the MVD and Investigative Committee, operativniki and investigators from the FSB have been involved in investigating trafficking, including some of the largest international cases. They have also been involved in investigating trafficking cases that use

---

26. For a more complete history of the KGB and the FSB, see Knight 1996; Soldatov and Borogan 2011; and Taylor 2011.

27. Presidential Order no. 308, "O merakh po sovershenstvovaniiu gosudarstvennogo upravleniia v oblasti bezopasnosti Rossiiskoi Federatsii," of March 11, 2003 (SZ RF 2003, no. 12, item 1101).

Russia as a transit point for trafficking to third countries, because they violate the border regime. The Criminal Procedure Code gives investigative jurisdiction over cases of illegal border crossing (Article 322) and organizing illegal migration with aggravating factors to the FSB.

Federal Migration Service

Though it does not have any investigative powers, the Federal Migration Service bears mentioning in the list of law enforcement agencies that may be involved in human trafficking cases. A 2004 presidential order removed the responsibility for overseeing migration issues from the MVD and placed it on the newly created FMS.[28] With 37,342 people working for it as of July 13, 2012, the FMS is the central coordinating body for migration policy, particularly the prevention and control of illegal migration. It also gives out passports, visas, and foreign work permits; registers foreigners and migrant workers; and monitors whether they have overstayed their visas. Although the FMS has no power to conduct any investigative activities, it does have the power to write up violations of the migration regime under the Administrative Code and handle deportation proceedings. Thus the FMS may become involved in trafficking cases if the case has to do with victims who are in Russia illegally.

Institutional Machinery

All government agencies, including law enforcement, have their own organizational norms, policies, and practices that constrain and shape the behaviors of their agents (March and Simon 1958). It is impossible to understand what motivates law enforcement's behavior in human trafficking cases without having an understanding of this institutional environment—the structure, culture, and incentive systems that make up what I call the institutional machinery. The structure and culture of Russian law enforcement agencies have an important impact on their ability and willingness to pursue certain types of criminal cases. Agents are socialized into a strict, militaristic hierarchy, in which subordination to the chain of command trumps all other considerations, thereby limiting officers' ability to be creative and take initiative. In addition, they are socialized into an entrenched culture of corruption, which can lead them to act outside the law. But by far the most important factor influencing their behavior is the system of

---

28. Presidential Order no. 314, "O sisteme i strukture federal'nykh organov ispolnitel'noi vlasti," of March 9, 2004 (SZ RF 2004, no. 11, item 945).

performance assessment and accountability that relies primarily on quantitative indicators. Success is a cleared case or a conviction; anything else is considered a failure. This belief not only affects an individual agent's own reputation and prospects for career advancement, but all of his superiors' as well, since all quantitative indicators are aggregated up to the very top of the hierarchy. This system is a carryover from the Soviet period, as are many of the patterns of behavior that it creates in day-to-day practice.[29]

Performance Assessment

Referred to as the *palochnaia sistema* (stick system), Russian law enforcement's system of assessment focuses on the number of activities completed (e.g., cases cleared, citations written, searches conducted, people arrested) to assess whether they are performing their duties adequately, at both the individual and department levels. This is accompanied by onerous paperwork requirements for documentation. Statistics are aggregated up the hierarchy, so there is significant pressure from above for them to look good, which leads at best to failure to perform police duties and at worst to manipulation and falsification (Khodzhaeva 2011; Maksimova 2011; Paneyakh et al. 2012; Paneyakh 2014). The perverse effect of the *palochnaia sistema* is to drive law enforcement agencies to collude in lowering the effectiveness of the criminal justice system.

Three statistical indicators—number of cases cleared (*raskryvaemost'*); number of cases investigated within time limits (*srok*) set by the Criminal Procedure Code; and number of cases/activities in comparison to the previous reporting year (*analogichnyi pokazatel' predydushchego goda*, APPG)—form the basis for assessing all actors in the criminal justice system. They affect individual officers' chances for promotion or punishment and departments' reputation within the agency and access to resources (Paneyakh et al. 2012, 63). Although each agency is affected in slightly different ways by these statistical requirements, these basic comparative indicators are consistent across agencies.

A case is considered cleared (*raskryto*) in the system once a suspect has been identified and charged with a crime.[30] Operativniki and investigators have slightly different points at which they can consider a case cleared. For an operativnik, it is the moment at which an investigator opens the case, but for an investigator, it is

---

29. For a discussion of Soviet-era law enforcement practices, see Solomon 1987; Shelley 1996; Beck and Robertson 2004; Schreck 2004; MT 2007; Abdullaev 2008b; and Wendle 2008.

30. This status is in contrast to being fully investigated (*rassledovano*) but not cleared (*ne raskryto*), when the evidence gathered reveals the circumstances surrounding the crime and allows the identification of a suspect but does not result in a charge (Paneyakh et al. 2012).

the moment at which a procurator signs off on the indictment (Paneyakh et al. 2012, 63). Perversely, the emphasis on this statistic can create disincentives for members of law enforcement to do good investigative work. As soon as a case has been uncovered, the operativniki, investigators, and sometimes even procurators try to gauge the prospects for clearing it and eventual conviction. This initial stage thus determines the future of the case, since once an investigation is set in motion, there is almost no room for honest mistakes, including discovery that the suspect has been charged in error (Paneyakh et al. 2012, 86). If the case falls apart at any point along the way, it will ruin the statistical output of all the departments involved. So instead of doing a strong investigation, putting together a solid case, and letting the court decide, agents try to avoid opening cases where it would be difficult if not impossible to identify the suspect or that they do not think will result in a conviction. Consequently they tend to focus on cases that are easy to investigate, have fairly certain prospects for conviction, and can be completed in a timely manner, rather than serious cases or those that require extensive investigative resources.

Although theoretically a performance assessment system like this could be helpful in standardizing practice and tracking outcomes (Eterno and Silverman 2012), in reality, if a case does fall apart, the extensive documentation pinpoints exactly who was responsible for the failure and should be punished. A failure may mean that a mistake is discovered by the next person in line, the time limit is violated, or the case cannot be forwarded or closed without serious consequences (Paneyakh et al. 2012, 62). But by far the worst failure in this system is an acquittal. Because performance indicators are focused on the completion of activities, not their quality or results, as soon as each agent/department is done with his or her part, he or she can pass the case on with little regard to whether it falls apart later because of shoddy or incomplete investigative work as long as it is closed by the standards that apply to that particular agency. At the same time, each agency recognizes its dependence on others for its statistical output and generally tries not to upset them by sending them cases that will ruin their statistics. If there is concern, agents will at least try to have informal conversations about the case's prospects first (Paneyakh et al. 2012, 107).

Statistics on violations of time limits established by the Criminal Procedure Code also have a prominent place in the annual reports of both the police and the court's activities and are closely monitored by the heads of investigative agencies. Every stage of the criminal process has a time limit attached, as I discuss in more detail below. There is also an emphasis on comparison over time. For each line of statistical information collected, next to it is the percentage increase or decrease from the previous year. Not surprisingly, there is pressure for the numbers to continue to go up, not down, regardless of the situation on the ground. This is especially true for the number of cases cleared.

A more general consequence of this assessment system is that it is impossible to get objective statistics on crime because all data are a potential way for superiors to assess lower-level law enforcement, and therefore the temptation to falsify or manipulate the statistics is significant (Paneyakh et al. 2012).[31] This was made clear in a 2010 report by the procurator general's office that demonstrated that crime statistics Russia-wide were full of distortions intended to inflate the number of cases cleared (including having dead people "confess" to committing crimes) and inflate the quality of investigative work (Procuracy RF 2010). In 2011, on completing a more thorough review and finding similar practices in eighty of eighty-three regions, Procurator General Yuri Chaika declared that "no one believes in the objectivity of criminal statistics anymore" (Makedonov and Faliakhov 2011; RAPSI 2011). Over time, the practice of falsifying statistics tends to reinforce itself, because it allows cases to be processed faster than if the investigative work is done properly. The driving need to clear cases can also lead to violence and coerced confessions (HRW 1999; Amnesty International 2006; Taylor 2011) and can discourage proactive policing. If a crime is prevented, there is no one to arrest and therefore no number to add to the statistics to reflect the work put in (Taylor 2014a).

Organizational Structure

Most law enforcement activity takes place at the regional and local levels in cities and towns. Because of the way the MVD is structured, departments are subordinated to both the head of their regional/local agency as well as all people above them in the service to which they belong. For example, traffic police in the city of Vladivostok in the Primorskii region are subordinate to and therefore accountable to the head of the Primorskii region MVD but also to the head of traffic police in Vladivostok, the Primorskii region, and the Russian Federation. In practice, this situation leads to a massive amount of paperwork, because agents have to account for their activities to multiple bosses, each asking for different, sometimes duplicative information.[32] The duplication results in conflicting priorities among superiors, especially when there are campaigns against particular types of crimes that come down one hierarchy of subordination but not another.[33]

---

31. Cooking the books is not unique to Russian law enforcement. There have been many reports of police departments in other countries, including the United States, in which pressure from above for crime clearance and lower rates of violent crime have led to manipulation of statistics (Eterno and Silverman 2012).

32. Paneyakh et al. (2012) note that many departments have to produce up to three reports a day to comply with demands from their various superiors.

33. These specialized law enforcement campaigns require that the agents focus their resources almost solely on whatever the target of the campaign is and usually occur after something scandalous has happened (Paneyakh et al. 2012, 25–29).

In addition, the fact that operativniki and investigators are often located in two different agencies poses significant problems in terms of the efficiency of criminal investigations. Even when the two types of agents are technically in the same agency, as in the MVD, functionally they are separated by significant intraagency barriers (Paneyakh et al. 2012). Furthermore, in human trafficking cases there are frequent situations of overlapping jurisdiction.[34] For example, if slave labor is occurring on a construction site, the FMS is empowered to enter the premises, do a document check, and start deportation proceedings. But if agents think there may be a crime involved, they must call in the operativniki to assess whether there is a crime and if so to collect evidence (Tiurukanova 2005a). There are also significant overlaps between the functions of investigators and procurators, especially at the point of opening a criminal case. Though procurators no longer have to approve the opening of a case, they do have the power to cancel the investigator's decision to open, therefore giving them "de facto veto power" (Burnham and Firestone unpublished).

Finally, because of the division of functions, significant acrimony exists among the various branches of law enforcement (and divisions within branches), which are often far from unified in their attitudes, priorities, and understandings as well as the role they see themselves playing in the administration of justice. Rivalries among law enforcement branches have been a long-standing problem in Russia. As Brian Taylor notes:

> KGB/FSB agents have always considered themselves the elite "blue bloods" among the law enforcement agencies . . . viewing the average cop as someone who is overburdened with unimportant grunt work and frequently corrupt. Police, in return, see themselves as the real fighters against crime, soldiers who shed blood while FSB agents and procurators just sit at their desks. Procuracy officials, for their part, see themselves as the linchpin of the system, with everything dependent on them . . . in reality they are often dependent on information provided by other agencies, the police in ordinary crimes and the FSB in high-profile cases (Taylor 2011, 67).

Keeping law enforcement agencies in conflict with one another may be a deliberate strategy to help reinforce dependence of each organization on the center (the president) and ensure that none of the agencies becomes too strong (Kosals 2010; Taylor 2011; Burnham and Firestone unpublished), but in practice it creates significant problems during the pursuit of criminal cases, especially complex ones.

---

34. These problems also play out in other agencies, especially in the narcotics sphere, where the Federal Drug Service and FSB often have turf battles (Matthews 2007; Burger and Holland 2008; Galeotti 2010b; Taylor 2011).

Organizational Culture

Police are by nature "hierarchical, secretive, jealous of external influence, and contemptuous of legal and procedural constraints on gathering evidence and treatment of suspects and criminals even in the most advanced countries" (Hinton and Newburn 2009, 5). They tend to do what they think is best to reach their desired goal—arresting and prosecuting criminals. Like law enforcement worldwide, Russian law enforcement agencies are quite conservative in their beliefs and attitudes. Despite the many attempts at reorganization and reform, the MVD's organizational culture has proved highly resistant to change. Though legally required to serve the people, police agents "appeared to consider it their main job to supervise, rather than protect citizens and maintain their own legitimacy" (Robertson 2004, 296). As Taylor notes, the post-Soviet Russian state has been unable to replace the ideology of the Soviet period with "a sense of professional ideals and ethics that would steer their [agents'] behavior away from corruption and predation" (Taylor 2011, 203). Like law enforcement around the world, Russian law enforcement agents are socialized into these norms through training at their respective agency academies and supervision on the job (Oberfield 2014).[35]

There are several defining features of Russian law enforcement's organizational culture that disincentivize prosecution. The first is what Leonid Kosals terms "militarization," in which the "command of one's superior is more important than the law or public interest" (2010, 2). This is exacerbated by the fact that there is no external oversight of police activities from either society or local governments. Superiors have direct control over assessment, promotion, and assignment of functions. The assignment of functions is particularly important because different types of jobs in different locations offer greater or fewer opportunities for career advancement by making it more or less difficult for agents to meet their quotas. Other assignments may make it more or less lucrative for officers to participate in corruption and line their pockets with bribes or extortion money (Kosals 2010).

Inherent in this militarized, hierarchical structure is an emphasis on subordination of lower ranks to higher ones and a culture of punishing people who deviate from their positions or roles (Khodzhaeva 2011; Maksimova 2011). It is rare for individual officers to take initiative without receiving the approval of their superiors, because the system punishes rather than rewards a creative approach, even when their behavior is wholly within the requirements of the law. In the context of trafficking, this has been both bad and good. Lower-level

---

35. All procurators are required to have a five-year legal education, usually obtained at a specialized Procuracy academy. Investigators are supposed to have a five-year higher legal education, usually from an MVD academy, but as of 2002, the last year with statistics available, only 60 percent actually did (Burnham and Firestone unpublished).

officers who have attended training sessions on human trafficking or are particularly committed to trafficking cases often cannot find support from their superiors because using a new and complicated statute has high potential to affect
the department's statistical output. They may risk reprimands, including wage
docking or demands to work overtime, if they do anything that is not approved
procedure. Furthermore, there is little protection for police whistleblowers or for
lower-level officers who disobey an illegal order from their superiors.[36] As one of
my interviewees, an academic in Saratov who had trained police on trafficking,
noted: "Even if an investigator has information about a trafficking case, he still
has to clear the investigation with his superior. What can one person do against
the entire system? Even if he wants to investigate it, the first question that the boss
will ask is 'How are you going to prove it?' If there is still a lot of investigating to
do, it will not get opened. There is a process of consultation with the boss, where
he will look at what information he has and go from there. The statistics of the
entire department reflect on the boss, so he has an interest in keeping them positive" (A2). In one trafficking case I heard about in my interviews, a senior MVD
officer allowed a rescued woman to sleep on his office floor during the investigation because she had nowhere else to go. A lower-ranking officer would probably
not have been willing to take this chance.

NGOs and academics who have worked with law enforcement in trafficking training sessions have noted who is willing or able to take risks given this
hierarchy and who is not. As one person described to me, the people who have
been most interested in trying out the human trafficking laws are those who are
conscientious, experienced, and principled. These tend to be law enforcement
agents of the older generation who feel responsibility and who are established
and do not have to worry about their careers. The younger agents are more concerned about their career prospects and do not want to take risks on these types
of uncertain cases (A2).

At the same time, because subordinate MVD divisions are required to carry out
orders from above, they must respond to demands from the federal-level MVD to
produce more human trafficking cases. Many of my interviewees noted that once
the human trafficking laws were enacted, there was an immediate demand from
above for results. Before the law was passed, the MVD usually sent lower-level

---

36. Technically, in Criminal Code Article 42, there is a provision that "failure to carry out a clearly
illegal order or directive may not be punished criminally," but in practice, defining what "clearly
illegal" means is difficult, as is asking the lower-level bureaucrats receiving the orders to go against
their superiors (Burnham, Maggs, and Danilenko 2012). In 2011 the Constitutional Court ruled that
state employees could not be punished for whistleblowing activities if those activities were done in
the public interest with no intent to defame or pursue political goals, but the court refused to define
"public interest" and no definition currently exists in Russian law (Bratersky 2011).

officers to conferences and training sessions run by international organizations and domestic NGOs as more of a goodwill gesture than because they had taken an active interest in the issue. After the law was passed, law enforcement became more pragmatic, open to cooperation with these organizations because they had expertise on how to work trafficking cases. In addition, promotion for active MVD officers is contingent on attending continuing education institutes once every two years to brush up their qualifications. This requirement presents an opportunity for education about human trafficking. The MVD continuing education institute in Moscow (Domodedovo) in collaboration with the International Organization for Migration (IOM) has developed a course on human trafficking for relevant divisions of the MVD which has been offered periodically since 2010.

Another defining characteristic of the MVD's organizational culture has to do with the acceptance and institutionalization of corruption.[37] Russian law enforcement agents have been described as following a model of "predatory policing," enriching themselves and the institution as a whole rather than protecting the public (Gerber and Mendelson 2008). Corruption in law enforcement has a long history in Russia, starting even before the communist period and persisting through today (Simis 1982; Shelley 1996). Scholars have cited low wages, a lack of respect for the law, and low legal consciousness as important contributing factors to the continued prevalence of low-level corruption in the police force (Shelley 1999; Robertson 2004). Corruption also is subject to the hierarchy, with low-level agents only keeping a small amount of the money that they extort while the rest goes to their superiors, who in turn pay their superiors. Whereas in the 1990s the Mafia tended to be the main extractor of protection money from businesses, by 2007 that role had largely been taken over by police (Kanev 2007).[38] In some ways, the performance assessment system has exacerbated this tendency. Once departments have hit their targets, their agents are free to spend the remainder of their time on activities that enable them to extract bribes (Favarel-Garrigues 2011; Taylor 2014a).

---

37. For an excellent outline of the major types of corruption practiced by Russian law enforcement, see Taylor (2011, 162–68). He outlines four major forms: (1) shakedowns, in which police stop someone on the street and ask for documents—when they do not have their paperwork in order they are offered the option of paying an on-the-spot "fine"; (2) roofing—providing protection to businesses; (3) forced takeovers—where one business pays for a case to be opened against his or her business rival; and (4) selling assets—information, documents, services, positions.

38. Local police patrolmen are heavily involved in extracting bribes from street traders, both individual sellers and the owners of street kiosks. Police officers usually receive a daily payment as well as in-kind payments of goods that the vendors are selling. In slightly higher-level businesses (small businesses, cafés, restaurants), the MVD's criminal investigation unit is often doing the extortion or providing the protection. The antieconomic crimes unit gets payoffs from people selling illegal CDs and DVDs or other counterfeit goods. Finally, the large warehouses and shopping malls are usually controlled by the district police precinct (Kanev 2007).

Further complicating the issue is the attitude of officers themselves to corruption. In a study of cadets and recently graduated officers, Beck and Lee (2002) found that many believe corruption is morally acceptable and/or justifiable under certain circumstances or for particular goals, generally when their crimes were victimless or when it was necessary to help friends and/or family. Many police felt justified in taking bribes to supplement their low wages (Taylor 2011).[39] In 2006 the *Moscow Times* reported the results of a survey of active MVD officers in which a majority of them considered it acceptable to use force against detainees and 20 percent had no objections to planting evidence (drugs or weapons) on a suspect (MT 2009a). An informal list exists of accepted costs for particular police activities including, among other things, dropping a criminal complaint, giving out classified information, forging documents, and providing protection to businesses (Taylor 2011). In another large study of current police, most reported earning more from nonstate actors than from the state budget and spending more time on illegal activities during working hours than in their free time (Kolesnikova et al. 2002).

As one of the procurators I interviewed suggested, "people in the police have different motivations than they once did. During Soviet times, they worked with only one objective, and that was to combat crime. If there was a complaint of someone's daughter gone missing, they'd have the guy in handcuffs in several hours. Now people work for themselves. It's a new system. Eighty percent of the people work on behalf of themselves, their family, to get ahead. They want material things. Of course, there are many good things about private property, but one of the consequences of that is that people are more self-interested than they once were" (P1). The entrenchment and systematic nature of corruption in law enforcement means that no one has any incentive to combat it, even though the government regularly expresses a desire and commitment to doing so.

Corruption has certainly played a part in facilitating human trafficking. It is well established that two of the main groups from which low-level police agents are known to extort money are migrant workers and those involved in the prostitution business, either as prostitutes or as brothel owners. These payoffs may cause agents to look the other way and not pursue cases. Additionally, corruption may cause human trafficking cases to drop out of the system even before they are registered or opened. During the initial investigation, there is often significant uncertainty about what type of case the evidence indicates, and it is easy for an investigator to close a case, for a price, under the provision of the Criminal

39. This has changed somewhat since pay increases began in 2005 (Taylor 2011).

Procedure Code that allows it if there are "no elements of a crime in the activities." Finally, corruption may affect the types of trafficking groups that law enforcement pursues, pushing agents to focus on small groups rather than larger groups with more significant organized crime connections. They may be able to extort more money from the large groups, so it actually becomes profitable to ignore them. They may be too afraid that the large groups have significant ties to people in power or have resources to buy protection. However, many of these behaviors may also be driven by other parts of the institutional machinery, like the fear of not being able to clear complex cases.

The Criminal Justice Process

In theory, the criminal justice process as outlined by the Criminal Procedure Code is straightforward. Acting on information received from either a report or through law enforcement activities, the operativniki gather evidence and then pass it on to the investigator who directs the investigation and assembles a case file. At the end of this process, the investigator writes up an indictment which is approved by a procurator. The case file is then passed on to a separate courtroom procurator (*gosobvinitel'*) who takes it to trial and presents the state's case (see Figure 3.1). However, in reality, the incentives created by the institutional machinery described above change what should be a simple process into one with pervasive problems.

Although each law enforcement agency is supposed to exercise independent decision making on the merits of the case in accordance with its role outlined in the Criminal Procedure Code, in practice they are in close contact from the moment they learn about a crime. Incentives created by the performance assessment system mean that agents are likely to try to avoid cases that they think will be difficult. According to one operativnik in Moscow speaking about human trafficking cases, "The investigators, procurators, and MVD do not want to take responsibility. The courtroom procurators do not want to support [the charges] in court because it is dangerous for their careers and their numbers. It is a minus for their movement up the ranks if they are not successful" (M14). This fear persists even though the great majority of trial judgments are convictions. In theory, any Russian law enforcement officer will say that he is obligated by law to charge the correct crime, and therefore if it is trafficking it will be charged as trafficking. In reality, the disincentives to look for trafficking are present right from the beginning, when agents receive a tip. The discussion that follows juxtaposes what is outlined in the Criminal Procedure Code with what actually occurs in practice.

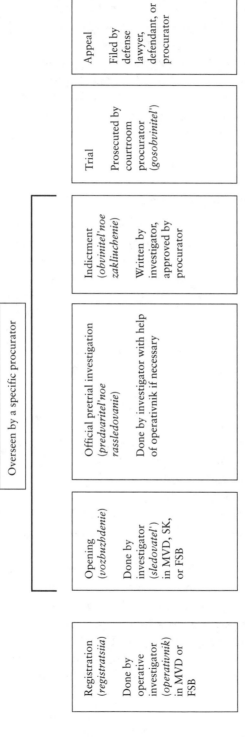

FIGURE 3.1 The criminal justice process

Registration of a Case

The first stage in the process is the registration of a crime. A crime can come to the attention of law enforcement in several ways. First, it can be reported by someone with firsthand knowledge about the planning or commission of a crime—usually a victim, witness, family member, or other interested party—by going to the police station or by calling the police hotline number (02).[40] Reporting a crime in this way requires an official written complaint (*zaiavlenie*) with the personal information of the person making the complaint and his or her signature (CPC Article 141).[41] Anonymous tips are not an acceptable basis for opening a criminal investigation in Russia (CPC Article 141[7]).[42] Second, a crime can be identified as a result of police work that uncovers a crime in preparation or one that has already been committed. It may also be identified based on information received from another agency. Third, a crime can become known to law enforcement through reports in the media. A suspect's voluntary admission that he or she has committed a crime can also be grounds for opening a criminal case.[43]

Although Russian law enforcement agencies are required by law to record any crime that comes to their attention, in reality this is often the first place where incentives created by the performance assessment system come into play. Registering a crime puts it in the system, which means it will have to be accounted for later. If the agent who receives the crime report is not confident that a suspect will be identified and apprehended and the case cleared, he will try his best not to officially register the crime or to delay long enough to create doubt about whether the crime actually took place (Paneyakh et al. 2012, 67).[44]

Agents have several tried-and-true methods of discouraging registration of crimes that they think they cannot solve. They may delay by sending the complainant to a different agency, saying the crime is not within their jurisdiction. They may pretend to register it and simply not make an entry in the registry.

---

40. About half of all crimes come to the attention of law enforcement in this way, especially theft, robbery, and assault (Paneyakh et al. 2012).

41. The complaint can come in oral or written form, but either way it must be signed by the complainant. The police are then required to give the complainant a receipt stating that the crime was registered.

42. This blanket prohibition is a consequence of the Soviet era, when anonymous tips and denunciations were one of the primary ways to convict people of crimes against the state, often without any other evidence (Figes 2007).

43. This provision is not clearly regulated and often leads to confessions made under police pressure. Nonetheless, a suspect may have an interest in admitting to the crime, because confession is often seen in court as a mitigating factor in sentencing decisions. In this way, it can help both the suspect and the investigators because it virtually guarantees that the case will go forward successfully (Paneyakh et al. 2012).

44. Using delay tactics can also be a way for both operativniki and investigators to extort bribes for either refusing to register a case or refusing to open it.

They may try to convince the complainant that registering the crime will lead to enormous headaches, but that they will still look into it and if they can find a suspect, the complainant can register the crime then (Paneyakh et al. 2012, 111–12). Agents actively discourage victims of minor theft of items like wallets or cell phones from registering the crime because they know that the likelihood of recovery is almost zero and the crime will hurt their statistics if it is registered but not closed. This behavior has also been reported in cases of domestic violence, where agents will frequently refuse to register the crime out of fear that the complainant will later withdraw the complaint because of reconciliation and the agency will be stuck with an open case (Amnesty International 2005; Johnson 2005b).[45] In contrast, if it seems clear that agents will be able to identify the suspect, they will usually register a complaint right away.

When cases are registered as a result of law enforcement activities, it is usually only after agents have gathered enough evidence to identify a suspect. If crimes are complicated and the case has any chance of falling apart, the operativnik usually confers with the investigator and sometimes even the procurator before filing the initial report. If his preliminary investigative work fails to yield a charge, he would have to account to his superiors for the period of time and the resources used when he worked and did not collect enough evidence to forward a case to the investigator. Likewise if the investigator decided not to proceed because the evidence the operativnik brought was shoddy or insufficient, that would be a black mark on the operativnik's record (Paneyakh et al. 2012, 22). Thus it behooves operativniki to be in touch with others very early in the process, especially if the case is not a common type, which human trafficking is not.

If law enforcement does register the complaint, agents will enter it into the official register with basic information, including their initial assessment of how they will charge the crime. Each department tries to "play with charges" in each case to ensure the utmost benefit for its statistical output (Paneyakh et al. 2012, 64–67). The operativniki, for example, want cases with greater levels of severity, because there is a separate line on their statistical report form for clearing cases of grave or especially grave crimes. In addition, these types of crimes give them more investigative tools. So, knowing that their charge can later be changed by someone farther along in the process, they tend to charge crimes at higher levels of severity than may otherwise be warranted. This tactic can be as simple as noting that the crime was committed by an organized group, which almost always moves it into the category of grave or very grave.

---

45. Police failure to register a complaint can be appealed to the Procuracy or the court (CPC Articles 124, 125, and 144).

Once a crime is registered, the agency that took the complaint has three days to look into it and determine whether enough grounds exist to pass it to an investigator to open an official investigation.[46] Agents usually try to accomplish this task quickly and make a determination about whether the case is worth expending resources on, by which they mean what chances it has of leading to a conviction. The decision to pass the case on to the investigator requires the permission of the head of that investigative department (*rukovoditel' sledstvennogo organa*), who is always attuned to how any given case may affect the department's statistical output. The process leading up to registration, then, often determines the course that the case will take through the system.

Opening of a Case

After the operativnik collects the initial evidence and information, he brings it to an investigator in whichever agency has jurisdiction over that type of crime. The investigator then decides whether to open the case.[47] At this point, the investigator usually applies his own formal and informal criteria about whether the case is likely to move forward through the system successfully and, if he thinks it will not, tries to find any way possible not to open it.[48] As a result, a suspect's guilt is essentially predetermined at the opening of the case (Paneyakh et al. 2012). Once a case is opened, it is, in practical terms, impossible to close it without the approval of the head of the investigative agency, who does not want to do this because it has the potential to damage the department's statistics.[49]

---

46. This term can be extended by ten days by the head of the investigative or inquiry unit, or by a procurator or the head of the investigative unit for thirty days if accompanied by an explanation of the concrete circumstances that require a longer time period (CPC Article 144[3]). In reality, these are almost always granted, because almost no case can be reasonably looked at in that period of time (Paneyakh et al. 2012, 115). This entire stage of investigative activity takes place outside the formal requirements of the CPC but is overseen in a general sense by the Procuracy and regulated by the law on operational-investigative activities. There is no specific procurator attached to a case until it is officially opened (Paneyakh et al. 2012, 60).

47. Before the 2007 reforms, approval to open a case had to be received from a procurator. Investigators complained that it was not always easy to get in touch with procurators in a timely manner (especially in rural areas) and that this extra step was an insult to the professionalism and education level of the investigators (Burnham and Firestone, unpublished).

48. Officially, investigators must decide whether a crime took place, what type of crime it was, whether the statute of limitations has been exceeded, and whether they have jurisdiction. Informally, they look at whether there are prospects for identifying and apprehending the suspect, whether there is likely to be enough proof to convict the suspect, and how much effort and time it will take to adequately investigate the case (Paneyakh et al. 2012, 116).

49. Although the head's approval is technically not needed to close a case, he can reverse a decision to close a case, giving him de facto veto power (CPC Article 213). Once opened, cases may be closed for reasons including settlement between the parties and active repentance of the accused (CPC Articles 25–29)

According to the Criminal Procedure Code (Article 140), the basis for officially opening a case is that there is "enough information showing the elements of the crime." In reality this means that law enforcement has quite a bit of discretion in determining whether the information it has is sufficient to proceed. For cases that appear to have little prospect of resulting in clearance and a successful conviction, the investigator tries to decline opening them based on one of the options outlined in the Criminal Procedure Code.[50] According to an academic I spoke with in Saratov, "Everything depends on the bosses and statistics. . . . They look at the case and the proof that they have very carefully before opening it, and if they do not think it will go to court, they decline to open it for 'formal' reasons and basically refuse to take the case" (A2).

If the agency does decide to open the case, a copy of the document with all information about the case, including the specific charge, goes to the procurator (CPC Article 146). Within twenty-four hours, he must review the case and decide if it was opened illegally or on insufficient grounds. If so, he can reverse the decision (CPC Article 146[4]). If the agency declines to open a case, that decision must be forwarded to the procurator who, within five days, must determine if the decision was made incorrectly (CPC Article 148).[51] Regardless of the decision, the results must be reported to the complainant.[52]

In addition to the informal negotiations that have already taken place with the operativniki before the case even reaches their desks, investigators may also confer with procurators about which Criminal Code article to charge a crime under before officially opening it. The openness of procurators to discussion with investigators at this stage varies from region to region, but negotiation saves everyone time and reduces the risk that cases are taken on which would be difficult to clear. It also creates an opportunity to resolve potential conflicts that may arise down the line in terms of charging or evidence (Paneyakh et al. 2012). For new laws or complicated cases, procurators are usually involved in the charging decision since it will ultimately be their agency that will be accountable for the charges being correct and for supporting them in court. For more standard

---

50. Acceptable grounds for declining to open a criminal case after a complaint is received are (1) no crime has been committed; (2) there are no elements of the crime in the activities of the accused; (3) the statute of limitations has expired; (4) the suspect has died (unless the trial is needed to clear his or her name); (5) there is no statement from the victim, and the case cannot be opened in any other way (unless the victim is a dependent or in a helpless position and cannot defend his or her rights and legal interests); and (6) the court has not granted permission to open a case against a state official (CPC Article 24).

51. If a procurator makes this determination, he must tell the person who declined to open the case why that person has made a mistake and what he needs to look at again.

52. The complainant can appeal the investigator's decision not to open a case to the Procuracy or the court (CPC Article 148[5]).

cases, there is usually less involvement by the procurator because the investigators already know what evidence they need to forward a case with that charge. The more severe the crime is, the more discussion necessary.

Often these informal negotiations result in charging a crime that is easier to prove with the idea that if agents uncover more evidence later, they can add or substitute other charges. Investigators know they can always fall back on the easier charge because they have at least enough evidence to support it. In reality, however, with the pressure to clear cases, the investigator will rarely take the time to look for additional evidence that would reveal a more serious or more complex crime if he feels that he has enough evidence to go forward with a simpler charge. In the situation of trafficking, for example, there is little incentive for an investigator to look into turning a recruitment into prostitution case into a human trafficking one.

After the investigator decides to officially open the case, the pretrial investigation stage begins. During this stage, the investigator manages the process of turning material collected by the operativniki into a case file that can be presented to the procurator.[53] At the moment of opening, the time limit begins. Any case being investigated for more than two months requires additional permission from above for an extension.[54] If the case is at all complex or uncertain, investigators try to delay officially opening it until they are fairly sure that they have the evidence they need to secure a conviction and will be able to collect and compile what they need within two months. Since there are no time limits on the operativniki for doing their initial investigative work, the investigator waits to officially open the case while the operativniki continue to gather evidence. This often results in long delays, sometimes years, between when a case is discovered and when it is officially opened.

In an arrangement available since 2003 for suspects accused of crimes punishable by no more than ten years imprisonment, the accused can agree to the

---

53. Before 2007, the Procuracy had the ability to actively supervise the case by giving instructions on its course to investigators through the threat of demanding the case file to check its compliance with the law. Now that function has been shifted to the investigators' superiors within their agency. The Procuracy still retains general supervisory powers over the criminal process and though they can initiate a check on the investigators' work, they usually only do it if there has been a complaint from a citizen, private entity, or law enforcement agency about the investigation (Burnham and Firestone, unpublished).

54. The head of the investigative agency can grant an extension of up to one month if the request is made at least five days before the time limit expires. If the investigation goes on for longer than three months, permission to extend it must be obtained at the regional level. The time limit can be extended up to twelve months by the head of the regional investigative agency. Anything longer is allowed only in rare instances and requires going even higher up the chain (CPC Article 162). Asking permission at the regional level inevitably brings scrutiny from above, so most investigators try to avoid it at all costs. There was more flexibility before the 2007 reforms. Then they had up to six months before an extension had to be approved at the regional level (Paneyakh et al. 2012, 36, 41).

charges against him in exchange for a sentence that does not exceed two-thirds of the maximum allowable punishment and an abbreviated court hearing (CPC Articles 314–17).[55] The victim, his or her representative, and the procurator must agree with the decision. This arrangement is particularly advantageous for investigators, because it means that no one will look closely at the case file and so they do not need to put in as much work. Agreement means a guaranteed clearance. It can also be advantageous for those accused, as it reduces the time they spend in pretrial detention. However, they give up their right to an appeal on the facts, though they can still appeal legal errors.

Since 2009 the accused may conclude a cooperation agreement (*dosudebnoe soglashenie*) with the procurator during the pretrial investigation stage. In this arrangement, the accused agrees to provide information about the crime's co-conspirators and/or reveal the whereabouts of assets to be confiscated as illegal profits from the crime. In exchange, he or she receives a sentence that is no more than half the maximum penalty. Based on the degree of cooperation, the judge may decide to give the defendant a sentence below the statutory minimum or no sentence at all.[56]

Indictment and Trial

After the investigator finishes putting together the case file, he writes up the indictment (*obvinitel'noe zakliuchenie*) outlining the evidence against the accused, which is then sent to the procurator for approval (CPC Article 220). Within five days, the procurator must make a decision on what to do with the case: approve or change the charge and send it on to trial, dismiss the case, send it to a higher level procurator if the case is serious enough or, send it back to the investigator for additional investigation or to change the charge (CPC Article 221).[57] If the procurator returns the case to the investigator, he must resubmit the case within one month. The return of a case is a significant blemish on the investigator's

---

55. Since the institution of this system, approximately half of all criminal cases that are eligible have been decided in this way. However, research suggests that defendants who choose this procedure receive treatment no different from those who do not. Because the maximum end of the sentence is rarely given out by judges to any defendants, the resulting sentences are similar for both groups (Titaev and Pozdniakov 2012). This process differs from the US sense of plea bargaining, which allows prosecutors and defense lawyers to negotiate over the charges, although such deals sometimes happen informally during charging in Russia (Pomorski 2005, 2006; Solomon 2012).

56. The type of cooperation that the defendant agrees to provide is written up in an agreement that he or she, the defense attorney, and the procurator must sign. The procurator must decide whether to accept or refuse the request for a cooperation agreement from the defendant within three days of receiving the information from the investigator (CPC Article 317[1–9]; CC Articles 61–64).

57. This period can be extended to thirty days by a higher-level procurator.

record.[58] In reality, procurators do not do this too often, because they do not want to have a contentious relationship with the people who bring them cases. Because of their role as the supervisory body over the activities and actors in the criminal justice process, the procurators realize that their agency's statistics are wholly dependent on operativniki and investigators (Paneyakh et al. 2012).

If the procurator signs off on the indictment, it is then passed to a courtroom procurator.[59] At the same time, the case file is given to the defendant and his attorney, who have an unlimited time to review it (CPC Article 217). However, if they are obviously dragging their feet, a judge can put a time limit on this stage, and the investigator can decide to move the case forward (CPC Article 217[3]). Unlike in many legal systems where the prosecutor who works on the case then takes it to court, the Russian system has a separate set of procurators who go before the court to argue the state's case. Courtroom procurators have not been involved in any stage of the investigation process up to that point and cannot call for further investigation, even if they deem it necessary to support the case. The decision about whether the case is worthy of going to court has effectively already been made when the indictment is signed. Prior to going before the court, the courtroom procurator receives the case file. At this point, the only option he has if he is uncomfortable with the case is to refuse to support the case in its entirety or a particular charge. With more complicated cases or new laws like human trafficking, the courtroom procurator may not have an incentive to support a specific charge if he fears that the judge will acquit the defendant, especially if there are other charges included with the indictment, which human trafficking cases usually have. An acquittal would negatively affect the courtroom procurator's statistics as well as the judge's if it was reversed on appeal.

Most human trafficking cases are heard first at the district court (raionny sud), unless they are particularly complex, in which case they are heard at the regional level.[60] The trial process is strictly regimented in terms of time limits, with judges

58. The investigator can appeal the procurator's decision to return the case within seventy-two hours of being notified (CPC Article 221[4]).

59. The particular courtroom procurator assigned to a case is decided by the head of the department. Though there is no formal set of rules for making this decision, there are informal ones. Generally the more complex cases are given to more experienced people. If a procurator specializes in a particular area of the law or has experience in a particular type of case, he will be given similar cases in the future. Finally, department heads consider the caseload that each of the procurators is carrying at the moment (Paneyakh et al. 2012, 49).

60. Russia has four levels of court: justice of the peace courts, district courts, regional (subject-level) courts, and the Russian Supreme Court. CPC Article 31 outlines which cases go to which courts of first instance. All Criminal Code articles that may be associated with human trafficking cases go to the local court of general jurisdiction. The only exception is for the most serious form of kidnapping, which would go to the Supreme Court of the region as the court of first instance.

facing similar pressures as other actors in the criminal justice system (Solomon 2012). When the judge receives the case file, he may schedule a pretrial hearing or go directly to trial.[61] He may also decide to return the case to the procurator to fix mistakes, which is a significant black mark on the procurator's record.[62] After approving the case, the judge must schedule the trial within fourteen days of receiving the case (within thirty days if it is a jury trial).

If the defendant has made an agreement with the state, either for cooperation or to admit his or her guilt, he or she still goes to court for a hearing, but the trial is heard in a special procedure (*osobyi poriadok*) without a full oral examination of the evidence in the case file, instead proceeding directly to the sentencing stage. This is advantageous for judges as it reduces the likelihood of appeal and keeps trials within the prescribed time period, since judges do not have to write out a full opinion. Also, the hearing does not take as much courtroom time, usually only about an hour (Solomon 2012; Titaev and Pozdniakov 2012). Jury trials are available for defendants accused of only the most serious crimes and must be the choice of the accused (CPC Article 31[3]).[63] Few traffickers have been eligible.

After the trial is complete, the judge prepares the document (*prigovor*) outlining the judgment and sentence in which she must justify the rationale for the decision on each charge and for each person and the evidence to support it.[64] This results in a detailed written record of the case, including descriptions of all the evidence and testimony given as well as in-court motions and activities. The final moment in court occurs when the judge reads the verdict to all the assembled parties, who stand throughout. A written copy of the verdict must then be delivered to the defendant and his or her attorneys (and any other interested parties). They have ten days to file an appeal to a higher court (CPC Article 312). Procurators have the right to appeal both guilty verdicts and acquittals, which they must do within the same time period.[65] If there is no appeal, the sentence takes legal

---

61. A pretrial hearing must occur if there are any motions to exclude evidence, if the defense requests that the case is returned to the procurator if there is reason to believe that the case should be closed or suspended, if the defendant has requested a jury trial, and for a handful of other reasons (CPC Articles 227–29).

62. The judge can make this decision if the indictment is in violation of the Criminal Procedure Code, if the indictment was not given to the accused, if the case needs to be combined with another case, or if the accused is not told of his rights to appeal certain decisions of the procurator (CPC Article 237).

63. For more on jury trials in Russia, see Thaman 1996 and 2007.

64. Due to time constraints judges often copy and paste much of this directly from the indictment document.

65. The appeals process is outlined in CPC Articles 379–80. Until 2013, appeals were made to the court of cassation for factual and legal review, including the presentation of new evidence. As of 2013, there has been a complete overhaul in the appeals procedure (Solomon 2013).

effect (*vstupit' v zakonnuiu silu*) ten days after the reading of the verdict. If the higher court rejects the appeal, the sentence takes legal effect immediately.

Russian law enforcement agents must do their jobs within a set of institutional constraints. Because of the basic institutional structure, it is easy to see why an ordinary, noncorrupt law enforcement official may have trouble investigating or prosecuting any case, let alone a trafficking case. It is difficult to care about the outcome of a case and follow it through the justice system when the functions of law enforcement are divided up into so many different agencies. Even if a person is very dedicated to the outcome of a particular case, it is out of his hands once he has fulfilled his function in the system. These incentive structures have important impacts on the course that human trafficking cases take through the system.

The fear of getting punished or not promoted because of poor statistical performance is strong. With the increased prestige and salary available as agents move up the ranks, they are hesitant to risk making any mistakes or trying new laws when there is uncertainty about the results. They are unlikely to look for more complex crimes than what they see and can immediately charge and clear from their desks. Uncertainty at any point in the system creates caution. This is best displayed by what happened during the reorganization and separation of the Procuracy into the Investigative Committee in 2008. There was a precipitous drop in the number of human trafficking cases registered in 2008 as agents were paralyzed by uncertainty over where they would end up, to whom they would be subordinated, and what the new institutional priorities would be. This drop in cases was not limited to human trafficking. The uncertainty caused by the anticipation of the change and the change itself led to a 12 percent overall drop in criminal cases opened during 2008 in comparison to the previous year (Interfax 2009).

As this chapter has shown, Russian law enforcement officials are not simply lawless, corrupt, willy-nilly enforcers of the law or interested only in collecting bribes. They are quite attuned to the technicalities of the law and concerned with following it closely, lest they feel the wrath of their superiors for poor work or not having a large enough completed caseload to qualify for promotion. They try to use the law's technicalities instrumentally to accomplish their desired ends. In many cases, trafficking included, law enforcement is literal to the extreme, sometimes overlooking the spirit of the law in favor of the letter of the law. This characteristic provides an important part of the explanation for why human trafficking cases are not often charged as such.

The next three chapters follow human trafficking cases through the criminal justice process, to show how the institutional machinery affects the pursuit of human trafficking crimes. These chapters explore the difficulties that Russia's law enforcement has had, the strategies agents have developed, and the results, covering the three main stages of a trafficking prosecution: finding and identifying a case as trafficking; investigating and gathering evidence; and prosecuting and sentencing. Although these processes may actually be going on simultaneously, I keep them conceptually distinct because the problems that arise in each stage are somewhat different.

THE IDENTIFICATION OF HUMAN TRAFFICKING CASES

In an interview with the newspaper *Komsomol'skaia Pravda* Dmitrii Ermoshin, an operativnik in Penza, told the reporter, "All of a sudden a man came running towards us. 'Help me!' he said. 'The slaveholder took my documents and is making me work. I barely managed to escape!' We said to him, 'What slaveholder? We don't live in the Caucasus, or in the fifteenth century. Have you gone nuts?' But then he described the 'slaves.' We assessed the situation: all the signs were there!" (Ladnyi 2002). Ermoshin's disbelief that slavery could still be happening in the twenty-first century in a region not historically connected with the phenomenon has, unfortunately, been a fairly common reaction to situations of human trafficking. The institutional machinery described in the previous chapter pushes law enforcement agents to internalize particular ways of thinking and acting, so the tendency to categorize human trafficking as some other crime with which they are already familiar is strong. Only in situations that seem out of the ordinary are agents' standard operating procedures shaken up, and they realize they are dealing with something new. Ultimately, they did categorize this case as human trafficking, but that is not always the outcome. This chapter focuses on the first and critical stages, finding and identifying cases of human trafficking. Law enforcement's determinations of whether a situation counts as trafficking or not produces the meaning of the law as applied in practice, determines to whom it applies, and ultimately determines the officially reported crime rates.

Most trafficking cases come to the attention of law enforcement through a report from the victims themselves or their friends and family. Less often, agents find out about a case through proactive police work, usually while looking at another case. Reports can also come from victim assistance organizations that have had contact with victims through their hotlines or assistance programs, but this has been difficult due to the contentious nature of the relationship between law enforcement and NGOs.

Even if information does come to the attention of law enforcement, agents may still fail to identify the situation as a human trafficking case or officially register it as such. In identifying a case as trafficking, agents must first apply the formal criteria of the law. But the newness and vagueness of that law mean that even the application of formal criteria requires a number of subjective judgments. Because human trafficking is a criminal process, rather than a crime that happens at a particular place and time, law enforcement agents may see a number of other crimes that, when put together, indicate human trafficking but when considered separately look like a series of stand-alone crimes. Always short on time and resources and pressured to clear cases quickly, they take the first good-enough option that they find for charging given the evidence. They have minimal incentives to check whether the crime they see at first glance is actually part of a larger, more complex human trafficking situation.

As a response to confusion about the formal requirements of the human trafficking statutes, law enforcement agents, as bureaucrats often do, have developed shorthand indicators of what "real" human trafficking cases look like. This chapter discusses several of these: the victim's ability to escape, his or her agency in entering the trafficking situation, and whether he or she has received any remuneration. These shorthand heuristics are often based on widely held societal stereotypes of trafficking and its most likely victims. This may result in discrimination against victims if they come from already marginalized groups such as migrants or prostitutes or more benign failure to recognize victims because the situations do not fit the informal criteria agents have developed.

Finding a Trafficking Case

Victims as an Information Source

Despite the fact that most of the human trafficking cases in Russia have been found as a result of victim reports, studies of human trafficking victims worldwide as well as my own interviews suggest that victims are wary of bringing information to law enforcement. Many victims of human trafficking do not see themselves as victims at all. I was told several stories of women who returned from being trafficked into prostitution abroad and told their treating psychiatrist that they were not victims, just unlucky (M13, N2, N22). Male victims of labor trafficking rarely consider themselves victims because the term is considered emasculating, "clearly highlight[ing] their perceived failures as a man (read: strong, self-sufficient, breadwinner, household head)" (Surtees 2008, 26). Both men and women view their complicity in accepting the initial job offer as something that indicates that they were not victimized but instead had agency in the process.[1] As one surprised investigator from the Amur region's Investigative Committee noted in a media interview: "We get information about other cases where people are being held [for labor], but when we go to verify it, we find that they have gone to work for the employer of their own free will, because of difficult life circumstances. . . . It turns out that they themselves are the most difficult to convince that they are victims" (Klimycheva 2010).

For victims of both sexual and labor exploitation, shame and embarrassment may be another reason why they do not approach law enforcement. Sex trafficking victims tend to repress memories, deny that they were prostitutes, or otherwise rationalize their behavior so that they do not have to admit that they fell prey to deception or were too naïve to realize what was really happening (N3, N43, N28). According to the head of the Investigative Committee, Alexander Bastrykin, the biggest problem that his investigators have had in trafficking cases is exactly this. "A number of victims are reluctant to be in contact with the investigators and categorically refuse to give statements, about both the circumstances of the crime and the people committing it, fearing exposure of their personal lives."[2] Male victims of labor trafficking also struggle with shame. Because they have gone abroad to be breadwinners, failure to bring home money is considered not just an individual failure but a disappointment to the entire family (Surtees 2007a). Many victims would rather take their chances again and bring home something than return with empty pockets, or worse, be in further debt because they have taken out loans to facilitate the trip or owe their traffickers money (Surtees 2007a).

Some sex trafficking victims may not be willing to come forward because they have an emotional attachment to their trafficker or are simply in disbelief that the person who trafficked them could have known what he or she was doing. In one story I heard, a victim had met her trafficker over the Internet and fell in love.[3] He arranged for her to visit him in Turkey.[4] At the airport she was met by

---

1. See McCarthy 2014b for a discussion of the victim/agent dichotomy surrounding human trafficking.

2. Bastrykin speech, on file with author.

3. This is a common way for traffickers and pimps alike to recruit their prostitutes. Especially in sex trafficking cases, the relationship between pimps and prostitutes is almost always significantly more complicated than that of exploiter to exploited (Hoyle et al. 2011; Lloyd 2011).

4. Destination country name changed.

a man claiming to be a friend of her boyfriend who then forced her into prostitution. Occasionally the boyfriend would visit her and they would spend time together, but she was always returned to her exploiter. On returning to Russia, she still trusted the boyfriend and believed he could not have possibly known what was happening to her (N25). These types of psychological attachments can mean that victims do not see themselves as victims and therefore do not go to law enforcement.

Another reason that victims are unlikely to come forward is fear of their traffickers. Traffickers explicitly threaten harm to the victims, their friends, and their families if the victims ever go to the police. Having seen the brutality of which most traffickers are capable, victims more often than not acquiesce to these demands. Traffickers also take advantage of victims' limited legal knowledge to keep them from going to police, suggesting that if the victim breaks his or her contract or does not repay his or her debts, the trafficker will use the legal process to have assets belonging to the victim's family taken away. Although this is not possible, since contracts to perform illegal activities are by nature not valid and therefore nonbinding, many victims do not know that. Most victims come from families with very little money, so this threat carries added weight. In fact, one of the most common reasons for agreeing to questionable job offers that may result in trafficking is the need to help keep the family financially solvent.

Fear of law enforcement is another reason why victims may not come forward. This is both general and specific. Most Russians view their law enforcement negatively. The police are regularly rated as one of the least trusted institutions in Russia, with about two-thirds of the population consistently reporting little to no trust (see Semukhina and Reynolds 2013 for an overview). "Russians believe that the very structures that are supposed to uphold the law are the most consistent violators of it" (Taylor 2011, 44). Members of the Russian public are deeply ambivalent about involving the police in their lives, contacting law enforcement only if absolutely necessary (Davis et al. 2004; Robertson 2005; Zernova 2012a; Semukhina 2014). According to one study, 73 percent of crime victims did not report the crimes to the police, most believing that nothing would be done (Gilinskiy 2005). Women who experience domestic or sexual violence are especially reticent about turning to law enforcement for help, given its long-standing indifference to these types of cases—usually blaming the victim, questioning her story, and engaging in delay tactics to try to get her to drop the complaint (Beninger-Budel and O'Hanlon 2004; Amnesty International 2005; Bigg 2005; Johnson 2005b). Even if they did approach police, many Russians are convinced that the state is incapable of "providing justice or the impartial resolution of conflict . . . [and their] behavior is directed towards the expectation of legal failure" (Kurkchiyan 2003, 27). They have long been used to going outside the system to achieve what they need (Ledeneva 1998, 2006).

In Russia, all cases require an official complaint to be investigated, which requires the name and passport information of the reporting party. Most traffickers immediately take the identity documents of their victims away under the pretenses of officially registering them and never give them back. This makes it difficult for victims to prove who they are if they do go to the police and makes the police suspicious that they are illegally in Russia because they have no documents.

If victims have been trafficked abroad, they will likely retain this generalized distrust of the police and fear approaching them for help. It is perhaps unreasonable to expect that victims would readily approach the same agency that has the power to fine them, arrest them, or deport them. Many victims of trafficking know they have broken laws in the process of being trafficked (N21, N28, O8, O29). They may be in the country illegally, having entered on tourist visas or overstayed their work visas. Even if they were to leave the country voluntarily to return to Russia, they might be subject to legal proceedings at the border or receive a deportation stamp which would severely curtail their ability to receive visas to travel internationally in the future. They may also be working in the sex trade, illegal in many countries. Finally, there may be a significant language barrier between the victims and anyone who could offer them help, including police. Likewise, if they have had bad experiences with law enforcement in their destination countries, they may be hesitant to go to law enforcement when they return to their country of origin (Farley 2004; Surtees 2007b). Many victims spend time in deportation facilities and are treated as criminals before they are identified as victims of trafficking, if they ever are (O29).

Some trafficking victims have had more direct experiences with law enforcement that may make them especially wary. Many women in prostitution have experienced law enforcement agents as clients (Waugh 2006, Tverdova 2011). In one situation, which is representative of many stories that I heard from victims and psychologists who worked with victims, a Russian policeman came to the victim as a client. When she told him she was there against her will and asked for help, he suggested that because she was there illegally, he could have her deported. To avoid this possibility she would have to service him and his friends. In another situation, this same victim had to service a group of police officers who then refused to pay and beat up the victim and the other women she was with (N28, O21). Migrants who are in Russia illegally or legally but not officially registered where they are living are also afraid of the police. Many have experienced shakedowns by police in which they are pulled aside to have their documents checked and have had to pay bribes when their illegal documents are discovered.

Traffickers keep victims from going to law enforcement by telling them that the police are "in their pockets," and would return the victims to the trafficker if they did try to report. Victims of sex trafficking know that the brothel owners pay monthly protection fees to the police in cash or in kind and have seen others who have escaped returned by those same police (A3). In one case in a rural area of the Kurgan region (no. 354), a victim managed to escape a particularly brutal labor trafficking situation and asked locals where he could find the authorities. They sent him to the head of the local village council, whom the victim asked to call the police. Instead, the council head called the trafficker who immediately came to retrieve the victim, beating him for his escape attempt (Ura.ru 2012).

Friends and relatives of the victims sometimes go to law enforcement to report potential trafficking situations, but often they do not have enough specific information to help law enforcement actually investigate, even if agents were willing. Others who have tried to report trafficking have encountered indifference and corruption from local law enforcement. In one situation, a Russian woman whose daughter had been trafficked abroad went to the police where an agent told her that finding the daughter was not their business. They then told her that the only way for her to get their help was to pay a large sum of money to have them "use their connections" and solve the case (N53, O20).

Sometimes, information from victims may get to law enforcement indirectly, through media coverage, and lead to a case.[5] In one example, a woman told her story to the press in Khabarovsk, and it resulted in an investigation by the police. If articles from the news media come to the attention of the federal operativnik unit on trafficking, they may decide to assist the local operativniki in their investigation. I witnessed several situations in which the International Organization for Migration found a story about trafficking on the Internet and reported it to the MVD's federal anti-trafficking unit to make sure that it was pursued in the region where it occurred. This process had varying levels of success.

Victim Assistance Organizations as an Information Source

Law enforcement may also receive information about possible trafficking situations from victim assistance organizations that run hotlines or are assisting victims if the victim consents. Given the disincentives described above for victims to come forward, this may be one of the most promising forms of obtaining information about these situations. Victim assistance organizations, which are mostly NGOs, are trained to identify indicators of trafficking and could serve as a filtering mechanism for law enforcement, saving its agents time and effort. In

---

5. The procedure for investigating a case when information comes from the media is outlined in CPC Article 144(2).

addition, assistance organizations are more likely to get information from the victims, because they seem friendlier, more willing to help, and focused on the victim's interests. Unfortunately, NGOs and law enforcement agencies are often at odds. Victim assistance organizations are primarily oriented toward victim recovery and empowerment, whereas law enforcement agencies are oriented primarily toward crime solving.[6] Consequently, these relationships have been difficult to build and sustain and have become even more so since 2006, when the Russian government began cracking down on NGOs.

Since the early 2000s, there have been a number of organizations in Russia dedicated to helping trafficking victims, some of which include human trafficking as part of a larger portfolio of activities helping women or migrants, others that focus specifically on human trafficking. These organizations can be divided into two groups, domestic Russian NGOs and international organizations like the International Organization for Migration and the Red Cross. Victim assistance has been provided by both types of organizations and is primarily financed by international donor organizations from the West. In some regions, victim assistance shelters have been intermittently opened by NGOs when they have had funding. The Angel Coalition, a Moscow-based anti-trafficking NGO, had a grant that supported shelters in several regions of Russia, but the funding ended in 2007.[7] In addition, the IOM, on a grant from the European Commission in Russia, ran a shelter in Moscow from March 2006 through November 2009 and opened shelters in Rostov-on-Don and Vladivostok, both of which were closed in 2013. In June 2013, the Russian Red Cross's branch in St. Petersburg, with support from the IOM and the local government, opened a small shelter for victims of both labor and sex trafficking with plans for possibly reopening a shelter in Moscow.

The inherent tension between victim assistance organizations and law enforcement stems from each side having very different goals. This divergence leads to mutual suspicion and blame for failure to investigate and prosecute more cases. NGOs are frustrated at law enforcement's single-minded focus on obtaining victim testimony so they can prosecute cases rather than on helping the victim recover and reintegrate back into society (N22). They fear that law enforcement will not properly take into account the physical and psychological trauma affecting victims and instead will further traumatize them by continuing

---

6. Here I am speaking only of relationships between NGOs and law enforcement that have developed around the issue of human trafficking. For a description of other productive relationships between Russian NGOs and law enforcement, see Taylor 2006.

7. Shelters were located in Yaroslavl, St. Petersburg, Petrozavodsk, Murmansk, Nizhny Novgorod, Kazan, Chelyabinsk, and Irkutsk.

to press them for information to help the investigation. If the victims are in the country illegally, there is concern that revealing them to law enforcement may lead to their deportation, or that the NGO itself may be harassed for harboring a criminal.

On the other side, law enforcement's main job is to gather a sufficient body of evidence so it can successfully prosecute a suspect and put him or her in jail. To do this, agents need hard facts to work with, and they need them in a timely manner, while it is still possible to collect evidence. Russian law enforcement has two complaints about working with NGOs. The first is that NGOs hold back crucial information that could help them uncover trafficking cases by not immediately reporting when they are assisting a trafficking victim (A8). The second is that NGOs tend not to give enough hard facts to start an investigation. This is particularly a problem since an official complaint is required for law enforcement to open a case. A complaint that does not specify names, dates, phone numbers, flight information, and so on gives law enforcement nothing to work from (M11). This can be a problem for NGOs that only run hotlines and do not have direct contact with victims. Often, the hotline operators cannot get enough information from callers before they hang up for an investigation to be pursued (N24). When the NGO then reports the situation to law enforcement, it is frustrated when law enforcement says it can do nothing.

At one training conference I attended in 2008 in Moscow, some of these problems came to a head in an argument between an NGO representative and a member of law enforcement. The NGO representative said that five years earlier, she had witnessed a situation that she thought was trafficking but did not know where to go with the information. The operativnik pressed her on why she did not go to the police and then somewhat sarcastically asked whether she would now be willing to submit an official complaint so the police could begin investigating the situation. "Well," said the operativnik, "Do you want to help or do you not want to help?" When the exasperated NGO representative said that she would not submit the complaint and sat down, the operativnik used the interaction to point out to the audience that this was exactly the problem with NGOs—they do not provide information when they have it, but then they get angry when law enforcement is not doing anything to fight trafficking. This, of course, is not the only side of the story. NGOs fear giving law enforcement personal information about victims because they cannot guarantee the victims' safety once the information is out of their hands. There is enough corruption, or perceived corruption, in the MVD that the NGOs feel that they may be exposing their clients or themselves to danger if the information gets into the wrong hands (N24).

The relationship between law enforcement and NGOs has become more contentious since the Russian state began cracking down on NGOs in 2006.[8] This campaign has made most domestic NGOs fearful of becoming involved with any representatives of state power out of concern that their organizations could be harassed or shuttered. The situation is made even more complicated by the fact that the law enforcement agencies in charge of trafficking investigations and prosecutions, particularly the Procuracy and the Investigative Committee, are the primary enforcers of the legislation placing limitations on NGOs. There is widespread distrust of NGOs that receive foreign funding due to the belief that they may engage in political activities that could threaten regime stability. This fear has been exacerbated by accusations that foreign-funded NGOs played an important part in the downfall of regimes in neighboring Georgia and Ukraine.

In 2012, the government passed the "foreign agent" law, which requires any domestic NGO that receives foreign funding and engages in political activity—loosely defined—to register with the Ministry of Justice as a foreign agent.[9] Failure to do so carries a steep fine. In addition to the Cold War–era connotations of treason and spying, being designated a foreign agent places onerous reporting requirements on organizations and requires that all their publications display the label prominently. In the aftermath of the law's passage, hundreds of organizations were inspected for compliance and several were fined (Najibullah 2014). With no organizations voluntarily registering, in 2014 the Ministry of Justice gained the power to unilaterally label them as foreign agents (Coalson and Balmforth 2014). Since much of the funding for human trafficking activities has come from foreign donors—including from the US Agency for International Development, which was forced to close its operations in Russia in 2012—development of a productive and cooperative relationship on human trafficking between the nongovernmental sector and law enforcement is unlikely any time in the near future.

---

8. In 2006, the Russian government passed a new law regulating the activities of NGOs. The law's provisions "restrict who may form an organization in the Russian Federation, expand the grounds on which registration may be denied, and expand the supervisory powers of the state over organizations" (ICNL 2006, 2). When it was first passed, there was significant concern that it was an attempt by the government to get rid of NGOs with whose politics they disagreed. In particular, the provisions that required all NGOs to re-register and increased reporting requirements caused concern since they created more opportunities for NGOs to be shut down because of small mistakes in their paperwork. For a nuanced assessment of the outcome of this law, see Javeline and Lindemann-Komarova 2010.

9. Federal Law no. 121-FZ, "O vnesenii izmenenii v otdel'nye zakonodatel'nye akty Rossiiskoi Federatsii v chasti regulirovaniia deiatel'nosti nekommercheskikh organizatsii, vypolniaiushchikh funktsii inostrannogo agenta" of July 20, 2012 (SZ RF 2012, no. 30, item 4172).

In a 2009 meeting with then-President Dmitrii Medvedev, the human rights activist Ella Pamfilova identified human trafficking as one of several issue areas where cooperation between law enforcement and NGOs could help law enforcement uncover crimes more effectively (Podrabinek 2009). Though few and far between, it is worthwhile noting some of the success stories of cooperation that have occurred. Even though each instance has taken place at the local level, they give some indication of the potential for cooperation if and when the political and legal climate allows for it.

Many NGOs have received grants for the specific purpose of educating law enforcement on trafficking and have tried to engage agents by running training sessions specifically targeted to their needs. In general, there was recognition of the importance of developing a pragmatic approach to dealing with law enforcement. One of my NGO interviewees in Moscow noted that in sessions with law enforcement the group tried to "convince the MVD that it is in its interest to help the victims so they will start talking . . . the victims can help uncover the crime. Especially at the regional level, talking about human rights is practically useless, because they [agents] are not interested in hearing about it" (N26). By aligning the incentives of the officers to get higher-quality victim statements so they could clear cases with the NGO's desire for more victim-oriented practices, these training sessions were quite successful.

Conferences and training sessions run by NGOs have had varying levels of attendance by law enforcement but have often created good connections between agents and the community. As one of my informants suggested, these conferences sometimes improved law enforcement's opinion of the local NGOs (N44). They also helped NGOs develop informal referral networks with law enforcement. However, the drawback to these sorts of relationships was that if particular agents left or were transferred to new positions the cooperation often ceased. This was a frequent complaint in many of my interviews with NGOs (N31, N43, N44). In turn, law enforcement has been known to contact NGOs for information on human trafficking and advice on how to work with victims (N20, N22, N24, N32, N44). At several conferences I attended that were run by NGOs, law enforcement agents stated publicly that they needed NGOs because the victims did not trust them but did trust the NGOs (M1, M19, M22). At these conferences, NGOs were praised by law enforcement for raising awareness in their cities and helping them learn about the intricacies of the crime and how to prosecute it more successfully (A3, M11, M13).[10] Nevertheless, local law enforcement is still hesitant to

---

10. It may be that the law enforcement agents were pandering in these situations. However, I attended several conferences where the law enforcement participants sat silently, appeared disinterested, and did not contribute, so I can only assume that they were being genuine in the cases where they did compliment the NGOs for their work.

sign anything that binds its agents to any activities that would require them to do more work or without explicit permission from above.

One of the closest relationships that I encountered was in Vladivostok. In early 2002, the Vladivostok branch of the Transnational Crime and Corruption Center (TraCCC) (then based at American University in Washington, DC, and operating a research center out of Far Eastern State University) introduced the issue of trafficking in the region. TraCCC was doing research on trafficking in cooperation with local law enforcement officials, especially border guards, who often dealt with human trafficking during that period. Another NGO activist's persistent attempts to approach the city and regional government about human trafficking then resulted in an international conference in Vladivostok on human trafficking in 2006 and a conference on migration politics, including human trafficking, in 2008. According to police, city officials, and NGOs, the 2006 conference led to increased awareness at all levels of government and an increase in cooperation among local anti-trafficking organizations, the city government, and local law enforcement (M11, M13, N7). This cooperation resulted in several prosecutions and an agreement from the city to take over financing of the local shelter when its grant period ended.[11] Unfortunately, the shelter was closed in 2013 for lack of funding.

In rare cases, local relationships like this have been institutionalized with memoranda of understanding between the local NGO and MVD outlining the responsibilities of each in fighting trafficking (Kazan, Karelia), but these are not permanent and still largely rely on individuals on both sides who are committed to upholding them. The hierarchical structure of the MVD means that local units may not have the autonomy to conclude agreements like this without permission of higher authorities.

The most successful cooperation between law enforcement and a victim assistance organization occurred between the IOM in Moscow and law enforcement agencies based in Moscow and the Moscow region. The IOM ran a victim rehabilitation shelter which operated from March 2006 until November 2009.[12] During this time, the shelter and its staff assisted 423 victims of trafficking, 37 percent men and 63 percent women, with about half (53 percent) victims of sexual exploitation and the rest victims of labor exploitation and begging schemes (IOM 2009).

---

11. The shelter was financed by the US government and the European Commission and was run through the IOM, which gave it to the city in 2010.

12. The shelter was funded by the European Commission in Moscow, the US State Department, and the Swiss Agency for International Development (SIDA). The goal was to have the city of Moscow or the federal government take over operation of the shelter once it was set up and running smoothly. When the grant money ran out, no city or federal governmental structure would take on the responsibility, and so the shelter closed.

In addition to the accomplishments in providing victim assistance, the IOM was able to develop a productive working relationship with law enforcement through official agreements with the local and federal level operativnik and investigative units. Many of the trust problems that plague NGO-police relations were mitigated because of IOM's status. As an international organization (Russia holds observer status but is not a full member), the IOM has a different standing in relation to law enforcement than a domestic NGO does. Whereas domestic NGOs are a part of civil society, pushing the government to make changes and often standing in opposition to the government, the IOM's mission is to work within the existing government structures to accomplish its goals. This makes it less of a perceived threat to the state's power than domestic, often foreign-funded NGOs (N19, N24). Furthermore, the head of the counter-trafficking project had been a career police officer in Italy before coming to the IOM, and several of the people working on the project had law enforcement experience. This history helped make connections with law enforcement easier. However, even with these advantages, developing a relationship with law enforcement was not without its difficulties. The MVD originally wanted the IOM to pass on information about every victim that came through the shelter, with or without the victim's consent. This, of course, was against IOM policy, but initially there was a significant amount of suspicion from the MVD that the IOM was committing an offense by harboring criminals, usually in relation to victims who were in the country illegally and receiving rehabilitation treatment at the facility (N1, N19).

The IOM process generally worked as follows. If victims consented to help they could either give basic information to help law enforcement find out if the crime was still ongoing or give and sign a more official statement (*pokazanie*), which meant that if the case went forward they could be called on to testify as official witnesses in court (N1, N28). If the victim agreed to give an official statement that would be admissible in court, it was usually done on video. Video made it clear that the interview complied with the requirements of the Criminal Procedure Code (N28) and helped ensure that the victim might not have to show up in court if the case did go to trial.[13] This was particularly helpful when the victim had been trafficked to Russia and returned to his or her origin country and could not or would not return to testify. Occasionally the IOM helped facilitate

---

13. Audio/video or film recordings of the victim's testimony are admissible if the victim fails to appear and the two parties agree. In some circumstances, however, including when a foreign national refuses or is unable to come to court, the judge can unilaterally decide to have the victim's statement read into the court record (CPC Article 81).

a Russian victim's return to his or her destination country to give testimony at a later trial (N25).

Victims were never sent to the police station; the officer always came to the rehabilitation center.[14] Before meeting the victim, the officer spent time speaking to the center's psychologist so that he (most, if not all, of the police who worked with the IOM were men) knew what lines of questioning would be too sensitive and/or inappropriate with that particular victim. If victims are pushed on subjects about which they are uncomfortable or before they are ready, they are likely to shut down psychologically and refuse to cooperate further. According to IOM staff, law enforcement agents accepted this and were generally willing to cooperate and abide by the advice of the psychologist. In fact, I was told several stories about when victims started to have emotional difficulties during questioning and the agent, instead of pushing, suggested that they take a break and he come back later.

The rehabilitation center's psychologist always participated in the interview with law enforcement and could help steer the conversation in a way that would not retraumatize the victim. In addition, sometimes the psychologist would bring up something that the MVD officer did not ask about but that she thought might be relevant to the case (N25, N28). The participation of a psychologist helped reduce the likelihood that victims would be retraumatized during questioning and made them feel more in control of the situation. This was a remarkable development, because the Russian police are not usually permitted to include other people in the questioning of a witness out of concern that a third party would compromise the ongoing investigation or create "a headache" (N19). In addition, Russian law makes it a criminal offense for any person to reveal information about the preliminary investigation, a risk that is increased by allowing outside participation in witness interviews (CC Article 310).[15] Having a psychologist present made sure there was no undue pressure placed on the victims to give statements and that law enforcement did not behave inappropriately—for example, by threatening victims with deportation or prosecution if they refused to talk (N21). According to Russian law, failure of Russian citizens to cooperate in an investigation is itself a criminal violation, so an agent could have easily used this argument to force victims to cooperate (CC Article 308; ODIHR 2008b). If the victim was in Russia illegally, agents had the upper hand because they could

---

14. Although best practices as recommended by the IOM (2007b) and others suggest that police not come to the shelter and instead meet the victim at a neutral location, this was the best deal that the IOM could negotiate with police in Russia and therefore considered preferable to having the victim go alone to a police station for questioning.

15. Investigators are required to tell participants that disclosing such information is a crime, and participants must acknowledge it in writing (CPC Article 161).

threaten deportation if the victim did not cooperate. Although law enforcement occasionally hinted at these possibilities, they never actually carried out any of their threats, though perhaps it was unnecessary given the power dynamic.

In these interviews the goal of the agents was to get as much detailed information as they could to help prove the crime. Agents focused their questions on the process by which the victims were trafficked: who sent them, who paid for their transportation, which documents they traveled on (their own or false, tourist visas or work visas), where they got the tickets, who escorted them, how they crossed the border, where they arrived, and so on (N28). If the victim was exploited in Russia, the agents would ask more specific questions about where he or she was held and how many other people were held with him or her, so that they could figure out if they needed to intervene to find more people. They would ask about the conditions of exploitation to help prove that exploitation had taken place: whether there was an option to leave or ask for help; whether victims had free access to their documents (N28). With the guidance of psychologists, agents learned to steer away from questions that probed victims' motivations, their level of willingness to do the work (especially with regard to prostitution), and their family backgrounds.

In my interviews, the staff at the IOM praised the Moscow city, Moscow region, and federal operativniki with whom they worked most closely for their sensitivity and cooperation with regard to the victims. At the outset, there was significant concern about how law enforcement would behave, since Russian law enforcement agents have a reputation for bullying witnesses to get the information that they want. As one staff member told me: "The stereotypes of law enforcement that the victims have . . . we all have them too. It's good that they didn't fulfill them" (N21). Despite some instances in which law enforcement did not behave respectfully, for the most part everyone seemed impressed (N28). The MVD agents working with the IOM shelter staff seemed to realize that threats and bullying were ineffective in getting the victim to talk. Instead they got more information by being friendly and compassionate. When the victim broke the law, usually by entering Russia illegally, the police tended to listen to the psychologists who explained to them that if the victim did break the law, he or she most likely did not do it willingly (N28). Unfortunately, this level of understanding and cooperation only really happened with law enforcement agents who had direct contact with the shelter victims and IOM staff.

Over the three years of the project, this relationship developed into a two-way street. Law enforcement got information it needed to pursue trafficking investigations, and victims were referred to the center by law enforcement for help. Of the 423 trafficking victims that were aided at the center during its operation, over a quarter were referred by law enforcement.[16] Fifty-nine percent cooperated in some way with law enforcement.[17] One IOM staff member told me that after talking to one of the federal level operativniki, a victim who had been very afraid of the police had completely changed her attitude toward cooperation (N21). The environment at the center produced surprising results in the form of a domino effect. Often if one person agreed to cooperate with law enforcement, then others also became willing (N25). In return, the IOM referred a number of situations that it suspected were trafficking (often from calls received on its hotline) to law enforcement for further investigation, thereby helping the police with their work.[18]

Over time, the relationship developed to the point where IOM staff could call the federal MVD unit of operativniki working on trafficking for help; they had similarly reliable contacts in the FSB. These contacts usually led to assistance for the victims but sometimes did not, as the requests were caught up (intentionally or unintentionally) in bureaucratic procedures. This relationship was strongest at the federal level and in Moscow and the Moscow region. In 2008, the model was deployed at new IOM-sponsored shelters in Rostov-on-Don and Vladivostok, both of which have since closed. According to Sergei Tveritnikov, then the head of the federal anti-trafficking unit: "In Moscow we have established a good relationship with the IOM. The IOM's rehabilitation center has helped over a hundred witnesses and victims in human trafficking cases. I hope that we can achieve similarly good cooperation in the Rostov region" (Kavkazskii uzel 2008).

As reflected in Tveritnikov's statement, there appeared to be a basic recognition that the psychological and physical rehabilitation that IOM provided helped produce better witnesses. Law enforcement agents, especially those who interacted with victims at the IOM shelter, learned that it could pay to be kind to victims. In some cases agents genuinely cared. One person who ran a training session for law enforcement expressed his surprise to find that it was not at all difficult to convince the agents that if they were more sympathetic, they would get better testimony from victims. As it turned out, this group of agents had

---

16. The exact figures are 22.2 percent by law enforcement organs and 3.1 percent by combined actions of IOM and law enforcement (IOM 2009).

17. Of these, 39 percent cooperated with Russian law enforcement, 15 percent cooperated with law enforcement in other countries, and 5 percent cooperated with law enforcement in both Russia and another country (IOM 2009).

18. The IOM hotline, with call centers in Moscow, St. Petersburg, Astrakhan, and Petrozavodsk, was a resource center for people considering working abroad or people who had come to Russia to work. Over the two and a half years of operation (May 2007–November 2009) they provided over 13,400 phone consultations. The hotline created another nexus of cooperation between the IOM and the authorities, most often the Federal Migration Service (IOM 2009).

plenty of sympathy toward the victims. They simply did not have the techniques or the experience to talk to them, help them, and make them feel safe (N31). In other cases, however, the good interactions were simply pragmatic. Despite the fact that trafficking victims can often be difficult from the point of view of law enforcement—they can be rude, hostile, violent, and/or addicted to drugs and sometimes do not speak Russian—they are by far the best source of information for evidence as well as places to look for more trafficking violations. Law enforcement's cooperation is not because its agents have "big hearts," as one interviewee told me, but because there is pressure from above to produce trafficking cases, and the officers know that this is their best and only avenue to do so (N24).

The biggest problem that the IOM encountered was that the MVD did not always follow up with the victims on the progress of the case. This was disconcerting for victims because they did not know if they needed to worry about their traffickers tracking them down once they left the rehabilitation center (N28). Most often the lack of communication occurred because the cases did not go forward or because they were charged as other crimes for which the victim's testimony was not as important. By law, the MVD investigator is supposed to inform the complainant about the decision that is made on the case, but this applies only if the case is officially opened (CPC Article 145[2]). Since much of the cooperation between victims and the police at the IOM shelter was informal and took place before the case was officially opened, this legal provision did not apply. Nevertheless, many victims and staff were frustrated by the lack of information on the progress of the investigation (N28).

Ultimately, by taking advantage of the incentive structures facing law enforcement, the IOM was able to accomplish the dual goal of aiding victims and getting better criminal justice outcomes. Achieving this level of cooperation depended on creating an institutionalized structure through an official agreement as well as having people on both sides who were committed to making it work. This combination is a rarity and probably only occurred because of IOM's status as an international organization. Nevertheless, it serves as a model of what might be possible someday if the relationship between NGOs and law enforcement becomes less contentious.

Law Enforcement Action as an Information Source

The final way that law enforcement may find a trafficking case is through proactive investigative activity (*operativno-rozysknaia deiatel'nost'*). These activities are specifically targeted at uncovering trafficking operations such as raids on brothels, massage parlors, large agricultural businesses, factories, and other places where victims may be found. To gather the appropriate intelligence to conduct such a raid requires a significant investment of time and resources (MVD 2008). When pressed from above to process cases quickly, agents may see this type of effort as a waste of time. Even if they do find evidence of human trafficking, they know that they will be in for a long and difficult investigation. Without exception, traffickers train victims to lie about working voluntarily. Law enforcement generally needs to spend significant amounts of time with the victims before they will admit to being forced, time agents do not always have. It may be easier for law enforcement to take victims at their word rather than dig deeper for evidence of victimization.

Within MVD units that are responsible for human trafficking, agents often emphasize crimes that they consider more serious, such as kidnapping or organized crime. This is not to suggest that if law enforcement receives actionable intelligence about people in danger, it will not act. I witnessed a number of examples in which the IOM submitted a complaint directly to the head operativnik at the federal anti-trafficking unit, and he immediately arranged an operation to free victims. However, this does not always happen.

If law enforcement wanted to be proactive in looking for human trafficking, it could be, at least in cases of sexual exploitation. Traffickers must advertise to recruit prostitutes and then to sell prostitution services (MVD 2008). Information on potential trafficking situations is readily available in magazines and newspapers, both nationally and locally, that run advertisements that may indicate trafficking recruitment schemes. Despite the pleas of NGOs, many newspapers are still willing to print dubious advertisements for jobs abroad. At one conference presentation I attended, several examples were pulled from print advertisements in Vladivostok: "Work in Japan! Looking for a good-looking woman between the ages of twenty and twenty-eight, with at least two years of hairdressing experience. Send us a photo of you. For details, e-mail . . ." Another read, "Looking for attractive, social women from twenty to thirty-five for work in the best night clubs and bars in Spain as hostesses. Pay: 1,500–2,000 euros a month. Credit available for your trip, guaranteed by contract" (Bazhenova 2008). Similar advertisements can be found on the Internet. These advertisements all offer salaries that are unrealistic for the jobs in countries where work visas are necessary, all characteristics which make them possible avenues for recruiting human trafficking victims.

Of course, even if agents wanted to actively look for human trafficking cases, it is very difficult to identify a case as trafficking during its early stages. Most human trafficking cases are identified only after the exploitation has taken place (Gallagher and Holmes 2008). As a manual for investigators in the MVD notes: "At the stages of recruitment and transportation uncovering human trafficking is practically impossible, and if the elements of the crime are there (at that stage) there is usually not enough evidence to make the case. Usually at this stage, the victims do not know what they are being prepared for" (MVD 2008). Most law enforcement officers that I spoke with emphatically made the same point.

Requests for information from police in other countries were an important source of information in several of the cases I looked at. In a case in the Primorskii region, the Uzbek police submitted a request to their colleagues in Russia for information because they were investigating a trafficking case in which a Russian citizen trafficked Uzbek women to Russia (no. 87). In this case, the investigation also resulted in a prosecution in Russia. In another example, Russian operativniki got information from police in Moldova about a woman who was being held in Moscow in sexual slavery. The Moscow operativniki sent a team to find and rescue her, but the case was eventually transferred to Moldova for prosecution (M14).

Identifying a Trafficking Case as Human Trafficking

As the preceding section demonstrates, finding a trafficking case is extraordinarily difficult. People who have information are reluctant to bring it to law enforcement, and the time and resource investment for law enforcement to proactively uncover a case is often prohibitive. However, even if a human trafficking case does come to the attention of law enforcement, it must be recognized as a trafficking case and actually registered as such. This has both a formal and informal component. Formally, agents must decide if the activities that they have uncovered constitute a crime as defined by the statute. Confusion over what the statute means and how it should be applied means that even the best-intentioned agent may simply not see human trafficking even though it is there. Informal criteria may also play an important role in determining whether a case is considered to be human trafficking. Like most people, law enforcement agents have particular ideas about what human trafficking looks like. Consequently, when encountering a possible human trafficking situation, they apply these criteria. This all takes place alongside a set of informal negotiations between the operativniki and the investigators over which charges to register the case under. If the case is seen as too complex and unlikely to result in a conviction, there may be resistance to registering it as human trafficking. Instead, agents may choose to pursue it under another statute or find a way not to pursue it at all.

Formal Criteria

Relying on the plain text of the law requires law enforcement to make a number of subjective judgments. There is overlap between the component parts of a human trafficking crime and other crimes that are on the books, so using the text of the law to categorize the crime as trafficking can be confusing and difficult. Because the text does not outline the means by which trafficking can be committed, law enforcement agents rely primarily on commentaries to the Criminal Code written by academics and judges which give more specificity about the crime's elements. Although law enforcement agents may and often do use these commentaries, the reality on the ground is that they are under so much pressure to clear cases, it is unlikely that they have the time to sit down and puzzle out how their evidence fits with the suggestions in the commentary. If they are unfamiliar with what to do in a particular situation, more than likely, they will find the first Criminal Code article that fits the situation well enough, or they will ask a colleague what to do. In this way, organizational practices get reinforced over time.

The crime of human trafficking is a process that unfolds over time and space, making it different from many other crimes that occur at a specific time and place and consist of a single illegal action such as murder, robbery, or assault. Crimes that are processes are, by nature, more difficult to investigate. Furthermore, because it is a process, the point in time where agents encounter that process can determine what crime they see and how they proceed in investigating it.

Identifying a case of trafficking as trafficking actually requires law enforcement agents to go against their initial instincts to identify the crime as something they already recognize. Under the previous system, when law enforcement agents found a foreign woman working in prostitution without identity documents, she would be fined for prostitution under Administrative Code Article 6.11, accused of illegal migration, and probably deported. Now, there is the possibility that she could also be a trafficking victim. What once seemed like a simple migration violation—foreign laborers without passports working on a farm—now has the potential to be a trafficking case. According to Tatiana Kholshchevnikova, one of the drafters of the human trafficking law, it is not that the MVD is disinterested in dealing with human trafficking, they just have problems seeing the "big picture" crime of human trafficking and not a series of smaller, individual crimes. The difficulty of distinguishing trafficking from prostitution was made clear by one NGO activist who told me that in a 2005 training session, regional police officers proudly reported that they had opened a lot of trafficking cases, thinking that Article 240 (recruitment into prostitution) was the same thing as trafficking (N22). I heard about many instances where once law enforcement agents had trafficking explained to them in training sessions, they immediately recognized past cases that they had encountered as trafficking (N22).

Human trafficking as defined in the Criminal Code has several distinct stages (buying/selling, recruitment, transportation, transfer, harboring, receiving) which in part or in whole comprise a human trafficking violation. Although the law technically states that any of the individual elements of human trafficking can be enough to charge the crime as human trafficking, each stage of the trafficking process can itself contain other violations that could be charged under other Criminal Code articles.

Figure 4.1 shows some of the overlapping laws that can be used at any individual stage of human trafficking. Depending on the point at which a law enforcement agent encounters the trafficking process, he could see one of a number of crimes, including but not limited to human trafficking. For example, at the recruitment stage, agents might charge a crime under Article 240 (recruitment into prostitution) or Articles 150 or 151 (recruiting a minor into committing a crime or into engaging in antisocial activities). At the transportation or transfer stage, the movement could be accomplished by means of false documents (Article 327), by crossing a border illegally (Article 322), or by organizing illegal migration (Article 322.1). The harboring or receipt stages of human trafficking could easily be charged as Article 127 (false imprisonment) or, if the victim was moved unwillingly in the process, Article 126 (kidnapping). Finally, at the exploitation stage, law enforcement may encounter crimes such as organizing prostitution (Article 241), rape (Articles 131–34) and/or physical assault (Articles 115–18). They may also see no crime, only the administrative offense of prostitution or pimping (AC Articles 6.11 and 6.12) or a violation of the Labor Code on working conditions or wages.

Most of these crimes are ones that law enforcement has had years worth of experience investigating and prosecuting and therefore are more likely crimes to identify in a situation of trafficking (A3, M8, N24, P6).[19] These different crimes also fall under the jurisdiction of different investigative bodies, as shown in Figure 4.1, which can make it difficult to identify the component parts as a larger trafficking case. Various agencies have jurisdiction over noncriminal fineable offenses in the Administrative Code. Any police officer may issue a citation for engaging in prostitution and pimping, but usually such crimes are the province of the local beat police, the *uchastkovyi* (AC Article 28.3[2.3]). Fines for labor violations are handed out by inspectors in the Ministry of Labor.

Moreover, some of these other crimes implicate not only the traffickers but also the victims. As a result, if law enforcement agents are not looking for human trafficking, they may arrest trafficking victims for the crimes they have committed in the process of being trafficked, such as crossing a border illegally, or fine them for engaging in prostitution. Although there may be a number of lesser

19. All but Article 322.1 (organizing illegal migration) existed before the trafficking laws were passed. Article 322.1 was added into the Criminal Code in December 2004 by Federal Law no. 187-FZ, "O vnesenii izmenenii v Ugolovnyi kodeks Rossiiskoi Federatsii, Ugolovno-protsessual'nyi kodeks Rossiiskoi Federatsii, i Kodeks Rossiiskoi Federatsii ob administrativnykh pravonarusheniiakh," of December 28, 2004 (SZ RF 2005, no. 1 [part 1], item 13).

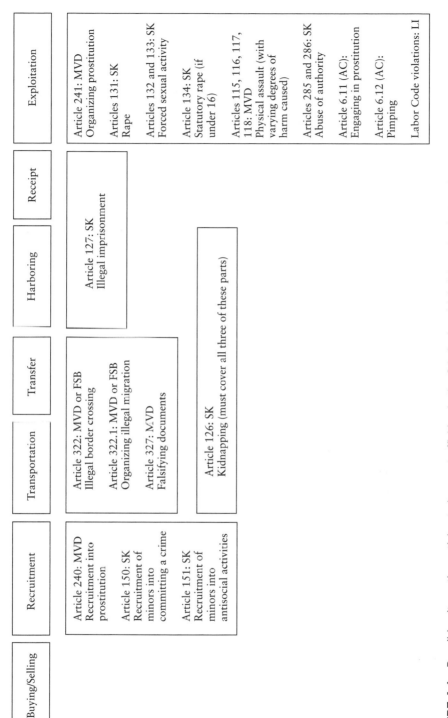

FIGURE 4.1 Possible alternative articles to human trafficking in the Criminal and Administrative Codes. SK = Investigative Committee; MVD = Ministry of the Interior; FSB = Federal Security Service; LI = Labor Inspector.

crimes committed in each stage of trafficking, each stage is not necessarily a crime in and of itself. For example, as one procurator noted, neither transportation nor transfer are crimes in themselves, so it is difficult to use them as foundations for a trafficking prosecution (P7).

In fact, according to many of my interviewees, trafficking cases are rarely opened as trafficking. Usually they are uncovered in the process of investigating another crime. One operativnik in Vladivostok noted: "Most of the cases are not originally charged as human trafficking. Usually we get information about a firm or more accurately a place where there are people being used as prostitutes. The initial work is to document the fact that there is organized prostitution going on . . . the case is opened as 240 or 241, at which point no one really knows about the fact that there was trafficking involved. But then in the course of interviews with the victims, the trafficking is uncovered and it is added as an additional crime" (M13). Given the lack of incentives to do this additional work, it is not a surprise that in reality this second step rarely takes place.

The only part of the human trafficking statute that does not have any overlap with other Criminal Code articles is the buying or selling of a person. In addition, a transaction is something that occurs at a particular place and point in time, which makes it easier for law enforcement to identify it as a crime. Even so, it is difficult to capture the moment of transaction without proactive policing, a strategy that is particularly time and resource intensive. Nevertheless, law enforcement agents seem to have become most focused on this aspect of the law, especially in domestic sex trafficking cases and cases of child trafficking. From 2004 to 2013, almost all domestic child and sex trafficking cases charged as human trafficking had a purchase or sale of a victim involved. According to an operativnik in Vladivostok: "Ten years ago, there was a lot of buying and selling of women going on between brothels, but now they fear doing it. The women can leave if they want. There are a lot of raids, and when the women are questioned, there is no evidence that they have been sold. They are free to leave. If there is no selling and no force involved, it is not trafficking" (M13).

Informal Criteria

Beyond the text of the law, informal criteria play an important role in whether Russian law enforcement agents identify a situation as trafficking. Law enforcement professionals, like those in many other occupations, use categories to help organize their everyday experiences and make their practice more efficient. An important part of categorization in criminal justice is the normalization of crimes, establishing "knowledge of the typical manner in which offenses of given classes are committed, the social characteristics of the persons who regularly commit them, the features of the settings in which they occur, the types of victims often involved, and the like" (Sudnow 1965, 259).[20] By normalizing what a crime looks like, law enforcement is able to use these shorthand methods to react more quickly to situations they encounter, especially under time, resource, and personnel constraints (Swigert and Farrell 1977). When something new is made a crime, the effort at normalization kicks in. The informal criteria that emerge serve as guides to law enforcement about when to use the new laws and when not to, although these criteria are not necessarily determinative. This is especially true for laws that are new, unclear, or confusing or in the absence of clear guidance from above.

Although trafficking is not a particularly common crime, agents have learned to apply their own normalization criteria to situations that they encounter to help determine when and how to use the human trafficking laws. This process has been critical in allowing them to distinguish the application of these new laws from what they did before. The conclusions law enforcement agents reach as they encounter these situations for the first time shapes how the law is implemented in the future, especially in their region. Teaching law enforcement how to recognize trafficking from situational cues was emphasized at every training session and discussion I attended or read about in Russia. However, even several years after the law was passed, law enforcement officials remained unclear about the parameters of trafficking (A2, A9, N19, N20).

While normalization takes into account the actual text of the law, it also includes societal stereotypes. In Russia, as elsewhere, the stereotypical victim of trafficking is an innocent, naïve girl from a village who is duped into working abroad and then forced into prostitution. At the same time, there is a stereotype that people who accept these jobs know that they carry a risk of forced prostitution or slave labor and therefore accept that risk by taking the job offer. These stereotypes color what agents see when they look for potential human trafficking victims. It also means that law enforcement may miss trafficking victims, categorizing them instead as illegal immigrants or prostitutes and then taking measures based on those classifications.

VOLUNTARINESS

One of the most common refrains I heard about sex trafficking from law enforcement was "she knew what she was getting into," with the implicit assumption that if the woman knew she would be working in prostitution, she could not be

---

20. Although Sudnow primarily refers to normalization with respect to commonly occurring crimes, I (and the literature using this concept) believe that the process is similar for any type of law that law enforcement must enforce or implement.

a real trafficking victim. This stereotype is in part fueled by the large numbers of women who engaged in prostitution full- or part-time during the 1990s to support themselves (Aral et al. 2003; Avgerinos 2006). Consequently, if there is any indication that the victim worked as a prostitute prior to the trafficking or if she agreed to work as a prostitute as part of the trafficking scheme, law enforcement may not consider her a victim of trafficking. Agents fail to recognize that even with the victim's consent, there is often recruitment or transfer with intent to exploit or exploitation involved, prosecutable offenses under the human trafficking statute. In the sex and labor trafficking cases that I examined, many victims did display some level of agency and consent to their exploitation. Although migrants from abroad are extremely vulnerable to trafficking, the fact that law enforcement seems to focus more on trafficking that occurs within Russia indicates the prevalent view that migrants consented to their exploitation by taking low-paying, potentially dangerous jobs in the first place.

Though it may be difficult for law enforcement to figure out whether a person consented to the initial stages of their eventual exploitation, the United Nations' protocol on trafficking, to which Russia is a signatory, offers some guidance. It specifies that if any of the means listed (the threat or use of force or other forms of coercion, abduction, fraud, deception, the abuse of power or of a position of vulnerability, or the giving or receiving of payments or benefits to achieve the consent of a person having control over another person) were used, the consent of the victim to any stages of the trafficking process is irrelevant. The story told at the beginning of this book about the disagreement between FSB agents over whether women who consented to work as prostitutes abroad counted as trafficking victims is an example of how these informal criteria come to bear on cases in real life.

The informal criteria of consent has some flexibility. For example, when looking at charging practices in international sex trafficking cases, the fact that the women went voluntarily and consented to work abroad as prostitutes did not seem to matter as much as interviews and discourse around Russia suggested that it might. In several successful international sex trafficking prosecutions, the women were specifically recruited to and agreed to be prostitutes abroad. But despite these exceptions, this stereotype is still quite strong and can inhibit identification and prosecution of cases at any stage of the criminal justice process. This may especially be the case if the victims do not self-identify as victims, either because they believe that their agency in the process made them responsible or because traffickers tell them to say that they are there willingly. The stereotype is so strong that procurators go to great lengths to show that the victim was, in fact, a real victim and was forced to be in or continue in prostitution. Conversely, the defense usually tries to show that the women had already displayed questionable sexual behavior, which made their real victim status suspect. This echoes a common practice in rape cases in Russia and elsewhere, in which often it falls to the victim to prove that she resisted sexual advances in order to be considered a "real" rape victim (Sperling 1990; Spears and Spohn 1998; Johnson 2001, 2004, 2005b).

One way that traffickers have adjusted to this informal criterion is to change their methods of recruitment, especially for international trafficking. Whereas in the 1990s and early 2000s they often recruited women into jobs that were clearly nonsexual in nature (nannies, hotel clerks, maids) and forced them into prostitution, in the later 2000s they changed their tactics to look for people who would be willing to accept jobs that carried some possibility of engaging in sex for pay. Women were recruited as hostesses and dancers and to chat up customers in lounges and get them to buy drinks. In the traffickers' recruitment pitches, there was an implication that the women could engage in paid sexual services on the side if they wanted. Women who agreed to jobs like this, I heard many times, should have known what the job offer really meant. Thus they were less real as victims than those who were recruited into and accepted more innocent jobs.

COMPENSATION FOR SERVICES

Another frequent issue in both sex and labor trafficking cases is whether the victim received any money for her services. If a prostitute or a laborer receives any money, law enforcement may not consider them to be victims of trafficking, even though by most objective standards they might have undergone exploitation. Frequently news articles on trafficking cases mention that the victims were paid only enough "for bread." Traffickers have noted these stereotypes as well and have made adjustments to avoid prosecution. As one interviewee told me, they now pay their laborers or prostitutes small amounts of money so that they cannot say that they were exploited (N28).

ABILITY TO ESCAPE

Another stereotype is that trafficking victims must have their freedom of movement completely curtailed, to the point where they are locked up and require "rescuing" by law enforcement. This means that if law enforcement believes that the victims could have escaped on their own—that there were no locks on the doors or they were not chained up—or had freedom of movement (e.g., were able to go to the store for groceries), they will not be considered trafficking victims. In reality, it is rare that victims are physically restrained to this degree. They may be allowed movement but only with accompaniment or have to follow strict guidelines when they go out. But there may be other reasons that a victim will not leave the situation, including threats of violence to them or their families, because they have had their documents taken away, or because they do not know where they are.

On encountering a potential human trafficking case, law enforcement's question is often: "Did they have a chance to escape? And if so, why didn't they?" The answer to this question is usually "yes, but . . ." Traffickers may bring their victims to places that are isolated or where it is difficult for them to communicate with anyone. So, although the victims technically have freedom of movement, in reality they have nowhere to go. In several slave labor cases in Russia, the labor took place deep in the forest, where the victims could not have found their way out even if they had wanted to (nos. 39, 202). Another case of labor exploitation took place on a boat, where twenty-five Ukrainian fishermen were held prisoner and forced to illegally fish crabs (no. 86). Many victims are people who are unlikely to have friends and family who are looking for them because they have long been isolated due to alcoholism or drug addiction or are abroad and are already isolated from contact with their family.

Although it is more frequent in cases of slave labor than in cases of sexual exploitation, chaining victims up is still not the dominant form of insuring subordination. Psychological and physical measures can be equally powerful, as is the fact that the victims have had their identity documents taken away. Unfortunately for investigators, chains are the best and most indisputable evidence for a labor trafficking charge, so they continue to employ the informal criteria of inability to escape to help solidify their cases. According to my interviewees, many investigators will only accept physical restraint (chains, handcuffs, etc.) to prosecute use of slave labor under Article 127.2, probably because physical restraints easily correspond to what they recognize as slavery. One operativnik in Moscow joked with me that slave labor prosecutions would be much easier if "we chained them up first and then rescued them" (M14). An NGO worker from Astrakhan confirmed this, suggesting that in cases of slave labor with foreign victims: "Article 322.1 [organization of illegal migration] is often used, not [Article] 127.2. The MVD has already gotten used to using 322.1. They think there needs to be some sort of pistol or blood involved for it to be 127.2" (N37). As one procurator in Vladivostok told me,

> We place a great emphasis on the characteristics of the person and the situation they are in. We give less weight when the person was free to leave than if they were locked up in a nonpopulated area. We pay a lot of attention to the statements of the victims. Were they forced? If they live in the city versus living in the taiga without any people nearby, if they're locked in. If they can freely come and go and meet with their friends, it is much harder to make the case that they were victims. . . . If they agreed to it, it is harder. If they went willingly, then we have to prove that they were held and were threatened or too scared. We have to prove the fear and this is very difficult. (P6)

This informal criterion tracks with the predominant societal understanding of slave labor as noted in one of Surtees's interviews with a victim: "Most people do not believe that it was really impossible to exit the slavery. . . . They think that if such things happened to you, you are stupid" (quoted in Surtees 2008, 27). Although her interviews took place in Eastern Europe, this also reflects the situation in Russia. Not everyone is as shocked and outraged as the police officer quoted at the beginning of this chapter. This informal criterion is highly gendered, corresponding with predominant ideas of manhood and masculinity. Real men would have tried with all their might to escape. Only those men who had been bested in physical strength with the use of chains are real victims. Women, in contrast, are presumed to be unable to escape situations of prostitution, and often threats are enough for law enforcement to consider them trapped.

A clear ability to escape or to call for help can undermine a trafficking charge. In one slave labor case in Moscow (no. 32) in which three men exploited teens with cerebral palsy who had aged out of state care, the procurator dropped the slave labor charge because the teen victims could have used their cell phones to call for help or could have run away because they were often left outside alone. Of course, the theoretical ability to run away in this situation was quite different from the actual ability, especially given the victims' medical condition and the fear the traffickers had instilled in them by locking them up in a bomb shelter.

Accomplishing the first step of a human trafficking case, finding it, is a difficult one. Law enforcement does not have the time or resources to pursue cases without some information from which to work. Although victims are the most direct way to get information about these situations, there are many reasons for them to fear coming forward. They are afraid of revenge, disclosure of embarrassing personal information, and mistreatment by the police. Because of the complex emotional relationships that usually exist in sex trafficking cases between pimps and their prostitutes, many women in these situations may not see themselves as victims at all. Victims of sex and labor trafficking may not see themselves as victims if they had agency in the process or accepted a job they felt they should have known would be risky. Unfortunately, since 2004, Russian law enforcement has relied almost exclusively on reports from victims in the cases they have pursued as human trafficking. This means that there are many more cases that they may never learn about because victims do not come forward.

Another source for information on human trafficking cases, victim assistance organizations, is not a promising avenue at the moment. The current relationship between NGOs and law enforcement is extremely contentious and becoming more so because of recent laws restricting NGO activity and funding sources. Even when there were no restrictive laws, the relationship was still difficult. Law enforcement is oriented toward getting as much information as quickly as possible to track down and prosecute suspects. Victim assistance organizations, in contrast, would rather forgo seeing the trafficker jailed if there is any risk that it may retraumatize the victim or further violate his or her rights. This fundamentally different orientation toward solving the human trafficking problem has made it difficult for these groups to work together. Productive relationships have been few and far between, but examining them, especially the experience of the IOM, shows the benefits for both victims and law enforcement that can come with formalized cooperation.

Law enforcement also has problems identifying cases as trafficking. So even if they do find one or receive information about one, they may not pursue it as such. Human trafficking falls into the category of cases from which law enforcement tries to shy away—complex, new, and resource intensive. The statute itself is unclear, and because human trafficking is a process, the point at which law enforcement encounters it matters a lot for whether agents even see human trafficking. This confusion makes evidence gathering difficult but also creates opportunities for law enforcement to pursue traffickers under the statutes that comprise its component parts. In situations of uncertainty, law enforcement turns to informal criteria to help define when it is appropriate to use the human trafficking laws, including a victim's ability to escape, voluntariness, and the receipt of compensation. Although these criteria exist nowhere in the statutory requirements of the law, or in any commentaries that I have reviewed, they have an enormous impact on the decision making of law enforcement agents when they encounter a trafficking situation.

A Comparative Note

How unique are the problems that Russian law enforcement faces in finding and identifying human trafficking cases? The limited research that exists in other countries (mostly the United States) suggests that this stage presents the largest barrier for combating trafficking worldwide. Getting reports of trafficking cases is difficult everywhere. Victim or citizen reports and accidental discovery of trafficking while investigating other cases remain the most common ways for police to find out about trafficking cases (Clawson et al. 2006; Verhoeven and Van Gestel 2011). In a small telephone survey of law enforcement agents in the United States who had worked on trafficking cases, only 5 percent came from information supplied by victim assistance organizations, highlighting that strained relationships between NGOs and law enforcement are not just a Russian problem (Clawson et al. 2006). Countries in Europe, encouraged by the Organization for Security and Cooperation in Europe, have tried to overcome this by instituting National and Transnational Referral Mechanisms that formalize cooperation between NGOs and government officials to improve delivery of victim services as well as criminal justice outcomes (ICMPD 2009, 2012).

In the United States, Farrell et al. (2012) find that agency readiness, preparation, and education are the strongest predictors for identifying human trafficking cases. But even with significant education, local-level law enforcement agents in the United States continue to display low awareness of the problem and minimal readiness to respond if they encounter a case (Farrell et al. 2012; Clawson et al. 2008). Stereotypes of the "typical victim" also affect law enforcement's ability to identify cases. Although each country has its own set of stereotypes—for example, the Brazilian "Myth of Maria" is of a gullible, poor woman of color who falls for a fake job offer from a European (white) prince—the tendency to look for the stereotypical victim is powerful (Haynes 2007; Blanchette et al. 2013) and has important effects on who is considered deserving of state protection and who is not. In particular, stereotypes of who is not a real trafficking victim have been shown to affect labor trafficking victims' access to services in Italy, the Netherlands, and the United States (Brennan 2010; Smit 2011; Caneppele and Mancuso 2013; Barrick et al. 2014). The ILO has created a list of operational indicators of trafficking to help identify victims, but it is unclear how regularly, if at all, these guidelines are being used by on-the-ground personnel anywhere (ILO 2009b).

THE INVESTIGATION OF HUMAN TRAFFICKING CASES

Even if a human trafficking case is successfully uncovered and identified as such, the challenge of investigating it still remains. This chapter explores the complications that law enforcement encounters as its agents try to put together a successful human trafficking case. Not only must they figure out how to collect evidence across regions or borders from frequently traumatized and unstable victims and witnesses, they must also anticipate how quickly the case will proceed through the system and whether it will be cleared. These challenges were substantial in the initial years that the law was in place. Very few people in the country, let alone in each individual region, had experience with trafficking cases. There was also significant ambiguity about how the human trafficking statute was meant to be applied, making it difficult for agents to know what the correct evidence was. As one interviewee noted: "The real problem is that [the evidence required] is unpredictable. There is no common formula for what works because nothing is outlined" (M5). The guidance that did exist came from internal agency orders and instruction manuals for law enforcement produced by nongovernmental organizations or law enforcement academies (Zhuravlev and Pigaev 2006; Dvorkin 2007; Shushkevich 2008), but these were spottily distributed and investigators did not always have the time to read them. As practice on trafficking has increased over time, law enforcement's behavior demonstrates how the demands of the institutional machinery have interacted with the reality on the ground.

The chapter is divided into two parts. The first discusses the challenges that law enforcement faces that are specific to investigating human trafficking cases and the tactics agents have used to obtain evidence. I discuss victim testimony, which law enforcement needs to prove that exploitation has taken place or that the trafficker intends to exploit the victim; the use of video to capture the transaction phase of the trafficking process; and the search for corroborating evidence to support the charges. In the second half of the chapter, I describe how the broader institutional environment of law enforcement influences human trafficking investigations, including the time limits imposed on the investigation, the division of functions among different enforcement agencies, and the added complications that come with investigating international and cross-regional cases. These factors are equally likely to be present in investigations of any serious or complex crimes and in applications of new laws.

Complications Specific to Human Trafficking Cases

One of the biggest problems identified by law enforcement in implementing the human trafficking laws was the confusion and uncertainty caused by imprecise wording. Until 2008, Article 127.1 of the Criminal Code defined human trafficking as: "buying/selling of a person, or the recruitment, transportation, transfer, harboring, or receiving of a person for the purpose of their exploitation." Most law enforcement and court interpretations believed this meant showing either that the intent of the trafficker was to exploit the victim *or* that the victim was actually exploited. For law enforcement, proving the latter could be fairly straightforward. If a victim was already being exploited and the accused could be directly tied to the exploitation taking place—as might happen, for example, with a brothel or factory owner—the proof was clear. Law enforcement then had to work backward to show that the exploitation happened because of one of the actions outlined (buying/selling, recruitment, transportation, transfer, harboring, or receipt). Of course, this still required agents to obtain testimony from victims to show that the exploitation had taken place along with corroborating evidence, but the evidentiary requirements were at least clear. For example, law enforcement agents could go undercover to purchase the services of prostitutes that they suspect are in a trafficking situation to show that exploitation is taking place.[1] During their time with the prostitute, they could ask her questions to find out if she had been sold into the situation (P7). In an example from a case in the city of Saransk, operativniki collected information on a prostitution ring by making

---

1. These controlled purchases (*kontrol'nyi zakupki*) are regulated by the law on Operational-Investigative Activities (Federal Law no. 144-FZ of 1995).

controlled purchases of prostitutes' time in saunas and private apartments, then asking questions about the prices charged and the operations of the prostitution agencies.[2] For each of the six times they did this, they requested prostitutes from a different agency, so they could get the most information possible and collect the evidence necessary for a successful prosecution.[3]

If the victim had not yet been exploited, and law enforcement instead had to prove the *intent* to exploit the victim, gathering proof was much more difficult. According to commentaries on the law, the accused does not have to directly exploit the victim, but they do have to have the knowledge that their actions will result in the person being exploited (Dolgolenko 2004; Lebedev 2004). According to many law enforcement professionals with whom I spoke, showing this intent is a significant challenge. At each stage in the human trafficking process, it would be easy for a trafficker to deny intent to exploit. At the recruitment stage, police could use questionable advertisements recruiting women into prostitution or with unrealistic job offers abroad as a clue that trafficking might be going on, but proving that the people placing those advertisements have the intent to exploit the women is difficult (N22). During the transportation or transfer stage, it can be difficult to show that a person arranging the travel or even accompanying the victim had the intent to exploit him or her because the middlemen can easily say that someone paid them to take the victim from one place to another and they had no idea what would happen to the victim (A4, A8).[4] Even if the suspect is a direct participant in the transaction, one procurator told me, it could still be difficult to prove the intent to exploit as the seller can always say he or she did not know or care about what happened to the victim after he or she was sold and therefore had no intent to exploit him or her (P7). Russian law enforcement also

---

2. Saransk is located in the Republic of Mordovia in the Volga Federal District.

3. It is unclear from the court documents whether the undercover police officers actually engaged in sexual activities with the prostitutes while collecting their evidence. It is possible that they did, considering that just talking with prostitutes is often considered a sign that something is amiss, especially since prostitutes frequently see police officers as clients. When the law enforcement personnel were undercover only to make the arrest, it seems more likely that there were not sexual activities involved. In several instances, the police officer paid for oral sex in a car with marked bills and arrested the woman as they drove away; in others, the prostitutes were brought to an apartment, and the arrests were made as soon as the money was exchanged. I have heard anecdotal evidence from NGOs working with victims that law enforcement officers demand sexual favors from prostitutes while busting prostitution rings.

4. In terms of gathering evidence, it matters who bought the ticket and whether the victim was accompanied by the trafficker on her journey. If the victim bought the ticket herself, this is not considered transportation for the purpose of exploitation and agents must find some other evidence of trafficking. If the victim traveled alone, without his or her trafficker, that also means he or she was not under the influence of the trafficker, and the action of movement (transportation or transfer) cannot be enough to show exploitation (P7).

encountered problems proving the intent to exploit in cases of child trafficking, which were mostly done for illegal adoptions. For many, it was unclear whether these activities even fell within the legal definition of human trafficking. Were babies who were being sold to adoptive parents being exploited or intended for exploitation? Although this last question was cleared up by the 2008 amendments, the difficulty of proving intent to exploit for any of the other activities still remains.

Victim Testimony

The need to prove exploitation or intent to exploit led law enforcement to prioritize the collection of victim testimony, which was, according to one of my informants, the "trump card" in any prosecution because it could show the exploitation (N26). Consequently, law enforcement strategies and the strategies of those organizations working with them were aimed at increasing victims' incentives to cooperate with law enforcement and training law enforcement officials to deal with traumatized, fearful victims. Both NGOs and law enforcement recognized that providing psychological, medical, and legal assistance to victims, establishing a system of temporary residence permits for victims, and providing shelter as victims recovered from their trauma were important ways to help build a trafficking case. However, in the absence of laws creating these measures, Russian law enforcement had a difficult time obtaining victim testimony. Although the shelter run by the IOM in Moscow provided a bridge between law enforcement and victims, it was open for only three years and was not government funded. Even if law enforcement could convince victims to cooperate by sharing information, and in some cases testifying, there were still problems with having the evidence the victims provided being considered reliable. This problem forced law enforcement to collect corroborating evidence (documentary, physical, witnesses), which had its own associated challenges.

Most victims are not particularly eager to participate as witnesses against their traffickers, making obtaining victim testimony difficult for law enforcement. The trauma inherent in trafficking is severe; until that trauma is dealt with, it can cause problems that can inhibit evidence collection. Of the 423 victims seen at the IOM rehabilitation center in Russia, 73 percent of them were diagnosed with post-traumatic stress disorder. A study of 207 female victims in Europe found that it takes at least ninety days post-trafficking for mental health problems even to begin to abate (Zimmerman et al. 2006). There can also be significant memory loss due to trauma.

In addition, for many of the same reasons that victims are unwilling to come forward to reveal the crime to law enforcement, they are also hesitant to talk to law enforcement once the crime has been discovered. They fear they will be judged for their actions, that law enforcement is untrustworthy, and that their traffickers will take revenge on them or their families. One operativnik told me about a woman who would cooperate only after bail of two million dollars was set for her trafficker (M15).[5] One of the biggest concerns expressed by victims about participating in the criminal justice process is that their identity will be revealed to their traffickers or that they will have to face their traffickers in court or during other parts of the investigation.[6]

The Criminal Procedure Code provides several options to protect victims during the process. The victims and witnesses can be given pseudonyms that appear in all the documents that the trafficker and his lawyer will see (CPC Article 166[9]).[7] During identification lineups there are provisions to make sure the person being identified cannot know who identified him or her (CPC Article 193[8]). Technically, victims and witnesses are supposed to appear to testify in the trial, but within Russian law, there are ways around this. Audio/video or film recordings of the victim's testimony are admissible if the victim fails to appear and the two parties agree (CPC Article 81). In some circumstances, however, the judge can unilaterally decide to have the victim's statement read into the court record, as long as the testimony was obtained in line with the Criminal Procedure Code.[8] If the victim does appear at court to testify, he or she can be questioned by the court away from the other participants (CPC Article 278[5]). However, all of these options require that the people investigating the case have enough experience to know when to use these tactics, the sympathy and desire to make the victims more comfortable, and the time to pursue these extra bureaucratic steps.

For victims to turn from traumatized, possibly unreliable witnesses to witnesses who are capable of testifying, psychological, medical, and legal assistance

---

5. One of the provisions of the new law on victim's rights, which went into effect on January 1, 2015, gives the victim the right to petition the court to hold the accused under arrest if he or she feels that the accused might pose a threat (Frolov 2014; Federal Law no. 432-FZ of 2013).

6. When there are inconsistencies between witnesses and defendants' testimonies, an investigator can request a confrontation (*ochnaia stavka*). In this procedure, the two are brought together to give their version of the events and, through the discussion, resolve the inconsistencies in their testimony (CPC Article 192).

7. New legislation on victims' rights strengthens these protections. Victims can petition to have their personal information excluded from court documents. Sometimes trafficking victims are not officially recognized as victims in the cases and are instead considered witnesses, so these provisions are equally relevant for both groups.

8. Other circumstances include death, severe illness, and natural disaster. Despite these requirements, judges frequently decide to read victims' statements into the court record anyway, giving broad application to the term severe illness. In one case I examined, the severe illness of one of the victims was that she was pregnant. In reality, it would not be difficult to show that a victim had a severe illness, given that most suffer from post-traumatic stress disorder or other ailments.

is critical. This requires a safe place to stay and temporary residence permits. If they are in danger from reprisals by their traffickers, they may need access to witness protection. Providing these types of assistance is part of Russia's obligation under the Transnational Organized Crime convention and its associated protocol on human trafficking, and is part of its membership in other international organizations (the OSCE, Council of Europe) which have issued directives on human trafficking that Russia is obligated to follow. Nevertheless, despite calls from law enforcement, NGOs, and the international community, the Russian government has not provided financing or created a legal infrastructure for this type of assistance.[9] Without this support, law enforcement must walk a fine line between not pressuring the victim too much too quickly and still getting timely evidence. In the time that victims are recovering and deciding whether to cooperate, vital evidence could disappear (M11).

Shelters and Residence Permits

Law enforcement consistently identified the absence of shelters, especially at the regional level, and temporary residence permits as hindering their ability to investigate and prosecute human trafficking crimes (M17). As one Moscow operativnik said at a conference: "The biggest problem—where to keep people? IOM's shelter has a twenty-one-day limit. Investigations take two months. Police do not want to think about rehabilitation. We entrust this to NGOs" (M22). Even when victims are locals, as often happens in cases of labor exploitation, there can be problems with shelter. According to an agent investigating a large labor trafficking case in the Perm region (no. 248): "We ran into unexpected problems: several of the victims did not have documents; some of them had passports and registrations, but their houses had been demolished and they had nowhere to live. Considering how big the investigation was and how long it took, we had to figure out tons of details, including organizing food and medical services" (Lobanov 2008). In some regions law enforcement has informally organized witness protection services, provided temporary places for the victims to live, and even helped several find jobs, but this was done on a case-by-case basis. The need for shelter was one point of common ground in the otherwise contentious relationship between law enforcement and NGOs.

Options for shelters in Russia are limited. The Russian state runs shelters for "women in difficult situations," but these are not in every region and their management is often reluctant to take former prostitutes or drug addicts, which many

---

9. This type of assistance was one of the pillars of the draft law on trafficking that was eventually not passed.

victims of trafficking are (N22).[10] The particular type of trauma experienced by trafficking victims is often cited as a reason that specialized trafficking shelters are necessary (Rosenberg 2006; Warnath 2007). In addition to the IOM's shelter, NGOs have run shelters in various Russian regions, but their funding has been mostly foreign and their period of operation limited by grant cycles. They also cannot take women with children or girls under eighteen because of legal regulations governing care of minors. In June 2013, the Russian Red Cross opened a small shelter in St. Petersburg which is currently the only shelter for trafficking victims in all of Russia.

There is no established system of temporary residence permits for human trafficking victims which would allow victims to legally remain where the investigation is being conducted. This is especially important in the Russian context, where a registration system applies to both citizens and foreigners. Freedom of movement, as well as access to state-funded social services, is regulated by a system of internal registration (*propiska*).[11] Russian citizens are each registered to a particular address, giving them access to medical care and other state benefits in their locality. If they are trafficked to another location, they are unlikely to be registered there, making the provision of temporary housing problematic from a legal standpoint. Furthermore, they cannot receive state-funded medical assistance anywhere but in the region where they are registered. I heard several stories of medical establishments refusing to take victims who were not registered locally. I heard about a handful of women's shelters that did have provisions to deal with temporary local registration, but they were certainly in the minority (N2). If the victims do return to their home region, registration data contained in their passports often does not correspond to their actual place of residence, so it is impossible for law enforcement to find them again if they need to follow up on the investigation.

With international victims who are in Russia illegally, there is no way to guarantee they can remain in Russia legally during the investigation and prosecution

---

10. This is related to a larger issue in Russia, the underfunding and underdevelopment of state-sponsored and private social assistance programs for people who have fallen on hard times or who have drug, alcohol, or mental health problems (McDaid et al. 2006; Bobrova et al. 2008). In addition, there are few programs for orphans and disabled children aging out of state care, who are particularly vulnerable to human trafficking (Rudnicki 2012; HRW 2014).

11. The *propiska* system is a holdover from Soviet times, when the government closely regulated allocation of housing and movement within the country. The Russian Supreme Court has declared the system unconstitutional several times when used in relation to Russian citizens who are granted freedom of movement in the Constitution. Nevertheless, its use has not abated, especially in large cities (Light 2010).

of the trafficking case.[12] Instead they are usually deported, a process handled by the Federal Migration Service (FMS). Although there have been some informal arrangements struck between the MVD and the FMS to give illegal migrants temporary legal status for the duration of the investigation and/or trial, this is far from the norm. In one situation in the Moscow region in 2008, thirteen victims were found in slave labor conditions. With the help of the IOM as mediator, the MVD and the FMS struck a deal that would allow the migrants to have one-year permits to work and stay in Russia from the FMS, as long as they continued to cooperate with the MVD's investigation. The men would be paid 2,000 rubles a month ($70) to clean the territory of an MVD facility and would be housed and fed for this temporary period, after which they would get their registration and be able to work legally. The deal fell apart when the victims arrived at the MVD facility and refused to work for the pay offered and in the working conditions provided. This outcome was unfortunate, since it was the first time that the cooperation between the agencies had been made so explicit. But there was also significant risk of retraumatization for the workers, who felt that they had been removed from one exploitative situation only to be placed in another, this time under the auspices of being helped. Both the MVD and the FMS were angry that their attempts at "humanitarian action" were unappreciated, leading them to be hesitant about making such efforts again.

Other informal agreements have been successful, however. In an international case investigated by the FSB, the agency asked a victim from a neighboring country to return to Russia to participate in an ongoing investigation. It allowed her to enter Russia without documents and go to the IOM rehabilitation center during her participation in the investigation and trial. The agency then helped bring her back to her country when her part in the investigation concluded (N19). But even if law enforcement wants the victims to return to give statements, many of them refuse, especially if they have already returned to their countries of origin.

The absence of a safe place to shelter victims and a system of temporary residence permits means that law enforcement must get the victim's story right away or within the time it takes to deport him or her. This restriction does not give agents much chance to question the victim, even if they do suspect trafficking. This point was brought home by one operativnik who suggested that the best way

---

12. According to the Presidential Administration, foreign victims who are participating in criminal proceedings should be able to stay in Russia during the criminal process, but this is not regulated by law. The administration says that law enforcement can ask the migration service for a permit and it should be granted (ODIHR 2008b).

for agents to have regular access to victims for questioning is if they are hospitalized for injuries sustained during trafficking:

> We cannot require [the victims] to be present and hold them, we must let them go after they do the initial interview. The only way we can keep them around is during the time they are getting medical services. . . . After that, the victim is only needed during the trial, so we have to let them go. And then they leave and we usually cannot find them again. The length of time that they stay under medical attention, of course, does not depend on us; it depends on the doctor. If the doctor says the woman is healthy and has no psychological problems, he or she lets them go. Even if the women have all these problems, they can still refuse treatment, unless they have certain infectious diseases, in which case they must stay in the hospital. As long as they are being treated, they are de facto under police control and we can work with them on the investigation. (M13)

Given the level of trauma necessary to require hospitalization, the victim is unlikely to provide a coherent story and accurate recall of events, not to mention the further trauma he or she might experience through questioning. Without any place for victims to stay and/or a guarantee of protection, they often disappear back to their region of origin or, worse, return to their trafficker, the only person they know in the city where they are currently located. Unlike in many other countries, there are no budgetary resources for funding services for crime victims, so it is difficult to find places for victims to stay during the course of the investigation. Many victims do not want to stay in touch with police, do not live where they are registered, or frequently change their contact information, making it hard to find them again. Because most victims come from the margins of society, they are also less likely to have a place and people to return to for support.

The difficulties in getting victims to talk, combined with an absence of supporting legislation on temporary residence permits and shelters, has made it difficult for law enforcement to obtain the critical piece of evidence to prove that exploitation occurred or that the trafficker had the intent to exploit the victim—the victim's testimony. Without this, law enforcement has little incentive to try to push forward a trafficking prosecution and may instead choose to charge the case as something else where the victim's testimony is less necessary or drop it altogether. The example of the cooperative relationship between the IOM's shelter in Moscow and law enforcement shows how a dedicated system of shelters can increase law enforcement's desire to use the human trafficking laws by helping agents obtain victim testimony to sustain a trafficking charge.

Creating and Increasing Incentives for Victim Testimony

According to my NGO interviewees as well as other research that has been done on trafficking victims, a number of factors may motivate a victim to participate in the criminal justice process. These reasons include saving other people from the same fate, getting justice for themselves, getting revenge against their traffickers, and wanting to exercise their legal rights (N21, N25; Bjerkan and Dyrlid 2006). Victims who have actually participated in the trials of their traffickers have expressed pleasure that the traffickers were punished and they got their revenge (N25).

There are several potential avenues for increasing the likelihood that victims will give testimony: participation in a witness protection program, opportunities to access civil compensation, and access to legal services. Traffickers are known for their brutality and their willingness to do anything to protect themselves and their business interests. So if a victim does decide to participate in a trial as a witness, his or her life could be endangered, especially if the trafficker finds out who snitched. Traffickers may threaten physical harm to victims or victims' families so the victims change or withdraw their statements. If the traffickers are convicted, they threaten that after they get out of jail they will find the victims and hurt them (N28). Although there are few concrete examples of these threats actually being carried out, most victims have, at a minimum, seen or experienced the traffickers use physical force to keep people in line or know that they have connections to local thugs, so the victims consider these threats real.

In a case of labor trafficking in the Khabarovsk region (no. 282), two men showed up at one victim's house and threatened to beat him unless he retracted the statement he had made to police by saying that the police had coerced it from him. He did what they asked but later returned to the police to tell them what had happened. In this case, most of the witnesses gave their statements under pseudonyms to avoid reprisal. In another case in the Republic of Karachaevo-Cherkessia (no. 334), the victim witness who was most crucial for helping law enforcement uncover and prosecute a sex trafficking case was found murdered the day before the sentence was handed down, her naked body beaten to death and without ears (Desiatichenko 2011). This was a clear message, intended to show that she was being punished for snitching. The accused may be more benevolent, instead trying to buy off the witnesses. In one slave labor case in Orel (no. 90), the victims' lawyer reported that the number of victim witnesses had dropped by half after many were bought off. In fact, procurators' motions to the courts to keep the accused in pretrial detention frequently mention the possibility that the trafficker may try to influence the victim.

In 2004 the Russian government enacted witness protection legislation that applies to victims, their legal representatives, witnesses, and other participants in the criminal process. It provides for personal security and security of dwelling, protection of confidential information, change of identity, relocation, and plastic surgery (these last three apply only to victims of grave or especially grave crimes), among other things.[13] The law, however, does not protect the witness after the verdict is handed down, nor does it protect any of the representatives of victim assistance organizations that may be helping the victim, unless they are acting as official witnesses in the case (M17).[14]

According to the law, witness protection can begin before the case is officially opened, but there is a significant gap between the law on the books and the law in practice. Most MVD officials with whom I spoke did not believe that the witness protection legislation applied while operativniki were gathering evidence and the investigator was deciding whether to go forward with the case (A9, N26). They believed that only when the case is officially opened can the victim be officially recognized as a victim (*poterpevshii*) and therefore qualify for witness protection.[15] But as previously noted, the official opening may not occur for several years after the case comes to law enforcement's attention, because agents want to make sure that the case will be cleared within the time limit before actually opening it. Other law enforcement agents believe that the legislation applies only to victims and witnesses who are officially cooperating with law enforcement in the investigation (ODIHR 2008b).

Expanded use of the witness protection legislation, even with some of its faults, could be a way to incentivize victim participation in criminal proceedings. However, a lack of funding and misunderstanding of the provisions of the legislation by those who are supposed to be implementing it means that it does not currently help make victims feel safer participating.[16] In addition, trafficking

---

13. Agencies responsible for providing witness protection include the MVD, the FSB, and the Federal Drug Service. See ODIHR 2008b; MT 2006. For the full text of the legislation, see Federal Law no. 119-FZ "O gosudarstvennoi zashchite poterpevshikh, sviditelei i inykh uchastnikov ugolovnogo sudoproizvodstva," of August 20, 2004. SZ RF 2004, no. 34, item 3534.

14. The new Law on Crime Victim's Rights now allows protection to be continued after the verdict is handed down, especially in cases of acquittal (Filimonov 2014; Federal Law no. 432-FZ of 2013).

15. In Russian law, a victim of a crime (*zhertvo*) can be legally recognized as a victim (*poterpevshii*) by the investigator during the investigation or by the court during the trial (CPC Article 42). Under Russian law, a person can receive the legal status of victim only if he or she is a citizen of the Russian Federation or of a country with which Russia has an agreement specifying that that country's citizens receive all rights of Russian citizens in criminal proceedings. Countries in the latter category include Moldova, Azerbaijan, and Kyrgyzstan (N22; ODIHR 2008a).

16. After some changes in the law, this program is becoming more effective. In 2008, a special subdivision was created in the MVD to provide state witness protection. See Presidential Order no. 1316, "O nekotorykh voprosakh Ministerstva vnutrennikh del Rossiiskoi Federatsii," of September 6, 2008 (SZ RF 2008, no. 37, item 4182). An addition to the federal budget in 2011 guaranteed perpetual financing for the program; in 2012, about $10 million was devoted to the program (average cost per witness is $3,500 per month) (RAPSI 2012; Falaleev 2013).

victims may not fit law enforcement's stereotypical model of a victim who needs witness protection, and agents may not want to protect victims of trafficking, thinking them undeserving of the scarce budgetary resources dedicated to the law (N21, N22). As one investigator noted at a conference I attended in Moscow, victims do not appear that interested in what is offered by the witness protection legislation. They do not want to change their place of residence, get plastic surgery, or take any of the more serious measures available through the law. For victims, a Moscow MVD officer suggested, it is easier and more practical not to participate in the process at all (M17). Use of witness protection was reported in only five of the 279 cases in the data set.

The possibility of civil compensation from the traffickers was mentioned by a number of my interviewees as another way to encourage victim cooperation (M15). Since most victims fall into trafficking rings because of economic necessity, the inducement of potential compensation for the harm they have suffered may encourage them to cooperate throughout the duration of the investigation and prosecution (A8, N22, N43; Bjerkan and Dyrlid 2006). This outcome requires that law enforcement or a victim advocate communicate these options early in the process. Despite the guarantee in Russia's Constitution that crime victims have a right to compensation for harm done (Article 52), only in December 2013 did the government pass a Victim's Rights Law fulfilling these obligations. In effect since January 2015, it permits victims to be officially recognized as such from the moment a case is opened, which allows law enforcement to start proceedings to confiscate property and other assets from the accused before they can hide it in anticipation of a court judgment on damages (Frolov 2014). On occasion, civil compensation has been awarded to victims in trafficking cases.

In Russian law, victims (and their lawyers) can play a much more active role in the criminal process than in other countries (CPC Article 22). Whereas in many countries, the prosecutor represents both the victim and the state, in Russia victims can pay for their own lawyers, who are given the same rights and privileges as defense attorneys (CPC Article 42). Although law enforcement is obligated by law to explain victims' rights to them, in practice agents usually fail to inform or do so inadequately, which means that victims are rarely represented. There are no provisions for state-provided free legal assistance for crime victims and no tradition of pro bono work done by lawyers (ODIHR 2008b). Some NGOs provide legal assistance, but it is not guaranteed and varies by region and funding. In addition to explaining and guiding victims through the criminal justice process more generally, providing them with legal representation could help increase victim participation in investigations by helping them navigate the civil compensation process. Legal representatives could explain to the victims what they are and are not eligible for, walk them through the process, and help guarantee that their rights are protected under Russian law.

Concerns about Victim Testimony

If victims do agree to cooperate with law enforcement, there is still another hurdle—the evidence that they provide is not always convincing to the courtroom procurator who presents the case in court or the judge who decides it. Knowing this, agents may be reluctant to pursue trafficking charges, believing that, even if they did get the "trump card" of a victim willing to testify, the victims would still be considered untrustworthy. Without exception, traffickers train victims to lie about their age, job, and consent to work, which means that initial denials that they are victims may change over time. In the absence of psychological help to deal with the trauma experienced during trafficking, victims can be unreliable witnesses. The trauma sometimes makes them unable to remember details or to remember some details but not others. As they recover psychologically, victims may remember other parts of the story that either contradict or call into question what they have said before. Trauma also makes it difficult to tell a linear story, which is precisely what law enforcement needs to be able to prosecute a case. Without an accurate understanding of the effects of trauma—which few police, procurators, and judges have—victims may appear to be guilty or at least complicit, trying out different stories that help them cover up either guilt or shame. Law enforcement does not want to take the chance that a victim will change his or her story during the investigation or, worse, recant his or her testimony entirely.

In addition, because traffickers operate covertly, the victims may not even be able to give the type of concrete evidence that law enforcement needs to show that a crime has taken place.[17] One victim told a story about how, when she was interacting with police in her destination country, she needed to "tell them everything—where I've been, who I am, name names. . . . From the beginning, when I told them the names, no one had heard of them. Of all these figureheads, I hadn't seen even one who was actually in charge and controlling these brothels. They said that at the very least, I needed to show them the place where I was held. But when we were brought there, we were transported behind closed windows across [the city] and did not see where we were going" (O20).

Trafficking victims often do not engender sympathy. Rather than naïve girls from the village, they are sometimes exactly the opposite. A procurator in Khabarovsk who had taken a trafficking case to court (which was eventually

---

17. The time, place, mode, and other circumstances of the commission of the crime must be proven along with the participation and intent of the accused (CPC Article 73[1]).

charged as recruitment into prostitution) told me that one of her main problems was that it was difficult to figure out how much weight she should assign to the victims' statements. Most of the victims had agreed to be prostitutes in China, thinking it would be an easy way to make money, after which they could return home (P4). She worried that because they had consented the court would not value the evidence. It seems that she was right to be concerned about this. As a judge in Vladivostok told me, "as witnesses these groups [of victims] are different. They may change their statements or what they say because they are bribed with money, and then they will just take the money and go away. . . . Most are unprotected and from bad families. They are a specific contingent. They start in prostitution because they want to be grown up and have everything right away" (J3).

By the time the investigations end and the trials begin, many of the women have moved on with their lives and do not want to publicly retell what they did and what was done to them (P4).[18] This can be especially true in small towns, where there would be no way not to have their personal information revealed. In one case (no. 74), opened in Kirov in 2008, the main organizer of the sex trafficking ring was not arrested until 2011. Despite good participation of victim witnesses in the trial of the traffickers who were prosecuted right away, by the time the organizer's trial occurred in 2012, fewer than half were still willing to testify. Procurators and judges may interpret victims' reluctance to testify as an indication of guilt or complicity.

Use of Video to Capture the Transaction

With all the difficulties inherent in collecting victim testimony and having it trusted by the other actors in the criminal justice system, it is perhaps no surprise that law enforcement has preferred other ways to gather evidence for human trafficking prosecutions. Capturing evidence of the moment of sale is one way to do this. The technique became even more common after 2008, when the human trafficking law was amended to state that the purchase or sale of a person was itself considered a crime, regardless of whether there was any intent to exploit that person.

This behavior is a rational response to law enforcement's organizational strengths of investigating a crime that occurs at a particular place and point in time. It is also a response to agents' incentive structure, allowing them to clear cases easily by presenting procurators with one piece of definitive evidence that

---

18. Trials of criminal cases that involve sexual crimes or in which it is necessary to ensure the security of trial participants can be closed by court order (CPC Article 241). In practice, such instances make up only a small percentage of the criminal cases heard every year in Russia. For example, in 2013 only 1 percent of cases were heard in closed hearings (http://cdep.ru/userimages/sudebnaya_statistika/Svedeniya_za_2013.xls).

proves the crime. If they build the case from multiple pieces of evidence, they are relying on the other people who handle the case to accept the story that they have put together. As one judge suggested: "The reason human trafficking cases are so rare is that they [agents] want to use a more understandable and clear charge. It's easier to prove that way. With human trafficking, you have to find the seller, the buyer, and the victim and question all of them and show the transactions. With other crimes—like kidnapping, where you just have to find the person and the victim—there is less of an evidence base that you need to gather" (J2).

In addition, focusing on the transaction fits closely with agents' informal understandings of what makes human trafficking different from other crimes—that money is exchanged. However, it too has its drawbacks. Without undercover work to conduct purchases, bookkeeping records that indicate that the transactions have taken place, or information that allows agents to track the trafficker and video record the transaction, it is very difficult to capture evidence of this phase of human trafficking. Capturing the transaction in real time requires proactive police work, not always a strength given the resource constraints and incentive structures facing most Russian law enforcement agencies. But with evidence of the transaction itself, little other evidence is required. As one investigator in Moscow told me in a follow-up interview in 2012, police strategy has increasingly focused on undercover purchases of victims precisely because it is so much easier to get a conviction if there is video evidence (M17).

The strategy of using undercover activity to get evidence of the sale is most developed in cases of child trafficking and represents the only spark of creative law enforcement practice surrounding the use of human trafficking laws. Because intent to exploit was difficult to find in cases of child selling (most often the children were going to parents who were infertile or could not otherwise have children), to prove the intent to exploit the children, agents arranged undercover purchases in which they told the sellers that they would be using the children to sell their organs or for prostitution or begging (all forms of exploitation outlined in Article 127.1). If the seller still went through with the sale, law enforcement could show that the sale was undertaken with the intent of exploitation and the human trafficking charge could be sustained (P7).

Establishing the intent to exploit in this way was a conscious strategy as explained by one operativnik from the Siberian Federal District. When asked by a reporter why he had to tell the seller that his ten-day-old daughter would be used for organ transplants, he said: "Without [telling them about the organs] we couldn't have put this 'father' behind bars. . . . In [the new Criminal Code] there is the buying and selling of people only for prostitution and other forms of sexual exploitation. But there is another point, buying and selling for 'removal of organs and skin.' To catch the trafficker here, we also had to prove that he sold [his daughter] for organs or prostitution; otherwise the criminal would only pay a fine" (Riabtsev 2005).

In this case the father was convicted to five years in prison, largely because he did not flinch when the terms of the sale were revealed by the undercover agent. Law enforcement seems to have identified this strategy early in their prosecutions of human trafficking cases. The first successful use of this strategy covered in the media was in 2005 in Bryansk, when the undercover agent making the purchase told the mother that the six-year-old girl she was selling would be used either for prostitution or for organ transplant. Those conditions did not deter her, and she was arrested after receiving the $10,000 from the agent. She was convicted and sentenced to six years in prison (no. 178).

Almost all cases of child trafficking have been brought down by undercover operations, although after the law was amended, the strategy of inventing a form of exploitation disappeared entirely. Now after receiving a tip that someone is looking to sell his or her child, law enforcement immediately arranges an undercover purchase. The operativniki usually pose as an infertile couple looking to adopt a child. Before the meeting takes place, the operative team sets up a video camera so they can capture the transaction in real time. Video recordings are particularly important, since many of the transactions involved in trafficking operations, especially domestic ones, take place outside normal banking channels (M14). Agents use marked money for the exchange, and as soon as the money and the child change hands, the suspects are arrested.

This evidence is compelling to judges. After the amendment to the law, almost all cases of child trafficking charged under the human trafficking laws had successful convictions. In 2010 four of five were convicted, in 2011 six of six, and in 2012 ten of twelve, with one still ongoing at the time of publication. In 2013 these figures were four of seven with three still ongoing.[19] After all, who can dispute video evidence of parents selling their child seemingly without remorse? In one case in the Kaluga region (no. 333) the sentencing document showed that only three pieces of evidence were needed to prove the case: the video of the transaction, the marked money used in the exchange, and the child's birth and vaccination certificates, which were given to the undercover officer at the time of the sale. In some ways it is not surprising that law enforcement has pursued these types of cases so successfully. They fit the type of case that agents like: short, simple, and with a high probability of conviction. In addition, crimes against children have special resonance in Russia, as elsewhere.

19. In 2009, the first year after the change, I could not find outcomes for three of the six cases opened. In the others, two cases had defendants who were convicted of human trafficking, and one was closed because the defendant was sent for psychiatric treatment (no. 364).

Although not as frequently, law enforcement has made undercover purchases for other types of trafficking. In Taganrog in the Rostov region (no. 47), Alexander Sviridov sold five men for 225,000 rubles ($8,035) to undercover agents to be used for slave labor. For the ones with documents, he charged 50,000 rubles each ($1,785). For the ones without documents, he offered a discount, selling them for 25,000 each ($893). The victims did not know they were being sold and thought they were being offered paid work in construction. In recruiting the men, Sviridov looked for strong men who could withstand the demands of construction work. When making the sale, he reportedly told the undercover officers: "They're strong, they work hard and eat little. You don't even have to pay them and can feed them the minimum. The expenses are minor, maybe some cigarettes. They're not going to give you trouble and if they try to run away, we'll find them, don't worry" (Samsonova 2007). Sviridov was charged with human trafficking, but the outcome of the case is unclear.

Corroborating Evidence

Prosecutions that pit a victim against an abuser can be very difficult to prosecute without corroborating evidence (Lievore 2004). According to one operativnik, the investigators with whom he has worked on trafficking cases have tended to view cases with only victim testimony as evidence warily, saying that they do not trust what victims say. Without other forms of evidence, the operativnik claimed, a procurator would not support a trafficking charge in court (M8). At the same time, law enforcement practice around the world has shown it is difficult to sustain a trafficking charge without victim testimony (Gallagher and Holmes 2008). That additional evidence beyond victim testimony is critical was confirmed by a judge in Vladivostok, who said: "What we look for as judges is the corroborating evidence. . . . For example, if there was physical restraint, some sort of bruises were documented. We also look for witnesses that can show objectively that the crimes happened and can support the statements of the victims . . . [and] that all the statements are also supported by expert analysis" (J3). But as one procurator noted, this is often just the problem: "With murder, we know what expert analyses to order and how to prove the case, but with human trafficking, it's a lot harder" (P3). The lack of experience and absence of investigative and judicial practice connected to the human trafficking laws means that these understandings are still not fully developed.

Other types of evidence that can be collected to help support a trafficking charge include physical evidence, other witness testimony, and medical evidence. Collecting these types of evidence is also a challenge and time consuming, which means that there may not be an incentive for law enforcement to put in the extra work required to turn a case they could easily charge and clear under a different statute into a human trafficking case. These problems are compounded if the trafficking case has an international dimension and the necessary corroborating evidence is located in one or several other countries.

PHYSICAL EVIDENCE

Even the routine gathering of physical evidence can be a challenge in a human trafficking case. Human traffickers are both businessmen and criminals. They are generally smart and know how to hide their tracks well. Investigators must be familiar with the different ways that trafficking rings can operate and know what types of evidence could be valuable for proving the trafficking charge. Seemingly unconnected pieces of evidence, at least in the eyes of an operativnik doing a crime scene search, can later be put together to show a trafficking scheme. Accounting records, work schedules, travel documents, and confiscated passports can all contain evidence of exploitation (M19). Being able to show the physical place victims were being exploited is crucial. Especially in cases of sex trafficking, evidence of the exploitation, such as condoms or other sex paraphernalia, can be valuable. Any objects that show that the victims were beaten or held—such as bats, night sticks, or handcuffs—are also important, especially since in deciding whether to support a human trafficking charge, procurators and judges often use the informal criterion of ability to escape (M8).

A manual written by the MVD for investigators of trafficking cases adopts a comprehensive approach to evidence gathering, suggesting: "during searches for human trafficking crimes, there is one recognized method—so that nothing is missed, it is necessary to seize everything. Later, you can always return what was taken" (MVD 2008).[20] Technology can be a valuable source of information. The manual suggests that it all be seized and then taken to an expert who can examine the hard drives, Internet activity, e-mail, and cell phone records on the suspect's computers. To add to the evidentiary base, law enforcement can wiretap phone conversations and film locations where they think exploitation is taking place (M19, M13, P4). If the exploitation did take place abroad, recorded phone calls can be a good way of proving it (P3). Several cases explicitly mentioned that law

---

20. Searches (*obysk*) and seizures (*vyemka*) can be carried out on the order (*postanovlenie*) of an investigator. If the search takes place in a home or residence, it requires a judicial warrant, unless that home or residence is also the crime scene. During the search, any items deemed to be related to the crime can be seized. After the search is conducted, it must be recorded in a document (*protokol*) outlining the location and circumstances of the objects, documents, or valuables that were discovered and whether they were surrendered voluntarily or without consent. All objects seized must be listed, specifically described, and shown to all parties before being seized (CPC Article 182–83). This entire process must take place in the presence of two attesting witnesses (*poniatoi*) (CPC Article 170).

enforcement had used wiretaps to secure evidence of the traffickers' intent to sell victims.

Documentary evidence of the financial schemes that support the trafficking operation can help prove human trafficking. In fact, practitioners and scholars have suggested that with a clear money trail, the victim's testimony becomes less critical in proving the trafficking charge (Levchenko 2009). However, tracking a trafficking scheme through the financial documents requires a dedicated forensic accountant. Russia has specialists in this area, but not many, so their time is scarce. Forensic accountants are more likely to investigate things like money laundering and tax fraud, which are higher priorities for the state. Law enforcement may be wary of depending on this type of evidence, knowing there will likely be a backlog and they may not get the information they need in time to complete the investigation.

If someone in law enforcement is dedicated to pursuing the case as human trafficking, often the initiative for further evidence collection lies with him or her. One procurator explained to me that she personally traveled to Moscow to gather the evidence at the embassies of the countries to which the women were sent so she could get documents such as visa applications to show that they were issued on false passports. In that case, the falsified passports were critical for proving the guilt of one participant in the trafficking ring, whose main role was to falsify documents to enable the women to travel abroad (P3). However, this type of dedication is infrequently rewarded in a system that stresses speed and certainty in processing cases over precision of conviction under particular Criminal Code articles.

OTHER WITNESSES

Finding other witnesses is important but difficult, especially if they have been involved in the crime. In one case, the procurator told me, women were taken from Khabarovsk through Moscow to their destination, but instead of buying a normal airline ticket from their city to Moscow, the traffickers bribed an army pilot to take them on a military plane. Although the pilot ended up being one of the witnesses in the trial, it was difficult for his testimony to be admitted as evidence. He was considered untrustworthy because he had also committed crimes, including taking a bribe and misusing state equipment. Other witnesses frequently include prostitutes working voluntarily and drivers who knew the crime was being committed but were not technically part of the trafficking ring. Their testimony is viewed with similar skepticism by judges and procurators. Although a potentially rich source of information, the law enforcement personnel I spoke to said they did not generally use the clients of the prostitutes as witnesses because of similar concerns about reliability (M17, M19). Witnesses may also be frightened to cooperate if the trafficking was conducted by an organized criminal group because they are afraid of reprisal or violence (M5).

Another source of information that law enforcement could use in cases where the trafficking rings are highly organized is lower-level participants who could reveal information about others higher up in the trafficking chain. After 2009, when a law was passed allowing law enforcement to reward suspects who cooperate in this way, this approach has been used quite successfully in trafficking cases (Tumanov and Shmaraeva 2009). The data set includes twelve cases in which information provided by suspects led to significantly better investigative outcomes. For example, in a case in the Chuvash Republic only through the cooperation of the woman ringleader of a sex trafficking operation was law enforcement able to find the rest of the group, which included several law enforcement officials (no. 319).

MEDICAL AND FORENSIC EVIDENCE

Other evidence that can be convincing is medical evidence, both physical and psychological. Evidence of sexually transmitted diseases, damage to the female reproductive organs, skin problems, problems with the nervous system, infections, lung problems, and bruising can all be signs of physical trauma induced by human trafficking. In addition, there may be evidence of digestive problems because of the feeding regimes imposed on the victims by their traffickers (Zimmerman et al. 2006; Zimmerman 2008). Russian law outlines the procedures for having expert testimony and analysis (*ekspertiz*) accepted into the case file. According to the Criminal Procedure Code, forensic expert analysis must be done by a government institution, not a private expert like a doctor at a rehabilitation clinic (CPC Article 195).[21] In trafficking cases, this can be a disincentive for gathering this type of evidence since the victim may have to voluntarily submit to multiple invasive medical or psychological examinations just so they can be included in the case file as official evidence. Complicating this situation, there is usually only one certified location in each city, which means victims have to travel significant distances to get the proper examinations (Khodzhaeva 2011).

Broader Institutional Problems in Investigations
Inexperience and Lack of Guidance

After the trafficking law was passed, the greatest problem plaguing law enforcement was a lack of experience in putting together a human trafficking case.

---

21. This is also the case in France and many other civil law systems. See McKillop 1997 and Merryman and Perez-Perdomo 2007.

As one academic I spoke with suggested: "The problem is not that they [agents] don't want to start using this law; the problem is that it's a new norm and they don't know how to use it. A lot of it is procedural, and there are a lot of changes to work though" (A3). In both my interviews and in news reports from early cases, investigators specifically mentioned that they had nowhere to turn for advice or help. In response to a question about whether agents had asked other regional law enforcement agencies for assistance in putting together their first case, one officer told me: "Whom would we have asked for help? We figured it all out ourselves; we didn't go to anyone for help. This was the first case, a precedent. We had no experience—not in the FSB, not in the Procuracy—and no one to turn to for information. We learned how to do it ourselves. There were probably lots of mistakes, which is why it took so long" (O30).

Yet the case that this officer was working on in Mari El was opened in December 2006, a year after the first successful trafficking prosecution in Saratov (no. 161)—opened in June 2004 and finished in April 2005—and several others had been completed. Information was available, but without an easily accessible centralized information-sharing system the agents in this case were essentially starting from scratch. This is part of a broader problem of information sharing across regions.[22] In my interviews, people from at least three different regions claimed to have opened the first trafficking case in Russia (Khabarovsk in January 2005, Saratov in June 2004, and Mari El in December 2006). News media reports cited another region that claimed to have the first case in Russia, opened in September 2005 (no. 272). In this case, the courtroom procurator in Kurgan, Andrei Banshchikov, said: "In the Urals region this is the first case like this. We tried to find similar experience in other regions in Russia, but we couldn't find anything. So we can say this is the first one in the country" (Efimov 2006). The uncertainty of using a new law is increased significantly if you think you are the first one using it.

In the MVD, information tends to go down but not back up the hierarchy. There is little sharing of practice horizontally among regions, so often individual local agents have to develop practice on their own through trial and error. This

---

22. This situation has improved somewhat because of the 2008 law requiring courts to publish their decisions online to increase transparency. See Federal Law no. 262-FZ, "Ob obespechenii dostupa k informatsii o deiatel'nosti sudov v Rossiiskoi Federatsii," of December 22, 2008 (SZ RF, 2008, no. 51 (part 1), item 6217). However, the project in its current state is hindered by the ability to search country-wide under particular Criminal Code statutes and the failure of many courts to list anything beyond basic information (defendant name, charges, dates of court proceedings). Some decisions have been made available at the Supreme Court level with the victims' names blacked out, but at the regional and local levels such an outcome may require too many resources. Some independent Web sites have stepped in to categorize and make court decisions searchable, but they are limited by what is released by the courts.

leaves curious, ambitious law enforcement with only one option, calling around to find an office that has seen a human trafficking case. Especially in the first few years, the number of offices that fit this description was small, and those who had been successful were even fewer. If agents can get their hands on them, informal guidance from previous case files and court decisions can be extremely helpful in putting together a human trafficking case. These documents outline possible evidence and ways to connect that evidence to show elements of the trafficking crime. Unsurprisingly, the time pressures of clearing a case quickly make officers unlikely to do this, though occasionally I heard about and talked to dedicated agents who did put in this level of effort, some going as far as to research Russia's obligations under the Palermo protocol to try to make their trafficking cases better.

It does seem, however, that once a case has been investigated and prosecuted in a region, others in that region rely on that experience. The decisions made in early cases create path dependencies, as human trafficking is a rare enough crime that if it is discovered a second or third time it will likely be assigned to the investigator who dealt with it the first time around. Within one year in Mari El, for example, two enormous trafficking rings were brought down. Both trafficked women to the EU for sexual exploitation. There were rumors that some of the participants may have known and learned from one another, but if so, law enforcement learned too. The first case—in relation to Nikolai Shirchenko, Vadim Petrov, and his tourist firm Puma—began in June 2006 (no. 29). Only a few months later, in November 2006, a similar case, that of Alexander Semyonov and Valentina Arkhipova and their tourist firm Piligrim, was opened (no. 30). In interviews, agents who worked on the Puma case suggested that the difficulties that they had encountered during the process were all lessons that the investigators of the Piligrim case were able to learn and consequently do their work much more efficiently (O30, P3). Despite being opened almost six months later, the Piligrim case was sent to court three months earlier than the Puma case. The final cases looked almost identical, with similar numbers of victim witnesses and similar types of evidence collected. When the cases were decided, the Piligrim ringleaders were convicted of more years on the trafficking charge than the Puma leaders were. In an interview after the Puma verdict was handed down, one of the procurators expressed frustration and vowed to appeal based on the fact that the sentences for this case were lower but the crimes were nearly identical (O30, P3).

Time Limits and Division of Functions

The long chain of people through which a case must pass creates a lack of ownership over that case. No link in the chain really has any incentive to follow a case through or fight to keep a crime charged under a particular article of the Criminal Code. No matter how much hard work agents put in, the charge could be changed by the next person in the chain. So, even if a law enforcement agent thinks he has a human trafficking case and collects what he thinks is evidence to support it, another actor in the system may disagree and will not support the decision to charge human trafficking. There are at least five points during the investigation and prosecution at which a case could have its charge changed.[23] After opening a case, and during the investigation, the investigator can change the charges from those under which the case was originally registered. The head of the investigative agency to which the investigator belongs can change it during oversight. The procurator can change it when he or she looks at the indictment. The courtroom procurator can also refuse to support the charges in court. Finally, the judge can change the charges on hearing the case. This means that no one has an incentive to put in extra effort at any stage of the process. This pattern is evident looking at official MVD statistics. In 2006, only 47 of the 125 total cases registered under human trafficking and use of slave labor were officially opened. In 2007, 54 of a possible 139 total cases were opened. In addition, because investigative jurisdiction over human trafficking is split between the Investigative Committee and the MVD, the issue of cross-agency cooperation affects the decision to open any given case.

One problem that this separation of functions creates is that there must be a shared understanding of what the elements of the crime are among the people who work on the case. Unlike murder or kidnapping, where there is generally agreement on what constitutes the crime (a dead body or a missing one), trafficking is more complicated. There are multiple elements (buying/selling, recruitment, transportation, transfer, harboring, receipt), and as outlined in previous chapters, the law is not exactly clear on which ones must be satisfied to constitute the crime. My interviews uncovered wide variations in what people thought was required to prove human trafficking, views not consistent across agencies or regions. Some believed that if you cannot prove that money was exchanged, trafficking did not happen or cannot be conclusively proven (A2). Others felt that the exploitation was the most important evidentiary requirement. Still others believed that you cannot have a case of human trafficking for sexual exploitation if the women are not sent abroad (M8). An even more conservative interpretation of the statute that I heard from several people was that all the actions had

23. In theory, these divisions are meant to act as internal checks within the system so that innocent people are not mistakenly prosecuted or sent to jail. Before the 2001 Criminal Procedure Code, this result was accomplished by the overarching principle of finding the truth (*istina*), whereby the procurator was supposed to collect both incriminating and exculpatory evidence in each case (Paneyakh et al. 2012, 10).

to be proven as well as the intent to exploit or exploitation (N19, U1). There is no resolution from the Supreme Court standardizing the proper interpretation of either of the human trafficking statutes. As a result, the next person in the criminal justice process could legitimately have a different interpretation of the statute and even draw on existing judicial practice to support that interpretation.

Operativniki do not collect the initial evidence for a case in a vacuum. They have some idea of what type of crime they have encountered and what evidence they need for a successful investigation of that crime. With trafficking cases, they could waste time doing extensive police work on a charge that may not be sustained. If the case is never opened, their work will not be reflected in the statistics (Paneyakh et al. 2012, 61). Communication between the investigator and the operativnik to ensure that the necessary evidence is gathered for a trafficking charge may occur, but usually takes place informally, since investigators are technically not supposed to be involved in the case until it is officially opened. More often, however, the splitting of functions means that an operativnik will hand over the evidence he has gathered to the investigator and be done with his part in the case. The investigator can choose whether to open the case and what to charge, if anything. This can be particularly problematic if the operativnik is part of an elite unit which specializes in collecting evidence on a particular type of crime but then encounters a "generalist" investigator who does not know that particular article of the Criminal Code well and may be less inclined to take the time to read all the commentaries on how to use it. The investigators may also be lazy and not care or may indeed have a different interpretation of what the law says than the operativnik.

I heard several stories of operativniki who fought with investigators to make sure that trafficking charges were included, but such behavior is more the exception than the rule. In one case in Vladivostok where two female victims were rescued, federal operativniki intervened to have the case opened. Immediately after the rescue, the local MVD had already prepared a statement for the women to sign declining to register a complaint. The local procurator also refused to open the case, saying there was no evidence of a crime. Without the help of a local anti-trafficking NGO and several dedicated upper-level regional operativniki, the case would not have moved forward at all. Only when the federal operativniki became involved was the case opened—but as recruitment into prostitution, not as trafficking (A5, M13, N7). Many operativniki with whom I spoke expressed frustration at the fact that investigators frequently refused to go forward with trafficking charges after they had worked hard to gather evidence.

All this negotiation and evidence gathering takes place within the strict time limits imposed by the Criminal Procedure Code. Once a case is officially opened, investigators have two months to complete their investigation before they must

TABLE 5.1 Length of trafficking cases charged under trafficking laws, n=187

	NUMBER OF CASES				
LENGTH OF CASE	INTERNATIONAL SEX	DOMESTIC SEX	INTERNATIONAL LABOR	DOMESTIC LABOR	CHILD
< 6 mos.	2	5	1	5	17
6 mos.–1 yr.	5	16	1	21	12
1–2 yrs.	9	21	5	20	2
> 2 yrs.	9	20	4	10	1
Average (in mos.)	24.3	20.4	23.7	18.3	7.3

request permission from above to continue. Table 5.1 shows the length of human trafficking cases from opening to final disposition. The average case, including appeals, took about 19.3 months to complete, with the longest lasting 61 months and the shortest 2 months.[24] This is significantly longer than the average case for a grave crime investigated by a local law enforcement body, such as murder or rape. In such cases pretrial investigation and trial proceedings combined usually take from six months to a year.[25] The one organ trafficking case with a final disposition was completed in three months and is not included below.

Human trafficking cases tend to get more rather than less complex as they are investigated. During the investigation, law enforcement usually realizes that the exploitation is more extensive and has gone on longer than previously thought. Agents then have to spend significant time identifying and finding additional victims. Newspaper articles often describe the complexity of the cases by referring to how many volumes of material each case took up, sometimes over a hundred.[26] Newspaper articles also describe the difficulties associated with prosecuting labor trafficking cases in which victims are foreign and do not speak Russian well. Delays are attributed to translation, finding victims, housing them, and convincing them to testify. In international cases, especially those in which the Russian traffickers are arrested with their foreign partners, there are significant procedural delays for translation and gathering of documents, extradition, and so on. Because failure to abide by the time limits is reflected in statistical reports as a violation, much of the investigative activity takes place before the official

---

24. Length of case was calculated from the date the case was officially opened to the date the verdict was handed down or the date the conviction went into legal effect (after all appeals were exhausted or ten days after the verdict if the defendant chose not to appeal). I used the arrest date as the date of opening if I did not have the opening date. It is illegal to arrest someone without opening a formal case against them. I did not always have data on when the sentences went into legal effect so if anything, this underestimates the length of these cases.

25. There are no official statistics on this point. This information comes from informal conversations with members of law enforcement.

26. Each volume of a case file contains a maximum of five hundred pages and must be hand-sewn together by the investigator.

opening of the case. Therefore, these numbers are probably an underestimation of how long it takes trafficking cases to go through the system.

International and Cross-Regional Cases

When trafficking occurs across international borders, the case becomes even more complex, especially if it involves more than one other country. Traffickers are not limited by national borders, but Russian law enforcement is. As one procurator noted: "The biggest problem with these cases is that Russian law enforcement agencies work on our territory and half the criminals are in other countries" (P3). Financial records and proof of exploitation may also be abroad. Once the trafficking is outside national borders, law enforcement must rely on the notoriously slow and cumbersome procedures of Interpol to get information from its colleagues in other countries, unless Russia has a Mutual Legal Assistance Treaty (MLAT) with the other country involved (N3, N20). Even though Interpol has made human trafficking a priority, according to one investigator with whom I spoke, it is more focused on finding criminals on the run than facilitating the exchange of documentary evidence among countries (M8). Like all law enforcement agencies, Interpol is also limited by time and resources.

In addition, Russian law enforcement also faces a pervasive distrust from the international law enforcement community with respect to information sharing, especially with the increase in politically motivated prosecutions. Consequently, agents have an incentive to try to pursue the case under statutes that allow them to prosecute domestically.

The time limits imposed on investigations can make the time required to gather information from other countries prohibitive, since a case must be officially opened in Russia before Russian law enforcement can make official requests to other countries. One procurator in Khabarovsk explained to me why she chose not to bring in evidence from China, where the victims were exploited: "Every piece of evidence has to go through Moscow's central Interpol bureau, be translated, officially stamped, and sent to the other country. And for any clarifying questions like getting the exact address [where they were exploited], you get back a whole stack of documents in Chinese" (P4). This resulted in her not pursuing a human trafficking charge. Instead she used the recruitment into prostitution charge, which required only showing that the victims were taken across the border, not the specifics of their exploitation abroad. Consequently it is perhaps unsurprising that fewer international cases of trafficking are prosecuted in Russia than domestic ones. The international cases that are pursued tend to be large and investigated by high-level security services, such as the FSB, that have significantly more resources at their disposal. The FSB was involved in investigating ten of the fifty-one international cases in the data set.

If the suspect is abroad, the situation is even more complicated. Cooperation on the extradition of suspects to or from Russia can be challenging and time consuming. In one large international sex trafficking case (no. 262), the accused, Ludmila Nesterova, organized a trafficking ring that brought twelve Russian women to Spain from Nizhnii Novgorod, promising them good, high-paying jobs. Instead, they were forced into prostitution, then kept there by a system of debt bondage and their inability to speak the language. When one of the women managed to contact her relatives, they reported it to the Russian police who placed Nesterova on the international wanted list and contacted their counterparts in Spain. In December 2008, Nesterova was detained there and the procurator general's office requested her extradition to Russia. The Spanish government agreed but wanted to put her on trial in Spain first. In December 2009, she was sentenced to four years in prison and began to serve her time in Spain. The following March, while still imprisoned in Spain, she was transferred to Russia to stand trial in Nizhnii Novgorod, the region where most of the recruitment had taken place, alongside her accomplice, Tatiana Borodavina. In July 2011, Nesterova was convicted, to a term of 9.5 years in prison (Borodavina received 8.5 years), and immediately returned to Spain to finish her sentence there. In April 2013, almost five years after she had first been caught and after serving the full sentence handed down by the Spanish court, she returned to Russia to serve her Russian sentence.

The Russian Constitution does not allow extradition of its citizens to face criminal charges abroad unless they have a bilateral extradition treaty with the requesting country. The Criminal Procedure Code does have provisions for trials of Russian citizens in Russia for crimes committed abroad with the participation of foreign experts, but these are rare (Harding 2007). Russia has sent a number of citizens from the Commonwealth of Independent States (CIS) back to their own countries to face charges. There have been a number of cases of extradition to Uzbekistan in which the exploitation occurred in Russia, but because both the traffickers and the victims were Uzbek citizens, prosecution was pursued there.

Investigations of trafficking crimes within the CIS are aided by an agreement for cooperation on criminal matters.[27] With states outside the CIS, the only way around having to use Interpol is an MLAT. MLATs establish a structure for information exchange during investigations and define the limits of what sorts of information can be exchanged. Russia has agreements with Israel, the United Arab

---

27. The CIS signatories to this agreement are: Azerbaijan, Armenia, Belarus, Kazakhstan, Kyrgyzstan, Moldova, Russia, Tajikistan, Turkmenistan, Ukraine, and Uzbekistan (CIS 1994). Georgia ended its relationship with the CIS in 2009; as of 2014, Ukraine and Moldova are ending theirs. The convention can be found at http://cis.minsk.by/main.aspx?uid=614.

Emirates, India, Spain, and the United States, among others, but their effectiveness may vary with the political winds. According to one senior investigator in Moscow, agents rarely work with countries with which they have no agreement (M17).

Another way around international cooperation through Interpol is personal contacts. Throughout the years, there have been numerous international conferences in Russia and abroad in which law enforcement agents were invited to exchange experiences fighting trafficking. Almost all these conferences end with exchanges of personal phone numbers and promises of assistance if necessary. In one case, connections made between Turkish law enforcement and law enforcement agents in the Tatar Republic in Russia led to the rescue of a girl trafficked from Kazan to Turkey. When the Russian police called, the Turkish officer was able to facilitate finding and freeing the woman (N44). But these personal contacts are more the exception than the rule.

Even with cases within Russia, there can be problems with jurisdictional boundaries across regions.[28] In one case (no. 82), two sixteen-year-old girls were taken under false pretenses from Tula to the Moscow region by two men whom they had just met. Instead of going to the city where they thought they would be meeting the men, the girls were taken to a cottage on the outskirts of Moscow, joining several other girls who were already there, and told they would have to work as prostitutes or else they would be beaten. One of them escaped and went to the police, after which the Tula and Moscow regional police staged a joint operation to rescue the rest of them. But after the raid, the cross-regional cooperation fell apart. The case was bounced from procurator's office to procurator's office between the regions as they tried to decide who had jurisdiction to prosecute and which charges to press. According to Alexander Korneev, a procurator who worked on the case in the Moscow region,

> The case was difficult because it was passed between different courts. At first it was investigated in the place where most of the witnesses lived, in Donsk [Tula region]. Then it came to our court [according to another interview, because the suspects lived there]. The suspects were charged with Article 126 [kidnapping]. But the court did not agree with that charge. The investigation fell apart, and by law, we could not keep the suspects under arrest any longer. The maximum amount of time we can

---

28. The Criminal Procedure Code outlines which region's police will have jurisdiction if the crime is committed in multiple places, but even with this guidance, it is not always clear. If the crime starts in one location and finishes in another, the investigating agency should be the one in the final location (CPC Article 152[2]). If the crime occurs in two places simultaneously, the investigating agency with jurisdiction is the one where the majority of the crime took place or where the most serious of the crimes took place (CPC Article 152[3]).

> keep them under arrest is a year. That time ran out, and so we had to free
> them. (Gumbert 2010; Korneev and Romanova 2010)

Eventually the case was closed entirely.

There have also been some positive examples of interregional cooperation. In another case (no. 160) where the women were trafficked from the Voronezh region to the outskirts of Moscow, the UBOP officer Evgenii Shekhovtsov noted: "This variant of the crime is very rare. In this situation, the sale was committed by a resident of Borisoglebsk [in the Voronezh region], and the buying was done by someone from Noginsk [in the Moscow region]. The Noginsk UBOP had to conduct a joint operation with the Borisoglebsk UBOP to arrest the buyer and the seller" (voronezh.rfn.ru 2004). There have also been several cross-regional investigative groups set up in the North Caucasus to deal with child trafficking rings there.

The complications surrounding evidence collection, when combined with the incentive structures of Russian law enforcement, make it unsurprising that trafficking prosecutions are few and far between. These cases are time consuming and complicated, and the system does not reward or encourage their pursuit. The average length of a case charged as human trafficking or slave labor is over eighteen months. Although this total varies somewhat by type of trafficking, law enforcement knows it will be in for a long and complex investigation if it opens a case as trafficking. Agents will inevitably have to ask for extensions beyond the time limits imposed by the Criminal Procedure Code, extensions that must be granted by the head of the regional MVD. Such requests lead to more scrutiny from above, something that agents try assiduously to avoid. Because trafficking is a process, evidence may be scattered over multiple regions or multiple countries, necessitating cross-regional or international cooperation and costing even more time. The need for such a heavy investment of time and effort in a system that rewards the rapid completion of cases makes it unlikely that agents will choose to pursue a case as trafficking when they have other, simpler, more familiar options. The division of functions and the ambiguity of the language of the law means that others in the system, having legitimately different interpretations of the statute's language, may decide not to pursue human trafficking charges because they seem inappropriate.

Evidence gathering is also fraught with difficulties. Victim testimony is the surest way for law enforcement to prove that a person was exploited or that there was some intent to exploit, but such testimony can be hard to obtain. With international and cross-regional cases, the absence of places to shelter victims can inhibit their ongoing participation in investigative activities. Law enforcement rarely gets all the information it needs from one interview with a victim. Unfortunately, the effects of trauma and marginal social backgrounds can make victim testimony unreliable in the eyes of procurators and judges. Victims may change their stories, lie, or refuse to continue cooperating. Without shelter and psychological assistance, neither of which law enforcement is equipped to provide, victims may simply disappear. Obtaining evidence that a transaction has taken place is convincing to both judges and procurators, but this outcome requires that law enforcement know about the transaction in advance, so that agents can videotape it or participate in it undercover. In sum, the combination of institutional incentives and the difficulties of gathering evidence for a trafficking case make it completely logical that law enforcement would try to avoid trafficking charges and instead charge trafficking crimes under other statutes.

A Comparative Note

Although the procedural requirements and the particular institutional incentives described here are Russian, the difficulty of gathering evidence to prosecute a crime as complex as human trafficking makes pursuing it a challenge around the world. In fact, the US Department of State calls human trafficking cases the "most labor and time intensive matters undertaken by the Department of Justice" (quoted in Farrell et al. 2012, 8). Law enforcement agencies in the United States, Germany, and the Netherlands have all noted that trafficking cases are long, uncertain, and complicated to investigate and therefore a likely waste of scarce resources (Farrell et al. 2008; Herz 2011; Oude Breuil et al. 2011; Verhoeven and van Gestel 2011; Farrell and Pfeffer 2014). The difficulty of producing victim witnesses whose testimony will be considered reliable in court causes prosecutors to give up cases altogether or prosecute under other statutes instead of trafficking ones (Warren 2012). As in Russia, countries like the United Kingdom (Kelly and Regan 2000), Germany (Herz 2006), and Australia (David 2007) are experimenting with proactive investigation techniques that do not rely as heavily on victim testimony.

Law enforcement worldwide complain about the lack of options for sheltering victims and keeping them in the country for the duration of the investigation, but most have made more progress than Russia. In fact, Russia is the only country in the post-Soviet region without some sort of shelter provisions for human trafficking victims (Dean 2014). Many countries, especially in Europe, offer temporary residence permits and reflection periods for victims to decide whether to cooperate with law enforcement; in others (United States, Belgium, Austria, and Serbia, among others), permits are contingent on cooperation with law enforcement (Craggs and Martens 2010; Simeunovic-Patic and Copic 2010).

INDICTMENT, TRIAL, AND SENTENCING

In 2004 the Omsk region had one of the first successful convictions under the new slave labor statute in Russia (no. 164). The accused, Mukan Zhuandykov, had promised four local Russian men good pay but then locked them up, chained one to a bed, and forced them to work for free in his garden, barely feeding them and housing them in horrible conditions—slavery by any standard. When the appeals court reduced the conviction of four years imprisonment to seven months because there were no "severe consequences" to Zhuandykov's actions, the reporter covering the case noted: "If the procurator is at peace with the decision of the appeals court [to reduce the sentence to seven months from four years] and does not seek another review of the sentence, this guardian of law will have to acknowledge that the first pancake always has to be thrown out."[1] Using a favorite Russian idiom—that the first time doing something new is almost always a failure—he expressed the fear of every procurator and judge in Russia regarding a new law, that the conviction will not stand and their performance statistics will be negatively affected.

This chapter explores the final stages of a trafficking case, the indictment and trial. It is important to remember that if a trafficking case has gotten this far and is still being pursued under trafficking or slave labor charges, it is a surprise. It will have passed through several different people, each with his or her own

---

1. Quoted in a weekly roundup of news from Omsk from an article called "He Doesn't Consider Himself a Monster," published on October 6, 2004 (Regnum.ru 2004).

concerns about moving the case forward as human trafficking and the power to reclassify the case as something else. It is not, however, a surprise that having made it through the process under any charge, trafficking cases often result in convictions. The Russian system is strongly biased toward conviction, in large part because of the assessment system, with an acquittal rate of less than 1 percent for cases that end up in court (Paneyakh 2014). This chapter begins by outlining the various choices about charging that investigators and procurators make at the indictment stage and the alternative paths that have been pursued in both sex and labor trafficking cases. As has been made clear throughout the book, the choice to use alternative articles and stick close to the familiar is quite logical given the incentives that everyone in the system has to ensure that cases are cleared and convicted.

Even if the procurator approves a trafficking charge and it moves forward to trial, there are still two more people in the criminal justice chain who have the power to make a trafficking case into something else—usually a less serious crime—or to simply remove the human trafficking charge altogether and pursue the case as something different. The first is the courtroom procurator, who, of all the actors in the system, may have the greatest incentive to get rid of the human trafficking charges because he or she has the most at stake. Courtroom procurators' sole job is to secure a conviction in court, and they base their assessments on this fact. If they are nervous about the case or uncertain about the evidence fitting neatly into the Criminal Code article as understood by the judge, it is easier to simply refuse to support the trafficking charge in court and proceed with other charges than take the chance that they will not get a conviction. This is one reason why most human trafficking cases are brought with multiple charges.

Judges are formally the final decision makers about the strength of a trafficking charge and the evidence collected to prove it. Their careers, too, are assessed based on statistical indicators: the number of reversals by higher courts, the number of acquittals, and whether they keep within the time limits imposed by the Criminal Procedure Code (Solomon 2012). In a system without guidance from precedent, judges have to hedge their bets, uncertain about how a higher court will interpret their decisions on appeal. With a new law or one that is rarely used, like trafficking, judges may have an incentive to find that the human trafficking charge is not supported by the evidence, but some other charge that is more familiar and less likely to be rejected on appeal is supported. This is not to suggest that judges will not convict someone on human trafficking charges if those charges are warranted, but that if there is any uncertainty whatsoever about how the law should be interpreted, they too will err on the safe side.

The second part of the chapter looks at cases that have gone to trial, discussing the strategies that procurators and defense lawyers use in court and on appeal as well as the reasoning that judges cite when they convict or acquit defendants of human trafficking. It also tracks the sentences that traffickers have received for their crimes. Russian law allows for variation in judicial practice across regions. Looking at judicial reasoning can give us important insight into what this group of actors does and, perhaps more important, does not see as human trafficking. Technically, the judge's role in the Russian, Roman-law-based legal system is limited to applying the facts to the statute to see if they fit or not, but there is significant room for interpretation given the somewhat unclear wording of the trafficking and slave labor statutes.

While the Russian legal system does not have formal precedent, the decisions made by judges at the local and regional levels can have an important impact on future practice. First, they contribute to judicial practice on the specific Criminal Code article. When practice diverges too much among regions, the Presidium of the Supreme Court may collect all the cases and issue a resolution about the proper interpretation of the law to guide lower-court judges. Second, there is an important local impact for future cases of trafficking. Trafficking is a rare enough crime that whenever a case of trafficking is uncovered, it is likely that investigators, procurators, and judges will look to previous cases (if there are any) within the region for guidance. Finally, there may be informal advice shared among law enforcement agents when a trafficking case is uncovered and being investigated, based largely on how previous cases have proceeded through the system.

Although I have framed many of these moments as "choosing" to use particular articles of the Criminal Code rather than others, most Russian law enforcement agents do not consider this a choice. Instead, they take a doctrinal approach in which discretion is completely absent. The following is a typical response that I received from a procurator at a conference: "As to whether one [statute] is preferred over the other, it depends on how serious the crime is, whether there is enough evidence and if all the grounds exist" (P2). In the mind of law enforcement agents, the decision of what to charge is very technical. If the elements of the crime are there and they have evidence to support each element, they will charge that crime. However, with complex crimes like human trafficking, there are several possible interpretations of the evidence, each leading to different, equally legitimate charges. It is under these circumstances, where there are multiple possible charging options, that we can most clearly see the institutional machinery at work.

The Charging Decision

After all the evidence is gathered and placed into a case file by the investigator, the indictment (*obvinitel'noe zakliuchenie*) is written up and approved by a procurator. This document contains the final decision on the charges the investigator and procurator have deemed appropriate for the case. Approval of the indictment can be a formality, but as the overseers of the criminal justice system, procurators are ultimately responsible for the statistics and therefore success rates of prosecutions in that system. This means that they are acutely aware that a human trafficking charge could be difficult to prove in court and may decide to change the charges or send the case back and encourage the investigators to choose simpler ones. Of course, this does not mean that law enforcement avoids trafficking cases entirely. Agents must balance the likelihood that cases are cleared with other statistical assessment categories such as the comparison to the previous year's numbers. A significant drop in the number of trafficking cases from year to year does not look good for the criminal justice system either.

Alternative Charging Practices

Rather than expend the time, energy, and resources investigating cases as human trafficking, law enforcement agents who are unwilling or unable to take risks are likely to employ a deliberate strategy of charging under alternative articles of the Criminal Code. The practice of charging with alternative articles is evidenced by the fact that the data set, which captured any incident that was labeled human trafficking, use of slave labor, or commonly substitutable terms in the media contains 111 cases of sex and 121 cases of labor trafficking that were opened under alternative Criminal Code articles, almost as many as were opened under human trafficking statutes. The circumstances of each of these cases would have just as easily fit under human trafficking charges but for the disincentives to use those laws. Ironically, these are many of the same charges that law enforcement personnel used to prosecute traffickers before the human trafficking laws were adopted. The only type of trafficking that is not covered by any other statute is child trafficking for illegal adoption, unless it can be proven that the child was kidnapped first.

Another strategy used by law enforcement is to double up, charging both trafficking and another charge "for insurance" (M17). This can include any of the charges previously mentioned or a charge of organizing or participating in a criminal conspiracy or criminal organization (Article 210). Of the cases charged as trafficking, 65 percent of labor trafficking cases and 77 percent of sex trafficking cases were brought with additional charges. In Russian legal practice, it is less common to bring multiple charges against a suspect because each charge stands independently of the other charges and must be proven and, perhaps equally important, written up separately with its own body of evidence. Charging multiple crimes, then, increases the complexity of the case and the time that must be spent investigating it, which is another disincentive for adding trafficking charges to a case. The major exception to this is cases of child trafficking, in which only 15 percent were brought with additional charges. This is a reflection of the relatively straightforward nature of child trafficking cases in which a clear transaction takes place.

On one hand, the prospect of significant sentences may be one reason that investigators might choose to charge under one statute rather than another. After all, one of law enforcement's main jobs is convicting criminals and putting bad guys in jail. Furthermore, the system rewards convictions for grave and especially grave crimes, which human trafficking became after the 2008 amendments. As one of my MVD interviewees suggested in 2012, law enforcement was becoming frustrated with pursuing child and labor trafficking cases because the sentences ended up being so low (M17).

On the other hand, because of the perverse effects that institutionalized corruption has on law enforcement, perhaps it is a good thing that the sentences for trafficking are not high. Increasing the possible sentences for a crime may have the effect of lowering the number of cases brought because it creates opportunities for corruption. The increased risk of landing in jail for a longer period of time makes a suspect willing to pay more for the case not to be opened in the first place. This dynamic has been seen in the fight against corruption, with the price of bribes increasing as the penalties for engaging in corrupt behavior have increased (Krainova 2010). It is probably safe to assume a similar dynamic might be at work with other types of criminal cases, including trafficking.

The possible sentences for human trafficking and human trafficking-related articles are listed in table 6.1. Although the penalties for trafficking correspond with penalties worldwide and those required by international conventions, they are not that different from the penalties for crimes committed under articles that law enforcement uses as alternatives. In some cases, the alternatives carry even larger sentences than the trafficking statutes would. Given all the disincentives for pursuing a trafficking case as trafficking, the difference in possible sentences does not seem significant enough to get law enforcement to change its practice and begin using the human trafficking statutes in any case that might fit. As one operativnik in Moscow told me, "240 is only a little less harsh [than 127.1]. It is not a big difference in the sanctions, so why try harder?" (M14). When combined with the uncertainty of how a judge will react to a human trafficking charge, it is not a surprise that law enforcement agents would continue to take the safe bet, charging crimes they understand well.

ALTERNATIVE CHARGES FOR SEX TRAFFICKING CASES

Because my data collection methodology registered all incidents mentioned in the news media as trafficking (see appendix A for detail), I followed a number

TABLE 6.1   Possible maximum sentences under Criminal Code articles

	BASIC	1ST-LEVEL AGGRAVATING FACTORS	2ND-LEVEL AGGRAVATING FACTORS
127.1 (human trafficking)	up to 5 yrs., after 2008 6 yrs.	3–9 yrs.	8–15 yrs.
127.2 (use of slave labor)	up to 5 yrs.	3–9 yrs.	8–15 yrs.
240 (recruitment into prostitution)	up to 3 yrs.	up to 6 yrs.	3–8 yrs.
241 (organizing prostitution)	100,000 to 500,000 ruble fine	up to 6 yrs.	3–9 yrs.
127 (false imprisonment)	up to 2 yrs.	3–5 yrs.	4–8 yrs.
126 (kidnapping)	up to 5 yrs.	5–12 yrs.	6–15 yrs.
285/286 (abuse of authority/official position)	up to 80,000 ruble fine	up to 3 yrs.	up to 10 yrs.
322 (illegal border crossing)	up to 200,000 ruble fine	up to 5 yrs.	none
322.1 (organizing illegal migration)	up to 200,000 ruble fine	up to 5 yrs.	none

of cases that appeared on their face to be trafficking but did not end up being charged as such. Looking at these cases helps elucidate how law enforcement has learned to use the human trafficking laws and differentiate them from previously existing laws.

Especially in domestic sex trafficking cases, law enforcement rarely uses the human trafficking charge unless an actual monetary transaction has taken place, with the woman being sold by one person to another. Although there are many domestic cases of kidnapping or deceitful recruitment with the victims being forced into prostitution, it is rare that these cases are charged as human trafficking. Most of them ended up being charged (and often convicted) under prostitution-related statutes, though the accused could easily have been brought up on trafficking charges as well. In these cases, the activities (recruitment, transportation, transfer, harboring, and receipt of people) are all directed at involving the victim into some sort of sexual exploitation, the key criteria for a trafficking charge. In the data set of sex trafficking cases, there were 111 cases that could have qualified as human trafficking under Article 127.1 but were instead charged as other crimes. Most of these were domestic trafficking.

Laws on prostitution-related offenses are more familiar to law enforcement and are quicker and easier to investigate. Furthermore, most actors in the criminal justice system have experience with them, which means it is less likely that there will be confusion about the wording of the statute. Overall, this means the cases are more likely to be cleared and reflect well on agents' performance. Though they had tried to use the same statutes to prosecute traffickers before the trafficking laws were passed, they found them to be inadequate. Only with the amendments in 2003 did they become easier to use. These practices have been reinforced by the federal-level MVD, as they have conceptualized human trafficking as a suite of crimes that encompass the human trafficking articles but also include articles dealing with prostitution-related offenses and pornography as well as those facilitating illegal migration.

In an example of how this practice works, a man and a woman organized brothels in Astrakhan, forcing minors into prostitution through violence and threats (no. 106). The victims were deceitfully recruited through newspaper advertisements promising them high-paying jobs and then kept in an apartment and forced into prostitution. Although the organizers were charged with recruitment into prostitution, organizing prostitution, and false imprisonment and received sentences of 6 and 7.5 years, they also could have been charged with human trafficking. Using the trafficking statute, these men could have been charged with recruitment or harboring for the purpose of sexual exploitation. Aggravating factors might have included the threat of using or using force, trafficking in relation to two or more people (there were six victims), and/or trafficking in relation to a known minor (several of the victims were minors). Crimes that are charged as recruitment into prostitution do not appear to be any less violent or use any different means of coercion to keep the victims in the trafficking situation than cases charged as human trafficking.

One of the operativniki I spoke with in Khabarovsk made a similar complaint about a case in his region. In this case two contract soldiers forced two young women into a car, brought them to their apartment, and raped them (no. 275). They later decided to start prostituting the women, so they took pictures, sent them out by text message, and started selling their services. The women could not leave but somehow managed to send a message to one of their friends about what had happened, and the friend went to the police. The case was charged as kidnapping, not human trafficking. When I asked why, the operativnik said somewhat disdainfully, "It was investigated by the Procuracy and they didn't want to open it as 127.1 [human trafficking] (M8)."[2] This was a clear demonstration of interagency tensions, but also a clear example of why having a unified understanding among agencies of the definition of human trafficking is so important.

Increased ease of using the recruitment into prostitution statute for both domestic and international sex trafficking has enabled law enforcement to pursue

---

2. This incident took place before the investigators from the Procuracy were separated out into the Investigative Committee.

a significant number of cases in this way. Whereas before the 2003 changes, law enforcement did not see this statute as covering international cases, now there is a specific aggravating factor of "transport across Russian borders or illegal holding of someone abroad" attached to it. For the purposes of international sex trafficking, this makes these articles virtually interchangeable. The result has been particularly attractive to law enforcement personnel because the recruitment is usually the activity that occurs on Russian soil. In addition, the most difficult part of international investigations is retrieving evidence that the exploitation had taken place abroad. Gathering this evidence is unnecessary if agents use the recruitment into prostitution statute with the crossing borders aggravating factor, because they do not have to prove exploitation.

To cite one example, Sergei and Alexander Lazkov and Olga Krylova ran a trafficking operation from 2003 to 2006 in which they advertised high-paying jobs as masseuses, waitresses, dancers, and models in Spain to women from Novosibirsk. Once the women arrived, they were told they had to work off the debt paid to get them there (between 5,000 and 8,000 euros) in prostitution. Those who refused were threatened that they would be used for organ transplants or that their relatives' houses would be set on fire. One of the women managed to call her sister, who was married to a policeman in Madrid, and the women were eventually freed and returned to Russia (no. 249). Despite the fact that this case included all the "traditional" elements of trafficking, it was charged under Article 240: specifically, recruitment into prostitution with the aggravating factors of crossing the border and holding the victim abroad and after a premeditated agreement.[3] The practice of using recruitment into prostitution as the primary charge for international trafficking has declined over time. Now it is mostly used as a backup charge for international sex trafficking cases being charged under the human trafficking statutes.

The interchangeability of these two Criminal Code articles can also be seen by directly comparing charging decisions across regions. For example, in the following two cases, the scenarios were nearly identical, but the cases were charged under different statutes. Both men recruited women who were already in prostitution (St. Petersburg, no. 245) or who owed them money and were willing to work as prostitutes to pay it back (Saratov, no. 161) to go to Germany. The women were promised good money and living conditions and told that the recruiters would pay to get the necessary documents and plane tickets to get them

---

3. Despite the fact that some of their activities were committed before the trafficking law was enacted, human trafficking would have been a possible alternative charge, since the aggravating factors of recruitment into prostitution with which the defendants were charged were added to the Criminal Code at the same time as trafficking.

there. In the Saratov case, several of the women took up the accused several times on his offer, often obtaining new travel documents under false names after they had been deported from Germany for migration violations. In both cases, once in Germany, the women worked off the money and repaid it. When they got there, however, many of the women had to give more money to their pimps than they had agreed on, had a difficult time paying back the money, and became trapped in a cycle of debt bondage. In the St. Petersburg case, they were threatened with harm to themselves and their families if they did not continue to work, including through sales to Turkish pimps, who were considered notoriously cruel to prostitutes. Even though this case appeared to be more serious, the St. Petersburg police decided to charge a "lesser" crime, recruitment into prostitution (with aggravating factors of violence or threat of violence, transport across Russian borders or illegal holding of someone abroad, and by a group with a premeditated agreement). The Saratov case was charged with human trafficking with the aggravating factor of using false documents. Nevertheless, the cases turned out similarly. Savitskii in Saratov was sentenced to 3.5 years in prison and Pastorov in St. Petersburg to 4 years in prison. This result shows that there is not always a need for law enforcement to use the more complicated trafficking charge over the tried-and-true articles of the Criminal Code.

Another indicator that Russian law enforcement is using alternative Criminal Code articles to prosecute sex trafficking is the immediate and significant increase in the number of prostitution-related cases right after the trafficking laws were enacted in December 2003 (figure 6.1). Although there had been a steady increase in crimes prosecuted under these two articles between 2000 and 2003, there was a significant jump between 2003 and 2004. Crimes of recruitment into prostitution (Article 240) had a 187 percent increase and crimes of organizing prostitution (Article 241) a 174 percent increase. Given the widespread acceptance of prostitution throughout Russian society and its profitability to the police, it seems unlikely that the drastic change in the numbers indicates a new interest among law enforcement agents in combating this crime. If anything, cases of prostitution should go down over time as the rings, once broken up, take some time to re-form, as we can see starting in 2008. Instead, the trend shows that law enforcement is using the laws on prostitution-related offenses to pursue human trafficking cases, which they were incentivized to do after the passage of the trafficking laws. Though it is hard to say definitively whether all these cases could have been charged as trafficking, using these Criminal Code articles seems to be an effective strategy for prosecuting traffickers without having to confront the disincentives created by the trafficking law.

This practice is backed up by my interview data. At a conference I attended in Moscow, the head of a law enforcement unit in the Nizhnii Novgorod region

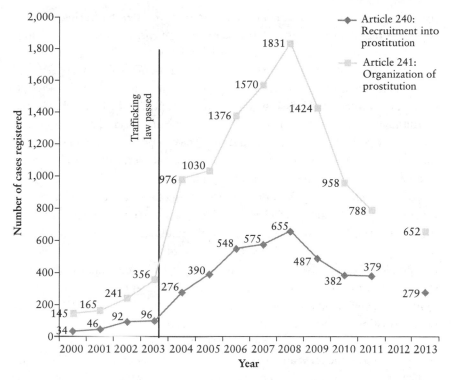

FIGURE 6.1 Cases registered under prostitution-related statutes, 2000–2013. 2000–2003 and 2013 data on file with author; 2004–2008 data from Vinokurov et al. 2010; 2009–2011 data from Chirkov 2012. Data from 2012 unavailable.

said that his region had had no experience with Article 127.1 because agents opened all trafficking cases under Article 240 to stay on the safe side (M20). And, according to an operativnik in the federal anti-trafficking unit in Moscow, approximately half of the cases of recruitment into prostitution that it deals with could probably have been charged as trafficking but were not because of resource concerns. As if to confirm how real these considerations are, he then added that his unit had to make a tradeoff: prosecute ten cases of recruitment into prostitution or one case of trafficking. To him, the choice seemed clear. The more criminals that could be prosecuted, the better (M14).

There have been arguments in the law enforcement academic community over how and when Articles 240 and 127.1 overlap, when they should be used together, and when one should be chosen over the other (Alikhadzhieva 2008). One of the important distinctions between the articles is whether or not the prostitution has already taken place (A4). For a human trafficking charge, the crime is considered to have been committed at the moment that any of the activities outlined take place (buying/selling, recruitment, transportation, transfer, harboring, receipt) regardless of whether the exploitation actually happens. With recruitment into prostitution, there is disagreement about how many times the victim must engage in acts of prostitution, but there is no question about the fact that the exploitation (i.e., prostitution) must take place for the statute to be used.[4] As a result, the human trafficking charge can be used for attempted trafficking, whereas the recruitment into prostitution statute cannot. Several Russian academics argue that any activity of a pimp could (and should) be charged as trafficking based on the fact that harboring with the goal of exploitation is covered under the broadest interpretation of the trafficking statute (Pysina 2005).

Some academics and practitioners suggest using the ambiguity between statutes to law enforcement's advantage, allowing agents to strengthen the charges by using both articles or widen their application (Mizulina 2006, 201). According to one of my interviewees, "there is overlap between 240 and 127.1, but it should not be a problem. You can use both as cumulative charges . . . this way, you can get all stages of the process" (A4). Others take a more cautious approach to this overlap of norms, believing it best to play it safe and charge one or the other (P7). Either way, the distinctions are quite technical, and it seems completely reasonable that given time and resource constraints, an investigator would not spend the time trying to unravel the mess and would instead default to the more familiar of the two charges, recruitment into prostitution.

One procurator I spoke with suggested that there may be an added incentive for the MVD (operativniki and investigators) to charge recruitment into prostitution rather than human trafficking—to keep the trafficking case within the MVD rather than sending it to the Procuracy (or Investigative Committee). Because investigative agencies are held responsible for any case that they open, if the MVD were to send it to the Procuracy and the Procuracy did nothing with the case, the MVD would be stuck with an open case that was not closed in its statistics (P1). In reality, the only way that the MVD could keep the case is by charging it as something that it has sole jurisdiction over (organizing or recruitment into prostitution) or charging it as trafficking with no aggravating factors. But it is rare that human trafficking is found without aggravating factors.

ALTERNATIVE CHARGES FOR LABOR TRAFFICKING CASES

Cases that register in the media as slave labor but are not charged under Article 127.2 are usually charged either as kidnapping, false imprisonment, organizing

---

4. While some commentaries on Article 240 suggest that the act of prostitution must be systematic—that is, it must happen at least three times (Naumov 2007)—others say that one time is sufficient (Rarog 2011).

illegal migration, illegal border crossing, or abuse of authority/official position. These were the primary charges in the 121 cases in the data set that contain elements of labor trafficking but were not charged as such. In contrast to cases charged as slave labor, which usually have multiple victims and significant rights violations, cases charged under other articles tend to be smaller-scale violations or individual-on-individual violence and often occur over shorter time periods. However, this is not always the case. The three cases described below all involve single victims exploited in farm labor, each of which was charged under a different Criminal Code article: kidnapping, false imprisonment, and using slave labor.[5]

In 2008 in Mordovia a man was kept as a slave for a month and a half by someone who was not satisfied with the job he had done fixing a car. They argued about it for three months, and then one night the accuser came with some friends to the victim's shop. They told the victim that if he did not pay back the money, they would take him and force him to work on one of their parents' pig farm, which they then did. The farm was guarded by dogs, and he was threatened that if he ran away they would destroy his auto repair shop, so he started working for them. After a month and a half he ran away and went to law enforcement (no. 110). The farmer, his wife, and their son were all charged with kidnapping.

In a case in the Kursk region in 2005, two Azerbaijanis held a fifty-year-old man as a slave after deceitfully recruiting him with promises of good money. They originally recruited several men but after a month did not pay them anything, so the others left. They forced the remaining one to work and the rest of the time kept him chained to a cow trough, giving him only a pillow and blanket. They barely fed him. He managed to escape after about two months. It was his second attempt. After the first they caught him, returned him, and beat him (no. 276). The Azeri men were charged with false imprisonment with respect to two or more people.

In a similar case in Volgograd, a man was held as a slave from 2006 to 2008. In February 2004 he had gone looking for work tending horses and was promised fair money and good living conditions. But during the time he was working, seven horses died. The boss demanded that he work off their value, 100,000 rubles in total. His passport was taken, and when he refused to work and/or tried to escape, he was beaten and returned to work. His relatives went to law enforcement, which was able to free him from the situation (no. 126). The farmer was charged with using slave labor, by means of blackmail, and with the confiscation of identity documents.

---

5. It is unclear what happened in any of these cases as I was not able to track down their final disposition.

These three cases display the fluidity of charging practices and different possibilities that law enforcement could use and still have charged correctly. Overall, looking at alternative charging practices for both sex and labor trafficking demonstrates that in these situations law enforcement actually has quite a bit of leeway in deciding what to charge a trafficker with. The tendency to go with what they know rather than the unfamiliar is strongly incentivized by the pressure to clear cases quickly and with minimal effort.

Human Trafficking Trials

Assuming that the courtroom procurator agrees to take the human trafficking charge forward, the case will go to trial. As many of my interviewees noted, trafficking is a business, and the traffickers are shrewd businessmen. When they are caught, they hire experienced, expensive lawyers to defend them, a fairly unusual practice in Russia where defense lawyers have traditionally played a minor role in courtroom proceedings (Jordan 2005). During the trial stage the unspoken stereotypes and informal criteria that are often used by law enforcement personnel to determine whether a case is trafficking become vocalized and used as evidence. Questions about whether the victims accepted the jobs willingly, how easily they could escape, and whether or not they were compensated feature in the strategies of both the prosecution and the defense and sometimes in judicial reasoning. Based on an in-depth reading of court documents from 106 cases in forty-six regions of Russia, it is possible to identify some of the patterns that have developed.[6] The major questions at issue in human trafficking trials appear to be about charging (was the case charged correctly? was the statute applied by the judge correctly?); procedural issues (were there violations of the Criminal Procedure Code during the investigation or trial stage?); and issues of witness credibility.

Charging Questions

In the early years of the human trafficking law, procurators often charged the most serious of the aggravating factors when they used the human trafficking statutes—human trafficking committed by an organized group. There was almost never an attempt to charge the defendants with organizing or participating in a criminal conspiracy or criminal organization (Article 210) in addition to

---

6. This set includes forty-five conviction documents in which all victim testimony and court proceedings are detailed, as well as eighty-seven appeal documents in which both the prosecution and defense have the opportunity to outline the legal shortcomings of the case. See appendix A for details.

the trafficking charge.[7] However, the court usually relied on the definition of a criminal organization as outlined in Article 210 to prove activities done by an organized group. This article requires that the group has a clear (*chetkoe*) delineation of roles, has created durable contacts among the members of the group (*ustoichivost'*), and has the intent to commit grave or especially grave crimes as a group. Prosecution strategies consequently focused on outlining who served what role and showing that the roles had been clearly and specifically delineated in the trafficking operation.

It was clear from examining case documents that although most trafficking is committed by a group, proving that the group is organized is difficult. Perhaps for this reason, the use of this aggravating factor has declined over time. The most common problem has been showing the durability of the criminal contacts over time. In one case in Saransk in the Republic of Mordovia (no. 75), the trafficking charge was lowered from trafficking as an organized group, the most serious aggravating factor, to the most basic level of trafficking because the judge said that the procurators needed to show more constant contact among the members of the group and a clearer organizational structure. The prosecution had tried to prove durability and intent by showing that the accused had a clear plan to conceal their crime: registering the sauna at which the prostitution took place under someone else's name. But according to the judge, this one-time act was not enough. In another case in Mari El (no. 29), the prosecution was able to prove durability of contacts through phone records and recorded phone conversations over several months and was able to secure a conviction for trafficking committed by an organized group.

When the human trafficking charge is brought with other charges, it appears to be a double-edged sword. On one hand, it helps make sure there is a conviction if the judge is not convinced by the human trafficking charge. On the other hand, it gives judges more opportunity to avoid convicting under the trafficking charge for fear their decisions will be overturned on appeal. For example, in a case in Izhevsk in the Udmurtia (no. 609), the judge decided that the evidence showing the women had been transported for the purpose of prostitution actually fell under the organizing prostitution charge and therefore could not be used to support the trafficking charge. In the same case, the accused were found to have created an organized group to recruit women into prostitution and organize

---

7. This behavior seems to reflect a more general trend in Russia of hesitancy to use this article of the Criminal Code. Despite reports of thousands of organized criminal groups in Russia, between 2004 and 2008 there were relatively few crimes registered under this statute (2004–224; 2005–244; 2006–255; 2007–337; 2008–325) and even fewer convictions of organized criminal group members (2004–20; 2005–44; 2006–60; 2007–54; 2008–96) (Ovchinskii 2007).

prostitution, but not to traffic them. In another example, from the Primorskii region (no. 281), the judge said that the buying/selling of the victim was intended to fulfill the goal of organizing prostitution, not human trafficking. In both cases, the trafficking charges were dropped by the court. This also happened in a case of slave labor (no. 336) in the Republic of Karelia in which the head of a psychiatric hospital forced his disabled patients to work on his private garden plot. The man was originally convicted of using slave labor, but the decision was overturned on appeal because the appellate judge said that the victims could not refuse the work (a key part of proving slave labor) because they were mentally ill, not because the accused had put them in a situation of slavery. In only one case that I reviewed did the lower-court judge in Tiumen decide to fold the alternative charge of false imprisonment into the trafficking charge, saying that the false imprisonment was a part of harboring, as defined by the trafficking statute (no. 61). This interpretation was later upheld by the Supreme Court in another case (no. 25) from the Komi Republic in which the court suggested that the exploitation of a person as defined in the human trafficking statute by nature included false imprisonment, so an additional charge of false imprisonment was unnecessary.[8]

Judges seemed to be most convinced by human trafficking charges that focused on the buying/selling of the victim for the purpose of exploitation. Consequently, before the 2008 amendment made this irrelevant, the defense regularly tried to show that the buying/selling was not related to exploitation. A common defense was that the woman voluntarily moved to the accused's prostitution business and that the money was exchanged because the new pimps were paying off her debt to the previous pimps. For example, in a case in Saransk, Mordovia (no. 75), the woman who was sold had stolen a mobile phone from the pimps that sold her. At trial, the pimps who bought her insisted that the money that was exchanged was to pay back her debt and was not intended to be a purchase of the prostitute herself. In this case, the judge did not accept this argument, and the defendants were convicted of trafficking.

Another defense strategy both in the initial trial and on appeal was to question whether the charges were being applied correctly. Because there is confusion over the wording of the law and how and when it should be applied, a strong argument that the trafficking article is being applied incorrectly could be convincing to a judge, especially since no resolution has been issued by the Plenum of the Supreme Court on proper interpretation. In a Mari El case (no. 29), the defendants insisted that the human trafficking statute required that the victim be kept in a dependent condition, which the judge dismissed as not being required by the law.

---

8. Decision of the Supreme Court of the Russian Federation of July 9, 2012, no. 3-D12-6.

Recruitment, the judge said, could stand alone as the key element for convicting under human trafficking. In the same case, the defendants also tried to argue that because the victims had not lodged a complaint against the defendants, they should not be considered victims. The judge did not accept this reasoning either, referencing the UN protocol that states that if any of the means outlined in the protocol are used, a victim can still be a victim even if she consented to the exploitation against her. In a case of labor trafficking in the Sakhalin region, the defendant willingly admitted to beating the victim but insisted it was for personal reasons and was not intended to make him work as a slave, a key element in proving use of slave labor (no. 50).

Procedural Questions

In almost all cases, defense attorneys asked the judge to throw out some evidence that they said was obtained in violation of the Criminal Procedure Code. Occasionally, the court did this, but generally these motions were dismissed. A common defense argument was that the police violated procedural rules by exerting pressure on the defendants to sign false confessions, as a result of which their statements from the pretrial investigation stage contradicted what they said at trial.[9] Other defense lawyers alleged that the case was fabricated. Because the defendants did not pay protection money to the police, they said, the police had found and forced people to testify against them. On appeal, the defendants and their lawyers often complained that the judge did not adequately take into account mitigating factors like the existence of dependents at home or positive characterization by friends, neighbors, associates, and co-workers. In a case in Sakhalin, the defendant tried to show that he was a good person by referring to an incident in which he had saved two fishermen from drowning several years earlier (no. 50). When procurators appealed, which is permitted under Russian law, it was usually to protest that the judge had not applied the statute correctly or to protest that the sentence given out was too low, although in rare circumstances it was to protest a sentence that was too harsh.

Witness Credibility

Another factor that seems to be important in making the prosecution's case successful, particularly in cases of sex trafficking, is proving that the women were

---

9. Statements from the pretrial investigation can be read into the record at trial to confront the witness/defendant/victim with inconsistencies in his or her statement or because he or she refuses to answer questions on the stand, which participants have a constitutional right to do (CPC Article 281).

"real" victims, reflecting stereotypes about their willingness and knowledge about working in prostitution. In most of the sentencing documents the judges are clear about the fact that the women were working either unwillingly or tried multiple times to leave the situation but were unable to. In a case in the Primorskii region (no. 87), for example, the women were brought into the police station for questioning after the Ussuriisk police received word from their counterparts in Uzbekistan that the women were being kept in Russia against their will. When asked if they were being held, the indictment notes, the women all said that they were working there willingly. But the indictment then goes on to say that they were afraid of what their trafficker would do to them if they answered truthfully, reasoning that the judge accepted in convicting the accused. In a different case in the same region (no. 281), the judge noted that one of the young women had accepted the offer to work in prostitution because she "didn't have enough life experience" to know to act differently.

In response, the defense tried to show that the victims were not real victims by insinuating that they had been involved in questionable sexual behavior prior to the trafficking situation, especially if the victim was a minor and had been sexually active in the past. In one case, the court made sure to note that although one of the victims had been a prostitute in the past, that she had given up the profession and had been working in an ordinary job, with the underlying implication that if she had been working as a prostitute when she had been recruited into the trafficking situation, there would have been less sympathy for her. In a case from Bashkortostan, this tactic was successful, with the judge excluding one part of the trafficking charge because the woman had been a prostitute before (no. 149).

In labor trafficking cases, defense attorneys argued that the victims willingly agreed to the work, so it was not possible that there was slave labor going on. Others suggested that the work was actually an in kind exchange for housing and food and therefore not exploitation. In a more creative defense, several defendants admitted to using the free labor of the victims but suggested that rather than exploiting the victims, they were taking pity on them, housing and feeding them when they were down and out and had nowhere to live or in areas where there was high unemployment. They accused the victims of being ungrateful for their display of generosity. In one particularly remarkable case from a village in the Chelyabinsk region (no. 13), the defendants insisted that the victims were bad workers, so it was necessary to threaten them and lock them up so they would not steal anything or drink themselves silly. Judges did not seem to accept these lines of reasoning as valid. As in sex trafficking cases, the defense also questioned the character of witnesses and victims in labor trafficking cases, suggesting that they were unreliable and prone to lying because they came from asocial backgrounds or were addicts.

Defense attorneys also tried to use evidence that the victims had the freedom to escape, to show that they must have remained voluntarily. One operativnik in Khabarovsk remarked on this phenomenon:

> The real problem comes when the judge and the defense lawyer [*advokat*] for the other side ask whether they [the victims] had the possibility of escaping or running away. But there are two understandings of what it means to be held. There is the psychological type of being held where they might have the physical opportunity to run away but understand that if they do and are caught, they'll be beaten. In addition, they don't have papers or anything else, so what would they do if they did run away? But inevitably the judge and the lawyer from the other side ask if they could run away, if they answer yes, then they ask why they didn't run away. The judges have a very subjective opinion on all of this. For them, fear and psychological pressure are not enough to overcome the fact that they didn't run away. This is a fault in our law. These people are normally really scared. (M8)

Despite what I often heard from law enforcement officials in my interviews about victim testimony being unreliable, there was a surprising level of trust in the victims' stories in the court documents. For example, when the aggravating factor "trafficking a known minor" was used, the courts tended to trust the victims' statements that they had said they were underage or that the traffickers should have known because they were friends or acquaintances. The courts were usually skeptical if the victim changed his or her story at trial from what he or she said in the pretrial investigation, but not in a negative way. This contradicts some of what I heard in my interviews, where at least one judge noted that victim testimony was often untrustworthy because it changed frequently. Instead, in case documents, the judges noted that victims had probably changed their statements because the defendants had tried to pay them not to testify or because the victims had sympathy for the defendant. They did not suggest that victims were inherently untrustworthy because they came from bad backgrounds or had participated in immoral activities. Of course, these statements are only what is officially on record in the trial documents and may not represent the actual interaction in the courtroom.[10]

Looking at acquittals can also show how informal criteria apply to judicial decision making. In a case in the Primorskii region from 2005 (no. 202), the de-

---

10. Courtroom sessions are not recorded or transcribed verbatim. Although quite detailed, the sentencing document is the judge's summary of the facts of the case and the courtroom interaction and does not include word-for-word exchanges.

fendants were accused of recruiting three men with promises of well-paid work picking nuts in a local forest. Once there, the victims were beaten and threatened with physical reprisals if they did not work well, and one of the victims was eventually beaten to death. In a somewhat strange interpretation of the law, the judge found the defendants not guilty of using slave labor because the men had been beaten so badly that they could not work. Even though they were kept in the forest and were supposed to be slaves, they were not working, and therefore the crime had not been committed. The court suggested that because the men had consented to the work, there was no basis for the use of slave labor charge. In this case, the defendants were punished harshly for the murder, notwithstanding the acquittal on charges of slave labor. However, the symbolic function of using the slave labor charge in addition to the murder charges was lost.[11] A strict interpretation of the law on slave labor that seems to require involuntary entry into work makes it seem as though this judge, at least, was relying on an eighteenth-century definition of what slave labor means, rather than understanding its contemporary manifestations. If this interpretation becomes dominant, it will be difficult to prosecute slave labor charges in cases where the victims originally consented to the work, especially in the case of irregular migrants, who, studies have shown, usually enter voluntarily into what later become slave labor situations (Tiurukanova 2005a).

In a 2004 case in the Kemerovo region (no. 92), a trafficking charge was pursued alongside a murder charge, an important symbolic gesture. This was another forestry case in which the defendants used the slave labor of the victims to illegally log in the forests around Kemerovo. The men they recruited were homeless people and alcoholics; all were alienated from their families. They were promised good jobs in the fresh air and good working conditions, but in reality they lived in a garage, slept on the floor, and were fed once a day and forced to work long hours in harsh conditions. When the victims tried to escape, they were caught, returned, beaten harshly, and forbidden access to medical assistance. Several were eventually murdered, and the defendants burned the bodies to cover up their crimes. They then recruited more victims, one of whom managed to escape and tell the police what was happening. In an appeal to the Russian Supreme Court from 2008, the defense argued that because the men could leave their place of work freely, the slave labor charges were unsubstantiated. But the Supreme Court left the trial court decision largely unchanged, thereby validating

---

11. Something similar occurred in a high-profile case in Nizhnii Tagil in which teenage girls had been reporting missing by their parents and law enforcement did nothing. The girls were later found dead in a forest, having been killed when they refused to work as prostitutes for the men who held them captive in apartments in the town. The case was prosecuted as murder, not trafficking, and the killers were eventually sentenced to life in prison (Blinova 2007).

an interpretation of the law in which people could be considered enslaved even if they were not physically restrained.

Overall, these issues show how in flux interpretations of the human trafficking laws still are. In the first few years, if investigators and procurators did overcome their hesitancy to use the human trafficking charge, they seemed willing to use it aggressively, charging with the highest aggravating factor (organized group) and testing out expansive uses of the flexible definition. Over time, however, based on the feedback from procurators who refused to support the charges in court and judges who either acquitted on human trafficking charges or folded them into other charges, agents have revised their strategies downward. The questions about procedure, witness credibility, and charging that have repeatedly come up in trials and appeals appear to make not using human trafficking charges the path of least resistance.

Trial Outcomes

This section examines the sentences that traffickers have received in cases that were charged as human trafficking between 2004 and 2013.[12] Although most of the time it is possible to distinguish between cases in which at least one person was convicted of human trafficking and those where the human trafficking charges did not hold up, there is rarely enough detail in news reports to distinguish how much of the sentence is for human trafficking and which defendants in the group were convicted of trafficking.[13] Consequently, when necessary I separate the sentencing data below into two groups—cases in which at least one person was convicted of human trafficking and cases in which there were convictions, but not under human trafficking charges. The Judicial Department of the Russian Supreme Court does keep statistics on the number of people convicted under the human trafficking statutes and their sentence length (see appendix B), but it does not include cases where human trafficking was not the primary charge, nor does it break them down by type of trafficking.

There are four basic categories of sentences available in the Russian Criminal Code: imprisonment, fines, corrective labor (wage garnishing), and conditional sentences (CC Articles 43–59).[14] Imprisonment takes place in either a regular,

---

12. Basic information about all of these cases is available online at http://people.umass.edu/laurenmc/traffickingjustice.

13. If a defendant is convicted of multiple crimes with prison sentences, there is a procedure for those sentences to be cumulated (CC Articles 69–70).

14. A conditional sentence is deferred pending the defendant staying out of trouble for a set period of time. If it is successfully completed, there is no criminal record for the defendant.

minimum security regime (*obshchii rezhim*) or a harsh, medium to maximum security regime (*strogyi rezhim*) in a correctional colony.[15] There is also the option of imprisonment in a prison colony (*kolonii poselenie*) for those convicted of minor offenses or an educational colony (*vospitatel'naia koloniia*) for juvenile offenders (Piacentini and Pallot 2012). Throughout the system, there has been an increase in the number of cases that have been heard in special procedure and do not go to a full court hearing—the Russian equivalent of plea bargaining. While it is difficult to separate this out in the data, since not all media outlets note when this happens, studies have shown that in reality, it may not make a significant difference in sentencing (Titaev and Pozdniakov 2012; Solomon 2012).

Domestic Sex Trafficking Cases

Of the 130 cases of sex trafficking that were charged under the human trafficking law between 2004 and 2013, 102 were domestic cases in which the trafficking occurred inside Russia. I was able to find sentencing information on 261 defendants in fifty-nine of those cases. There were 192 defendants in cases where at least one person was convicted of human trafficking and 66 in cases where no one was convicted of human trafficking, but were convicted of something else. There was one case where it was unclear what ultimately happened with the human trafficking charge (no. 27), but the three defendants did receive significant sentences of nine to ten years each. In total, 113 defendants were sentenced to imprisonment in a regular regime, ranging from 1.25 to 14 years (average 6.1).[16] An additional fifty-five received sentences in a harsh regime, ranging from 2.5 years to 21 years (average 9.3). Ninety-three defendants (36 percent) received conditional sentences of between 1.3 and 8 years (average 2.6) and lost varying privileges for some specified time as part of their sentences. Several lost the ability to be employed in the tourism industry. Those in official positions sometimes lost rank or the ability to be employed in government service. Figure 6.2 shows

---

15. Men and women go to separate prison colonies in regular regime imprisonment. Strict regime imprisonment is only for men and is generally used for those who are repeat offenders or who have committed especially grave crimes. Neither of these types of custodial sentences is cell-based. Instead, prisoners live in dormitories on closed premises. For the most dangerous criminals, there is the option of the special regime (*osobyi rezhim*), a maximum security, cell-based imprisonment for dangerous repeat offenders and those serving terms of life imprisonment (Piacentini and Pallot 2012).

16. Those with unknown sentence lengths were not included in the average. If the sentence type was unknown, I assumed it to be prison in a regular regime, the modal category for these cases. If there was a range of sentence lengths given, (i.e. the defendants were convicted to between X and X years), I took the middle of that range and applied it to everyone.

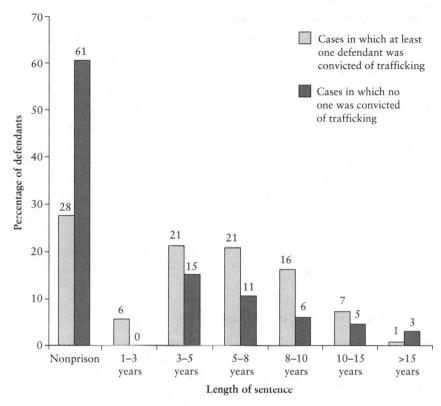

FIGURE 6.2 Percentage of domestic sex trafficking defendants in sentencing categories, by conviction status (n=261)

the percentage of defendants falling into each sentencing category, grouped by the conviction status of the case.[17]

These data suggest that having at least one person convicted of human trafficking in a case increases the severity of the case in the eyes of the judge since defendants in these cases seem to be convicted at a higher rate and to longer sentences. On the whole, domestic sex trafficking cases are much more likely to have each component part of the trafficking process charged separately. The trafficking charges are usually reserved for the people who have engaged in buying/selling, with others in the ring charged according to their roles. This may explain the higher number of conditional sentences in cases where no one was convicted of human trafficking. These cases are probably seen as "ordinary" prostitution

---

17. Here I combine all types of prison sentences to contrast them with conditional, nonprison sentences.

rings; consequently most of the participants are convicted under organizing prostitution charges, which is usually punished with a conditional sentence.

Most of the highest sentences in this category were coupled with other charges that could also raise the sentences. For three of the highest sentences, news articles explicitly mentioned that the three defendants were acquitted of human trafficking because there were no elements of the crime in their activities. In this case, the defendants had kidnapped and forced at least twenty women into prostitution, including minors. They threatened to and actually carried out violent acts against the women, slashing the faces of five of them as an example to the others. Over time the operation grew from its home base in Ulyanovsk and began sending prostitutes to Moscow, St. Petersburg, and Samara. Few victims wanted to testify because they were so scared (no. 197). In this case it seems likely that the procurator or judge expected that trafficking would include a monetary exchange; otherwise it is difficult to understand how the defendants could not be found guilty of trafficking.

International Sex Trafficking Cases

In the twenty-eight cases of international sex trafficking charged as human trafficking, I was able to find sentencing information for seventy-three defendants in twenty-six different cases. Forty defendants received regular regime sentences ranging from 1.5 to 19 years (average 6.9), and an additional fifteen received harsh regime sentences ranging from 4.5 to 12 years (average 8.4). A lower percentage of defendants in international sex trafficking cases received conditional sentences than those in domestic ones (25 percent in the former compared to 36 percent in the latter). For those who did, sentences ranged from 3 to 7 years (average 4.6). As in domestic cases, several were barred from working in tourism for a specified number of years.

Figure 6.3 shows the sentencing data for these defendants. Unlike in the domestic trafficking cases, where defendants were often convicted under other statutes, all but one of these international cases had at least one defendant charged and convicted under Article 127.1. This suggests that international trafficking more closely reflects what law enforcement agents think of as "real" trafficking, especially the belief that it must cross borders, even though Russian law does not require this as an element of the crime. But, as in domestic sex trafficking cases, law enforcement agents still used additional Criminal Code articles as backup.

Labor Trafficking Cases

In the 101 cases charged as labor trafficking, I was able to find sentencing information for 148 defendants in 63 different cases. There were 125 defendants

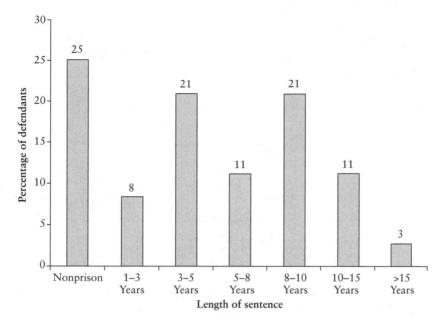

FIGURE 6.3 Percentage of international sex trafficking defendants in sentencing categories (n=73)

in cases where at least one person was convicted of trafficking and 23 in cases where no one was convicted of trafficking, but was convicted of something else. Overall, fifty-nine defendants received a sentence of prison in a regular regime, ranging between 7 months and 11 years (average 4.5 years), and thirty-nine received sentences in a harsh regime ranging from six months to 27.5 years (average 9.1 years). Two defendants received life sentences—one in a regular regime, one in a harsh regime.[18] Another group of defendants, five in total, received sentences in a prison colony and one received a sentence in a prison colony for minors. Forty-eight received conditional sentences (32 percent) ranging from two to eight years (average four). Figure 6.4 shows the percentage of defendants in each sentencing category by conviction status. Here I combine the international and domestic cases because there are so few defendants in international cases (twenty-seven total) that it is difficult to do a finer-grained analysis. It does appear that defendants in international cases are more likely to be convicted of trafficking charges—only two were convicted of other charges—but generally receive lower sentences: an average of 4 years, compared to the domestic average of 6.9. Nine of the twenty-seven received conditional sentences.

Looking more closely at the sentences shows that the harshest sentences were usually given in cases in which there were aggravating circumstances and

18. I did not include the life sentences in the averages.

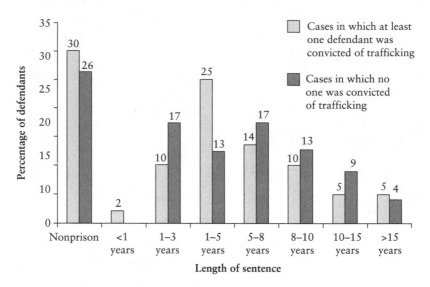

FIGURE 6.4 Percentage of labor trafficking defendants in sentencing categories, by conviction status (n=148)

additional charges. Those sentenced to a harsh prison regime all had multiple charges including a number of other serious crimes, such as participating in an organized criminal group, kidnapping, false imprisonment, drug trafficking, and/or murder. This practice reflects both the uncertainty of bringing a new charge without the backup of other, more familiar charges and the fact that many of these situations are extremely abusive and exploitative, involving significant rights violations which can be charged under more than one article of the Criminal Code. In one case in the Murmansk region (no. 39), the procurator chose not to support the trafficking charge, presumably because it was superfluous given the large sentence expected for murder. In another in the Primorskii region (no. 202), the defendants were acquitted of trafficking but convicted of several other serious statutes. This is reflected in figure 6.4, which shows that in cases where no one was convicted of human trafficking, defendants were convicted more frequently and received harsher sentences. This result is the opposite of what we see in domestic sex trafficking cases. There were also several cases in the data set where the defendants were charged with murder but the trafficking charges were still pursued, possibly as a symbolic gesture, considering the harsh sentences that the murder convictions would bring on their own (nos. 92, 367).

Child Trafficking Cases

In the forty-six cases of child trafficking charged under trafficking laws, I was able to find full sentencing information for forty-one defendants in thirty different cases. Figure 6.5 shows the percentage of defendants falling into each sentencing category. Like international sex trafficking cases all of these cases had at least one defendant charged and convicted of human trafficking. Most of the defendants (twenty-nine) received a sentence of prison in a regular regime, ranging between 2 and 10 years (average 3.7 years). Another group of defendants, eleven in total, received conditional sentences ranging from 3 to 5 years (average 3.6 years). Only one defendant received a harsh regime sentence of ten years, but his trafficking charge was paired with a more serious kidnapping charge (no. 218). This was one of the few cases before the 2008 amendments in which someone was successfully prosecuted for child trafficking. In this case an undercover officer in Novosibirsk contacted the seller, Dmitrii Olenev, and offered him $3,700 for his two-year-old son to be used as an organ donor for his sick child. They even brought the child for a medical examination to make sure he was healthy. After getting his wife drunk, Olenev kidnapped the child and brought it to the point of sale, after which he was detained. The other high-sentence case also involved kidnapping. Aksana Dashkaeva of Chechnya was sentenced to ten years in prison for kidnapping and selling an acquaintance's child, despite cooperating with the investigation and admitting her guilt.

The sentencing data here seem to contradict what many law enforcement personnel told me: that people who sold their children were not receiving harsh sentences. Although these parents may not be sentenced to the statutory maximum,

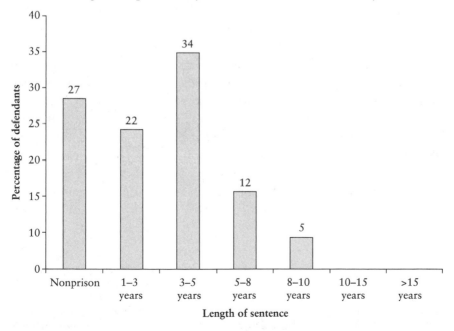

FIGURE 6.5 Percentage of child trafficking defendants in sentencing categories (n=41)

73 percent are seeing some sort of prison time. Just as law enforcement takes situations of child trafficking very seriously, so too do the courts.

Civil Compensation

The Russian system awards compensatory damages as well as damages for moral harm.[19] In cases charged as trafficking, judges awarded damages in six labor and five sex trafficking cases. In one labor case, the damages went to the dead victim's brother for funeral expenses (no. 202). Awards ranged in size and often had to be split among several victims. Although there are only a few cases to analyze, compensation to victims of labor trafficking seems to be slightly higher than to victims of sex trafficking. In one labor case, the victim received 144,000 rubles ($4,750) in compensation (no. 46), but the other awards were between 42,500 and 100,000 rubles. In the three cases of sex trafficking where compensation amounts were specified, the payments were lower, between 20,000 and 50,000 rubles per person. Perhaps this difference occurs because in slave labor cases, victims are performing a job for which there is knowledge of what wages are appropriate—unlike prostitution, which exists in the shadow economy.

If the victim wants to present a civil claim for moral and/or material damages, he or she must do this at the same time that the criminal proceedings are initiated. It is not possible to add a civil claim later. Nor is it possible for the procurator to initiate the civil claim on the victim's behalf unless the victim is a minor (ODIHR 2008a). Furthermore, while the procurators are obligated to collect enough evidence to prove the criminal case, the burden of proving the damages suffered by the victim falls to the victim him- or herself. For women who have been exploited in prostitution to receive compensation for material damages, they would have to prove that they have experienced physical harm that could be compensated, often a change in their health, as a result of the trafficking (Civil Code Article 1064). Such harm is often difficult to document, especially the longer-term health effects that may result from things like pimps pumping victims full of antibiotics until they become resistant (N22).

Judges usually consider civil claims only at the time of the sentencing in the criminal case, so if for any reason it is stalled or dismissed, the civil claim cannot

---

19. Russian law divides damages into material and moral. Material damages comprise compensation for losses either in kind or in monetary value. This could include property, lost wages, hospital bills, and so on. Moral harm is defined as "physical or mental suffering" by Article 151 of the Civil Code and refers to violations of an individual's "nonproperty" rights such as life, health, dignity, personal inviolability, honor and good name, business reputation, or privacy (Burnham, Maggs, and Danilenko 2012; Civil Code Article 150).

go forward (ODIHR 2008a).[20] If there is no criminal case, victims can sue their traffickers, but the process is cumbersome, expensive, and seldom successful. The statute of limitations on filing a civil claim in these circumstances is three years. Most victims have no idea that they might be eligible for compensation—in part because they do not have lawyers, but also because there is significant confusion over when and how they might qualify for compensation in a trafficking situation.

Looking at the indictment and trial stages of human trafficking cases shows that procurators and judges are equally cautious in the face of uncertainty as other actors in the criminal justice system. With a new law, there is theoretically more room for experimentation, because it is new and unfamiliar to everyone in the system. On one hand, procurators can encourage judges to interpret the statutes in a particular way through the rationale presented in the indictment. On the other hand, there remains a deep concern over what the judge will actually decide; this fear leads to a mostly conservative approach to employing new statutes. As in the investigation process, uncertainty also allows for informal stereotypes and criteria to enter the courtroom. Victims' willingness to perform the work and their ability to escape are included nowhere in the trafficking statutes as elements of the crime or in any of the commentaries that I have read about the law, but they seem to comprise an important part of the prosecution and defense's arguments and the judge's reasoning.

As a response to this uncertainty, procurators frequently charge multiple statutes as backup to the human trafficking statute, even though the trafficking statute, with its wide scope, was designed to cover all the actions reflected in the other charges. These are not necessarily charging errors. Indeed, all the alternative charges are clearly present in the activities of the accused in these trafficking rings. More interesting is the decision not to use the human trafficking statute even though it would require less time and paperwork than writing up the evidence for each charge separately. However, given the fact that the sentences are similar and the alternative articles are more familiar and less complicated, it is not a surprise that law enforcement would pursue cases that way rather than devoting the time and resources to investigating human trafficking with its attendant risks—that the courtroom procurator will not support the charge or the judge will not accept it.

---

20. If a case is dismissed because the procurator refuses to prosecute, a separate civil suit is still a possibility, but it depends on the court's view of why the case was dismissed. This is similar for an acquittal. If the defendant is acquitted because the procurator has failed to prove the defendant committed the crime, the civil case is dropped. If the acquittal is for another reason, the civil suit can be pursued by the victim independently (Burnham, Maggs, and Danilenko 2012).

Defendants in cases that are charged with trafficking receive meaningful sentences, regardless of whether they are ultimately convicted of trafficking, although they rarely receive the statutory maximum.[21] The average prison sentence for sex trafficking cases (domestic and international) was 7.2 years, with an additional 32 percent of defendants receiving conditional sentences. In labor trafficking, the average was slightly less: 6.4 years in prison, with an additional 30 percent of defendants receiving conditional sentences. In incidents of domestic sex trafficking, cases in which at least one person was convicted of human trafficking seemed to bring longer and harsher sentences than those in which defendants were convicted, but not of human trafficking. Labor trafficking cases showed the opposite effect. Child traffickers saw lower prison sentences, averaging 4.5 years, but had a similar rate of conditional sentences: 27 percent. Even though law enforcement takes child trafficking the most seriously of the three types, defendants in child trafficking cases are usually caught in the act rather than after the child has been sold and thus can be charged only with attempted trafficking. Furthermore, because the proof is so solid in these cases, many of the defendants decide to make a deal with procurators to admit their guilt, have a speedy court procedure, and accept a sentence of no more than two-thirds of the possible maximum.

A Comparative Note

The strategies used by investigators and procurators in Russia in selecting charges for trafficking cases do not differ significantly from law enforcement practice in other countries. In the United States at both the state and federal levels (Albonetti 2014; Farrell et al. 2012) and in many European countries (Wade 2011), prosecutors tend to rely on criminal statutes that predate trafficking laws and cover component parts of the crime rather than the whole trafficking process. As in Russia, these alternative charges tend to provide greater certainty of conviction because they are familiar to all participants in the criminal justice system, whereas human trafficking laws are untested in the courts and often difficult to interpret. It is therefore a common practice to double up on charges, making sure to charge component parts of the crime in addition to the overall trafficking

---

21. A 2007 article in *Ogonek* shows that this is not a surprise. Even for the most serious types of crimes, few convicted defendants receive the maximum possible time in prison. For murder, only about 3.5 percent of those convicted received the maximum possible sentence (2004–2008) and for intentional infliction of serious bodily harm, only two people received the maximum possible sentence (2004–2008), and only 35 percent received any sort of prison time at all (Ovchinskii 2007).

charge. Judges in other countries also struggle to apply the laws on the books to actual situations. Research on court cases in jurisdictions as diverse as Norway and Ukraine has shown how judges have struggled to apply abstract concepts such as exploitation and vulnerability to real-life situations (Pyshchulina 2005; Skilbrei 2010). Much like law enforcement agents, judges may be unfamiliar with trafficking laws and fall prey to the same sorts of stereotyping as their on-the-ground colleagues. As Angelo Constantinou (2013) shows in a study of sex trafficking cases in Cyprus, testimony is often discredited by judges if the victim does not show the "appropriate" amount of remorse, shame, or traumatization.

Sentencing of traffickers in Russia does not appear to differ significantly from other countries around the world. Although most countries have strict penalties for trafficking on the books, it is rare that the statutory maximum is handed down to those convicted of trafficking (Gallagher and Holmes 2008; Wade 2011). Even in the United States, which has probably the strictest penalties on the books for human trafficking—conviction on federal charges can bring sentences of twenty years to life imprisonment—the average sentence is significantly lower. A report on the forty-five human trafficking suspects sentenced in 2007 and 2008 showed that 36 percent of them received probationary sentences or jail time under a year. Only five were sentenced to more than ten years, with the rest being somewhere in between (Kyckelhahn et al. 2009). In the United Kingdom as of 2009, the average conviction for trafficking cases was 4.7 years, though as in Russia, many defendants were serving additional years for other offenses (Lipscombe and Beard 2014). On the other end of the spectrum is the Netherlands, where the average sentence is only twenty-five months (Dept. of State 2013b).

It is difficult to obtain cross-national data on sentencing over time. The *Trafficking in Persons Report* from 2013 gives statistics on the achievements of the previous year for all countries around the world (Dept. of State 2013b). If we look at countries in Russia's neighborhood, Ukraine has been the most aggressive at pursuing trafficking cases, convicting 115 people of trafficking in 2012, with 65 of them receiving prison terms and 42 receiving suspended sentences. In the same year, Moldova convicted thirty-five traffickers, but Belarus convicted only one. In Latvia, only three of eighteen convicted traffickers were sentenced to prison terms, whereas in Lithuania the seventeen convicted traffickers were all sentenced to prison terms of between four and seven years. Armenia sentenced eight convicted traffickers to prison terms of four to eleven years, while Azerbaijan sentenced six of twelve traffickers to prison time, but Georgia prosecuted no traffickers. Overall, the wide variation in sentencing practices suggests that Russia is well within the average of patterns and rates of sentencing for trafficking cases in its region and in the world more generally.

CONCLUSION

From initial denials that human trafficking was a Russian phenomenon to the passage of a law in 2003 that criminalized it, Russia has made progress in combating this significant problem. Having a law on the books was clearly an important first step. But to understand how Russian law enforcement has responded to human trafficking, we must also explore the institutional context in which it operates—the internal logic of incentives and the ways that new policies are grafted onto the institution's existing practices and standard operating procedures. As this book shows, it is in studying where the rubber meets the road—the implementation and enforcement of the laws—that we can learn not only about the response to human trafficking but also how law enforcement's inner workings shape its response to many problems. Looking at a new, complex crime like human trafficking, where there are multiple "correct" charging options, lays bare the way that law enforcement's institutional machinery creates a framework that limits the possibilities for decision making in a way that studying less complex cases might not allow us to see. This book delineates the contours of that institutional machinery, both formal and informal, and demonstrates how it leads to the on-the-ground construction of policy as it is applied to citizens. This conclusion summarizes these findings and their implications, then discusses the possibilities for changes in the institutional machinery and improvements in the prosecution of human trafficking cases.

Trafficking in Russia

Russian law enforcement has pursued three main types of trafficking: sex trafficking, labor trafficking, and child trafficking for illegal adoption. Sex trafficking cases show a clear delineation between those where the trafficking occurs within Russia and those where women are trafficked across the border, either into or out of Russia. Domestic operations are run by small organized groups, mostly operating in urban population centers. They recruit their victims from nearby towns and villages and coerce them into working in prostitution through threats, violence, and the use of debt bondage. However, without a monetary transaction taking place—the women actually being bought and/or sold—law enforcement agents have tended to charge these cases under the prostitution-related Criminal Code statutes, recruitment into or organizing prostitution, not human trafficking.

International trafficking rings are considerably more complex, traffic significantly larger numbers of women, and operate for longer periods of time. They recruit Russian women through advertisements or job placement agencies for work abroad. Many of the women know that they are going into an occupation where sexual services may be included. Like the women in domestic sex trafficking cases, they are held abroad through debt bondage, threats of violence, and actual violence. In addition, they are often in the destination country illegally, having overstayed their entry visas, and may not have the language skills or freedom of movement to ask for help. The situations of women trafficked into Russia are similar. Although law enforcement does not always manage to bring down the full trafficking ring in these cases because partners are often abroad and beyond their reach, this type of case most closely corresponds to the way trafficking is portrayed in the media, so is more likely to register on law enforcement's radar as "real" trafficking. Thus agents have tended to consistently charge these cases under human trafficking laws.

Labor trafficking cases have two main types of victims: foreign migrants either brought into Russia or already present in Russia; and Russian citizens who are at the margins of society because of alcoholism, homelessness, or drug addiction. In most labor trafficking cases, the exploitation usually needs to be so egregious that it jars law enforcement out of its normal institutional repertoires of dealing with migrants and those at the margins of society—indifference or repression. Aspects of the crime that remind law enforcement of eighteenth-century conceptions of slavery tend to have the most resonance. Situations that feature beatings, chains, overseers, excessive hunger, mistreatment, and inhumane living conditions tend to be those that law enforcement calls labor trafficking or, as the Criminal Code defines it, use of slave labor.

Finally, trafficking for illegal adoption occurs in one of two ways. First, there are organized groups with some connection to a maternity hospital where they have access to newborns. They either find new mothers who are giving up their babies already or deceitfully convince new mothers to give up their babies. The second type of child trafficking happens when desperate parents try to find people to buy their children because they do not have the means to support them or because they simply do not want them. Crimes against children are taken especially seriously in Russia, so it is no surprise that law enforcement agents have been more keen to pursue cases with what they consider to be totally innocent and helpless victims. However, an important part of the success story on child trafficking actually came at the initiative of law enforcement. When the human trafficking law was originally passed in 2003, confusion over the wording made law enforcement reticent to use it to prosecute cases of child trafficking, thinking they were not covered under the wording of the law. They lobbied heavily for a change to the law to clarify it and, after an amendment in 2008 that fulfilled their demands, have had tremendous success prosecuting the buying and selling of children for illegal adoption.

The Institutional Machinery and Its Effect on Trafficking Cases

Viewing Russian law enforcement as street-level bureaucrats responding to institutional incentives places my work within a larger tradition of looking at the difficulties that extant bureaucratic and organizational norms and practices present to policy implementation in Russia. This body of work has identified successes and failures across a broad range of policy areas (Appel 2004), including health policy (Twigg 2007), banking (Johnson 2000, 2002), statistical record keeping (Herrera 2010), domestic and international courts (Solomon and Foglesong 2000; Hendley 2004, 2005, 2013; Trochev 2008; Sperling 2009), and tax collection (Easter 2002; Gehlbach 2008). Law enforcement personnel are not fundamentally different from personnel in these other bureaucracies. Like other bureaucrats, law enforcement personnel respond to their institutional environment in making decisions. When faced with overwhelming, excessively complicated regulations, they often find the first "good enough" solution rather than weighing all the possible alternatives and choosing the optimal one.

The institutional machinery of Russian law enforcement—a combination of organizational structure, culture, and statistical performance assessment— drives behavior in predictable ways. Agencies emphasize the number of cases cleared, the completion of investigative activities within the time limits set by the Criminal Procedure Code, and a comparison to the previous year's statistics.

This approach leads law enforcement to be cautious in using new laws. Agents are risk averse to the extreme, concerned that pursuing a case with any degree of uncertainty will jeopardize their department's performance statistics. This problem is exacerbated by an organizational culture that prioritizes hierarchical subordination. Each superior is responsible for the statistics of his subordinates and the department as a whole, and those numbers are aggregated up the chain of command. This leads to significant pressure from the top for the case clearance statistics to look good and not vary significantly from year to year. This combination of factors leads law enforcement agents to look for cases that are quick and easy to clear with a fairly certain chance of conviction. They are loathe to waste resources, especially time, on collecting evidence for cases that have uncertain prospects for making it all the way through the system. Finally, law enforcement agents tend to stick to the familiar. Learning the requirements of new laws is complicated and comes with uncertainty, as different actors in the criminal justice system may have different and conflicting interpretations of what a new law means and when it should be applied.

As a complex crime taking place over time with multiple suspects and victims, human trafficking does not fit any of the criteria on which law enforcement agents focus when looking for an ideal case. The crime is not straightforward, not quick to investigate, and has victims who may be difficult witnesses and whose testimony may not be believed by the judges assessing the evidence. In addition, the crime is, by and large, unfamiliar to most law enforcement agents who might encounter it. This is true worldwide.

Finding and investigating a trafficking case is difficult. Even though most cases in Russia have been brought to law enforcement's attention by a victim report, victims often do not see themselves as victims, are traumatized, and fear getting in trouble. Victim assistance organizations find it difficult to trust an institution that prioritizes processing of cases over the well-being of victims. In the Russian context this problem has been exacerbated by the crackdown on NGO activity that began in 2006. Even if law enforcement agents had the information they needed to find a trafficking crime from one of these sources, important challenges still remain in identifying the case as human trafficking. Proper identification requires that law enforcement personnel look for a process rather than look at the more immediately visible crime, all while under pressure from their institutions to clear cases quickly. The formal criteria for a human trafficking charge as outlined in the wording of the statute are ambiguous enough to leave significant room for interpretation in both identifying a case as human trafficking and gathering evidence. Without practical guidance from above about how the law is supposed to be implemented on the ground, and in the face of uncertainty and fear of using new laws, law enforcement has produced its own set of informal criteria to judge whether the situation it has encountered is a "real" trafficking case or not. These criteria often hinge on the moral reputation of the groups from which the victims come. Prostitutes and migrants are seen as knowing what they were getting into, or at least as people who should have known, and therefore not as victims. Instead, most are regarded as potential criminals.

Gathering the correct evidence when there is so much confusion about what the statute means is a challenge for even the best-intentioned investigators, since it requires balancing the needs of the criminal justice process with the welfare of the victim. Ten years of practice have revealed that investigators look for victim testimony and/or evidence of the transaction to conclusively prove human trafficking in the court. But those who have worked with trafficking victims realize that they will often not get anywhere without a healthy victim who is willing and able to testify, which requires victim assistance services and places for the victims to live during the investigation.

Because the trafficking law is new, the evidentiary requirements are uncertain. How different people in the criminal justice system will interpret that evidence in light of the new law is also uncertain. As a result, law enforcement has been extremely cautious in its use of the new human trafficking statutes. But despite perceptions that Russian law enforcement has done little to fight trafficking, it is in fact investigating cases and imprisoning traffickers by prosecuting *human traffickers*, not *human trafficking*. Given the disincentives described throughout the book, agents have adopted a strategy for dealing with human trafficking that allows them to continue to use Criminal Code articles with which they have experience, as well as using the new trafficking articles in situations that the other articles do not cover fully. This ability was enhanced with the passage of amendments to the Criminal Code articles on prostitution-related offenses, giving them added teeth and making them more relevant for use in prosecuting human trafficking crimes.[1] The feedback from the court system, in the form of judicial opinions, reinforces this cautious strategy for using the human trafficking laws. Judges have interpreted the human trafficking statutes as narrowly as possible in most of the cases that have made it to trial.

Law enforcement is constrained by existing institutional norms and practices whenever it encounters a new issue. It does learn to deal with new criminal threats over time, but that learning does not always take place in the way that we would want it to. Rather than a "race to the top," in which over time ambitious

---

1. It is unclear why the prostitution-related statutes were changed when the trafficking laws were added. The predominant framing of trafficking as mainly for exploitation in prostitution may be part of the explanation, though nothing is clear from the transcripts surrounding the discussion of the draft law. Furthermore, the final version of the draft law did not even use the language that eventually ended up in the changes to the two prostitution-related statues. I have asked everyone I can find who was involved in the drafting of the law, but no one has any recollection of how or why this happened.

agents overcome their risk aversion and use the human trafficking laws successfully, there may be instead a "race to the bottom," where they learn over time that
pursuing trafficking cases with trafficking laws is not worth it. Those who try to
use the laws are slapped down by their superiors for wasting time and investigative resources on a complicated charge when they could be using something
simpler. Instead of learning how to use trafficking laws properly, they learn not
to use them at all. This type of learning then gets reinforced as they successfully
clear cases using other charges. As a result, agents do not apply trafficking charges
again. This sequence of events does appear to explain some of what is happening,
as some of my interviewees explicitly stated. One agent noted that his region had
never opened a human trafficking case under human trafficking laws and instead
always used recruitment into prostitution laws. Another underlined the direct
tradeoff of resources to investigate each type of case—ten cases of recruitment
into prostitution versus one case of human trafficking.

At the same time, something else is also at work. Although it is true that law
enforcement agents respond most strongly to the stimuli created by the institutional environment in which they work, they also experience a sense of pride in
a job well done. Human trafficking cases are noteworthy events. They rarely go
without a press release by the agency that uncovered them. In newspaper articles,
press releases, and interviews, law enforcement agencies are eager to share that
they are investigating and prosecuting the first trafficking case in their regions.
They make a point of showing how much work the cases involve by noting how
many volumes of evidence the case file took up, how long the investigation lasted,
and how many witness interviews, investigation procedures, and so on they had
to undertake. In addition, some stress the importance of creating precedent for
these types of investigations. In one case in Udmurtia (no. 203), Assistant Procurator Andrei Sutkin emphasized the importance of getting the first trafficking case right: "if we manage to prove that the accused really trafficked people,
similar cases will start being opened in all of Russia, because we can share our
own practice with colleagues, since [practice] doesn't yet exist in this country"
(Antonova and Peshkova 2005). In a system that does not value firsts but instead
prefers to concentrate on annual totals, it is telling that law enforcement agencies
find it important to publicize their accomplishments, showing that they do have
some reasons to pursue human trafficking as such, even if it is only pride.

In addition, we can see the ways in which the institutional machinery interacts
with and creates ideas about who deserves to access the state's protection and
enforcement resources. On one hand, potential victims are people whom law
enforcement agents are already inclined to regard with suspicion (prostitutes,
migrants, or other vulnerable groups) and who may have committed criminal
offenses themselves. They are not particularly sympathetic victims. On the other

hand, they are some of the state's most vulnerable populations and therefore some of the most deserving of state protection. Unfortunately, law enforcement's existing organizational repertoires surrounding these groups are well established. In cases of sexual violence against women, Russian law enforcement agents tend to be either indifferent or blame the victim, asking what she did to provoke an assault rather than focusing on the perpetrator. Trafficking is not much different. Women who do not fit the innocent victim profile are generally treated by law enforcement as if they must have known what they were getting into and are therefore less deserving of law enforcement's scarce resources. With migrants, Russian law enforcement shares the prevailing attitude of much of Russian society today: that migrants are parasites on the state, commit a significant amount of the crime in Russia, and ought to be returned to their countries of origin. Thus the organizational repertoires that attach to migrants are in many ways even more repressive than those that attach to women working in prostitution. They generally include rounding migrants up, detaining them, fining them, and then either letting them go to repeat the cycle again or turning them over to migration authorities. To be considered trafficking by law enforcement, then, a situation must be well outside the boundaries of what personnel are used to seeing.

However, there is some room for optimism. Both my interviews and media reports quoting law enforcement agents show that those who have been exposed to trafficking cases are deeply personally affected by what they encounter. This holds true for all types of trafficking. In one international sex trafficking case (no. 168) from the Vladimir region, an FSB agent involved in the investigation said: "When the victim told us the details of these horrors, our hair stood on end. Failing health—that's all they have left of their dreams of a beautiful life abroad. Well, and perhaps a pretty suitcase and a bit of their foreign clothing" (Newsru. com 2005a). At least some of those who encountered the victims firsthand were keen to put the traffickers in jail. An FSB agent who worked on a labor trafficking case in Penza said: "All of this occurred right in front of other people. Most of the workers there knew about it, but they all accepted it. . . . Honestly, this case is not part of our profile but what we saw was so astonishing to us, I decided to lead the investigation to the end" (no. 72; *Rossiia Penza* 2007; Shilov 2007). In an early child trafficking case in Taganrog in the Rostov region, police stumbled on an advertisement on the Internet for a two-and-a-half-year-old boy with all his documents (no. 214). They were so surprised by the ad that they called and arranged a meeting. They expected no one to show up, thinking it was a joke, but just in case told the sellers that they were an infertile couple and asked them to bring a photograph of the child. When the parents arrived and seriously discussed the sale of their son, the operativniki were shocked but arranged a second meeting to buy the boy. They arrested the couple after the transaction took place (Pavlova 2006; Poteria 2006; Sidorova 2006).

Implications of the Institutional Machinery

Understanding Russian law enforcement's institutional machinery gives insight into a number of areas beyond the implementation of human trafficking laws. First, it demonstrates how law enforcement could be incentivized to pursue particular types of crimes. The risk aversion that comes with using a new law can be overcome by extensive pressure from above to produce a particular type of case. This campaign logic was a notable characteristic of Soviet-era law enforcement practice (see Favarel-Garrigues 2011 on the campaign against economic crime) and has continued to this day. The best example of this point is Russian law enforcement's implementation of the law against extremist activity. After significant amendments in 2007, the law set out criteria for organizations and printed material to be declared extremist and banned and for people who committed extremist activity to be fined or imprisoned. Like the human trafficking law, the extremism law was broad and ambiguously written and quite complex to prove, but enforcing the law on extremism, unlike human trafficking, was a political and law enforcement priority.[2] Because of the hierarchical subordination within law enforcement, when the orders came down, law enforcement agents, especially low-level agents who were not in antiextremism units, boldly charged ahead to find extremism violations, even though they did not always fully understand the law's provisions. Again as with human trafficking, the wording of the law is so vague that agents have developed informal criteria to help guide them. According to some experts, they focus on finding keywords that indicate extremism on blog postings and other social networking Web sites which are harmful to almost no one and try to have them removed so they can fill the statistical boxes and show they are doing something. This comes at the expense of doing more extensive, longer-term investigations that may take more resources but will lead to higher-quality evidence of actual extremist groups.

Juxtaposing the response to extremism, which has been extremely politicized, with the response to human trafficking, which has not, shows the two possible consequences of the statistical assessment system.[3] In the extremism situation, the *palochnaia sistema* becomes the lever by which the state encourages prosecution of a particular type of crime. In the human trafficking situation, the *palochnaia sistema* does just the opposite, creating a strong fear of punishment

---

2. Extremism is defined as "any crimes motivated by political, ideological, racial, ethnic, or religious hatred or animosity, or by hatred or animosity toward any social group mentioned in this code" (CC Article 280).

3. Extremism charges have been used to limit free speech and freedom of religion as well as to ensnare political opponents of both local and national elites by banning Web sites, blogs, and social media postings of those who are critical (Kravchenko 2013). At the same time, the law has been used to bring down dangerous, violent groups—which has resulted in a decrease in hate crimes, according to Alexander Verkhovsky, head of the SOVA Center (personal conversation).

and failure to meet performance targets because of the vagueness of the law and uncertainty about how its use will be interpreted. In 2006 law enforcement did take a step toward using this lever on human trafficking by issuing an internal order (*prikaz*) to add a specific human trafficking data field (*stroka*) into annual report forms rather than just counting it in the broader category "Crimes against Freedom, Honor and Dignity of the Person." This step has indicated to lower-level law enforcement throughout Russia that human trafficking is something it needs to take seriously, but without a corresponding campaign it seems not to have had much effect.

Understanding law enforcement's institutional machinery also highlights the challenges Russian law enforcement faces and will continue to face in implementing its international commitments to criminal justice policies like fighting organized crime, money laundering, and terrorism. These crimes have similar characteristics that make them equally difficult to pursue in the criminal justice system. Like trafficking, they are processes that occur over time, rather than an individual crime that occurs at a set moment. Even though Russia has created specialized units with skillfully trained specialists to focus on some of these categories of crime, the structure of overlapping jurisdiction and agency rivalries can make them hard to pursue. So even if human trafficking is not a priority for Russian law enforcement agencies or agents themselves, it is important to recognize that these disincentives are likely to affect practice in other areas as well—including in the security sphere, an area in which the Russian government has always taken a keen interest.

On a more global scale, this book shows that implementing international commitments in a domestic institutional context can be difficult. In the rush to integrate into the international community, many countries, including Russia, have taken on obligations in the form of treaties and agreements that explicitly outline policies that must be adopted at the national level, like the human trafficking protocol. Even in a highly securitized world in which most countries are committed to addressing and eradicating transnational organized crime, these efforts still require support at the domestic level from actors who respond to their own institutional incentives. It is critical to understand that the resistance does not always come from the implementers' opposition to the policy or the norms it represents but from the difficulties in implementing the policy that result from organizational factors at the domestic level. In failing to prosecute human trafficking cases, Russian law enforcement is not intentionally engaged in undermining international agreements because it inherently has undemocratic values. Instead it is responding to the incentives of its domestic institutions, which may not be aligned with domestic or international policy makers' goals.

Understanding what motivates Russian law enforcement also has practical applications for domestic civil society actors. Women's and migrants' rights groups often need to engage law enforcement to improve the criminal justice response to issues like domestic violence, rape, and other forms of abuse and exploitation. Understanding law enforcement's mindset and incentive structure becomes critical for creating productive cooperative relationships. As many of the NGO representatives with whom I spoke noted, trying to evoke empathy for victims or use the language of human rights to persuade law enforcement to do something on trafficking was often pointless. Instead, by showing pragmatically how agents could gain something by treating victims well, the NGOs indirectly helped promote better treatment of victims, especially at the IOM shelter. Although some areas of the law are highly politicized, there are a number of nonpolitical areas that may be more open for engagement between civil society and law enforcement, including human trafficking.

What Is to Be Done?

It is worth mentioning that laws and the criminal justice system are not a panacea for solving problems. Although a better-constructed law and better incentive structures for law enforcement personnel may improve prosecution rates, they may not deal with the causes or consequences of human trafficking. Moreover, criminal justice is not always victims' justice. Provision of medical and psychological aid and employment training assistance to victims as part of a comprehensive rehabilitation package may do more to bring justice to the victims than prosecuting their traffickers ever will. Nevertheless, it is still important to ask how law enforcement's institutional machinery might be modified to help agents pursue complex crimes like human trafficking more effectively. Here I discuss the possibilities for changing each piece of the institutional machinery—the organizational culture, the organizational structure, and the statistical assessment system—then turn to what could be done to improve human trafficking prosecutions.

Organizational Culture

Changing years of entrenched institutional culture is not an easy task, and if it does occur, it takes place at a glacial pace. Thus it is unrealistic to expect that this will be the area in which Russian law enforcement agencies will improve their on-the-ground practices. The strict hierarchy and emphasis on subordination are something that law enforcement and the state have paid little attention to improving. Unfortunately this leads to a situation in which law enforcement officers are often trained for a reality that does not exist. Strict subordination in the ranks means that officers are afraid to use their own judgment and make decisions on their own for fear of being punished by their superiors. But, their job, especially for those on the front lines of law enforcement, inherently involves subjective, discretionary judgments. There has been consistent resistance to devolution of decision-making power to lower-level law enforcement agents to better reflect local needs, especially in the situation of local beat police (McCarthy 2014a). Despite a significant police reform in 2011, the organizational structure has proven highly resistant to change. If anything, the emphasis on hierarchical subordination has become stronger in the new postreform police, with superiors now supposed to take "personal responsibility" for their subordinates' behavior. Although in other contexts this approach could be a good thing, when introduced on top of Russia's already fearful culture of subordination, it is likely only to increase the fear of doing anything that may result in not clearing cases or meeting other performance targets.

The other aspect of organizational culture, widespread tolerance of corrupt practices, has been endlessly discussed within law enforcement agencies and by the government. In 2010, a frank report by Procurator General Yuri Chaika noted that the anticorruption drive within law enforcement had been a failure, with the price of average bribes increasing and few law enforcement officials being investigated and convicted of corruption (Oliphant 2010). Since then, regulations have been put in place to control corruption and numerous agencies created to oversee anticorruption drives, the most recent an office directly within the Presidential Administration established in December 2013 (d'Amora and Pfeifer 2013). The acceptance of corrupt practices as a normal part of policing activity has been a part of law enforcement's institutional culture at least since the 1990s. Since then, there has been little change in attitudes toward corruption within the force. The hierarchy guarantees that a cut of the now ubiquitous police protection rackets goes up the chain, which means that few insiders have any incentive to change the system. The system benefits those at the top and keeps lower-level agents relatively satisfied. Thus modifications that have a real impact on corruption will probably require some sort of stimulus from outside the agency as well as political will within the agency. This could happen through external review by local and regional government bodies or by citizens. Law enforcement has shown significant resistance to both.

Organizational Structure

It may seem as though the division of functions and the issues with overlapping jurisdiction are part of a poor organizational plan. In reality, the system that causes these problems is a consciously designed system of checks and balances to make sure that law enforcement agents can be held accountable for their actions. In fact, for most cases the organizational structure as designed by the 2001 Criminal Procedure Code works just fine. Its adoption was supported enthusiastically by the European Commission and the United States and was meant to limit Soviet-era excesses. During the Soviet period, there was almost no accountability at any stage of the criminal justice process, and police operated with near total discretion, doing whatever they needed to do to get cases cleared and meet their quotas. Now, theoretically, law enforcement agents at each stage know exactly what they need to do to successfully process the case through the system, and judges can throw out evidence collected in violation of the code. Unfortunately, with newer and more complex crimes the organizational structure seems to hinder law enforcement's ability to pursue these types of crimes successfully without resorting to old Soviet-style investigatory practices (especially in cases of terrorism or extremism) or by avoiding these charges completely and using other statutes with which they are familiar (Firestone 2010).

For over a decade the government has considered centralizing investigative functions in one agency, leaving the other agencies to do their jobs. At this point, it seems clear that if this were to happen, the functions would be moved to the Investigative Committee. Of course, none of the agencies that would be involved has any interest in giving up its investigative powers, so the struggle may continue for some time. On one hand, this sort of centralization could go a long way in taking at least one link out of the chain of uncertainty by making sure that the investigative function is contained within one agency. For human trafficking crimes and other crimes that have split jurisdiction between investigators in the MVD and the Investigative Committee, this change would certainly help standardize practice and concentrate experience in one location. On the other hand, the creation of an all-powerful investigative body that takes orders directly from the president, as the Investigative Committee does, may be used for political purposes and against perceived enemies of those in power. As the Investigative Committee has gained more power and independence from the Procuracy, this appears to be exactly what is happening. The Investigative Committee has been the primary vehicle for pursuing cases against participants in and organizers of the December 2011 street protests in Moscow in response to fraudulent Duma elections and in May 2012 after Putin's return to the presidency.

Statistical Assessment System

The system of statistical performance indicators plays a crucial role in shaping law enforcement's response to not only human trafficking crimes but crimes of all types. It can be used as a lever of power by the higher-ups in law enforcement agencies to induce lower-level officials to pursue particular types of crimes, but in the absence of strong encouragement from above, it tends to make agents cautious about taking risks, preferring to stick to investigating familiar and straightforward types of crimes when possible.

Despite numerous attempts to reform the *palochnaia sistema*, it has stayed in place. Why? According to Vadim Volkov (2010), without it there would be no accountability in police agencies, and law enforcement functions would become completely commercialized, with agents working for themselves rather than the state. Because there is no external oversight of law enforcement agencies (governmental or nongovernmental) and no transparency in their activities, there would be no check on their behavior without this system.[4] A less cynical explanation is that a system that measures performance statistics has the potential to create a virtuous circle in which, recognizing their debt to other actors in the system for good statistics, law enforcement agents at all stages do the best investigative work possible. Unfortunately, with the extreme hierarchical nature of Russian law enforcement, the emphasis on punishment and subordination, the separation of functions between agencies, and interagency rivalries, the creation of a virtuous circle is unlikely. Instead the system results in law enforcement agents colluding to charge less complicated statutes, or agreeing not to take cases forward, rejecting them on technicalities. As demonstrated above with the example of extremism charges, although the *palochnaia sistema* can be a hindrance, it is also incentivizing, if a blunt instrument at best. It can be a useful way to signal to lower-level law enforcement personnel the importance of pursuing a particular type of crime.

There have been several attempts to change the method of assessment in the MVD in particular, but even with changes, assessment criteria still fundamentally rely on counting the numbers of activities performed and comparisons to the previous year. In 2011 and 2012 the *palochnaia sistema* was changed to include comparison of departments across and within regions rather than just the comparison to the previous year. Other indicators of performance have been added: expert assessment by a body composed of senior MVD officers, public opinion surveys, and checks by inspectors.[5] But for the most part, these new standards still rely on quantitative indicators, and there is pressure for them to improve every year. In addition, they are primarily centered within the agencies and have little outside input either from local government or the public whom they are supposed

---

4. The only oversight is by the Procuracy under its powers of general supervision (*nadzor*) over the legal process and all its participants, but it usually steps in only in response to a complaint or some sort of serious transgression.

5. For a breakdown of this new system, including the specific statistics that are being assessed, see Paneyakh et al. 2012, 66–67.

to serve. There are models in other countries for incorporating qualitative assessments into law enforcement's assessment mechanism, but thus far Russian law enforcement has been resistant to employing them, since most of them involve horizontal accountability by way of external control and supervision over law enforcement activities.

How to improve the *palochnaia sistema* has been a long-running debate within the MVD. No one has come up with an alternative. Law enforcement agencies around the world employ some sort of statistical assessment tool to monitor and evaluate the police. Why is this activity so destructive in the Russian context? The combination of statistical assessments with the strong culture of hierarchy and subordination means that all law enforcement priorities end up being set from the center. In addition, the extensive documentation requirements required to maintain the system leave police, especially at the ground level, with little time to do anything else (McCarthy 2014a; Volkov 2014). These constraints hinder the development of local initiatives that may benefit certain regions that experience particular types of problems (Taylor 2014a). Human trafficking is one area where devolution of priority setting could be helpful. According to interviews and data from the news media, there does appear to be some geographic regularity to human trafficking cases, with some regions having a higher concentration of them than others. With more ability to set priorities locally, those regions that have high migration flows, for example, might devote more time and investigative resources to pursuing labor trafficking cases. Regions with higher levels of prostitution may devote more resources to pursuing sex trafficking cases. This change would require a massive reorientation of the goals of policing away from state protection and more toward a problem-oriented policing strategy and the devolution of some power to the local level, steps that Russian law enforcement agencies seem reluctant to take.

Improving Human Trafficking Prosecutions

Even with over a decade of practice on human trafficking under their belts, significant gaps remain in the ability of law enforcement personnel across agencies to find, identify, investigate, and prosecute human trafficking cases. According to Anne Gallagher and Paul Holmes (2008), specialized law enforcement capacity and expertise for investigating human trafficking crimes is a critical piece in an effective criminal justice response to the problem. Although Russia has taken a step in this direction at the level of the operativniki, it has no specialized investigators or procurators. Informally, if an investigator or procurator has worked on a particular type of case before, especially something uncommon like human trafficking, he will likely get future cases, but there is no guarantee. This system wastes valuable experience that has been built up on these complex investigations, experience that could be used to improve future cases.

In thinking about how to accomplish the needed reforms, the experience of anti-extremism units can be instructive. After establishing elite units of operativniki specializing in uncovering and collecting evidence on extremism crimes, law enforcement realized that often these specialist officers were running into generalist investigators who did not understand the extremism statute well enough to take the evidence they had collected and turn it into a prosecutable case. After ten years of practice, the government and law enforcement agencies created a corresponding specialized unit of investigators in the Investigative Committee and procurators at the federal and regional levels. In this case, specialization has mitigated the problems that the institutional division of functions causes, even though it also has drawbacks. Another alternative that could enable human trafficking prosecutions is to change the Criminal Procedure Code so that all trafficking violations fall under the jurisdiction of one investigative agency instead of being split between the MVD and the Investigative Committee. A third option would be to make human trafficking courses mandatory for certain groups of investigators and procurators in the continuing education programs that they must complete before being promoted, ensuring that more people would be able to recognize trafficking if they encounter it. Though these courses do exist, they are few and far between, being offered at only some continuing education academies.

A centralized point of contact with law enforcement can also be important and helpful in building trusting relationships with victim assistance organizations, which are likely to be the primary conduit between law enforcement and victims and an important source for information on trafficking cases. However, this result requires cooperation in a way that is uncomfortable for both the NGOs and law enforcement, because it requires some compromise over their primary activities and the development of mutual understanding of each other's needs and duties. The three years of cooperation between the IOM and Moscow's city, regional, and federal law enforcement agencies is a testament to the possibilities for improving trafficking investigations and prosecutions in this way. Institutionalization and agreement on the contours of these relationships is crucial; otherwise they will continue to be based on personal contact and the trust that has built up between a particular victim assistance organization and the individual law enforcement agent who regularly interacts with it. When one of these people leaves his or her position, the cooperation tends to cease and the trust must be rebuilt from scratch. The current state of the relationship between civil society and law enforcement means that this outcome may not be as likely as it once was. In addition to basic distrust of each other's goals, there is now the added issue of labeling organizations that receive foreign funding "foreign agents" and the consequent shuttering of many of the foreign grant-giving organizations in Russia. Most of the trafficking assistance provided in Russia since 2000 has been the result of grants from foreign organizations to local organizations to perform educational and rehabilitative services for trafficking victims.

The Future of Human Trafficking in Russia

Despite Russia's rhetoric and commitments to dealing with trafficking made at the regional (CIS, Council of Europe, OSCE) and international (UN) level, there is still much to be done. Widespread recognition within law enforcement of the need for shelter and rehabilitative services to help the police pursue trafficking cases has largely been ignored by state agencies that could fund these services. A center to coordinate law enforcement activity on trafficking proposed by the MVD's Investigative Committee in May 2008 has yet to materialize and as of 2014, there is only one active shelter for trafficking victims located in St. Petersburg (Novye izvestia 2008). The buck passing among government agencies about whose responsibility trafficking is continues and the legislator Elena Mizulina, who was the primary champion of further legislation on trafficking-related causes, has moved instead toward championing legislation on conservative morality-based issues such as prohibiting adoption for foreigners, increasing the role of the church, and preventing "gay propaganda" from being spread to children. The long-standing debate about whether trafficking victims should be the subject of special legislation or part of a broader legislative package providing compensation and rehabilitation to victims of crime more generally was resolved in favor of the latter point of view with the passage of a law in 2011 that granted compensation to crime victims from a state-run fund. The fund comes from the assets confiscated from crimes, but implementing legislation and budgetary funding have been slow in coming (Krainova 2011). If the law is anything like the witness protection program, it will be several years before it is up and running, and even then it will continue to be woefully underfunded.

There has also been reticence to seeing labor trafficking as a problem affecting Russia, but according to the 2013 Global Slavery Index, the first worldwide count of enslaved people, Russia ranks in the top ten for the absolute number of people in modern slavery, with estimates between 490,000 and 540,000 (Walk Free 2013). Many of these are victims of labor trafficking. The most likely victims of labor trafficking are migrants, but the strong antimigration sentiment prevalent throughout Russia means that migrants are not seen as particularly deserving of state resources in any context. In a particularly egregious example in Vladivostok, an undocumented Uzbek immigrant woman in labor was turned away from a state hospital because she did not have papers. In this case, it was the police who eventually forced the clinic to accept her. After giving birth, she fled and was later found. Deportation hearings began soon after (Arutunyan 2013). Antimigrant protests and even riots have increased for several years, and the police have encouraged this fear by blaming migrants for committing a large share of crime (Pravda.ru 2012). As a result, exploitative situations that rise to the level of trafficking and use of slave labor are less likely to be reported—migrants fear the police most of all—and the exploitation will be driven further underground, making migrants all the more vulnerable.

Nevertheless, there has been some interesting civil society movement on the issue of human trafficking. The direct action civil society group, Alternativa, has been staging rescue operations of men and women enslaved in sex and labor situations, primarily focusing on the North Caucasus and in some cases even cooperating with the police. They have reportedly freed over a hundred slaves since their inception, most of whom were ethnic Russians (Quinn 2014). Although their rescues have rarely resulted in criminal charges against the exploiters, they have received widespread exposure in the media for their daring and have drawn attention to the issue of trafficking in a way that has been lacking in the Russian context.

In 2013, for the first time since 2002, Russia fell from the Tier 2 watch list to Tier 3, the lowest tier of the *Trafficking in Persons Report* rankings (Dept. of State 2013b).[6] It was cited for "not making significant efforts to comply with the minimum standards," and particularly for its lack of progress in protecting and assisting victims and undertaking programs to prevent trafficking. Despite the MVD's August 2012 campaign in which it handed out pamphlets about human trafficking at train stations and on the streets, it seems that the state of affairs for pursuing trafficking in Russia has leveled out. Law enforcement regularly registers between seventy and a hundred cases of trafficking a year, but by agents' own admission, few of the defendants are ultimately convicted of trafficking (see official statistics in appendix B). Understanding how the institutional machinery of law enforcement causes personnel to be cautious about using trafficking laws explains this result. According to my data, of the cases reported in the media, law enforcement has chosen to use trafficking laws to pursue suspects in only

_____

6. Russia was placed on the Tier 2 watch list from 2004 to 2012 after one year on Tier 2 (Dept. of State 2003, 2004b-2013b). Starting in 2011, the Trafficking Victims Protection Reauthorization Act of 2008 required any country that would have received a Tier 2 watch list placement but had already been on the Tier 2 watch list for more than two years to be automatically downgraded to Tier 3. For the first two years, 2011 and 2012, Russia received a waiver because it had a written plan that, if implemented, would bring it into compliance, but the legislation limits waivers to two consecutive years. Russia remained on Tier 3 in the 2014 report (Dept. of State 2014).

about half of the cases that could fit the legal definition of human trafficking. Agents have made discretionary decisions, based on their institution's incentive structure, about when it is worthwhile to take the risks of using a relatively untested law. The good news is that for every trafficking case not pursued under human trafficking laws, agents frequently pursue and convict traffickers under other related laws. Ultimately, the great irony of Russia's human trafficking laws is that they have been simultaneously ineffective and yet have had their intended effect—bringing traffickers to justice—an effect that would not have happened without their passage.

METHODOLOGY

In this appendix I outline the challenges I faced in getting access to closed organizations and discuss the research strategy I developed to deal with these challenges. I also explain the data collection process for my data set of human trafficking cases, which allowed me to track the human trafficking situation throughout Russia, not just in the regions I visited. Through each of these approaches, I was able to gain different pieces of information that, when combined, gave me a full picture of Russian law enforcement's efforts to combat human trafficking. I include this appendix not only to explain my methods in more detail but also to pull back the curtain on how research is actually done in places like Russia and the creative solutions one must come up with in situations when the ideal data are either not available or your research subjects refuse to talk to you. It is my hope that graduate students and other scholars who read this will find some comfort in the honesty that comes with admitting that doing fieldwork is not as smooth and seamless as many finished manuscripts make it seem.

The data gathering for this book was anything but straightforward. In Russia, law enforcement agencies continue to operate in a nontransparent fashion and are reluctant to open up their practices to scrutiny by outsiders. There is a pervasive fear of speaking to foreigners (probably inherited from the Soviet era) that persists today with almost all state officials. The difficulty in penetrating Russian law enforcement is increased for an issue like human trafficking, which has garnered widespread international attention largely because of the government's and law enforcement's failure to act. Anyone doing research on policing must contend with the "blue curtain" of silence and secrecy in law enforcement agencies (Fox and Lundman 1974; Fleming 2010). I must admit, however, that during my ten months in Russia doing the primary research for this book (September 2007–July 2008), I found Russian law enforcement a particularly tough nut to crack.

I chose Moscow as the base for conducting my research because the federal-level agencies of the MVD and Procuracy are located there, as were a number of international and nongovernmental organizations working on human trafficking. I entered the field in September 2007 with a list of NGOs that had been listed as working on human trafficking as well as lists of law enforcement agents who had attended various conferences on human trafficking over the previous five or so years. I also had contacts through the work of Louise Shelley's Transnational Crime and Corruption Center (TraCCC), which then operated out of American University (Washington, DC) and now is based at George Mason University. Since the mid-1990s, TraCCC had been heavily involved in research on human trafficking and centers existed in several cities I visited (Saratov, Khabarovsk, Vladivostok, and Stavropol). Finally, I had contacts from previous time in Russia doing internships with the Angel Coalition, an anti-trafficking organization in Moscow, and at USAID in Washington, DC.

When I first arrived in Moscow, my initial attempts to speak with law enforcement were made through a series of letters that I faxed to agents who I knew had had some involvement in the drafting of the anti-trafficking legislation. In follow-up phone calls, I spoke with these agents. My requests to meet were met with brusque refusals. Some said they no longer worked on the issue but refused to speak with me about their previous experiences. Others hung up on me, presumably on hearing my accented Russian, before I could finish explaining who I was and why I was interested in speaking with them. I tried a similar tactic when I went on my first trip outside Moscow to Saratov because I thought that in the regions, people might be more willing to talk to me. In advance, I wrote a letter and faxed it to the local procurator's office, following it up with a phone call. I spoke with a very kind procurator who indicated that he would be happy to meet with me. But on the morning of our scheduled meeting, he called me apologetically to tell me that without permission from the federal-level procurator's office, he would not be able to talk to me. Despite my efforts, I was unable to contact the "proper" person at the federal level in time and had to cancel the interview.

This same pattern happened when I tried to get statistics through the official statistical agency of the MVD, the Main Information and Analytical Center (Glavnyi informatsionno-analiticheskii tsentr, GIATs). After submitting my request with letters of support from the Fulbright office in Moscow and the Russian university with which I was affiliated, I was given the run-around for several weeks. My request was transferred to several different offices and through several different people with whom I dutifully followed up each time. Finally, several months later, they said they could not help me. Other contacts who, I had originally believed, could set me up to talk with law enforcement agents also were unable to help. Law enforcement officials' busy schedules and their disinterest in speaking with people like me who "had nothing to offer them" were cited as reasons for not helping me make these connections.

Access was so difficult that after about two months of silence punctuated by a handful of meetings with tangentially related organizations, I called my dissertation adviser to tearfully report that I was going to have to change my topic because no one would talk to me. Out of desperation, I began compiling a data set of human trafficking cases reported in the media, hoping to at least have something to work with (see below for more discussion of these data). But miraculously, about two weeks after the tearful phone call with my adviser and a furious spurt of data entry, my persistence paid off as two important channels opened up to me. In late October, I was finally able to meet with the U.S. Department of Justice's attaché in Moscow, who had done a significant amount of work on human trafficking. I had made these contacts through a summer of interning at the Europe and Eurasia Division of USAID in Washington, DC, for a project on domestic violence and human trafficking. In the meeting, he told me that his office was arranging and sponsoring conferences on human trafficking education for law enforcement and invited me to their upcoming conference at the MVD academy in Stavropol. I quickly procured a third-class ticket on the same train, the cheapest one available, made a reservation at a Soviet-era hotel and was on my way. Ultimately, through these contacts I was invited to multiday conferences at law enforcement academies in Stavropol (twice) and Kazan. In addition, at the invitation of the Embassy, I attended conferences run by NGOs, which brought together stakeholders in the fight against human trafficking, giving me access to more law enforcement agents. These took place in Moscow, Irkutsk, and Vladivostok. At the latter two I was an invited speaker.

Meeting people in the conference context helped with access because they were already ready and willing to talk about the issue. Approaching officers in precincts or on the street randomly to ask about human trafficking would have been fruitless for several reasons. First, most of them would never have encountered human trafficking, and second, they would have been completely unwilling to speak to me. Instead, by introducing myself at conferences and asking to talk later, either at the conference or in a separate meeting, I gained more credibility as a researcher. Law enforcement agents to whom I spoke during lunches or coffee breaks often agreed to meet with me later for a more formal conversation about the human trafficking laws. In each location, I stayed longer than the conference to conduct more interviews and meet with representatives of local organizations.

The conference invitations gave me both an excuse and the funding to travel and meet with representatives of these organizations, many of which had rich histories of working on women's issues, including trafficking.

The second piece of my research strategy was to make contacts and begin doing volunteer work at the International Organization for Migration (IOM), which was running the most comprehensive anti-trafficking program in Russia at the time. The IOM program—funded by the European Commission in Russia, the US State Department and the Swiss government—had opened a shelter for trafficking victims in Moscow and was working with government officials and law enforcement agencies to improve their implementation of the trafficking laws. My time at the IOM mostly consisted of collecting data and translating and editing research that had been done by the IOM from Russian into English. By being there on a regular basis, I gained access to meetings, conferences, and interviews with officials and law enforcement agents, especially those at the federal level, to whom I would otherwise not have had access.

At these conferences and workshops, my status as a guest of the US Embassy or the IOM elevated my importance in the eyes of the law enforcement agents to whom I spoke. I was no longer a lowly graduate student whom they could ignore, but someone with whom they could speak on an official level. I was "in" enough, but not so much that I was one of them. I saw the law enforcement agents behave very differently with my American friends and colleagues who had law enforcement backgrounds. The brotherhood of police and prosecutors seems to be international. I was also not identified as a part of the NGO community which many law enforcement agents view suspiciously. Building trust was a fundamental piece of my research work with law enforcement, and agents do not trust people whom they think have an agenda, especially one that they associate with Western-funded, "feminist" organizations.[1] The trust and connections that I built in this year of research allowed me to continue to access the same people in my follow-up visits in 2009, 2012, and 2013 and to contact them in the meantime via e-mail with any questions that arose about new cases or other information that was unclear.

There were certain advantages to being an outsider (though a privileged outsider, because of my connections with the Embassy and IOM). People were curious about me. They wanted to know why I was there. What was I trying to

---

1. In Russia, feminism has a negative connotation and is considered a Western-oriented project at odds with traditional Russian values. During the Soviet period, it was identified with lesbianism and aggressive women who reject men and the family and has continued to have that association during the post-Soviet period (Sperling 1999; Kay 2000).

accomplish? After several conversations in which I was asked how we did things in the United States, I realized people did not understand why I was interested only in Russia. In fact, it seemed insulting to many people with whom I spoke that I was focusing on the trafficking problem in Russia when we had the same problem at home. Unwittingly, I found I needed to also become knowledgeable about US anti-trafficking law. This approach opened a lot of doors for me because I could use the comparative information to ask law enforcement agents how and why they did things the way they did, while giving them information on how it was done in the United States. By serving a function at these conferences, I was more accepted, and people were more interested in what I had to say. In fact, based on this supplemental research, I wrote a paper that compared Russian and American law enforcement practices on human trafficking. This paper was published in Russian (McCarthy 2008), and its reception at a June 2008 conference in Vladivostok on migration gave rise to invitations to speak at a series of conferences in other cities in Russia.

In addition to conference invitations—which took me to a variety of cities throughout Russia, some of which had had trafficking cases and some of which had not—I decided to visit several cities where I knew there had been trafficking prosecutions. I started by going to Saratov for a week where I had contacts with an affiliate of TraCCC who had done some of the first research work on human trafficking. The institute was affiliated with the Saratov State Law Academy, one of the most prestigious law schools in Russia. Several of the professors working with the center had participated in the drafting of the human trafficking law. They had also conducted training sessions for law enforcement personnel. In addition to talking to the people who worked in the center, they were able to arrange meetings with some of their local affiliates. Saratov also had one of the first successful prosecutions of human trafficking in Russia, decided in 2005.

The second city, Yoshkar Ola in the Republic of Mari El, was one that I discovered as a result of my data collection on human trafficking cases. As I put the data set together, I realized that this formerly closed city had had two successful major sex trafficking prosecutions in which the defendants had been sentenced to significant prison terms. I was interested to find out what was going on, so I decided to take a week-long trip there to visit a friend who was teaching English locally. Through a chain of informal contacts, I was able to get in touch with law enforcement agents who had been involved in investigating these cases. I coincidentally arrived the day before the sentencing hearing for one trafficking case and was able to attend the hearing and speak to the procurator and defense lawyers afterward. I also was able to interview one of the convicted traffickers in jail and examine the court documents and evidence films.

Finally, I went to the Russian Far East for a month, where I visited the cities of Vladivostok and Khabarovsk. According to MVD statistics from 2007, the Far Eastern Federal District had by far the greatest number of registered human trafficking cases, although on arriving I found that in reality it was only a few cases, each with a lot of victims. Furthermore, TraCCC has a center in Vladivostok, and I had previous contacts with one of the people who worked there. She was able to help me arrange interviews with attendees from previous law enforcement training sessions that the center had conducted. I also had several contacts with local NGOs working on human trafficking, which were able to help me make other contacts for interviews. In addition, I was invited to write and present a paper there for the 2008 international conference on migration politics. The session in which I presented focused on human trafficking and included law enforcement personnel from the MVD and Procuracy with whom I was later able to speak more formally. In Khabarovsk, I encountered a similar situation. My main contact was a person who had worked with TraCCC. He was able to contact people who had worked on trafficking cases for me to interview. I also spoke with local NGO representatives who had been working on trafficking since the early 2000s.

There were advantages and disadvantages to doing this research as a woman. In the male-dominated world of Russian law enforcement, there were often moments where the agents I was with acted with pity and condescension toward me because I was "just" a woman and could not possibly understand how things really worked. They would then try to take me under their wing and proceed to explain to me, as if to a child, exactly how and why things worked as they did. In these instances, although it went against my instincts, I usually played along and consequently found this to be incredibly helpful in getting more complete information because they did not see me as a threat or someone with whom they had to act hypermasculine, as they tended to do with other law enforcement personnel (see Johnson 2009b). However, in my interactions with law enforcement, I often had to put aside my personal beliefs in women's rights (especially on the topic of domestic violence) to gain better access to what law enforcement agents thought and felt and not make them feel as though I had an agenda.

Many people have wondered about my safety while doing research on the topic of human trafficking. I consciously chose not to investigate the process of trafficking, which might have exposed me to danger in the underground criminal world. However, doing research with Russian law enforcement had the potential to be dangerous because of their often unconstrained power and nontransparency. If they had felt that I was too pushy or straying into uncomfortable territory, it was entirely possible they could have arrested me. In fact, during my fieldwork, I was once invited in for questioning by the FSB in Moscow, but it was unclear whether it was related to my research or part of a larger inquiry into visa procedures for visiting students. Although I never personally felt unsafe, there was no guarantee to my safety. When confronted with situations in which my personal security might have been at risk, I made the decision to be a "good enough researcher with good enough information" rather than pursuing information that might put me in danger (Johnson 2009b, 323). I was unquestionably a "known entity" to the security services because I needed clearance to enter many of the conference sites. Without it, I would not have been able to attend these closed conferences.

I also believe that the timing of my research was particularly auspicious. For an American talking to Russian government officials, access is usually available only when the broader political relationship is positive. My fieldwork was conducted during the 2007–2008 academic year, a time during which there was little controversy between the US and Russian governments. Had I attempted to do this research the following year, after the war between Russia and Georgia, or any later time in the context of an increasingly strained relationship between the countries, I feel certain that the access that I got would have been nearly impossible. In addition, I had the advantage that the issue of trafficking had become less politicized as pressure on Russia from the United States and the international community to pass a comprehensive anti-trafficking law had largely died down, and the focus had shifted to better implementing the existing law. This timing gave me an opening that previous scholars researching human trafficking laws in Russia may not have had, because many of them were researching the topic in the aftermath of the nonpassage of the Working Group law, when there was heightened sensitivity about it. The only time I saw politics become involved in human trafficking while I was there was when the US *Trafficking in Persons Report* was released, which was met with angry remarks from the Ministry of Foreign Affairs. The topic of human trafficking was sensitive enough to law enforcement personnel, who recognized that their case numbers on human trafficking were low, but not so sensitive that they were unwilling to talk about it and explain why they had such a difficult time implementing the laws. Finally, during the time I was in Russia, human trafficking was a priority for the US Embassy in Moscow and had been for at least five years. The end of my fieldwork period coincided with trafficking becoming a lower priority for the Embassy, with fewer resources dedicated to sponsoring conferences and other events.

Another challenge that I had to overcome to get information was the emphasis on strict positivism in law enforcement. Most officers are educated in a system that emphasizes rote memorization of codes, which means that they are conditioned to find the one, correct answer, as I quickly learned when I tried to do a survey at an early law enforcement conference that I attended. Trying to see how agents would charge different types of situations under the Criminal Code, I gave them several hypothetical scenarios with open-ended answers, asking which article in the Criminal Code they would use and why. I tried to use situations that I had seen charged as recruitment into prostitution or organizing illegal migration but which I thought could be charged as trafficking. When I received the surveys back (only 15 of the 150 attendees at this particular conference bothered to fill them out), they all identified 127.1 and 127.2 as the proper articles, exactly as they were trained to do, especially in the context of a conference focused on human trafficking. This was the beginning and end of my use of surveys. My methodology of in-depth interviews and participant observation allowed me to move beyond agents taking out the code book to answer my questions and find out what they did on a day-to-day basis when dealing with trafficking. In this way, I learned that officers' answers on the survey about the appropriateness of using the human trafficking articles rarely corresponded to practice. Most officers were hesitant to use the human trafficking laws in most instances and preferred to fall back on more familiar articles.

Many people went to great lengths to help me with my research and were incredibly generous in sharing their time and connections with me. Many invited me into their homes and shared their lives and families with me, especially when I was in regions outside Moscow. There were many twists and turns during my year of research, and I found that my greatest asset was being able to go with the flow and take whatever opportunities were presented to me. This meant talking to just about anyone and sometimes finding myself in uncomfortable and unexpected situations. For example, in Khabarovsk my main contact arranged what I thought was a sham conference so that I could speak with a judge who, he thought, would be helpful to me. Much to my surprise, when the conference day came, I was the featured speaker to a captivated audience of about fifty college students who delighted in watching the American present in Russian. I was then interviewed about my research for the college's newspaper. My research diary was full of entries like "Today I went to what I thought was a meeting, but it turned into a conference with the Head of the MVD." Often, when I thought I'd be meeting with one person and had prepared questions for him or her, several people showed up. Once, in Kazan, I was set up for a meeting with a medical organization that distributed condoms to local prostitutes, a far cry from what I was working on. When they asked me why I was interested in talking to them, I struggled to answer the question. It was by far the most awkward meeting I had.

In total, I spoke with 140 people involved in some way with human trafficking. This included police in the MVD, procurators and Investigative Committee members, agents in the security services, NGOs offering rehabilitative services to trafficking victims, and Russian and foreign experts on human trafficking. I also had the opportunity to speak with the Albanian trafficker mentioned in

TABLE A.1   Interview sources

INTERVIEW SOURCE	NUMBER
Russian academic/expert (A)	9
Judge (J)	5
MVD (M)[a]	23
NGO and international organization (N)[b]	53
Other (O)[c]	30
Procuracy (P)[d]	9
Foreign expert (U)	7

[a] Includes operativniki, investigators, and professors at MVD institutes
[b] Includes domestic Russian NGOs, foreign NGOs with branches in Russia, and international organizations working in Russia
[c] Includes victims of trafficking, representatives of the Presidential Administration, FSB
[d] Includes investigators, courtroom procurators, and professors at Procuracy institutes

the book's opening story after his conviction, as well as victims in several regions. This gave me the comprehensive perspective that I needed to assess law enforcement's behavior. For the protection of my information sources, I refer only to their agency and city of employment when describing my conversations with them. Quotations throughout are based on handwritten notes from each interview, which I typed up immediately afterwards. While it would have been preferable to record, I quickly found that recording interviews made subjects uncomfortable. Table A.1 shows the types of informants and the numbers of each type with whom I spoke along with their category code used throughout this book.

Data Set of Trafficking Cases

As noted in the first part of this appendix, my data set of trafficking incidents identified by the news media began in desperation when my interview strategy initially failed. Little did I realize at the time what a rich source of data it would become. Using online, publicly available national and local Russian news media articles (television transcripts, newspapers, online reporting) and information from court Web sites, I tracked how trafficking incidents fared through the criminal justice process. The data set includes all the incidents that I could locate from the passage of the law in December 2003 through December 2013, a total of 527 discrete cases from over 5,200 news articles. All articles that used the words "human trafficking" (*torgovlia liud'mi*) or "use of slave labor" (*ispol'zovanie rab-*

skogo truda), the official wording of the Criminal Code articles, or other terms that connote human trafficking, such as sexual slavery (*seksual'noe rabstvo*), sex slave (*seks rabyn'*), slave trade (*rabotorgovlia*), slaveholder (*rabovladelets*), and trafficking (*treffiking, traffiking*) were coded if they involved Russians, either as victims or as perpetrators, and/or if the destination country was Russia. For practical purposes, I exclude from discussion the many mentions in the media of attempted trafficking into Russia that were stopped at the border and are being pursued in the legal systems of the countries where the victims originated. Though I collected some information on them, it proved to be too difficult to track these cases in the countries where they were being pursued. In addition, they have little to do with the practices of Russian law enforcement agencies, which are the primary focus of the book.

From September 2007 to December 2013, all articles with any of these keywords were delivered to my e-mail in-box every day from Yandex, a Russian indexing service that provides daily topic e-mails for free. I subscribed to a similar service from the news agency Novoteka. Articles about earlier trafficking incidents were located through extensive search procedures on online news sites that had national or regional coverage (Newsru.com, Regions.ru, Regnum.ru, Interfax, RIA Novosti, Gzt.ru, Komsomol'skaia pravda, Novyi region, Nr2.ru). I also ran a search from 2004 to 2008 for the same terms in the Eastview database of Russian national and regional newspapers.

My inclusion criteria for the data set were based on a broad reading of the wording of the Russian law—any situation that the broadest possible interpretation of the human trafficking statute would cover was included. This also allowed me to track the alternative charging practices that law enforcement used, as I could follow some of the cases that ended up not being charged as human trafficking but still had trafficking-like elements. For example, women recruited into prostitution and forced to stay with threats of or use of violence were included, because they included one element of trafficking (usually recruitment) and one form of exploitation (prostitution or slave labor) as defined by the Russian Criminal Code. They also usually included one or more aggravating factors as outlined in the human trafficking law (e.g., threat or use of violence; using a minor, etc.). My data search methodology did not pick up cases where alternative articles of the Criminal Code were used but the cases were never labeled with my search terms. This means that the many cases of recruitment into prostitution with aggravating factors that could make them qualify as trafficking (e.g., victims were forced to continue in prostitution through threats or use of violence) were not included. An incident was considered to have been charged as human trafficking if a specific trafficking charge (including both article number and/or aggravating factors as worded in the Criminal Code article) was mentioned in any of the newspaper articles referring to that case or the case was reported as opened (*vozbuzhdeno*) as either human trafficking or use of slave labor, using the specific language of the Criminal Code.

Each incident was registered as its own separate entry in an Access database. I could then connect any future articles about it with the information that already existed in the database. Most of these incidents turned into officially opened criminal cases, either under human trafficking laws or other laws. Some did not and after the initial report were never mentioned in the news media again. In some situations, one or several defendant's cases were separated out of the main case, either because the defendant concluded a cooperation agreement with the investigator or because he or she fled and was caught after the other members of the group had been tried. I kept situations like this together in one entry, tracking each case's progression separately in my description. Especially with large, complex trafficking rings, this was easier said than done, as different parts of the case were often found and opened separately and only later combined when investigators realized they were connected to a larger trafficking scheme. Though there is some possibility of double-counting incidents, it is unlikely given the level of detail and careful checking that I have done for all entries in the data set.

Before 2008, copies of the news media articles were kept in an EndNote database and after 2008, in Zotero. All news articles were coded by region and type of trafficking, and I logged as many details about each case as were available from the news reports and court documents. Table A.2 describes the data fields recorded for each case.

TABLE A.2 Data fields

BASIC CASE INFORMATION	OFFENSE-SPECIFIC INFORMATION	DEFENDANT/VICTIM INFORMATION
Type of trafficking	Specific charge under 127.1	Officials involved?
City and region of origin/	or 127.2	Women involved as
destination	Convicted of 127.1 or	suspects?
Court of first instance, appeal	127.2?	Number of suspects involved
and case nos.	Other charges?	Sentence length and type (for
Summary of case	Convicted of other charges?	each defendant)
Key dates (date opened, arrested,		Number of victims and basic
sent to court, convicted/		info (age, origin region,
acquitted, took legal effect)		etc.)
Length of case		Minors involved?
Investigating agency		

Putting this data set together required a great deal of detective work as there were varying amounts of information for each case. Sometimes I had all the details, including the names of the defendants. For others, I had only a brief mention of the case's existence, which contained little detail and was therefore difficult to follow up on. For many cases, the crime was only mentioned once, and despite my best efforts, I could find no follow-up information anywhere on the Russian Internet. Mostly the data gathering process was one of working back and forth among multiple data sources. For example, some media reports of cases did not include defendants' names, but I was able to locate the names by looking up the specific charge and the dates on the court Web sites. In other instances, I was able to find a defendant's name with a human trafficking charge on the court Web sites and work backward through a Yandex search to find out more information about the case.

All the included cases started during the time period of the study, but some did not have a final resolution by the time the study period had closed. Ongoing cases are included, with a final search to tie up all loose ends conducted in October 2014. Because of the spotty nature of some of the information, I was not able to find out what happened in a number of cases. I classify a case as having an unclear resolution if I could find no further information in Yandex or court Web site searches at least eighteen months after the last mention of that case in the media. Otherwise it is, perhaps optimistically, categorized as ongoing.

I performed several cross checks to make sure that the information contained in the data set was accurate and complete. One of my main concerns was to make sure that I was picking up approximately the same number and location of trafficking cases that law enforcement reported in their official data. I was able to obtain the MVD's regional breakdown of cases registered from 2005 to 2009, which I compared to my data for those years. This exercise turned out to be more difficult than I had expected, since the MVD counts cases differently from me. I count an incident of human trafficking as one case, regardless of the number of victims, if it was committed by the same group of people. The MVD (and other law enforcement agencies) may either count each victim as a separate registered case or may count several victims in one registered case depending on the circumstances. It was only when I lined up the number of victims in the cases I had in my data set with the MVD's number of cases registered that I was able to compare the numbers. Although I did not have a perfect match, the numbers were close enough for me to believe that most human trafficking cases registered by the MVD are also being picked up in the Russian media and therefore are contained in my data set. Most cases in the data set have at least one press release from a law enforcement agency in the group of articles used to create the data-set entry, and almost all of them cite sources in law enforcement for their information.

In fact, if each individual victim is counted as a case, my data set picked up more cases that were charged as human trafficking than were registered by the MVD. There are a number of reasons that this may be the case. The media may have used my search terms to refer to situations that I ultimately judged not to be trafficking or that were eventually registered as some other type of case. Also, some of the cases in my data set referenced situations where a criminal case had not yet been or was never initiated.

The second check I performed was for the accuracy of the reports contained in the media. For each case, I cross-referenced stories from different media outlets to make sure I had the basic facts correct, doing additional Yandex and Google searches to turn up more information. Many of the cases had seemingly huge numbers of reports on them, but it turned out that many smaller media outlets reproduced verbatim what a larger media outlet reported, making many of the news articles repetitive rather than confirmatory. In all cases, however, there were enough reports from reliable media sources to gauge what was actually happening.

In addition, for cases where I had information on the court of first instance, I looked at the court Web sites to get basic information on the cases when it was available. This information usually included the articles of the Criminal Code under which defendants were charged and convicted and the dates for key moments in the criminal process, but sometimes the records did not have even this information. For those cases where the name of the court of first instance was not specifically mentioned, sometimes I was able to figure it out through other information such as the town where the trafficking took place or the law enforcement agency that investigated it.[2] Though Russian courts are now required by law to post basic information on their Web sites (defendants, charges, court dates), not all of them have put their backlog of past cases online yet (Federal Law no. 262-FZ of 2008). Most do not start until 2009. I was able to find more information in these sources for cases in the later part of my study period.

Unfortunately, the way the Russian courts have set up their Web-site system, it is not possible to search for one Criminal Code article in all courts in the country.

---

2. If it was a local MVD or Procuracy unit, I assumed that meant it would have had its first hearing in the district court and searched accordingly. If the case was investigated at the regional level, I assumed it would have had its first hearing at the regional court.

Each individual court has its own Web site. Initially, many of the court Web sites were not even searchable by Criminal Code article, although this changed in the later years of my study.[3] In the early years, then, I mostly ended up searching by defendant's last name, which I sometimes did not have. Knowing that trafficking cases are usually appealed, I looked on appellate court Web sites for the regions where the first instance courts operated, both for the specific cases contained in the data and then in a broader search for any trafficking charges as that function became more widely available. In a handful of instances this turned up human trafficking charges that I was unable to connect to any other information either in the data set or on the Russian Internet, so I did not include them in my final count. Finally, I searched the Russian Federation Supreme Court Web site, which is not searchable by Criminal Code article.[4] For cases with named defendants, I searched by defendant's last name. All these searches combined enabled me to find a number of cases and court documents beyond those that I had found in the news or was given personally while doing my fieldwork. I also looked through Web sites that aggregated court documents, including Reshenie-sudov.ru and G-courts.ru, searching under both the title of the human trafficking statutes and the statute number. In addition to data from the news media articles, I collected 161 documents from 155 different cases spread over 46 regions of Russia, with some cases having multiple types of documents. Table A.3 describes the types and number of documents.

There are limitations to the methodology of studying human trafficking using media reports that should be acknowledged. Allowing the media to define the

TABLE A.3   Court documents

TYPE OF COURT DOCUMENT	CHILD	SEX	LABOR	TOTAL
Sentence	9	20	15	44
Appeal/decision from Cassation Court	8	36	22	66
Russian Supreme Court appeal	0	12	4	16
Other[a]	9	13	7	29

[a] Includes documents given to me personally by law enforcement, official speeches and presentations done by law enforcement for which I have the text, one indictment document, and one Constitutional Court appeal.

3. Local and regional courts in Russia can be accessed through the gateway Web site, http://www.sudrf.ru/index.php?id=300. Although there is a template provided for each court to utilize, each individual court defines which fields its records are searchable by and each court has made different progress toward digitizing past court records.

4. Documents from the Criminal Division of the Russian Federation Supreme Court are accessible at http://www.vsrf.ru/vs_cases2.php. They can be searched by case number, defendant name, and date of hearing. In most cases, the only information I had of these options was the defendant's name.

universe of cases may mean that only incidents that are stereotypically human trafficking—those where innocent women are sexually exploited abroad—or are particularly egregious are reported on by media outlets. Research in other countries has suggested that this may be a problem (Denton 2010; Rao and Presenti 2012). The data from Russia, however, show a wider range of situations that have been described as human trafficking than the stereotypical narrative. Media reported on cases in which women willingly took jobs as prostitutes and on cases that took place in Russia as well as abroad. In addition, there was significant reporting on cases of men forced into labor trafficking. It is possible that the recognition of what slavery or trafficking is may have increased over time, such that early media reports more closely reflect stereotypical notions of human trafficking. It is also possible that those reports with the widest reach tend to depict more stereotypical situations of human trafficking.

In Russia in particular, there are significant concerns that the media is primarily state owned and therefore politicized and biased. Although this is certainly true in reporting of political stories, it is not true at all levels of media. In collecting my data, I include a diversity of media from local, regional, and national news sources, some of which are primarily online. Some of the news outlets that are known for being politicized in other areas of reporting, in particular *Komsomol'skaia pravda*, have taken a special interest in human trafficking stories and have done extensive investigative reports on many cases—interviewing law enforcement, victims, witnesses, and other people involved. I also found that some of the local and regional news media outlets often followed cases in much closer detail than their national counterparts.

Another limitation has to do with the level of detail reported by the media. One of the limitations to using newspaper articles rather than official court documents (which are extremely difficult to obtain) as a basis for gathering data is that it is sometimes unclear whether the conviction was under the trafficking statute or under other statutes. For a case to be opened, there must be a charge attached to it, but that does not mean that it will be further investigated or that the charge will not change during further investigation. In addition, without court documents, if the conviction was for human trafficking, it is unclear what proportion of the sentence was a result of the human trafficking charge, especially since most of these cases were brought with multiple charges. It may also mask whether or not the eventual disposition of the case included a guilty verdict for trafficking at all. In most of the charged cases, I was able to find the specific part of the trafficking statute under which the defendants were charged. However, it does not necessarily mean that the conviction, if they were convicted of trafficking, matched that charge.

Ultimately, although the limitations of this methodology should certainly be taken into account, there is simply no other way to reliably document the variety of human trafficking incidents that occur, the ways that traffickers operate, and the types of traffickers and victims involved. Official statistics from the MVD, Investigative Committee, Procuracy, and courts are focused on the various outcomes of the criminal process; although they include data on sentencing, they do not reflect the variety of ways that traffickers are brought to justice in Russia—often through the use of other Criminal Code articles.

OFFICIAL RUSSIAN LAW ENFORCEMENT STATISTICS ON HUMAN TRAFFICKING CRIMES

TABLE B.1 MVD statistics on crimes registered under Articles 127.1 and 127.2

YEAR	2004	2005	2006	2007	2008	2009	2010	2011	2012	2013	TOTAL
Article 127.1: Human trafficking	17	60	106	104	57	94	103	50	70	66	727
Article 127.2: Use of slave labor	8	20	19	35	10	8	15	17	17	13	162
Total	25	80	125	139	67	102	118	67	87	79	889

Source: MVD, on file with author.
Note: The number of crimes registered by Russian law enforcement includes every individual crime that may exist within the eventual criminal case, but statistics on investigations and prosecutions usually combine these individual crimes into one case and count those. For example, if three women were sold into prostitution by the same person in one transaction, there would be three crimes registered, but only one criminal case officially opened (Paneyakh et al. 2012). This helps explain the disparity in numbers between this and the following table and between this and my data set.

TABLE B.2 Trafficking cases investigated by MVD and Procuracy/SK

	2004	2005	2006	2007	2008	2009	2010	2011	2012	2013
Article 127.1 Human trafficking										
—completed investigations (MVD)	6	3	6	5						
—completed investigations (SK, Procuracy)	5	56	102	65	67					
—number of criminals uncovered	4	24	45	55	67	86	53	26		44
Article 127.2 Use of slave labor										
—completed investigations (MVD)	1	2	6	0						
—completed investigations (SK, Procuracy)	6	12	16	24	14[a]					
—number of criminals uncovered	5	10	15	22	14	13	9	11		14

Sources: MVD data 2004–2007 and 2013 on file with author and from IOM 2006; Procuracy data 2004–2008 on file with author; data on number of criminals from 2009–2011 from Chirkov 2012. Blank cells indicate that data was unavailable.
[a] In 2008, the statistical calculations were changed. Instead of counting the number of completed investigations, they counted the number of cases sent to court which also includes cases that may have continued over from previous years, but since these are by nature completed, I use this number.

TABLE B.3 Judicial Department statistics on trafficking convictions and sentences under Articles 127.1 and 127.2

	2004		2005		2006		2007		2008		2009		2010		2011		2012		2013	
	127.1	127.2	127.1	127.2	127.1	127.2	127.1	127.2	127.1	127.2	127.1	127.2	127.1	127.2	127.1	127.2	127.1	127.2	127.1	127.2
Primary charge	1		3	5	4	9	12	6	36	3	27	10	31	9	27	7	29	5	28	4
Secondary charge[a]		1					7		12	3	39	6	11	5	5	4	11	1	8	4
Prison	1		2	2	4	2	7	5	26	2	16	6	24	7	17	1	22	4	19	4
<1 yr.							1	2						1			1			
1–3 yrs.				1	4		3	2	5		3	2	8	2	4		9		6	1
3–5 yrs.	1		2	1		2	3	1	10	2	9	4	7	1	4	1	8	2	9	1
5–8 yrs.									9		1		3	1			3	2	4	2
8–10 yrs.									2		3		6	2	5					
10–15 yrs.															4		1			
Conditional sentence	1		1			7	5	1	10	1	11	4	7	2	8	6	6	1	9	
Other[b]													1		2		2			
Closed											1		1			1				
Acquitted									1											

Source: Judicial Department of the Supreme Court of the Russian Federation, forms 10a, 10.3 and 10.3.1: 2004–2008 statistics on file with author, 2009–2013 statistics available online (www.cdep.ru).

a Only those with human trafficking as a primary charge are reflected in the sentencing statistics below.

b Includes psychiatric institutionalization or exemption from serving the sentence for health reasons.

Legal Sources (by Date)

RUSSIAN LAW SOURCES

Codes

Grazhdanskii kodeks Rossiiskoi Federatsii, chast' vtoraia of January 26, 1996, no. 14-FZ. SZ RF 1996, no. 5, item 410 [Civil Code of the Russian Federation, Part 2].

Ugolovnyi kodeks Rossiiskoi Federatsii of June 13, 1996, no. 63-FZ. SZ RF 1996, no. 25, item 2954 [Criminal Code of the Russian Federation].

Ugolovno-protsessual'nyi kodeks Rossiiskoi Federatsii of December 18, 2001, no. 174-FZ. SZ RF 2001, no 52 (Part 1), item 4921 [Criminal Procedure Code of the Russian Federation].

Kodeks Rossiiskoi Federatsii ob administrativnykh pravonarusheniiakh of December 30, 2001, no. 195-FZ. SZ RF 2002, no. 1, item 1 [Code of Administrative Violations of the Russian Federation].

Trudovoi kodeks Rossiiskoi Federatsii of December 30, 2001, no. 197-FZ. SZ RF 2002, no. 1 (part 1), item 3 [Labor Code of the Russian Federation].

Laws and Presidential Orders

Federal Law no. 2202-1, "O prokurature Rossiiskoi Federatsii," of January 17, 1992. SZ RF 1995, no. 47, item 4472 [On the Procuracy of the Russian Federation].

Federal Law no. 144-FZ, "Ob operativno-rozysknoi deiatel'nosti," of August 12, 1995. SZ RF 1995, no. 33, item 3349 [On operational-investigative activities].

Federal Law no. 92-FZ, "O vnesenii izmenenii i dopolnenii v Ugolovnyi kodeks Rossiiskoi Federatsii," of June 25, 1998. SZ RF 1998, no. 26, item 3012 [On additions and changes to the Criminal Code of the Russian Federation].

Presidential Order no. 308, "O merakh po sovershenstvovaniiu gosudarstvennogo upravleniia v oblasti bezopasnosti Rossiiskoi Federatsii," of March 11, 2003, SZ RF 2003, no. 12, item 1101 [On measures to improve the state organs for security of the Russian Federation].

Draft Law. "Proekt Federalnyi zakon 'O protivodeistvii torgovle liud'mi'" of March 18, 2003. http://www.sartraccc.ru/Traffic/i.php?oper=read_file&filename=law_project/0001.htm.

Federal Law no. 162-FZ, "O vnesenii izmenenii i dopolnenii v Ugolovnyi kodeks Rossiiskoi Federatsii," of December 8, 2003. SZ RF 2003, no. 50, item 4848 [On the introduction of changes and additions to the Criminal Code of the Russian Federation].

Presidential Order no. 314, "O sisteme i strukture federal'nykh organov ispolnitel'noi vlasti," of March 9, 2004. SZ RF 2004, no. 11, item 945 [On the system and structure of the federal organs of executive power].

Federal Law no. 26-FZ, "O ratifikatsii Konventsii Organizatsii Ob"edinennykh Natsii protiv transnatsional'noi organizovannoi prestupnosti i dopolniaiushchikh ee Protokola protiv nezakonnogo vvoza migrantov po sushe, moriu i vozdukhu i Protokol o preduprezhdenii i presechenii torgovli liud'mi, osobenno zhenshchinami i det'mi, i nakazanii za nee," of April 26, 2004. SZ RF 2004, no. 18, item 1684 [On the ratification of the United Nations Convention against Transnational Organized Crime and the additional Protocol against the Illegal Smuggling of Migrants by Land, Sea, and Air and the Protocol to Prevent, Suppress, and Punish Trafficking in Persons, Especially Women and Children].

Federal Law no. 119-FZ, "O gosudarstvennoi zashchite poterpevshikh, sviditelei i inykh uchastnikov ugolovnogo sudoproizvodstva," of August 20, 2004. SZ RF 2004, no. 34, item 3534 [On state protection for victims, witnesses, and other participants in the criminal justice process].

Federal Law no. 187-FZ, "O vnesenii izmenenii v Ugolovnyi kodeks Rossiiskoi Federatsii, Ugolovno-protsessual'nyi kodeks Rossiiskoi Federatsii i Kodeks Rossiiskoi Federatsii ob administrativnykh pravonarusheniiakh," of December 28, 2004. SZ RF 2005, no. 1 (part 1), item 13 [On the introduction of changes to the Criminal Code of the Russian Federation, the Criminal Procedure Code of the Russian Federation, and the Code of Administrative Violations of the Russian Federation].

Federal Law no. 87-FZ, "O vnesenii izmenenii v Ugolovno-protsessual'nyi kodeks Rossiiskoi Federatsii i 'O prokurature Rossiiskoi Federatsii,'" of June 5, 2007. SZ RF 2007, no. 24, item 2830 [On the introduction of changes to the Criminal Procedure Code of the Russian Federation and On the Procuracy of the Russian Federation].

Presidential Order no. 1316, "O nekotorykh voprosakh Ministerstva vnutrennikh del Rossiiskoi Federatsii," of September 6, 2008. SZ RF 2008, no. 37, item 4182 [On several questions concerning the Ministry of Internal Affairs of the Russian Federation].

Federal Law no. 218-FZ, "O vnesenii izmenenii v stat'iu 127.1 Ugolovnogo kodeksa Rossiiskoi Federatsii," of November 25, 2008. SZ RF 2008, no. 48, item 5513 [On the introduction of changes to article 127.1 of the Criminal Code of the Russian Federation].

Federal Law no. 262-FZ, "Ob obespechenii dostupa k informatsii o deiatel'nosti sudov v Rossiiskoi Federatsii," of December 22, 2008. SZ RF 2008, no. 51 (part 1), item 6217 [On the right of access to information about court activities in the Russian Federation].

Federal Law no. 404-FZ, "O vnesenii izmenenii v otdel'nye zakonodatel'nye akty Rossiiskoi Federatsii v sviazi s sovershenstvovaniem deiatel'nosti organov predvaritel'nogo sledstviia," of December 28, 2010. SZ RF 2011, no. 1, item 16 [On the introduction of changes to several legal acts of the Russian Federation connected with improving the activities of investigative agencies].

Presidential Order no. 38, "Voprosy deiatel'nosti Sledstvennogo komiteta Rossiiskoi Federatsii," of January 14, 2011. SZ RF 2011, no. 4, item 572 [On questions about the activities of the Investigative Committee of the Russian Federation].

Presidential Order no. 90, "Ob obshchei shtatnoi chislennosti organov prokuratury Rossiiskoi Federatsii," of January 25, 2011. SZ RF 2011, no. 5, item 710 [On general staffing of the organs of the Procuracy in the Russian Federation].

Federal Law no. 3-FZ, "O politsii," of February 7, 2011. SZ RF 2011, no. 7, item 900 [On the Police].

Federal Law no. 420-FZ, "O vnesenii izmenenii v Ugolovnyi kodeks Rossiiskoi Federatsii i otdel'nye zakonodatel'nye akty Rossiiskoi Federatsii," of December 7, 2011. SZ RF 2011, no. 50, item 7362 [On changes to the Criminal Code of the Russian Federation and several legal acts of the Russian Federation].

Federal Law no. 14-FZ, "O vnesenii izmenenii v Ugolovnyi kodeks Rossiiskoi Federatsii i otdel'nye zakonodatel'nye akty Rossiiskoi Federatsii v tseliakh usileniia otvetstvennosti za prestupleniia seksual'nogo kharaktera, sovershennye v otnoshenii nesovershennoletnikh," of February 29, 2012. SZ RF 2012, no. 10, item 1162 [On changes to the Criminal Code of the Russian Federation and several legal acts of the Russian Federation with the goal of strengthening punishment for crimes of a sexual nature committed against minors].

Federal Law no. 121-FZ, "O vnesenii izmenenii v otdel'nye zakonodatel'nye akty Rossiiskoi Federatsii v chasti regulirovaniia deiatel'nosti nekommercheskikh organizatsii, vypolniaiushchikh funktsii inostrannogo agenta," of July 20, 2012. SZ RF 2012, no. 30, item 4172 [On changes to several legal acts of the Russian Federation with regard to noncommercial organizations fulfilling the functions of foreign agents].

Federal Law no. 432-FZ, "O vnesenii izmenenii v otdel'nye zakonodatel'nye akty Rossiiskoi Federatsii v tseliakh sovershenstvovaniia prav poterpevshikh v ugolovnom sudoproizvodstve," of December 28, 2013. SZ RF 2013, no. 52 (Part 1), item 6997. [On changes to several legal acts of the Russian Federation with the goal of improving the rights of victims in the criminal justice process].

Supreme Court Decisions

Decision of the Criminal Division of the Supreme Court of the Russian Federation of April 28, 2005, Case 86-005-5 (Opredelenie Sudebnoi kollegii po ugolovnym delam Verkhovnogo Suda RF ot 28 aprelia 2005 g. no. 85-005-5).

Decision of the Criminal Division of the Supreme Court of the Russian Federation of July 9, 2012, Case 3-D12-6 (Opredelenie Sudebnoi kollegii po ugolovnym delam Verkhovnogo Suda RF ot 9 iulia 2012 g. no. 3-D12-6).

Transcripts of Legislative Sessions and Conferences

Golitsyno. 2002. Stenogramma Mezhdunarodnaia nauchno-prakticheskaia conferentsiia: Problemy bor'by s torgovlei liud'mi i perspektivy sovremennogo razvitiia Rossii [Transcript of International Academic-Research Conference: Problems in Fighting Human Trafficking and Prospects for Current Development in Russia], Golitsyno, Russia, October 27–29, 2002.

Yaroslavl. 2002. Stenogramma Kruglyi stol: Zakonoproekt o protivodeistvii torgovlei liud'mi: Obshchestvennye slushaniia [Transcripts of Roundtable on the Law on Countering Human Trafficking: Public Hearings] Yaroslavl, Russia, December 9–11, 2002.

Moscow. 2003a. Stenogramma Soiuz iskusstva i prava v bor'be protiv torgovli liud'mi [Transcripts of the Arts and the Law United in the Fight against Human Trafficking], Moscow, Russia, May 12, 2003.

Moscow. 2003b. Stenogramma parlamentskikh slushanii, provodimykh komitetom po zakonodatel'stvu na temu "O proekte federal'nogo zakona o protivodeistvii torgovle liud'mi" [Transcript of the Parliamentary Hearing in the Legislative Committee on the Federal Draft Law on Counteracting Human Trafficking]. Moscow, Russia, February 13, 2003.

Poiasnitel'naia zapiska. 2003. Poiasnitel'naia zapiska k proektu federal'nogo zakona "O dopolnenii stat'ei 126.1 [sic] Ugolovnogo kodeksa Rossiiskoi Federatsii" [Explanatory note to the Federal Draft Law "On the addition of Article 126.1 [sic]"].

State Duma. 2003. Stenogramma zasedaniia Gosudarstvennoi Dume, 21 noiabria 2003 g. [Transcripts of Hearings of the State Duma on November 21, 2003].

Federation Council. 2003. Stenogramma sto shestnadtsatogo zasedaniia Soveta
    Federatsii, 26 noiabria 2003 g. [Transcript of Hearings of the 116th Federation
    Council, November 26, 2003].
Poiasnitel'naia zapiska. 2008. Poiasnitelnaia zapiska k proektu federal'nogo zakona "O
    vnesenii izmenenii v stat'iu 127.1 Ugolovnogo kodeksa Rossiiskoi Federatsii,"
    Project no. N476214-4 [Explanatory note to the Federal Draft Law "On changes
    to Article 127.1 of the Criminal Code of the Russian Federation"].
State Duma. 2008a. Stenogramma zasedaniia 19 marta 2008 g. [Transcripts of
    Parliamentary Hearings on March 19, 2008].
———. 2008b. Stenogramma zasedaniia 25 oktiabria 2008 g. i 7 noiabria 2008 g. O
    proekte federal'nogo zakona no 476214-4 "O vnesenii izmenenii v stat'iu 127.1
    Ugolovnogo kodeksa Rossiiskoi Federatsii" (v chasti utochneniia poniatiia
    "torgovlia liud'mi" a takzhe usileniia otvetstvennosti za dannyi vid prestupleniia
    [Transcripts of Parliamentary Hearings on October 15, 2008, and November 7,
    2008: On the Federal Draft Law 476214-4 "On changes to article 127.1 of the
    Criminal Code of the Russian Federation" (with the goal of clarifying the
    wording "human trafficking" and strengthening sentencing for this type of
    crime], 5th session.
Federation Council. 2008. Stenogramma dvesti tridtsat' chetvertogo zasedaniia Soveta
    Federatsii, 12 noiabria 2008 g. [Transcripts of Hearings of the 234th Federation
    Council, November 12, 2008].

US LAW SOURCES

TVPA. 2000. Victims of Trafficking and Violence Protection Act of 2000, Public Law
    106–386, 106th Cong., 2nd sess. (October 28, 2000).
TVPRA. 2003. Trafficking Victims Protection Reauthorization Act of 2003, Public Law
    108–193, 108th Cong., 1st sess. (December 19, 2003).
———. 2005. Trafficking Victims Protection Reauthorization Act of 2005, Public Law
    109–164, 109th Cong., 1st sess. (January 10, 2006).
———. 2008. William Wilberforce Trafficking Victims Protection Reauthorization Act
    of 2008, Public Law 110–457, 110th Cong. 2nd sess. (January 5, 2007).

References

Abdullaev, Nabi. 2008a. "Anti-Organized Crime Unit Dissolved." *Moscow Times*, September 11.
——. 2008b. "Caucasus Cities Called the Safest." *Moscow Times*, August 27.
——. 2009. "Prosecutors Caught in 'Clan' War." *Moscow Times*, December 21.
Abdullaev, Nabi, and Alexander Bratersky. 2010. "Investigative Superagency Unveiled." *Moscow Times*, September 24.
Albonetti, Celesta A. 1986. "Criminality, Prosecutorial Screening, and Uncertainty: Toward a Theory of Discretionary Decision Making in Felony Cases." *Criminology* 24 (4): 623–44.
——. 1987. "Prosecutorial Discretion: The Effects of Uncertainty." *Law and Society Review* 21 (2): 291–313.
——. 2014. "Changes in Federal Sentencing for Forced Labor Trafficking and for Sex Trafficking: A Ten Year Assessment." *Crime, Law and Social Change* 61 (2): 179–204.
Aledzieva, Patimat. 2009. "Faktov prinuzhdeniia k trudu ne vyiavleno." *Dagestanskaia pravda*, August 14. http://www.dagpravda.ru/rubriki/obshchestvo/7789/.
Alikhadzhieva, Inna. 2006. "Nedostatki zakonodatel'noi reglamentatsii ugolovno-pravovoi bor'by s torgovlei liud'mi." *Ugolovnoe pravo* (5): 4–7.
——. 2008. "O razgranichenii torgovli liud'mi i vovlechenie v zaniatie prostitutsiei (stati 127.1 i 240 UK Rossii)." *Ugolovnoe pravo* (1): 4–8.
Allison, Graham. 1971. *Essence of Decision: Explaining the Cuban Missile Crisis*. Boston: Little, Brown.
Amnesty International. 2005. *Nowhere to Turn to: Violence against Women in the Family*. EUR/46/056/2005.
——. 2006. *Russian Federation: Torture and Forced "Confessions" in Detention*. EUR/46/056/2006.
Andreas, Peter, and Kelly Greenhill. 2010. *Sex, Drugs, and Body Counts: The Politics of Numbers in Global Crime and Conflict*. Ithaca, NY: Cornell University Press.
Antonov, A. G. 2011. "Spetsial'noe osnovanie osvobozhdeniia ot ugolovnoi otvetstvennosti pri torgovle liud'mi." *Zakonnost'* (3): 35–37.
Antonova, Evgeniia, and Mar'iana Peshkova. 2005. "Tsivilizovannoe rabstvo." *Rossiiskaia gazeta*, April 20.
Appel, Hilary, ed. 2004. *Evaluating Success and Failure in Post-Communist Reform*. Claremont, CA: Keck Center for International and Strategic Studies.
Aral, Sevgi O., Janet S. St. Lawrence, Lilia Tikhonova, Emma Safarova, Kathleen A. Parker, Anna Shakarishvili, and Caroline A. Ryan. 2003. "The Social Organization of Sex Work in Moscow, Russia." *Sexually Transmitted Diseases* 30 (1): 39–45.
Aronov, Nikita. 2013. "Propavshie v rabstvo." *Kommersant*, December 2. http://kommersant.ru/doc/2352306.
Arutunyan, Anna. 2009. "Let's Get Ethical Say Top Cops." *Moscow News*, March 13.
——. 2013. "Uzbek Woman Goes into Labor at Hospital Entry, Flees with Newborn." *Moscow News*, August 11.

Ashwin, Sarah, ed. 2006. *Adapting to Russia's New Labor Market: Gender and Employment Behavior.* New York: Routledge.

Avgerinos, Katherine P. 2006. "From Vixen to Victim: The Sensationalization and Normalization of Prostitution in Post-Soviet Russia." *Vestnik, the Journal of Russian and Asian Studies* (5): 17–39.

Barrick, Kelle, Pamela K. Lattimore, Wayne J. Pitts, and Sheldon X. Zhang. 2014. "When Farmworkers and Advocates See Trafficking but Law Enforcement Does Not: Challenges in Identifying Labor Trafficking in North Carolina." *Crime, Law, and Social Change* 61 (2): 205–14.

Bayley, David H. 1971. "Police and Political Change in Comparative Perspective." *Law and Society Review* 6 (1): 91–112.

——. 2001. *Democratizing the Police Abroad: What to Do and How to Do It.* Washington, DC: US Dept. of Justice, Office of Justice Programs.

——. 2002. "Law Enforcement and the Rule of Law: Is There a Tradeoff?" *Criminology and Public Policy* 2 (1): 133–54.

Bazhenova, Svetlana. 2008. "Dal'nevostochnyi tsentr razvitiia grazhdanskikh initsiativ i sotsial'nogo partnerstvo." Paper presented at Trudovaia migratsiia v Evraziiskom regione: tendentsii, problemy i puti sotrudnichestva, Vladivostok, Russia, May 29–30, 2008.

Beck, Adrian, and Ruth Lee. 2002. "Attitudes to Corruption amongst Russian Police Officers and Trainees." *Crime, Law, and Social Change* 38 (4): 357–72.

Beck, Adrian, and Annette Robertson. 2005. "Policing in Post-Soviet Russia." In *Ruling Russia: Law, Crime, and Justice in a Changing Society*, ed. William Alex Pridemore, 247–60. Lanham, MD: Rowman and Littlefield.

Benninger-Budel, Carin, and Lucinda O'Hanlon. 2004. *Violence against Women: Ten Reports/Year 2003.* Geneva: World Organization against Torture.

Bernstein, Jonas. 2008. "Medvedev Restructures the Interior Ministry." *Eurasia Daily Monitor* 5 (173).

Bigg, Claire. 2005. "Russia: Domestic Violence Continues to Take Heavy Toll." *Radio Free Europe/Radio Liberty*, December 15. http://www.rferl.org/content/article/1063891.html.

Bjerkan, Lise, and Linda Dyrlid. 2006. *The Courageous Testimony: Trafficked Women's Motivations for and Experiences from Testifying against their Traffickers.* Oslo: Fafo Institute.

Black, Donald J. 1970. "The Production of Crime Rates." *American Sociological Review* 35 (4): 733–48.

Blanchette, Thaddeus Gregory, Paula Ana Silva, and Andressa Raylane Bento. 2013. "The Myth of Maria and the Imagining of Sexual Trafficking in Brazil." *Dialectical Anthropology* 37 (2): 195–227.

Blinova, Valentina. 2007. "Propashchie." *Ogonek*, February 12, 18–21. http://www.ogoniok.ru/4983/17/.

Bobrova, Natalia, Urij Rughnikov, Elena Neifield, Tim Rhodes, Ron Alcorn, Sergej Kirichenko, and Robert Power. 2008. "Challenges in Providing Drug User Treatment Services in Russia: Providers' Views." *Substance Use and Misuse* 43 (12–13): 1770–84.

Borisov, A. B., ed. 2012. *Kommentarii k Ugolovnomu kodeksu Rossiiskoi Federatsii (Postateinyi) s postateinymi materialami i prakticheskimi raz"iasneniiami ofitsial'nykh organov.* 5th ed. Moscow: Knizhnii mir.

Boyd, Elizabeth A., Richard A. Berk, and Karl M. Hamner. 1996. "'Motivated by Hatred or Prejudice': Categorization of Hate-Motivated Crimes in Two Police Divisions." *Law and Society Review* 30 (4): 819–50.

Boyne, Shawn. 2014. *The German Prosecution Service: Guardians of the Law?* New York: Springer.

Bratersky, Alexander. 2011. "Top Court Backs Whistleblowers." *Moscow Times*, July 1.

Brennan, Denise. 2010. "Key Issues in the Resettlement of Formerly Trafficked Persons in the United States." *University of Pennsylvania Law Review* 158 (6): 1581–1608.

Bridger, Sue, and Rebecca Kay. 1996. "Gender and Generation in the New Russian Labor Market." In *Gender, Generation, and Identity in Contemporary Russia*, ed. Hilary Pilkington, 21–38. New York: Routledge.

Brilliantov, A. V., ed. 2010. *Kommentarii k Ugolovnomu kodeksu Rossiiskoi Federatsii (postateinyi)*. Moscow: Prospekt.

Brunovskis, Anette, and Rebecca Surtees. 2007. *Leaving the Past Behind? When Victims of Trafficking Decline Assistance*. Oslo: Fafo Institute.

Buckley, Mary. 2007. "Press Images of Human Trafficking from Russia: Myths and Interpretations." In *Gender, Equality and Difference During and After State Socialism*, ed. Rebecca Kay, 211–29. New York: Palgrave Macmillan.

——. 2008. "Human Trafficking from Russia: Political Responses and Public Opinion" *St. Antony's International Review* 4 (1): 115–34.

——. 2009. "Public Opinion in Russia on the Politics of Human Trafficking." *Europe-Asia Studies* 61 (2): 213–48.

Burger, Ethan S., and Mary Holland. 2008. "Law as Politics: The Russian Procuracy and Its Investigative Committee." *Columbia Journal of East European Law* 2 (2): 143–94.

Buriak, Maria. 2006. *Torgovlia liud'mi i bor'ba s nei*. Vladivostok: Dal'nevostochnogo universiteta.

Burnham, William, and Thomas A. Firestone. Unpublished."Investigation of Criminal Cases under the Russian Criminal Procedure Code." On file with author.

Burnham, William, Peter Maggs, and Gennady Danilenko. 2012. *Law and Legal System of the Russian Federation*. 5th ed. Huntington, NY: Juris Publishers.

Caldwell, Gillian, director. 1997. *Bought and Sold: An Investigative Documentary about the International Trade in Women*. Film. Witness.

Caldwell, Gillian, Steven Galster, and Nadia Steinzor. 1997. *Crime and Servitude: An Exposé of the Traffic in Women for Prostitution from the Newly Independent States*. Washington DC: Global Survival Network.

Caneppele, Stefano, and Marina Mancuso. 2013. "Are Protection Policies for Human Trafficking Victims Effective? An Analysis of the Italian Case." *European Journal of Criminal Policy Research* 19 (3): 259–73.

Caparini, Marina, and Otwin Marenin, eds. 2004. *Transforming Police in Central and Eastern Europe: Process and Progress*. New Brunswick, NJ: Transaction Publishers.

Chekalin, A. A., ed. 2006. *Kommentarii k Ugolovnomu kodeksu Rossiiskoi Federatsii*. 3rd ed. Moscow: Iurait-Izdat.

Chirkov, Dmitrii K. 2012. *Kharakteristika kriminal'noi situatsii v Rossii, sviazannoi s torgovlei liud'mi*. Presented in Vladivostok. On file with author.

Chuang, Janie. 2006. "The United States as Global Sheriff: Using Unilateral Sanctions to Combat Human Trafficking." *Michigan Journal of International Law* 27 (2): 437–94.

Chumarnaia, Elena. 2013. "Vlasti Severnoi Osetii kontroliruiut rassledovanie prodazhi mladentsa." *Argumenty i fakty Stavropol'*, April 10. http://www.stav.aif.ru/society/news/81043.

Clawson, Heather J., Nicole Dutch, and Megan Cummings. 2006. *Law Enforcement Response to Human Trafficking and the Implications for Victims: Current Practices and Lessons Learned.* Washington, DC: ICF International.

Clawson, Heather J., Nicole Dutch, Susan Lopez, and Suzanna Tiapula. 2008. *Prosecuting Human Trafficking Cases: Lessons Learned and Promising Practices.* Washington, DC: ICF International.

Coalson, Robert, and Tom Balmforth. 2014. "Leading Russian NGOs Muzzled by 'Foreign Agents' Label." *Radio Free Europe/Radio Liberty*, July 23. http://www.rferl.org/content/russia-muzzles-ngos-foreign-agent-law/25467789.html.

CIS. Commonwealth of Independent States. 1994. Konventsiia o pravovoi pomoshchi i pravovykh otnosheniiakh po grazhdanskim, semeinym i ugolovnym delam.

Constantinou, Angelo G. 2013. "Human Trafficking on Trial: Dissecting the Adjudication of Sex Trafficking Cases in Cyprus." *Feminist Legal Studies* 21 (2): 163–83.

CoE. Council of Europe. 2005. Convention on Action against Trafficking in Human Beings and Its Explanatory Report. Public Law 16.

Craggs, Sarah, and Ruzayda Martens. 2010. *Rights, Residence, Rehabilitation: A Comparative Study Assessing Residence Options for Trafficked Persons.* Geneva: International Organization for Migration.

Cronin, Shea, Jack McDevitt, Amy Farrell, and James J. Nolan. 2007. "Bias-Crime Reporting: Organizational Responses to Ambiguity, Uncertainty, and Infrequency in Eight Police Departments." *American Behavioral Scientist* 51 (2): 213–31.

D'Amora, Delphine, and Ezekiel Pfeifer. 2013. "Putin Creates New Anti-Corruption Department." *Moscow Times*, December 4.

Danilkin, Aleksandr. 2006. "Zhenu otdai diade . . ." *Trud*, March 21.

David, Fiona. 2007. "Law Enforcement Responses to Trafficking in Persons: Challenges and Emerging Good Practice." *Trends and Issues in Crime and Criminal Justice* (347).

Davis, Robert C., Christopher W. Ortiz, Yakov Gilinskiy, Irina Ylesseva, and Vladimir Briller. 2004. "A Cross-National Comparison of Citizen Perceptions of the Police in New York City and St. Petersburg, Russia." *Policing* 27 (1): 22–36.

Dean, Laura A. 2014. "Beyond the Natasha Effect: Determinants of Human Trafficking Policy Variation in the Post-Soviet Region." PhD diss., University of Kansas.

Demin, I. V. 2004. "K voprosu o protivodeistvii torgovle liud'mi." In Konstitutsionnaia zashchita grazhdan ot prestupnykh posiagatel'stv, realizuemaia normami ugolovnogo i ugolovno-protsessual'nogo zakonodatel'stva: Materialy vserossiiskoi mezhvedomstvennoi nauchno-prakticheskoi konferentsii, 19–20 fevralia 2004 g., 398–402. Moscow: Moskovskii universitet MVD Rossii.

Denton, Erin. 2010. "International News Coverage of Human Trafficking Arrests and Prosecutions: A Content Analysis." *Women and Criminal Justice* 20 (1–2): 10–26.

Dept. of State. 2001. *Victims of Trafficking and Violence Protection Act of 2000: Trafficking in Persons Report 2001.* US Department of State, Office to Monitor and Combat Trafficking in Persons. http://www.state.gov/j/tip/rls/tiprpt/2001/index.htm.

———. 2002. *Victims of Trafficking and Violence Prevention Act 2000: Trafficking in Persons Report 2002.* US Department of State, Office to Monitor and Combat Trafficking in Persons. http://www.state.gov/j/tip/rls/tiprpt/2002/index.htm.

———. 2003. *Victims of Trafficking and Violence Prevention Act 2000: Trafficking in Persons Report 2003.* US Department of State, Office to Monitor and Combat Trafficking in Persons. http://www.state.gov/j/tip/rls/tiprpt/2003/index.htm.

———. 2004a. *The US Government's International Anti-Trafficking Programs, Fiscal Year 2003*. Washington, DC: US Department of State, Office to Monitor and Combat Trafficking in Persons.

———. 2004b. *Victims of Trafficking and Violence Protection Act of 2000: Trafficking in Persons Report June 2004*. US Department of State, Office to Monitor and Combat Trafficking in Persons. http://www.state.gov/j/tip/rls/tiprpt/2004/index.htm.

———. 2005a. *The US Government's International Anti-Trafficking Programs Fiscal Year 2004*. Washington, DC: US Department of State, Office to Monitor and Combat Trafficking in Persons.

———. 2005b. *Victims of Trafficking and Violence Protection Act of 2000: Trafficking in Persons Report June 2005*. US Department of State, Office to Monitor and Combat Trafficking in Persons. http://www.state.gov/j/tip/rls/tiprpt/2005/index.htm.

———. 2006a. *US Government Funds Obligated in FY2005 for Anti-Trafficking in Persons Projects*. Washington, DC: US Department of State, Office to Monitor and Combat Trafficking in Persons.

———. 2006b. *Trafficking in Persons Report 2006*. US Department of State, Office to Monitor and Combat Trafficking in Persons. http://www.state.gov/j/tip/rls/tiprpt/2006/index.htm.

———. 2007a. *US Government Funds Obligated for Anti-Trafficking in Persons Projects, Fiscal Year 2006*. Washington, DC: US Department of State, Office to Monitor and Combat Trafficking in Persons.

———. 2007b. *Trafficking in Persons Report 2007*. US Department of State, Office to Monitor and Combat Trafficking in Persons. http://www.state.gov/j/tip/rls/tiprpt/2007/index.htm.

———. 2008a. *US Government Funds Obligated for Anti-Trafficking in Persons Projects, Fiscal Year 2007*. Washington, DC: US Department of State, Office to Monitor and Combat Trafficking in Persons.

———. 2008b. *Trafficking in Persons Report 2008*. US Department of State, Office to Monitor and Combat Trafficking in Persons. http://www.state.gov/j/tip/rls/tiprpt/2008/index.htm.

———. 2009a. *US Government Funds Obligated in Fiscal Year 2008 for Anti-Trafficking in Persons Projects*. US Department of State, Office to Monitor and Combat Trafficking in Persons. http://www.state.gov/j/tip/rls/reports/2009/121506.htm.

———. 2009b. *Trafficking in Persons Report 2009*. US Department of State, Office to Monitor and Combat Trafficking in Persons. http://www.state.gov/j/tip/rls/tiprpt/2009/.

———. 2010a. *US Government Funds Obligated in Fiscal Year 2009 for Anti-Trafficking in Persons Projects*. US Department of State, Office to Monitor and Combat Trafficking in Persons. http://www.state.gov/j/tip/rls/reports/2010/137248.htm.

———. 2010b. *Trafficking in Persons Report 2010*. US Department of State, Office to Monitor and Combat Trafficking in Persons. http://www.state.gov/j/tip/rls/tiprpt/2010/index.htm.

———. 2011a. *USG TIP Projects with Funds Obligated in FY 2010*. US Department of State, Office to Monitor and Combat Trafficking in Persons. http://www.state.gov/documents/organization/160227.pdf.

———. 2011b. *Trafficking in Persons Report 2011*. US Department of State, Office to Monitor and Combat Trafficking in Persons. http://www.state.gov/j/tip/rls/tiprpt/2011/index.htm.

———. 2012a. *US Government TIP Projects with Funds Obligated in Fiscal Year 2011*. US Department of State, Office to Monitor and Combat Trafficking in Persons. http://www.state.gov/j/tip/rls/reports/2012/205888.htm.

———. 2012b. *Trafficking in Persons Report 2012*. US Department of State, Office to Monitor and Combat Trafficking in Persons. http://www.state.gov/j/tip/rls/tiprpt/2012/index.htm.

———. 2013a. *US Government TIP Projects with Funds Obligated in FY 2012*. US Department of State, Office to Monitor and Combat Trafficking in Persons. http://www.state.gov/j/tip/rls/reports/2013/228856.htm.

———. 2013b. *Trafficking in Persons Report 2013*. US Department of State, Office to Monitor and Combat Trafficking in Persons. http://www.state.gov/j/tip/rls/tiprpt/2013/index.htm.

———. 2014. *Trafficking in Persons Report 2014*. US Department of State, Office to Monitor and Combat Trafficking in Persons. http://www.state.gov/j/tip/rls/tiprpt/2014/index.htm.

Desiatichenko, Irina. 2011. "Sviditelia po delu o torgovle liud'mi ubili v KChR." *Life News*, December 6. http://lifenews.ru/news/76370.

DeStefano, Anthony. 2008. *The War on Human Trafficking: US Policy Assessed*. New Brunswick, NJ: Rutgers University Press.

D'iakov, S. V., and N. G. Kadnikov, eds. 2008. *Kommentarii k Ugolovnomu kodeksu Rossiiskoi Federatsii (postateinyi)*. Moscow: Iurisprudentsiia.

Dolgolenko, Tat'iana. 2004. "Ugolovnaia otvetstvennost' za torgovliu liud'mi." *Ugolovnoe pravo* (2): 23–25.

Dvorkin, A. I. 2007. *Torgovlia liud'mi v Rossiiskoi Federatsii: kvalifikatsiia, preduprezhdenie, rassledovanie*. Moscow: Iurist.

Easter, Gerald. 2002. "Politics of Revenue Extraction in Post-Communist States: Poland and Russia Compared." *Politics and Society* 30 (4): 599–627.

Efimov, Vitalii. 2006. "U sosedei devki slashche?" *Kur'er Belomor'ia*, July 11. http://www.arhpress.ru/kurbel/2006/7/11/15.shtml.

Erokhina, Liudmila, and Maria Buriak. 2002. *Torgovlia zhenshchinami i det'mi v sotsial'noi i kriminologicheskoi perspektive*. Moscow: Profobrazovanie.

Eterno, John A., and Eli B. Silverman. 2012. *The Crime Numbers Game: Management by Manipulation*. New York: CRC Press.

Falaleev, Mikhail. 2005. "MVD primenit silu. No—s umom." *Rossiiskaia gazeta*, September 29.

———. 2013. "V maske i pod prikrytiem." *Rossiiskaia gazeta*, April 23.

Farley, Melissa, ed. 2004. *Prostitution, Trafficking, and Traumatic Stress*. New York: Routledge.

Farrell, Amy, Jack McDevitt, and Stephanie Fahy. 2008. *Understanding and Improving Law Enforcement Responses to Human Trafficking: Final Report*. Boston: Northeastern University.

Farrell, Amy, Jack McDevitt, Rebecca Pfeffer, Stephanie Fahy, Colleen Owens, Meredith Dank, and William Adams. 2012. *Identifying Challenges to Improve the Investigation and Prosecution of State and Local Human Trafficking Cases*. Boston: Northeastern Institute on Race and Justice.

Farrell, Amy, and Rebecca Pfeffer. 2014. "Policing Human Trafficking: Cultural Blinders and Organizational Barriers." *Annals of the American Academy of Political and Social Sciences* 653: 46–64.

Favarel-Garrigues, Gilles. 2011. *Policing Economic Crime in Russia: From Soviet Planned Economy to Privatization*. New York: Columbia University Press.

Favarel-Garrigues, Gilles, and Anne Le Herou. 2004. "State and Multilateralization of Policing in Post-Soviet Russia." *Policing and Society* 14 (1): 13–30.

Feeley, Malcolm M. 1973. "Two Models of the Criminal Justice System: An Organizational Perspective." *Law and Society Review* 7 (3): 407–26.

Feifer, Gregory. 2010. "Russia Boosts Powerful Investigative Agency." *Radio Free Europe/Radio Liberty*, September 24. http://www.rferl.org/content/Russia_Boosts_Powerful_Investigative_Agency_/2167559.html.

Figes, Orlando. 2007. *The Whisperers: Private Life in Stalin's Russia*. New York: Metropolitan Books.

Filimonov, Anton. 2014. "Rashirenie prav i garantii dlia poterpevshikh ot prestuplenii." Garant.ru, January 22. http://www.garant.ru/article/520854/#ixzz3FyRiNUfU.

Firestone, Thomas A. 2010. "Armed Injustice: Abuse of the Law and Complex Crime in Post-Soviet Russia." *Denver Journal of International Law and Policy* 38 (4): 555–80.

Fleming, Jenny. 2010. "Learning to Work Together: Police and Academics." *Policing* 4 (2): 139–45.

Fox, James C., and Richard J. Lundman. 1974. "Problems and Strategies in Gaining Research Access in Police Organziations." *Criminology* 12 (1): 52–69.

Frohmann, Lisa. 1991. "Discrediting Victims' Allegations of Sexual Assault: Prosecutorial Accounts of Case Rejections." *Social Problems* 38 (2): 213–26.

Frolov, Anton. 2014. "Poterpevshie izbaviatsia ot 'kompleksa zhertvy.'" Pravda.ru, January 13. http://www.pravda.ru/accidents/13-01-2014/1188030-law-0/.

Galeotti, Mark. 1993. "Perestroika, Perestrelka, Pereborka: Policing Russia in a Time of Change." *Europe-Asia Studies* 45 (5): 769–86.

——. 2010a. "Medvedev Pulls Investigative Committee Close." *Radio Free Europe/Radio Liberty*, October 12. http://www.rferl.org/content/Russias_Medvedev_Pulls_Investigations_Committee_Close/2188702.html.

——. 2010b. *The Politics of Security in Modern Russia*. Burlington, VT: Ashgate.

Gallagher, Anne. 2001. "Human Rights and the New UN Protocols on Trafficking and Migrant Smuggling: A Preliminary Analysis." *Human Rights Quarterly* 23 (4): 975–1004.

——. 2010. *The International Law of Human Trafficking*. New York: Cambridge University Press.

——. 2011. "Improving the Effectiveness of the International Law of Human Trafficking: A Vision for the Future of the US Trafficking in Persons Reports." *Human Rights Review* 12 (1): 381.

Gallagher, Anne, and Paul Holmes. 2008. "Developing an Effective Criminal Justice Response to Human Trafficking: Lessons from the Front Line." *International Criminal Justice Review* 18 (3): 318–43.

Gehlbach, Scott. 2008. *Representation through Taxation: Revenue, Politics, and Development in Postcommunist States*. New York: Cambridge University Press.

Gerber, Theodore, and Sarah Mendelson. 2008. "Public Experiences of Police Violence and Corruption in Contemporary Russia: A Case of Predatory Policing?" *Law and Society Review* 42 (1): 1–43.

Gilinskiy, Yakov. 2005. "Police and the Community in Russia." *Police Practice and Research* 6 (4): 331–46.

Girko, C. I. 2005. *Kommentarii k Ugolovnomu kodeksu Rossiiskoi Federatsii (postateinyi)*. Moscow: Dashkov i Ko.

Golianova, Natalia. 2008. "Starshaia sestra prodala mladshuiu v seks-rabstvo za 10,000 rublei." *Komsomol'skaia pravda*, December 18. http://kp.ru/daily/24217.3/419056/.

Gordon, Linda. 2001. "Who Deserves Help? Who Must Provide?" *Annals of the American Academy of Political and Social Sciences* 577: 12–25.

Granville, Johanna. 2004. "From Russia without Love: The "Fourth Wave" of Human Trafficking." *Demokratizatsiya* 12 (1): 147–55.

Griaznova, Ol'ga. 2007. "Russian Residents' Attitudes Toward the Law-Enforcement Agencies: A Review of Recent Research" *Russian Politics and Law* 45 (3): 74–104.

Gromov, C. V. 2005. "Nekotoroe voprosy kvalifikatsii prestuplenii—torgovlia liud'mi i ispol'zovanie rabskogo truda." *Ugolovnoe pravo* (3): 26–28.

Gumbert, Aleksandr. 2010. "Zhitel'nitsa Tuly popala v seksual'noe rabstvo v Podol'ske." *Podol'sk Today*, January 26. http://podolsk.bezformata.ru/listnews/seksualnoe-rabstvo-v-podolske/242351/.

Hahn, Gordon. 2010. *Medvedev's Investigation Reforms: Towards the Rule of Law?* Russia: Other Points of View, October 19. http://www.russiaotherpointsofview.com/2010/10/medvedevs-investigaton-reforms-towards-the-rule-of-law.html.

Harding, Luke. 2007. "Russian Law Prevents Extradition." *The Guardian*, May 22. http://www.theguardian.com/world/2007/may/22/russia.lukeharding.

Haynes, Dina F. 2007. "(Not) Found Chained to a Bed in a Brothel: Conceptual, Legal, and Procedural Failures to Fulfill the Promise of the Trafficking Victims Protection Act." *Georgetown Immigration Law Journal* 21 (3): 337–81.

Hemment, Julie. 2004. "Global Civil Society and the Local Costs of Belonging: Defining Violence against Women in Russia." *Signs* 29 (3): 815–40.

——. 2007. *Empowering Women in Russia: Activism, Aid, and NGOs.* Bloomington: Indiana University Press.

Hendley, Kathryn. 2004. "Business Litigation in the Transition: A Portrait of Debt Collection in Russia." *Law and Society Review* 31 (1): 305–47.

——. 2005. "Accelerated Procedure in the Russian Arbitrazh Courts: A Case Study of Unintended Consequences." *Problems of Post-Communism* 52 (6): 21–31.

——. 2006. "Assessing the Rule of Law in Russia" *Cardozo Journal of International and Comparative Law* 14 (2): 347–91.

——. 2009. "'Telephone Law' and the 'Rule of Law': The Russian Case" *Hague Journal on the Rule of Law* 1 (2): 241–64.

——. 2013. "Too Much of a Good Thing? Assessing Access to Civil Justice in Russia" *Slavic Review* 72 (4): 802–27.

Herrera, Yoshiko. 2010. *Mirrors of the Economy: National Accounts and International Norms in Russia and Beyond.* Ithaca, NY: Cornell University Press.

Herz, Annette. 2006. *Trafficking in Human Beings: An Empirical Study on Criminal Prosecution in Germany.* Freiburg: Max Planck Institute for Foreign and International Criminal Law.

——. 2011. "Human Trafficking and Police Investigations." In *Human Trafficking: Exploring the International Nature, Concerns, and Complexities,* ed. John Winterdyk, Benjamin Perrin, and Philip Reichel, 129–52. Boca Raton, FL: CRC Press.

Highlights. 1999. "Highlights from the Duma Roundtable on Trafficking." *Organized Crime Watch* 1 (2): 2–4.

Hill, Heather C. 2003. "Understanding Implementation: Street-Level Bureaucrats' Resources for Reform." *Journal of Public Administration Research and Theory* 13 (3): 265–82.

Hinton, Mercedes S., and Tim Newburn, eds. 2009. *Policing Developing Democracies.* New York: Routledge.

Hodgson, Jacqueline. 2005. *French Criminal Justice: A Comparative Account of the Investigation and Prosecution of Crime in France.* Portland, OR: Hart.

Holmes, Stephen. 1999. "The Procuracy and Its Problems." *East European Constitutional Review* 8 (1–2): 76–78.

Hoyle, Carolyn, Mary Bosworth, and Michelle Dempsey. 2011. "Labelling the Victims of Sex Trafficking: Exploring the Borderland between Rhetoric and Reality." *Social and Legal Studies* 20 (3): 313–29.

HRW. Human Rights Watch. 1999. *Confession at any Cost: Police Torture in Russia.* New York: Human Rights Watch.

——. 2013. *Race to the Bottom: Exploitation of Migrant Workers in Advance of the 2014 Winter Olympic Games in Sochi.* New York: Human Rights Watch.

——. 2014. *Abandoned by the State: Violence, Neglect, and Isolation for Children with Disabilities in Russian Orphanages.* New York: Human Rights Watch.

Hughes, Donna M. 2000. "The Natasha Trade: The Transnational Shadow Market of Trafficking in Women." *Journal of International Affairs* 53 (2): 625–52.

——. 2002. *Trafficking for Sexual Exploitation: The Case of the Russian Federation.* Geneva: International Organization for Migration.

ICMPD. International Centre for Migration Policy Development. 2009. *Cooperation beyond Borders: Development of Transnational Referral Mechanisms for Trafficked Persons.* Vienna: International Centre for Migration Policy Development.

——. 2012. *The Way Forward in Establishing Effective Transnational Referral Mechanisms: A Report Based on Experiences in Cases of Human Trafficking in South-Eastern Europe.* Vienna: International Centre for Migration Policy Development.

ICNL. International Center for Not-for-Profit Law. 2006. *Analysis of Law no. 18-FZ on Introducing Amendments to Certain Legislative Acts of the Russian Federation.* Washington, DC: International Center for Not-for-Profit Law.

ILO. International Labor Organization. 2009a. *The Costs of Coercion.* Geneva: International Labor Organization.

——. 2009b. "Operational Indicators of Trafficking in Human Beings." http://ilo. org/global/topics/forced-labour/publications/WCMS_105023/lang--en/index. htm.

——. 2012. *ILO Global Estimate of Forced Labor: Results and Methodology.* Geneva: International Labor Organization.

Interfax. 2009. "'Militsii prikhoditsia rabotat' v slozhnykh usloviiakh'" *Interfax,* July 14. http://www.interfax.ru/90036.

——. 2013. "Zhitelei Cheliabinskoi oblasti zapodozrili v ispol'zovanii truda soten rabov." *Interfax,* March 19. http://www.interfax-russia.ru/Ural/news. asp?id=388411&sec=1672.

IOM. International Organization for Migration. 2006. "Materialy, predostavleny Sledstvennym komitetom MVD RF: Analiz praktiki rassledovaniia ugolovnykh del o prestupleniiakh v sfere torvogli liud'mi."

——. 2007a. *Financial Report for the Year Ended 31 December 2007.*

——. 2007b. *The IOM Handbook on Direct Assistance for Victims of Trafficking.* Geneva: International Organization for Migration.

——. 2009. *Statistical Report: Assistance Provided to Victims of Human Trafficking from March 2006 to November 15, 2009.* Moscow: International Organization for Migration.

ITAR-TASS. 2013. "Sledovateli vyiavili novyi vid torgovli liud'mi—rabskii trud na morskikh sudakh," *ITAR-TASS,* April 15.

Javeline, Debra, and Sarah Lindemann-Komarova. 2010. "A Balanced Assessment of Russian Civil Society." *Journal of International Affairs* 63 (2): 171–88.

Jenness, Valerie, and Ryken Grattet. 2005. "The Law-in-between: The Effects of Organizational Perviousness on the Policing of Hate Crime." *Social Problems* 52 (2): 337–59.

Jenness, Valerie, and Beverly McPhail. 2005–2006. "To Charge or Not to Charge?—That is the Question: The Pursuit of Strategic Advantage in Prosecutorial Decision-Making Surrounding Hate Crime." *Journal of Hate Studies* 4 (1): 89–119.

Johnson, David T. 2002. *The Japanese Way of Justice: Prosecuting Crime in Japan*. New York: Oxford University Press.

Johnson, Janet Elise. 2001. "State Transformation and Violence against Women in Postcommunist Russia." PhD diss., University of Indiana at Bloomington.

——. 2004. "Sisterhood Versus the 'Moral' Russian State: The Postcommunist Politics of Rape." In *Post-Soviet Women Encountering Transition*, ed. Kathleen Kuehnast and Carol Nechemias, 217–38. Baltimore: Johns Hopkins University Press.

——. 2005a. "Public-Private Permutations: Domestic Violence Crisis Centers in Barnaul." In *Russian Civil Society: A Critical Assessment*, ed. Alfred B. Evans, Jr., Laura A. Henry, and Lisa McIntosh Sundstrom, 266–83. Armonk, NY: M. E. Sharpe.

——. 2005b. "Violence against Women in Russia." In *Ruling Russia: Law, Crime, and Justice in a Changing Society*, ed. William Alex Pridemore, 147–66. Lanham, MD: Rowman and Littlefield.

——. 2009a. *Gender Violence in Russia: The Politics of Feminist Intervention*. Bloomington: Indiana University Press.

——. 2009b. "Unwilling Participant Observation among Russian *Siloviki* and the Good-enough Field Researcher." *PS: Political Science and Politics* 42 (2): 321–24.

Johnson, Juliet. 2000. *A Fistful of Rubles: The Rise and Fall of the Russian Banking System*. Ithaca, NY: Cornell University Press.

——. 2002. *Agents of Transformation: The Role of the West in Post-Communist Central Bank Development*. Strathclyde, UK: University of Strathclyde.

Jordan, Pamela. 2005. *Defending Rights in Russia: Lawyers, the State, and Legal Reform in the Post-Soviet Era*. Vancouver: UBC Press.

Kaminskaya, Dina. 1982. *Final Judgment: My Life as a Soviet Defense Attorney*. New York: Simon and Schuster.

Kanev, Sergei. 2007. "Kak ustroeny 'kryshi' v Rossii." *Novaia gazeta*, October 22.

Kara, Siddharth. 2008. *Sex Trafficking: Inside the Business of Modern Slavery*. New York: Columbia University Press.

Kavkazskii uzel. 2008. "V Rostove-na-Donu reshaiut problemu reintegratsii zhertv rabstva." *Kavkazskii uzel*, October 28. http://www.kavkaz-uzel.ru/articles/145379.

Kay, Rebecca. 2000. *Russian Women and Their Organizations: Gender, Discrimination, and Grassroots Women's Organizations, 1991–96*. New York: Macmillan.

Kazantsev, Sergei M. 1997. "The Judicial Reform of 1864 and the Procuracy in Russia." In *Reforming Justice in Russia, 1864–1996: Power, Culture, and the Limits of Legal Order*, ed. Peter Solomon, 44–60. Armonk, NY: M. E. Sharpe.

Kelly, Liz, and Linda Regan. 2000. *Stopping Traffic: Exploring the Extent of and Responses to Trafficking in Women for Sexual Exploitation in the UK*. London: Home Office: Policing and Reducing Crime Unit.

Khodyreva, Natalya. 1997. "Education and Public Awareness Campaigns in Target Groups and Regions: Support of Trafficking Survivors." Presented at The Trafficking of NIS Women Abroad: An International Conference in Moscow, November 3–5, 1997.

Khodzhaeva, Ekaterina. 2011. "Chastnoe i publichnoe v prostranstvennoi organizatsii povsednevnykh praktik uchastkogo (Opyt etnograficheskogo opisaniia)." *Laboratorium* (3): 18–52.

Klimycheva, Iuliia. 2010. "Rabstvo 21-ogo veka." *Amurskaia pravda*, April 29. http://www.ampravda.ru/2010/04/29/025701.html.

Knight, Amy. 1996. *Spies without Cloaks: The KGB's Successors*. Princeton, NJ: Princeton University Press.

Kolesnichenko, Aleksandr. 2004a. "Klient vsegda vinovat." *Novye izvestiia*, November 30. http://www.newizv.ru/politics/2004-11-30/16195-klient-vsegda-vinovat.html.

———. 2004b. "Vsekh na prodazhu." *Novye izvestiia*, January 28. http://www.newizv.ru/society/2004-01-28/4201-vseh-na-prodazhu.html.

Kolesnikova, Natalia. 2013. "Rabstvo na Kavkaze: Kuda propadaiut liudi i pochemu ikh ishchut volontery." *Argumenty i fakty*, August 23. http://www.stav.aif.ru/society/law/159015.

Kolesnikova, O., Leonid Kosals, R. Ryvkina, and Iu. A. Simagin. 2002. *Ekonomicheskaia aktivnost' rabotnikov pravookhranitel'nykh organov postsovetskoi Rossii: Vidy, masshtaby i vliianie na obshchestvo*. Moscow.

Kolosov, Andrei. 2010. "Interv'iu zamestitelia General'nogo prokurora Rossiiskoi Federatsii A. G. Zviagintseva." *Argumenty i fakty*, February 24. http://genproc.gov.ru/smi/interview_and_appearences/interview/65680/.

Korablev, Boris. 2005. "Mladentsy pod razdachu." *Vremia novostei*, November 30. http://www.vremya.ru/2005/223/51/140253.html.

———. 2007. "Legalizatsiia mladentsev." *Vremia novostei*, March 16. http://www.vremya.ru/2007/45/46/174139.html.

———. 2008. "Dva goda na dva slova." *Vremia novostei*, March 18. http://www.vremya.ru/2008/44/46/199823.html.

Korneev, Igor', and Viktoria Romanova. 2010. "Mat' popavshei v rabstvo tuliachki boitsia mesti ee muchitelei." *Komsomol'skaia pravda*, January 22. http://kp.ru/daily/24428/597393/.

Kornia, Anastasiia. 2010. "Pretsedent v zakone." *Vedomosti*, July 15.

Kosals, Leonid. 2010. "Police in Russia: Reform or Business Restructuring?" *Russian Analytical Digest* (84): 2–5.

Krainova, Natalya. 2009. "Police Force to Improve Image with New Rules." *Moscow Times*, August 28.

———. 2010. "Cost of Bribe Nearly Doubles." *Moscow Times*, July 28.

———. 2011. "Initiative Makes State Compensate Victims of Crime." *Moscow Times*, May 27.

Kravchenko, Maria. 2013. *Inappropriate Enforcement of Anti-Extremist Legislation in Russia in 2012*. Moscow: SOVA Center. http://www.sova-center.ru/en/misuse/reports-analyses/2013/06/d27382/.

Kuehnast, Kathleen R., and Carol Nechemias, eds. 2004. *Post-Soviet Women Encountering Transition: Nation Building, Economic Survival, and Civic Activism*. Washington, DC: Woodrow Wilson Center Press.

Kurkchiyan, Marina. 2003. "The Illegitimacy of Law in Post-Soviet Societies." In *Law and Informal Practices: The Post-Communist Experience*, ed. Dennis J. Galligan and Marina Kurkchiyan. New York: Oxford University Press.

Kyckelhahn, Tracey, Allen J. Beck, and Thomas H. Cohen. 2009. "Characteristics of Suspected Human Trafficking Incidents, 2007–2008." *Bureau of Justice Statistics Special Report* 224526.

Laczko, Frank. 2005. "Data and Research on Human Trafficking." *International Migration* 43 (1–2): 5–16.

Ladnyi, Vladimir. 2002. "Za kochan kapusty—v raby." *Komsomol'skaia pravda*, October 24. http://kp.ru/daily/22661/21405/.

Larina, Alena. 2012. "V Ingushetii pytalis' prodat' dvukhletnego rebenka." *Rossiiskaia gazeta*, August 1. http://www.rg.ru/2012/08/01/reg-skfo/prodali-anons. html.

Lebedev, V. M., ed. 2004. *Kommentarii k Ugolovnomu kodeksu Rossiiskoi Federatsii*. 3rd ed. Moscow, Russia: Iurait-Izdat.

Lebedev, V. M., and A. V. Galakhov, eds. 2009. *Osobennaia chast' Ugolovnogo kodeksa Rossiiskoi Federatsii: Kommentarii, sudebnaia praktika, statistika*. Moscow: Gorodets.

Ledeneva, Alena. 1998. *Russia's Economy of Favors: Blat, Networking, and Informal Exchange*. New York: Cambridge University Press.

——. 2006. *How Russia Really Works: The Informal Practices That Shaped Post-Soviet Politics and Business*. Ithaca, NY: Cornell University Press.

Legislative Committee, State Duma of the Russian Federation. 2001. *Komitet Gosudarstvennoi Dumy po zakonodatel'stvu v 2001 godu: itogi, analiz, statistika*. Moscow.

Lehti, Martii, and Kauko Aromaa. 2006. "Trafficking for Sexual Exploitation." *Crime and Justice* 34 (1): 133–227.

Levchenko, O. P., ed. 2009. *Torgovlia liud'mi i legalizatsiia prestupnykh dokhodov*. Moscow: International Organization for Migration.

Levy, Clifford. 2010a. "Beaten Russian Editor Is Told to Say It's His Fault." *New York Times*, May 17.

——. 2010b. "Russian Mayor Irks Security Agency, and Suffers." *New York Times*, July 4.

——. 2010c. "Videos Rouse Russian Anger Toward Police." *New York Times*, July 28.

Lievore, Denise. 2004. "Victim Credibility in Adult Sexual Assault Cases." *Trends and Issues in Crime and Criminal Justice* (288).

Light, Matthew. 2010. "Policing Migration in Soviet and Post-Soviet Moscow." *Post-Soviet Affairs* 26 (3): 275–313.

Lipscombe, Sally, and Jacqueline Beard. 2014. *Human Trafficking: UK Responses*. House of Commons Home Affairs.

Lipsky, Michael. 1980. *Street-Level Bureaucracy: Dilemmas of the Individual in Public Services*. New York: Russell Sage Foundation.

Lloyd, Rachel. 2011. *Girls Like Us: Fighting for a World Where Girls Are Not for Sale. A Memoir*. New York: Harper Collins.

Lobanov, Mikhail. 2008. "Gubakhinskie 'raby' stali sviditeliami." *Kommersant*, August 23. http://www.kommersant.ru/doc/1016032.

Ma, Yue. 2002. "Prosecutorial Discretion and Plea Bargaining in the United States, France, Germany, and Italy: A Comparative Perspective." *International Criminal Justice Review* 12 (1): 22–52.

Macaulay, Stewart. 1984. "Law and the Behavioral Sciences: Is There Any There There?" *Law and Policy* 6 (2): 149–87.

Maggs, Peter. 2002. "Judicial Precedent Emerges at the Supreme Court of the Russian Federation." *Journal of East European Law* 9 (3): 479–500.

Makedonov, Lev, and Rustam Faliakhov. 2011. "U Chaiki vse khuzhe." Gazeta.ru, April 21. http://www.gazeta.ru/politics/2011/04/21_a_3591281.shtml.

Maksimova, Ol'ga. 2011. "Povsednevnye praktiki vzaimodeistviia sotrudnikov PPS i uchastkovykh upolnomochennykh s naseleniem." In *Militsiia i etnicheskie migranty: praktiki vzaimodeistviia*, ed. Viktor Voronkov, Boris Gladarev, and Liliia Sagitova, 136–72. St. Petersburg: Aleteiia.

Malarek, Victor. 2004. *The Natashas: Inside the New Global Sex Trade*. New York: Arcade.

March, James G., and Johan P. Olsen. 1984. "The New Institutionalism: Organizational Factors in Political Life." *American Political Science Review* 78 (3): 734–49.

March, James G., and Herbert Simon. 1958. *Organizations.* New York: John Wiley and Sons.

Massal'skii, Vadim, and Daniel Levin. 2009. "Prestupnost' v Rossii, 2009." *Voice of America,* December 24.

Mastrofski, Stephen D., and R. Richard Ritti. 1992. "You Can Lead a Horse to Water . . . : A Case Study of a Police Department's Response to Stricter Drunk Driving Laws." *Justice Quarterly* 9 (3): 465–91.

Matthews, Owen. 2007. "War Inside the Kremlin." *Newsweek,* December 1.

Maynard-Moody, Steven, and Michael C. Musheno. 2003. *Cops, Teachers, Counselors: Stories from the Front Lines of Public Service.* Ann Arbor: University of Michigan Press.

McCarthy, Lauren A. 2008. "Sravnitel'nyi analiz praktiki rossiiskikh i amerikanskikh pravookhranitel'nykh institutov v protivodeistvii torgovle liud'mi." In *Vne tolerantnosti. Torgovlia liud'mi i rabskii trud: metamorfozy starykh prestuplenii i novye metody ikh preodoleniia.* Vladivostok: Pacific State Economic University.

———. 2014a. "Local-Level Law Enforcement: Muscovites and Their Uchastkovyy." *Post-Soviet Affairs* 30 (2–3): 195–225.

———. 2014b. "Human Trafficking and the New Slavery." *Annual Review of Law and Social Science* 10: 221–42.

McDaid, David, Yevgeny A. Samyshkin, Rachel Jenkins, Angelina Potasheva, Alexey Nikiforov, and Rifat A. Atun. 2006. "Health System Factors Impacting on Delivery of Mental Health Services in Russia: Multi-Methods Study." *Health Policy* 79 (2–3): 144–52.

McKillop, Bron. 1997. "Anatomy of a French Murder Case." *American Journal of Comparative Law* 45 (3): 527–83.

McKinney, Judith R. 2009. "Russian Babies, Russian Babes: Economic and Demographic Implications of International Adoption and International Trafficking for Russia." *Demokratizatsiya* 17 (1): 19–40.

Medvedev, Dmitrii. 2009. "Rossiia vpered! Stat'ia Dmitriia Medvedeva." September 10. http://www.kremlin.ru/news/5413, accessed February 11, 2015.

Mendelson, Sarah, and Theodore Gerber. 2008. "Young Russian Women on Procreation, Trafficking, and Prostitution: Myths, Reality, and Policy Implications, Presentation." Center for Strategic and International Studies, Washington, DC, July 23.

Merryman, John, and Rogelio Perez-Perdomo. 2007. *The Civil Law Tradition: An Introduction to the Legal Systems of Europe and Latin America.* 3rd ed. Stanford, CA: Stanford University Press.

Mikhailova, Tamara, Dmitrii Vladimirov, and Vladimir Kuz'min. 2007. "Vladimir Putin: pozitsiiu Rossii gotov ob"iasnit detal'no." *Rossiiskaia gazeta,* June 5. http://www.rg.ru/2007/06/05/putin.html.

Mikhailovskaya, Inga. 1999. "The Procuracy and Its Problems: Russia." *East European Constitutional Review* 8 (1–2): 98–104.

Mizulina, Elena B. 2006. *Torgovlia liud'mi i rabstvo v Rossii.* Moscow: Iurist.

MT. Moscow Times. 2006. "Witnesses to Receive Bodyguards." *Moscow Times,* November 3.

———. 2007. "Police Should Chase Killers, Not Quotas." *Moscow Times,* October 26.

———. 2009a. "Survey on Police Force Hints Anti-Graft Drive Is Working." *Moscow Times,* June 10.

———. 2009b. "Police Must Pass Driving Tests." *Moscow Times,* July 30.

———. 2010a. "Medvedev Finalizes Investigative Committee." *Moscow Times*, December 29.

———. 2010b. "Bill on New Investigative Body Sent to Duma." *Moscow Times*, September 28.

MVD. Ministry of Internal Affairs. 2008. "Metodicheskie rekomendatsii po rassledovaniiu torgovli liud'mi (st. 127.1 UK Rossiiskoi Federatsii)." Unpublished, on file with author.

———. 2013. "Vladimir Kolokol'tsev pozdravil zhenshin, prokhodiashchikh sluzhbu v MVD Rossii, s nastupaiushchim prazdnikom." http://mvd.ru/document/2043551.

Najibullah, Farangis. 2014. "Russia Launches New Wave of Raids on NGOs." *Radio Free Europe/Radio Liberty*, May 14. http://www.rferl.org/content/russia-new-raids-ngos/25384948.html.

Naumov, A. 2007. "Razgranichenie prestuplenii predusmotrennykh st. 127.1 i 240 UK." *Zakonnost'* (6): 4–5.

Nesterova, Ol'ga. 2003. "Net sostava prestupleniia." *Trud*, April 30.

Newsru.com. 2005a. "'Versia': Sovremennaia rabotorgovlia prinosit 10 mlrd dollarov ezhegodno (Rasskazy devushek)." Newsru.com, March 21. http://www.newsru.com/russia/21mar2005/slaves.html.

———. 2005b. "Mat' prodala 3-letniuiu doch' za 80 rublei, chtoby kupit' vodku." Newsru.com, April 26. http://www.newsru.com/crime/26apr2005/doch_print.html.

———. 2009. "V istorii s maiorom Evsiukovym vinovaty 'likhie devianostye,' schitaet Nurgaliev." Newsru.com, August 30. http://www.newsru.com/russia/30aug2009/nur.html.

Novikov, A. P., ed. 2006. *Kommentarii k Ugolovnomu kodeksu Rossiiskoi Federatsii: Raschirennyi ugolovno-pravovoi analiz s materialami sudebno-sledstvennoi praktiki.* 5th ed. Moscow: Eksamen.

Novye izvestiia. 2008. "V MVD budet sozdan tsentr po bor'be s torgovlei liud'mi." *Novye izvestiia*, May 21. http://www.newizv.ru/accidents/2008-05-21/90388-v-mvd-budet-sozdan-centr-po-borbe-s-torgovlej-ljudmi.html.

NSC. National Security Council. 1997. *International Crime Control Strategy.* Washington, DC: National Security Council. http://clinton4.nara.gov/WH/EOP/NSC/html/documents/iccs-frm.html.

Oberfield, Zachary. 2014. *Becoming Bureaucrats: Socialization at the Front Lines of Government Service.* Philadelphia: University of Pennsylvania Press.

Oliphant, Ronald. 2010. "Chaika Says Graft War Failing." *Moscow Times*, October 14.

Ol'shanskii, Aleksei, and Iurii Kochemin. 2007. "Rab nashego vremeni." *Novye izvestiia*, June 21. http://www.newizv.ru/accidents/2007-06-21/71366-rab-nashego-vremeni.html.

Orlova, Alexandra V. 2004. "From Social Dislocation to Human Trafficking: The Russian Case." *Problems of Post-Communism* 51 (6): 14–22.

ODIHR. OSCE Office for Democratic Institutions and Human Rights. 2008a. *Compensation for Trafficked and Exploited Persons in the OSCE Region.* Warsaw: OSCE Office for Democratic Institutions and Human Rights.

———. 2008b. *Identification, Assistance, and Protection of Victims of Trafficking in the Russian Federation (Focusing on the Moscow Region).* Warsaw: OSCE Office for Democratic Institutions and Human Rights.

OSCE. Organization for Security and Cooperation in Europe. 2003. OSCE Action Plan to Combat Trafficking in Human Beings. Decision no. 557 (July 24).

———. 2013. Office of the Special Representative and Co-ordinator for Combating Trafficking in Human Beings. *Trafficking in Human Beings for the Purpose of Organ Removal in the OSCE Region: Analysis and Findings.* Vienna: Organization for Security and Cooperation in Europe.

Oude Breuil, Brenda Carina, Dina Siegel, Piet van Reenen, Annemarieke Beijer, and Linda Roos. 2011. "Human Trafficking Revisited: Legal, Enforcement, and Ethnographic Narratives on Sex Trafficking to Western Europe." *Trends in Organized Crime* 14 (1): 30–46.

Ovchinskii, Vladimir. 2007. "Kushchevskie klony." *Ogonek*, February 2. http://www.kommersant.ru/doc/1573608.

———. 2008. "Za chto borolis'?" *Ogonek*, September 22–28. http://www.ogoniok.com/5065/35/.

Paneyakh, Ella. 2014. "Faking Performance Together: Systems of Performance Evaluation in Russian Enforcement Agencies and Production of Bias and Privilege." *Post-Soviet Affairs* 30 (2–3): 115–36.

Paneyakh, Ella, Mikhail Pozdniakov, Kirill Titaev, Irina Chetverikova, and Marina Shkliaruk. 2012. *Pravookhranitel'naia deiatel'nost' v Rossii: Struktura, funktsionirovanie, puti reformirovaniia, chast' 1: Diagnostika raboty pravookhranitel'nykh organov RF i vypolneniia imi politseiskoi funktsii.* St. Petersburg: European University at St. Petersburg Research Institute for the Rule of Law.

Panfilova, Ol'ga. 2007. "Suprugu Bashkirskogo prokurora obvinili v ispol'zovanii rabskogo truda." *Novyi region*, August 15. http://newdaynews.ru/incidents/134765.html.

Pavlova, Larisa. 2006. "Rebenok po skhodnoi tsene." *Express Gazeta Online*, July 30. http://www.eg.ru/print/crime/8076/.

Piacentini, Laura, and Judith Pallot. 2012. *Gender, Geography, and Punishment: The Experience of Women in Carceral Russia.* New York: Oxford University Press.

Pinkus, Mikhail. 2007. "Trud iz pod palki." *Rossiiskaia gazeta*, October 12. http://www.rg.ru/2007/10/12/reg-ygural/rabovladelci.html.

Podrabinek, Aleksandr. 2009. "Shuty kremlevskie." *Ezhedevnyi Zhurnal*, April 20. http://www.ej.ru/?a=note&id=8994#.

Pomeranz, William. 2009. "Supervisory Review and Finality of Judgments under Russian Law." *Review of Central and East European Law* 34 (1): 15–36.

Pomeranz, William, and Max Gutbrod. 2012. "The Push for Precedent in Russia's Judicial System." *Review of Central and East European Law* 37 (1): 1–30.

Pomorski, Stanislaw. 2005. "Consensual Justice in Russia: Guilty Pleas under the 2001 Code of Criminal Procedure." In *Public Policy and Law in Russia: In Search of a Unified Legal and Political Space*, ed. Robert Sharlet and Ferdinand Feldbrugge, 187–98. Leiden: Koninklijke Brill NV.

———. 2006. "Modern Russian Criminal Procedure: The Adversarial Principle and Guilty Plea." *Criminal Law Forum* 17 (2): 129–48.

Poteria, Irina. 2006. "Mat' prodala rebenka za 20 tysiach dollarov." Taganrog.su, July 8.

Pravda.ru. 2012. "Kazhdoe vtoroe prestuplenie v Moskve sovershaiut migranty." Pravda.ru, November 6. http://www.pravda.ru/news/society/06-11-2012/1133519-migrant-0/.

Procuracy RF. 2008. "V Astrakhanskoi oblasti vynesen prigovor v otnoshenii gruppy lits, zanimavshikhsia torgovlei liud'mi." *Prokuratura News*, July 31. http://genproc.gov.ru/pda/news/news-62541/.

———. 2010. Doklad na zasedanii Soveta Federatsii Federal'nogo Sobraniia Rossiiskoi Federatsii.

Pustovoitov, Sergei. 2013. "Prodannyi v rabstvo Oleg Mel'nikov: Eto
    ne otchaianie, no . . ." Sobesednik.ru. http://sobesednik.ru/
    incident/20131031-prodannyi-v-rabstvo-oleg-melnikov-eto-ne-otchayanie-no.
Putin, Vladimir. 2003. "Bor'ba s torgovlei liud'mi: vstupitel'noe slovo Prezidenta Rossii
    na soveshchanii s chlenami pravitel'stva RF (otryvok)." Moscow, October 27.
    http://moscow.usembassy.gov/tip-transcript20.html.
Pyshchulina, Olga. 2005. "An Evaluation of Ukrainian Legislation to Counter and
    Criminalize Human Trafficking." In *Human Traffic and Transnational Crime:
    Eurasian and American Perspectives*, ed. Louise Shelley and Sally Stoecker, 115–
    24. Lanham, MD: Rowman and Littlefield.
Pysina, Galina. 2005. "Pravoprimenitel'naia deiatel'nost' v voprosakh realizatsii
    st. 127.1 UK RF." *Voprosy kvalifikatsii.*
Quinn, Allison. 2014. "How to Free a Modern-Day Slave in Dagestan." *Moscow Times*,
    January 16.
Rao, Smirti, and Christina Presenti. 2012. "Understanding Human Trafficking Origins:
    A Cross Country Empirical Analysis." *Feminist Economics* 18 (2): 231–63.
RAPSI. Rossiiskoe agentstvo pravovoi i sudebnoi informatsii. 2011. "GP otmechaet
    massovye fakty fal'sifikatsii statistiki prestupnosti v RF." April 21. http://infosud.
    ru/incident_news/20110421/252302382.html.
——. 2012. "Programma zashchity sviditelei v Rossii. Spravka." September 22. http://
    rapsinews.ru/legislation_news/20120922/264751821.html.
Rarog, A.I ed.. 2011. *Kommentarii k ugolovnomu kodeksu Rossiiskoi Federatsii*, 7th ed.
    Moscow: Prospekt.
Raymond, Janice G. 2002. "The New UN Trafficking Protocol." *Women's Studies
    International Forum* 25 (5): 491–502.
Regions.ru. 2002. "Penza. Domovladelets zastavlial vorov i p'ianits stanovit'sia
    rabami." September 18. Regions.ru. http://www.regions.ru/news/849211/.
——. 2004. "Rabotorgovtsa prigovorili k 5 godam lisheniia svobody." Regions.ru,
    October 25. http://regions.ru/news/1664906/.
——. 2011. "V Moskve osuzhdeny chleny bandy, prodavavshie zhenshchin
    v seksual'noe rabstvo." Regions.ru, April 27. http://www.regions.ru/
    news/2352919/.
Regnum.ru. 2004. "Obzor Omskoi pressy za 2–9 oktiabria 2004 goda." Regnum.ru,
    October 2–9. http://www.regnum.ru/news/339099.html.
——. 2006. "MVD predlagaet priniat' federal'nyi zakon 'O protivodeistvii torgovli
    liud'mi.'" Regnum.ru, May 16. http://www.regnum.ru/news/640566.html.
——. 2007a. "V Bashkirii otpravlen v otstavku glava Buraevskogo raiona." Regnum.ru,
    September 4. http://www.regnum.ru/news/880193.html.
——. 2007b. "Chitinskie pravozashchitniki prosiat osudit' eks-polkovnika za
    rabotorgovliu." Regnum.ru, June 21. http://www.regnum.ru/news/846013.
    html.
——. 2008a. "V Astrakhanskoi oblasti za torgovliu liud'mi osuzhdeny shest' chelovek."
    Regnum.ru, August 1. http://www.regnum.ru/news/1035058.html.
——. 2008b. "Vstupil v silu prigovor vziatkodateliu pytavshemusia podkupit'
    sledovatelia." Regnum.ru, June 26. http://www.regnum.ru/news/1020194.html.
Repetskaya, Anna. 1999. "The Trafficking of Russian Women and Children." *Organized
    Crime Watch* 1 (2): 4–5.
Reynolds, K. Michael, Olga B. Semukhina, and Nicolai M. Demidov. 2008.
    "A Longitudinal Analysis of Public Satisfaction with the Police in the Volgograd
    Region of Russia 1998–2005" *International Criminal Justice Review* 18 (2):
    158–89.

Riabtsev, Andrei. 2005. "Etu devochku prodavali na organy." *Komsomol'skaia pravda*, October 14. http://kp.ru/daily/23599.3/45525/.

Robertson, Annette. 2004. "Police Reform in Russia." In *Transforming Police in Central and Eastern Europe: Process and Progress*, ed. Marina Caparini and Otwin Marenin. New Brunswick, NJ: Transaction Publishers.

———. 2005. "Criminal Justice Policy Transfer to Post-Soviet States: Two Case Studies of Police Reform in Russia and Ukraine." *European Journal on Criminal Policy and Research* 11 (1): 1–28.

Rosbalt.ru. 2002. "Chtoby effektivno borot'sia s torgovlei liud'mi, neobkhodimo meniat' zakonodatel'stvo, schitaiut v MVD RF." Rosbalt.ru, August 27. http://www.rosbalt.ru/2002/08/27/61865.html.

Rosenberg, Ruth. 2006. *Domestic Violence in Europe and Eurasia*. Washington, DC: US Agency for International Development.

Rossiia Penza. 2007. "V Kuznetske sotrudniki FSB zaderzhali rabovladel'tsa." *Rossiia Penza*, May 11. http://penza.rfn.ru/rnews.html?id=2799.

Rudnicki, Ann A. 2012. "The Development of Russia's Child Protection and Welfare System." *Demokratizatsiya* 20 (1): 29–44.

Samsonova, I. 2007. "*Raby: kontrol'naia zakupka.*" *Gazeta Dona* 23 (442), June 5.

Schneider, Friedrich G. 2004. "The Size of the Shadow Economies of 145 Countries All over the World: First Results over the Period 1999 to 2003." IZA Discussion Paper Series, no. 1431.

Schreck, Carl. 2004. "Chopping Sticks Beats Solving Crimes." *Moscow Times*, May 20.

Semukhina, Olga. 2014. "Unreported Crimes, Public Dissatisfaction of Police and Observed Police Misconduct in the Volgograd Region, Russia: A Research Note." *International Journal of Comparative and Applied Criminal Justice* 38 (4): 305–25.

Semukhina, Olga, and Michael J. Reynolds. 2013. *Understanding the Modern Russian Police*. Boca Raton, FL: CRC Press.

Serdiukova, E. V. 2013. "Osnovaniia osvobozhdeniia ot ugolovnoi otvetstvennosti za torgovliu liud'mi." *Zakonnost'* (2): 54–57.

Sharapenko, Denis. 2009. "Estimation of the Shadow Economy in Russia." MA thesis, Central European University, Budapest.

Shelley, Louise. 1996. *Policing Soviet Society: The Evolution of Social Control*. London: Routledge.

———. 1999. "Post-Socialist Policing: Limitations on Institutional Change." In *Policing across the World: Issues for the Twenty-First Century*, ed. R. I. Mawby, 75–87. London: UCL Press.

———. 2002. "The Changing Position of Women: Trafficking, Crime, and Corruption." In *The Legacy of State Socialism and the Future of Transformation*, ed. David Lane. Lanham, MD: Rowman and Littlefield.

———. 2005. "Russia's Law against Trade in People: A Response to International Pressure and Domestic Coalitions." In *Public Policy and Law in Russia: In Search of a Unified Legal and Political Space*, ed. Robert Sharlet and Ferdinand Feldbrugge, 291–305. Leiden: Koninklijke Brill NV.

———. 2010. *Human Trafficking: A Global Perspective*. New York: Cambridge University Press.

Shelley, Louise, and Robert W. Orttung. 2005. "Russia's Efforts to Combat Human Trafficking." In *Ruling Russia: Law, Crime, and Justice in a Changing Society*, ed. William Alex Pridemore, 167–82. Lanham, MD: Rowman and Littlefield.

Shilov, Evgenii. 2007. "S tsep'iu na shee 34-letnii zhitel' Kuznetska stal rabom." *Trud*, May 17. http://www.trud.ru/article/17-05-2007/115994_s_tsepju_na_shee.html.

Shushkevich, Ivan. 2008. *Osobennosti predotvrashcheniia i rassledovaniia prestuplenii, sviazannykh s torgovlei liud'mi*. Moscow: Wolters Kluwer.

Sidorova, Ol'ga. 2006. "Reporter kupit syna." *Voronezhskoe kol'tso* 31 (123), August 3.

Simeunovic-Patic, Biljana, and Sanja Copic. 2010. "Protection and Assistance to Victims of Human Trafficking in Serbia: Recent Developments." *European Journal of Criminology* 7 (1): 45–60.

Simis, Konstantin. 1982. *USSR: The Corrupt Society. The Secret World of Soviet Capitalism*. New York: Simon and Schuster.

Simon, Herbert. 1957. *Models of Man, Social and Rational*. New York: John Wiley and Sons.

Skilbrei, May-Len. 2010. "Taking Trafficking to Court." *Women and Criminal Justice* 20 (1–2): 40–56.

Skolnick, Jerome H. 1966. *Justice without Trial: Law Enforcement in a Democratic Society*. Berkeley: University of California Press.

Smirnov, Aleksei. 2008. "Pravo na pretsedent. VAS sovershil protsessual'nuiu revoliutsiiu." *Gazeta*, February 15.

Smirnova, Lena. 2013. "Entrepreneurs See Dollar Signs in Garbage Piles." *Moscow Times*, June 12.

Smit, Monika. 2011. "Trafficking in Human Beings for Labour Exploitation: The Case of the Netherlands." *Trends in Organized Crime* 14 (2–3): 184–97.

Smith, Gordon. 1978. *The Soviet Procuracy and the Supervision of Administration*. Alphen aan den Rijn, The Netherlands: Sijthoff and Noordhoff.

——. 2005. "Putin, the Procuracy, and the New Criminal Procedure Code." In *Public Policy and Law in Russia—in Search of a Unified Legal and Political Space: Essays in Honor of Donald D. Barry (Law in Eastern Europe)*, ed. Robert Sharlet and Ferdinand Feldbrugge, 169–85. Boston: Martinus Nijhoff.

Snezhina, Svetlana. 2007. "Seks-Rabyn', pytavshikhsia sbezhat', urodovali nozhami." *Komsomol'skaia pravda*, December 17, 2007. http://www.kp.ru/daily/24019.5/88906/.

Sokovnin, Alexei. 2011. "Podpolkovnik GRU perepravlial devushek." *Kommersant*, March 25. http://www.kommersant.ru/doc/1607429.

Soldatov, Andrei, and Irina Borogan. 2011. *The New Nobility: The Restoration of Russia's Security State and the Enduring Legacy of the KGB*. New York: Public Affairs.

Solomon, Jr., Peter H. 1987. "The Case of the Vanishing Acquittal: Informal Norms and the Practice of Soviet Criminal Justice." *Soviet Studies* 39 (4): 531–55.

——. 1996. *Soviet Criminal Justice under Stalin*. Cambridge: Cambridge University Press.

——. 2004. "Judicial Power in Russia: Through the Prism of Administrative Justice." *Law and Society Review* 38 (3): 549–82.

——. 2005. "The Reform of Policing in the Russian Federation." *Australian and New Zealand Journal of Criminology* 38 (2): 230–40.

——. 2012. "Accountability of Judges in Post Communist States: From Bureaucratic to Professional Accountability." In *Judicial Independence in Transition*, ed, Anja Seibert-Fohr, 909–36. New York: Springer.

——. 2013. "Courts, Law, and Policing under Medvedev: Many Reforms, Modest Change, New Voices." In *Russia after 2012: From Putin to Medvedev to Putin—Continuity, Change, or Revolution?* ed. J. L. Black and Michael Johns, 19–41. New York: Routledge.

Solomon, Jr., Peter H., and Todd Foglesong. 2000. *Courts and Transition in Russia: The Challenge of Judicial Reform*. Boulder, CO: Westview.

Spears, Jeffrey, and Cassia Spohn. 1998. "The Genuine Victim and Prosecutors' Charging Decisions in Sexual Assault Cases." *American Journal of Criminal Justice* 20 (2): 183–205.

Spence, Matthew J. 2005. *The Complexity of Success: The US Role in Russian Rule of Law Reform.* Washington, DC: Carnegie Endowment for International Peace.

Sperling, Valerie. 1990. "Rape and Domestic Violence in the USSR." *Response to the Victimization of Women and Children: Journal of the Center for Women Policy Studies* 13 (3): 16–22.

———. 1999. *Organizing Women in Contemporary Russia: Engendering Transition.* Cambridge: Cambridge University Press.

———. 2009. *Altered States: The Globalization of Accountability.* New York: Cambridge University Press.

Stavropolye.tv. 2009. "Stavropol'skoi torgovke det'mi vynesli prigovor." Stavropol'e TV, June 16. http://www.stavropolye.tv/events/view/9127.

Stoecker, Sally. 2005. "Human Trafficking: A New Challenge for Russia and the United States." In *Human Traffic and Transnational Crime: Eurasian and American Perspectives*, ed. Sally Stoecker and Louise Shelley, 13–28. Lanham, MD: Rowman and Littlefield.

Sudnow, David. 1965. "Normal Crimes: Sociological Features of the Penal Code in a Public Defender Office." *Social Problems* 12 (3): 255–76.

Sunshine, Jason, and Tom Tyler. 2003. "The Role of Procedural Justice and Legitimacy in Shaping Public Support for Policing." *Law and Society Review* 37 (3): 513–48.

Surtees, Rebecca. 2007a. *Trafficking in Men, a Trend Less Considered––the Case of Belarus and Ukraine.* Geneva: International Organization for Migration.

———. 2007b. *Listening to Victims: Experiences of Identification, Return, and Assistance in South-Eastern Europe.* Vienna: International Centre for Migration Policy Development.

———. 2008. "Traffickers and Trafficking in Southern and Eastern Europe: Considering the Other Side of Human Trafficking." *European Journal of Criminology* 5 (1): 39–68.

Svetova, Zoia. 2008. "'Nas vyvozili v les, imitirovali rasstrel': chlen komissii po bor'be s korruptsiei derzhal v rabstve migrantov iz Uzbekistana." *Novye izvestiia*, March 5. http://www.newizv.ru/society/2008-03-05/85811-nas-vyvozili-v-les-imitirovali-rasstrel.html.

Swigert, Victoria, and Ronald Farrell. 1977. "Normal Homicides and the Law." *American Sociological Review* 42 (1): 16–32.

Tan'kova, Iaroslava. 2003. "Ia-seks-rabynia." *Komsomol'skaia pravda*, September 1–24. First article in series: http://www.kp.ru/daily/23105/22999/.

Tanner, Murray S. 2000. "Review: Will the State Bring You Back In? Policing and Democratization." *Comparative Politics* 33 (1): 101–24.

Taylor, Brian D. 2006. "Law Enforcement and Civil Society in Russia." *Europe-Asia Studies* 58 (2): 193–213.

———. 2011. *State Building in Putin's Russia: Policing and Coercion after Communism.* New York: Cambridge University Press.

———. 2014a. "From Police State to Police State? Legacies and Law Enforcement in Russia." In *Historical Legacies of Communism in Russia and Eastern Europe*, ed. Mark Beissinger and Stephen Kotkin, 128–51. New York: Cambridge University Press.

———. 2014b. "Police Reform in Russia: The Policy Process in a Hybrid Regime." *Post-Soviet Affairs* 30 (2–3): 226–55.

Thaman, Stephen. 1996. "Reform of the Procuracy and Bar in Russia." *Parker School Journal of East European Law* 3 (1): 1–29.

———. 2007. "The Nullification of the Russian Jury: Lessons for Jury-Inspired Reform in Eurasia and Beyond." *Cornell International Law Journal* 40 (2): 355–428.

Titaev, Kirill, and Mikhail Pozdniakov. 2012. *Poriadok osobyi—prigovor obychnyi: praktika primeneniia osobogo poriadka sudebnogo razbiratel'stva (gl. 40 UPK RF) v rossiiskikh sudakh.* St. Petersburg: European University at St. Petersburg Research Institute for the Rule of Law.

Tiurukanova, Elena. 2005a *Forced Labour in the Russian Federation Today: Irregular Migration and Trafficking in Human Beings.* Geneva: International Labor Organization.

———. 2005b. *Situatsiia s torgovlei liud'mi v RF: ugolovnoe zakonodatel'stvo i itogi pravoprimenitel'noi praktiki 2004g.* Moscow. http://www.sartraccc.ru/Traffic/i.php?oper=read_file&filename=scien_article/0003.htm.

———. 2006. *Human Trafficking in the Russian Federation: Inventory and Analysis of the Current Situation and Responses.* Moscow: UNICEF.

———. 2008. *Predotvrashchenie i protivodeistvie rasprostraneniiu rabstva i torgovlia liudmi v Rossiiskoi Federatsii.* Moscow: International Organization for Migration.

Tomin, V. T., ed. 2010. *Kommentarii k Ugolovnomu kodeksu Rossiiskoi Federatsii.* Moscow: Iurait.

Trochev, Alexei. 2008. *Judging Russia: Constitutional Court in Russian Politics 1990–2006.* New York: Cambridge University Press.

Tumanov, Grigorii, and Elena Shmaraeva. 2009. "Stukacham skostiat polsroka." Gazeta.ru, April 24. http://www.gazeta.ru/social/2009/04/24/2978651.shtml.

Tverdova, Yuliya. 2011. "Human Trafficking in Russia and Other Post-Soviet States." *Human Rights Review* 12 (3): 329–44.

Twigg, Judyth. 2007. *HIV/AIDS in Russia: Commitment, Resources, Momentum, Challenges.* Washington, DC: Center for Strategic and International Studies.

Tyler, Tom. 1990. *Why Do People Obey the Law?* Princeton, NJ: Princeton University Press.

———. 2004. "Enhancing Police Legitimacy." *Annals of the American Academy of Political and Social Science* 593 (1): 84–99.

———. 2007. *Legitimacy and Criminal Justice: International Perspectives.* New York: Russell Sage Foundation.

Ukolov, Roman. 2002. "Stanet li drevneishaia professiia legal'noi." *Nezavisimaia gazeta,* August 28. http://www.ng.ru/events/2002-08-28/7_trade.html.

UN. United Nations General Assembly. 2000. United Nations Protocol to Prevent, Suppress, and Punish Trafficking in Persons, Especially Women and Children, Supplementing the United Nations Convention against Transnational Organized Crime. Resolution 55/25.

UNODC. United Nations Office of Drugs and Crime. 2008. *Corruption and Human Trafficking: The Grease That Facilitates the Crime.* Vienna: United Nations Global Initiative to Fight Human Trafficking (UNGIFT).

Ura.ru. 2012. "Kakoi vek na dvore? V Kurganskoi oblasti fermer obviniaetsia . . . v rabovladenii." Ura.ru, November 2. http://www.ura.ru/content/kurgan/02-11-2012/news/1052149390.html.

UVD Amurskoi oblasti. 2003. Spravka o prinimaemykh UVD Amurskoi oblasti merakh po presecheniiu faktov vovlechenie v zaniatie prostitutsiei grazhdan, vyezzhaiushchikh za rubezh s territorii oblasti. On file with author.

Varese, Federico. 2001. *The Russian Mafia: Private Protection in a New Market Economy*. New York: Oxford University Press.

Vaughan, Diane. 1998. "Rational Choice, Situated Action, and the Social Control of Organizations." *Law and Society Review* 32 (1): 23–61.

Verhoeven, Maite, and Barbra van Gestel. 2011. "Human Trafficking and Criminal Investigation Strategies in the Amsterdam Red Light District." *Trends in Organized Crime* 14 (2–3): 148–64.

Vesti.ru. 2008. "Nurgaliev: Interpol—Naibolee effektivnyi mekhanizm protivostoianiia ugrozam." *Vesti.ru*, October 7. http://www.vesti.ru/doc.html?id=214363.

Vinokurov, S. I., N. I. Zherdeva, G. F. Koimshidi, A. P. Korotkov, A. A. Litvanov, O. V. Pristanskaia, V. N. Tishchenko, and Iu. G. Torbin. 2010. *Bor'ba s torgovlei liud'mi v Rossii: Prakticheskoe posobie*. Moscow: Academy of the General Procuracy.

Vlassis, Dimitri. 2002. "Global Situation of Transnational Organized Crime, the Decision of the International Community to Develop an International Convention, and the Negotiation Process." In *UNAFEI Annual Report for 2000 and Resource Material Series no. 59*, 475–94. Tokyo: United Nations Asia and Far East Institute for the Prevention of Crime and Treatment of Offenders.

Volchek, Dmitry. 2013. "Russia's 'Traditional Values' Lawmaker Faces Online Backlash." *Radio Free Europe/Radio Liberty*, August 14. http://www.rferl.org/content/russia-traditional-values-online-backlash-mizulina/25075288.html.

Volchetskaia, T. S., and Iu. Usenko. 2000. "Kriminalisticheskaia kharakteristika prestuplenii, sviazannykh s pokhishcheniem nesovershennoletnikh i torgovlei imi." In *Optimizatsiiu ugolovnogo sudoproizvodstva: sbornik nauchnykh trudov*, 89–92. Kaliningrad: Kaliningrad State University.

Volkov, Konstantin. 2007. "Torgovlia nesovershennoletnimi: Voprosy otvetstvennosti i sovershenstvovaniia praktiki pravoprimeneniia." *Rossiiskii sledovatel'* (10): 12–14.

Volkov, Vadim. 2002. *Violent Entrepreneurs: The Use of Force in the Making of Russian Capitalism*. Ithaca, NY: Cornell University Press.

———. 2010. "Palochnaia sistema: Instrument upravleniia." *Vedomosti*, February 19. http://www.vedomosti.ru/newspaper/article/2010/02/19/226253.

———. 2014. "MVD nuzhdaetsia v zamene modeli upravleniia." *Vedomosti*, October 6. http://www.vedomosti.ru/opinion/news/34285171/predely-kontrolya.

Voronezh.rfn.ru. 2004. "Zaderzhany prestupniki, vovlekavshie devushek v prostitutsiiu." *Voronezh.rfn.ru*, June 15. http://voronezh.rfn.ru/rnews.html?id=7677&date=15–06–2004.

Vystavkina, Mariia. 2013. "Biznesmeny zaderzhany za soderzhaniie 200 rabov" *Life News*, March 19. http://lifenews.ru/news/111873.

Wade, Marianne. 2011. "Prosecution of Trafficking in Human Beings Cases." In *Human Trafficking: Exploring the International Nature, Concerns, and Complexities*, ed. John Winterdyk, Benjamin Perrin, and Philip Reichel, 153–80. Boca Raton, FL: CRC Press.

Walk Free Foundation. 2013. *The Global Slavery Index: 2013*. Australia: Walk Free Foundation.

Warnath, Stephen. 2007. *Examining the Intersection between Trafficking in Persons and Domestic Violence*. Washington, DC: US Agency for International Development.

Warren, Kay B. 2012. "Troubling the Victim/Trafficker Dichotomy in Efforts to Combat Human Trafficking: The Unintended Consequences of Moralizing Labor Migration." *Indiana Journal of Global Legal Studies* 19 (1): 105–20.

Waugh, Louisa. 2006. *Selling Olga: Stories of Human Trafficking*. London: Weidenfeld and Nicolson.

Weber, Max. 2004. "Politics as a Vocation." In *The Vocation Lectures*, ed. David Owen and Tracy Strong. Indianapolis, IN: Hackett.

Wendle, John. 2008. "When Padding Police Statistics Proves Deadly." *Moscow Times*, October 29.

Williams, James L., and Adele S. Serrins. 1993. "The Russian Militia: An Organization in Transition." *Police Studies: The International Review of Police Development* 16 (4): 124–28.

Wilson, James Q. 1989. *Bureaucracy: What Government Agencies Do and Why They Do It*. New York: Basic Books.

Za demokraticheskuiu AGS. 2007. "Otkrytoe obrashchenie k General'nomu Prokuroru RF Iu. Ia. Chaike." http://ags.demokratia.ru/library/?content=book&id=104.

Zadvornykh, Ol'ga, and Anton Panov. 2013. "Zaderzhan biznesmen, ugrozhavshii szhech' sotrudnikov." *Life News*, April 4. http://lifenews.ru/news/112375.

Zakatnova, Anna. 2011. "Portret sud'i." *Rossiiskaia gazeta*, November 16. http://www.rg.ru/2011/11/16/sud-site.html.

Zavadskaya, Lyudmila. 1997. "Ministry of Justice Responds to Trafficking: Summary of Remarks." Presented at The Trafficking of NIS Women Abroad: An International Conference in Moscow, November 3–5, 1997.

Zernova, Margarita. 2012a. "Coping with the Failure of the Police in Post-Soviet Russia: Findings from One Empirical Study." *Police Practice and Research: An International Journal* 13 (6): 474–86.

Zernova, Margarita. 2012b. "The Public Image of the Contemporary Russian Police: Impact of Personal Experiences of Policing, Wider Social Implications and the Potential for Change." *Policing: An International Journal of Police Strategies and Management* 35 (2): 216–30.

Zhalinskii, A. E., ed. 2010. *Kommentarii k Ugolovnomu kodeksu Rossiiskoi Federatsii*. 3rd ed. Moscow: Gorodets.

Zhang, Sheldon X., and Samuel L. Pineda. 2008. "Corruption as a Causal Factor in Human Trafficking." In *Organized Crime: Culture, Markets, and Policies*, ed. Dina Siegel and Hans Nelen, 41–55. New York: Springer.

Zhuravlev, S. Iu., and S. K. Krepysheva. 2007. "Kvalifikatsionnye osnovy i soderzhanie otdel'nykh elementov kriminalisticheskoi kharakteristiki prestupnoi deiatel'nosti, sviazannoi s torgovlei liud'mi i ispol'zovaniem rabskogo truda." *Rossiiskii sledovatel'* (24): 3–6.

Zhuravlev, S. Iu., and A. M. Pigaev. 2006. *Torgovlia liud'mi: Mekhanizm prestupnoi deiatel'nosti, metodika rassledovaniia*. Moscow: Iurlitinform.

Zimmerman, Cathy. 2008. "The Health of Trafficked Women: A Survey of Women Entering Posttrafficking Services in Europe." *American Journal of Public Health* 98 (1): 55–59.

Zimmerman, Cathy, Mazeda Hossain, Kate Yun, Brenda Roche, Linda Morison, and Charlotte Watts. 2006. *Stolen Smiles: A Summary Report on the Physical and Psychological Health Consequences of Women and Adolescents Trafficked in Europe*. London: London School of Hygiene and Tropical Medicine.

Index

Page numbers followed by letters *f* and *t* refer to figures and tables, respectively.